GERMANY AS A CULTURE
OF REMEMBRANCE

- Class strata: 1830s-90s
- gender. (♀ in Heimat
  2. 68ers art.)

Russian Nat'lism
Japan - creating the nat -state

_____

War & Peace: ppl. fight for "Russia"

ALON CONFINO

GERMANY AS A CULTURE
OF REMEMBRANCE
PROMISES AND LIMITS OF
WRITING HISTORY

THE UNIVERSITY OF NORTH CAROLINA PRESS CHAPEL HILL

Manufactured in the United States of America

Set in Arnhem and Othello types

by Tseng Information Systems, Inc.

The paper in this book meets the guidelines for
permanence and durability of the Committee on
Production Guidelines for Book Longevity of the
Council on Library Resources.

Frontispiece: Ludwig Hohlwein, "Auf deutschen Staßen,"
ca. 1935. Courtesy of VG Bild-Kunst, Bonn 2006.

Library of Congress Cataloging-in-Publication Data

Confino, Alon.

Germany as a culture of remembrance : promises and
limits of writing history / Alon Confino.

p. cm.

Includes bibliographical references and index.

ISBN-13: 978-0-8078-3042-0 (cloth : alk. paper)

ISBN-10: 0-8078-3042-9 (cloth : alk. paper)

ISBN-13: 978-0-8078-5722-9 (pbk. : alk. paper)

ISBN-10: 0-8078-5722-X (pbk. : alk. paper)

1. Germany—History—1871—Historiography. 2. Memory—
Social aspects—Germany. 3. Memory—Political aspects—
Germany. 4. National characteristics, German. I. Title.

DD220.C66 2006

943.08072—dc22   2006005207

cloth   10 09 08 07 06   5 4 3 2 1
paper   10 09 08 07 06   5 4 3 2 1

For my parents
Hagar and Michael
And my children
Paolo and Davidi

This naïve craving for unity and symmetry

at the expense of experience . . .

—Isaiah Berlin, "Historical Inevitability"

CONTENTS

ILLUSTRATIONS

A selection of illustrations that also appear in color follows page 76.

PREFACE

In his essay on Tolstoy's view of history, Isaiah Berlin famously divided writers and thinkers, following the Greek poet Archilochus, into foxes who are fascinated by the infinite diversity of things and hedgehogs who relate everything to a central, unitary all-explaining system. Historians have provided these metaphors a life of their own in the fifty years since the publication of the essay by giving them a disciplinary bent. They often use them to represent historians as coming in two kinds: the hedgehogs who know about one topic superbly and the foxes who know many things but are experts in none. Berlin used the metaphors to describe different understandings of history, whereas historians have used them also to describe what historians do.

Since I came to my own historical senses, I have been a fox of the type described by Berlin. But I have doubted the popular professional use of the metaphor. The historian should know the ins and outs of his or her subject of study and master the specific archives and historiography. But to breathe life into his or her account and to offer an insightful interpretation, the historian must also know the broader historical framework of the society and age he or she studies—the social, cultural, political, and economic horizons and limitations available to people in the past. In this sense, the good historian should be a hedgehog and a fox.

What kind of animal metaphor this commingled existence can assume, I don't know. Marc Bloch portrayed the historian as an ogre to whom nothing human is foreign. There is much that is still appealing in this metaphor, coming as it does from a world of ancient fairy tales. A hedgehog, a fox, and an ogre: each representation captures a facet of the historian's work, but none quite captures an image of the historian as a human being at home in a complex world and at home in history. The modern historian seems to me more like a traveling juggler. The historian as a traveler is not an unknown description and may sound well worn, given the ubiquity of travel metaphors in our culture (let alone of the bad connotation carried by "tourist"). But as a description of the modern historian, it rings true. Like the traveler, the good historian must be curious about other people and cultures, taking seriously their hopes, fears, anxiety, and prejudices, however morally repulsive they may be. The historian is a traveler who moves deftly and comfortably among different pasts, societies, and disciplines. There is no obligation to leave one's desk (apart from the obligatory trip to the archives), but it is essential to travel in the imagination in order to understand, interpret, and narrate the people of the past. The historian, especially the modern one, is also a juggler of sorts. To give meanings to the pasts observed on the journey, the historian uses different methods, concepts, and narratives. Like a juggler he or she arranges these elements differently in any given interpretation, for there is no fixed arrangement of narratives and concepts that provides a unitary and universal explanation. The historian juggles the concepts and narrative into different combinations that interpret truthfully the fantastic diversity of life he or she encounters on the way. The sophisticated historian who navigates skillfully between methods and disciplines projects a modern and a postmodern air, while the image of the traveler who juggles, moving from village to village and perhaps avoiding the ogre on the way, has an air of times gone by. It may just be a fitting representation of the historian, whose vocation intermingles the present and the past.

The present book, a collection of new, old, and revised essays written between 1993 and 2004, represents my conviction of the historian as a hedgehog, a fox, an ogre, and a traveling juggler all folded into one. Consequently, it is organized in three concentric circles. The first circle presents my broad thinking about the craft of history. The prologue, "The Historian's Representations," is a theoretical reflection on historical representation in our time and provides an overall context and argument for how these essays were conceived in the first place. The aim of the prologue is therefore not, strictly speaking, to introduce the themes of the book. This is the task of the second circle, the introductions to parts I and II, that discusses the specific topics of the book, namely German nationhood and German memory since 1871. These introductions provide a historiographical discussion and place German nationhood and memory within a larger scholarly context. Finally, the third circle comprises the essays that explore in detail the topics of memory and nationhood.

The book explores the hybrid links between two powerful notions in modern culture and politics: nationhood and memory. Part I, "The Local Life of Nationhood: Germany as Heimat, 1871–1990," investigates the ways localness informed nationhood in modern Germany under different ideological regimes, and how Germans constructed in the idea of Heimat, or homeland, a symbolic manual that allowed them to feel German under any political ruler. Part II, "Memory as Historical Narrative and Method," explores how historians and laypersons understand and use the notion of memory, which has become central to articulate individual and group identity. My aim has not been so much to present a book about Germany per se, but to place the German case of nationhood and memory explicitly within the broader framework of modern historical and historiographical concerns over nationhood and memory. It is argued, through two broad case studies on nationhood and memory, that Germany is an extreme historical and historiographical case, but not a fundamentally different one, whose particular characteristics acquire general implications.

My aim also was not to gather previously published essays but, instead, to craft more of a new book. For this purpose, I wrote six new texts (the prologue, an introduction to each part, and chapters 4, 5, and 6. In addition, chapter 3 had been published only in German). Part I further sets this book apart from usual collections of essays, for it is conceived as an extended interpretative essay, a narrative whole of five interconnected essays about the modern Heimat idea. The reader who is interested in one or more distinct periods can read each of the five chapters individually and independently of one another; the reader who is interested in the vicissitudes of German identity over a long duration can read part I in its entirety. To make the book more lucid, I attempted to have the essays speak to each other. Some published essays were revised and updated, some were not. While the essays form a coherent body of work, they also demonstrate my changing opinions and interests. I have left the methodological and theoretical arguments unchanged as unembellished period pieces, even when my positions have changed. In remixing old and new material I conceived this book as a new creation: not as an isolated collection of essays but as a book whose whole is hopefully greater than its parts in the dynamic of the chapters and the additional meaning derived from combining them.

It is a pleasure to think alone, and life presents many and varied opportunities to enjoy doing so: on yet another flight from here to there, walking on a Tuscan or an Israeli beach, or on more mundane occasions. But thinking is ultimately an arid exercise if not shared with other people. I have been intellectually fortunate to be able to exchange ideas, whether in passionate disagreement or comfortable harmony, with a good many people who enriched my view of things. Some of them have read my work; with others I have had conversations that stretched over years. Yet others have made a point or told me a story that triggered within me a creative association or idea. I would not have been the scholar I am without their insights and criticism.

I have benefited in this way from the insights of Celia Applegate, Ori Dasberg, Jacques Ehrenfreund, Saul Friedländer, Michael Geyer, Elliot Neaman, Amnon Raz-Krakotzkin, Ajay Skaria, Siegfried Weichlein, and Maiken Umbach. One outcome of this book was the pleasure of getting to know Robert Moeller. With Richard Bessell, Paul Betts, Peter Fritzsche, and Rudy Koshar I have developed an intellectual and personal friendship that I cherish.

I gave the finishing touches to the book at the Institute for Advanced Studies at the Hebrew University in the fall of 2005, where I had the pleasure to be part of a research group on "Ethnography and Literature" that combined intellectual passion, debates, and friendship. I am indebted to my teammates Galit Hasan-Rokem, Carola Hilfrich, Arkady Kovelman, Christoph Markschies, Ronit Matalon, Ilana Pardes, and Amy Shuman. Emmanuel Sivan, who was a fellow at the institute at the same time, read the prologue and provided helpful comments. Yonatan Livne, the research assistant, made my life easier. The institute is one of my favorite research places in the world. I am grateful to Benjamin Z. Kedar and Eliezer Rabinovici, the past and present directors, and Pnina Feldman, the associate director.

Kristiane Klemm and Hasso Spode from the Historisches Archiv zum Tourismus am Willi Scharnow-Institut für Tourismus der Freien Universität Berlin were always generous and helpful. I am also grateful to the Berlin Program of the Social Science Research Council and the Humboldt Foundation for making it possible to spend two years in Berlin.

The University of Virginia has been extremely generous in supporting my intellectual endeavors from the first day I set foot there. Coming as I did from a very different Heimat, I have enjoyed a splendid professional and personal experience—one that shows academia at its best, when it has no boundaries and is both open minded and open ended. As tuition at private universities reaches irrational levels, it is all the more important to support and appreciate excellent public education, without which there will be no education at all worthy of the name in the United States and elsewhere. I thank Matthew Affron, Edward Ayers, Herbert Tico Braun, Bob Geraci, Krishan Kumar, Mel Leffler, Phyllis Leffler, Chuck McCurdey, Peter Onuf, Brian Owensby, Brad Reed, Sophie Rosenfeld, and Libby Thompson for their generous contributions to my work and for their friendship. Lenard Berlanstein, Allan Megill, and Erik Midelfort have read much of my work over the years with keen and critical insight; I owe much to their companionship and historical wisdom, so different, these three are, one from another.

At the University of North Carolina Press I have found over the years a wonderful, professional publishing home. My editor Chuck Grench saw the project through from beginning to end with steady hands and remarkable intellectual horizons, and I cannot think of a better team than Paula Wald, Katy O'Brien, and Brian MacDonald. The production of the book was assisted by grants from the Howell Fund at the Department of History and the Arts and Science Research Grant, both at the University of Virginia.

Haim, Muki, Roy, Guy, Yonatan, and Itamar, as well as Ofra, John, Didi, and Ariel have been a steady source of love and support; that my topics of study were not a subject of dinnertime discussion helped keep things in perspective. In Italy, I was fortunate to enjoy life with the extended Fiorani family.

This book is dedicated to my parents, Hagar and Michael, who in their own different ways have enriched me so much; their mark is all over my ideas. And it is also dedicated to my sons, Paolo and Davidi, who have brought enormous happiness to my life, and never stop teaching me new things. The presence of the past and the future made evident by these four has never been far from my mind as I wrote these pages over the years.

Francesca has made life and history meaningful.

Tel Aviv
Rosh Ha-shana 2005

GERMANY AS A CULTURE
OF REMEMBRANCE

PROLOGUE
THE HISTORIAN'S REPRESENTATIONS

All societies have been in different ways attentive to the past, that protean and essential factor of life: we depend on it and seek it, yet at times we cannot bear to face it. Our sense of individual and collective identity requires it, whether we decide to repress, embellish, or just lie to ourselves about it. Historians are also linked to the past, of course, but not quite in the same way as their fellow citizens: for historians have the vocation of representing the past accurately. They create narratives about the past using evidence and methods of verification as the primary material of their craft with the intention of telling true stories. The truth of their stories is never stable, for it is socially and culturally constructed, and their stories can never tell the whole truth about the past. But the foundation of all serious historical work is the intent for truth and fairness in the representation of the past.

And yet, because their stories are always linked to social and personal phenomena that stand outside the realm of scholarship, historians can never reach a cultural Archimedean point from which one can interpret the world from the "outside." They are always "inside" culture; they are a product of the intellectual tradition and historical mentality of their society, while attempting at the same time to explain and criticize it. And they always work with words that are at times ambiguous, even tricky. They create narratives, but their narratives don't always mean what they think they mean, and they don't always tell only the stories they think they tell.

In consequence, their final product is a narrative that mixes personal, public, and professional factors. It is not an arbitrary product, however. It has the beauty of narrative art, of storytelling, but it also makes, when it is properly crafted, a legitimate claim to accuracy. I would like to reflect, by way of introducing this collection of essays, on representations of the past made by historians as well as about representations of historians. I often tend to concentrate on Germany, not only because it is my major historical area of research, but also because modern German history, dominated as it is by the Third Reich and the Holocaust, is an extreme historical case, and extremes are sometimes useful for uncovering choices, views, and solutions.

The past exists out there—imagined, invented, actually experienced—for all to use. Historians make sense of it by creating narratives of the past that they shape, in my opinion, in three concentric circles of influence, namely, the personal, the public, and the professional.

The first circle consists of the historian's personal background, education, and memories. While the importance of this factor for determining a historian's interests, sensitivities, and approaches is evident, it is the least discussed. The profession is allergic to introducing personal considerations as justification for choices of method. These considerations are left to the preface and acknowledgments of books, or to informal discussions (and at times confessions) among colleagues. To be sure, there are exceptional cases such as autobiographies that sum up the lifelong vocation of a historian. It is probably desirable—even unavoidable—that the personal is kept separate from the strictly professional in historical studies. To link the two demands maturity and wisdom that comes with experience and an elegant style, as well as having something important to say. At the same time, it is unfortunate that the discipline cannot find an appropriate space in which to discuss this topic because, judging from historians' autobiographies, one can see how strong the link is between personal experience, upbringing, and memories, and professional and theoretical choices. The point is not to be narcissistically self-indulgent, but to take into consideration the historian's subjectivity in making choices that otherwise appear wholly theoretical, to articulate the conditions and interdependencies that limit and inform the historian's work.

The topic should be discussed among historians, although limits should be made clear. It is difficult to articulate any causal connections between the historian's past and the kind of historian he or she becomes. Thus, it is self-evident that Saul Friedländer's experience—born in 1933 in Prague, losing his parents in the Holocaust, surviving the war in a monastery preparing for the Catholic priesthood, and then discovering his Jewishness and emigrating to Israel—is related to his work on the Holocaust. But it is far from clear, based on Friedländer's autobiography, why his experience made him into the insightful historian that he became (and not into an angry Goldhagen, for example).

The historian cannot quite make this kind of psychological evaluation.[1] But he or she can make connections when personal experience is linked to professional life. Take the case of Henri Pirenne, the famous Belgian medievalist. Before 1914 Pirenne had been deeply and positively influenced by German scholarship, studied in Leipzig and Berlin, and had cultivated many friends and colleagues during his frequent participation in the German historians' annual meeting, the Historikertag. In a 1912 ceremony honoring his twenty-fifth anniversary at the University of Ghent, attended by colleagues from all over Europe, he asserted confidently that science had no borders. All this changed in August 1914, when the German army invaded Belgium. Pirenne lost a son at the beginning of the war. The University of Ghent was closed by the occupation authorities. And he was shocked by the October 1914 petition, signed by ninety-three of Germany's top intellectuals, that supported the nation's military and political goals and called for expansion of the German civilizing mission in Europe. Active against the occupiers, Pirenne was arrested several times and finally sent to Germany in March 1916, where he remained imprisoned until the end of the war. By then he had rejected much in German historical scholarship, judging even the good methodological tools it offered as badly executed politically and morally. He gave more weight than before to the individual in history, and saw Luther and Bismarck as the fathers of German militarism, chauvinism, and subservience to authority.[2]

The second circle of influence that shapes the historian's view is the dominant perceptions of the past in the surrounding culture. The birth of the historical discipline in nineteenth-century Europe, for example, took place just as nationhood was becoming a fundamental creed of political sovereignty and group identity. The historian thus became the grand priest of the nation and the ultimate recounter of its identity, roots, and immemorial existence. The line between careful historical inquiry and forging national identity was blurred. In our own period, two elements of public consciousness of the past seem particularly evident, and both have immediate bearing on German history. The first is the rise of memory as a key notion with which individuals and groups understand, explain, and interpret their identity. The second is the rise of the Holocaust to the status of a fundamental event in modern Judeo-Christian civilization, a foundational past that organizes (together with other representations of the past) the way people understand questions of history, morality, politics, and international relations (as, for example, in the influence of the Holocaust on the legal proceedings of the events in Rwanda and Bosnia).[3]

Many historians are influenced by the public representations of memory and the Holocaust, whether or not their immediate topic is German history.[4] Historians are both influenced by this general perception and participate in shaping it. Jacques Le Goff observed once that the medieval period may best be understood "by its inability to express itself apart from religious references." Our own period may well be understood by, among other things, its dependence—when expressing itself on a range of moral, historical, legal, and artistic issues—on memory and Holocaust references. How are historians of Germany to negotiate the burdensome closeness of their subject matter? How should they negotiate the concerns of the present with the commitment to describe accurately the world of Germans in the past?

It is widely assumed that the third circle of influence provides the professional tools to make this negotiation successful: to understand the past in spite of the personal and public bias of the historian. This circle includes the rules and modes of operation of the historical discipline as a vocation whose aim is to represent the past accurately. Using the tools of their craft, historians can do their best to reach an insightful, fair, and, as far as possible, truthful representation of the past.

The convergence of personal, public, and professional aspects of historical understanding came into sharp focus for me several years ago when I read Eugen Weber's *My France*, a collection of essays.[5] It was one of those periods in which debate flared up in German historiography about the appropriate way to study the Third Reich and remember the Holocaust. "My France," I thought, sensing very clearly the dissonance with modern German history. Weber's title moves between, on the one hand, the France that he loves and, on the other, the France on which he conducted historical work. Weber did not ignore France's unpleasant past during the Second World War; he had been a close student of Vichy and French fascism, but these did not prevent him from embracing "his France." There is an ease, a panache, and a self-confident lighthearted tone to Weber's introduction. Part of this, no doubt, owes to his skill as a historian and his sheer talent as a storyteller. But there is, I sensed, more to it than simply style; it is rather that even Vichy could not trample the notion of the presumed French *joie de vivre*. It reminded me of the persistent representation of Italy as the land of friendly people, romance, and *vino, pasta, e piacere di vivere*—which is all true enough (as I can attest firsthand) but often brackets out the brutality and murderousness of Italians during the twenty years of fascism.

For a historian of modern Germany, whose topics include the years 1933–45, "My Germany" would not be an impossible title, but would certainly be problematic. The title "my Italy" is not likely to elicit the reflexive question as to whether the author included Mussolini and the 1936 gassing of Abyssinians, whereas "My Germany" is likely to bring forth immediately the issue of how Hitler and Auschwitz are accommodated in the word "my." Such a title would require some explanatory words to avoid sounding uncritical, or apologetic, or even just to avoid being misunderstood. And this is true for all historians of Germany regardless of their background, while being particularly acute for those of German and Jewish background, because, as we all know, the German past of the Third Reich, to use an observation on American southern history made famous by William Faulkner and C. Vann Woodward, is not even past yet.[6]

At the same time, we can find in Weber's book indications of larger trends of public historical consciousness and disciplinary interpretative shifts. *My France*, published in 1991 and comprising essays written between 1958 and 1988, reflected a generation of scholars who studied fascism and were aware of the Holocaust in professional and personal ways; Weber, who grew up in Bucharest, left Rumania in 1940 and joined the British army in 1943. But this generation neither assigned the Holocaust the centrality it now possesses in the interpretation of modern European history nor lived in a culture that viewed the extermination of the Jews as the moral historical signifier of its age. In the immediate decades after 1945, the Holocaust was mostly perceived (if it was a topic of scholarly interest at all) as a unique, German affair having fundamental, perhaps insurmountable, problems of historical explanation, while the interpretative and public transformation of the past two decades has turned it from a German into a European affair, anchoring the German planning and perpetration of the Holocaust in a nexus of continental traditions, implementation, and participation. These days, a historian of France who aims at presenting a broader view and truthful interpretation of its twentieth century cannot but integrate and emphasize the French history and memory of the Holocaust. The acknowledgment of the centrality of the Holocaust necessarily means that "my France" acquires some of the meanings of "my Germany": the public, scholarly, and historical image of France is now made up also of the Vélodrome d'Hiver, the children of Izieux, and Louis Malle's *Au revoir les enfants* in a way it was not twenty years ago.[7]

Two lessons can be drawn from these reflections. First, and more generally, history writing is a dialectic between the personal, public, and professional. The three always exist in different combinations and configurations. There is always a personal inflection, one's memories and experiences, that commingle in a multitude of complex ways with the social, cultural, and political world around, with questions of justice and war, of life and death, as well as with the available professional choices of method and theory. In this respect, a historian should always ask how and why I think the way I do about the past. Often it is less the answer that is revealing than the journey in search of an answer. Second, and more specifically, German history poses, as is well known, particular problems of historical narration and explanation because of the years 1933–45. Still, the difference between German and other histories is not in kind but in degree and intensity. In many respects Germany is an extreme historical and historiographical case, but not a fundamentally different one, and its particular characteristics have general implications.

How are we to understand this past, which is at the same time so present? Understanding history, François Furet elegantly observed, "constitutes a dialectic between the experience of strangeness and the act of familiarization."[8] The past is out of reach like the river in Heraclitus's adage, "you cannot step twice into the same river." But at the same time, the historian should understand history from the viewpoint of people in the past, cultivating a certain familiarity with their tastes, attitudes, mentalities, values, and beliefs. Historians negotiate this dialectic with various degrees of willingness, resistance, and self-consciousness.

The most common strategy for understanding the past is to demand that the historian exercise detachment from the topic of study, avoiding emotions, personal inclinations, and ideological bias. It sounds appealing but is not necessarily always a good strategy. The work of two celebrated historians is revealing here. The most notable case in recent decades for emotional attachment to the object of study is the opening line of Fernand Braudel's *The Mediterranean and the Mediterranean World in the Age of Philip II*: "I have loved the Mediterranean with passion . . ." This was not Braudel's only declaration of love: "Let me start by saying once and for all," begins *The Identity of France*, "that I love France with the same demanding and complicated passion as did Jules Michelet; without distinguishing between its good points and its bad . . . but that passion will rarely intrude upon the pages of this book."[9] Of course his passion intruded. *The Identity of France* is now recognized as a flawed work because it assumes that rootedness has been the essential feature of the French people until recently. Today, historians of France recognize that immigration has always been a part of the French past and so has the myth of rootedness that Braudel helped to perpetuate.[10] But his attachment also endowed Braudel's books with an added depth, humanity, and the sincere attempt to familiarize with the past. A counterexample is Eric Hobsbawm's statement about his national sentiments in *Nations and Nationalism*: "Nationalism requires too much belief in what is patently not so. . . . [T]he historian [must] leave[s] his or her convictions behind when entering the library or the study. Some nationalist historians have been unable to do so. Fortunately, in setting out to write the present book I have not needed to leave my non-historical convictions behind."[11] What is presented as a positive detachment from the topic turns out to be a shortcoming: because Hobsbawm views nationalism as the opposite of historical reason, as a myth not to be believed in, his analysis lacks insights into the reasons why people in the modern world—how much of an exaggeration is it to say all people?—embraced nationhood with such tender emotions and destructive zeal. Hobsbawm made, in essence, no attempt to engage in a process of familiarization.

A delicate balance and complex mix exist, then, between the strangeness of the past and the process of familiarization, between personal sentiments and professional practices. These cannot be reduced to polar opposites. There is no single, correct formula for transforming evidence, via the rules of the historical discipline, into an enlightening interpretation. Detachment is a required element for the historian, but excessive detachment can deaden historical imagination and block access to the subjectivity of historical actors. A sense of personal involvement may add insights that come with intimate knowledge, but excessive involvement obscures critical analysis. The delicate balance exists in a state of tension but without a dissonance by the historian's possessing enough self-consciousness of his or her composite role as a representer of the past who is shaped by professional, public, and personal factors. Differently put, the issue of understanding the past cannot be solved by calling for detachment over personal involvement. Rather, the crucial aspect is often the questions we formulate and the things we seek to know about the past, and our engagement in a process of familiarization.

Precisely this problem of the strangeness and familiarity of the past has been crucial to German history because of the Third Reich and the Holocaust, which are the problem's locus classicus in modern historical thinking. For some historians and laypersons, the unbearable closeness of this past meant that no detachment was possible, that this was a past that could not go away, never became strange, and would therefore remain constantly present. When Elie Wiesel asserted, "The Holocaust? The ultimate event, the ultimate mystery, never to be comprehended or transmitted. Only those who were there know what it was; the others will never know," he challenged (if unintentionally) the basic procedures of historical understanding that assume that every human past is within reach of being comprehended, that experiencing a given event is not a requirement for understanding it, and that a process of historical familiarization takes place from an external position, that is, from a basic position of being distant from the past.[12]

Historical work on the Third Reich and the Holocaust has exhibited a dual sensitivity about the possibility and limits of historical understanding. On the one hand, historians have admirably and painstakingly reconstructed the period in spite of the enormous stress it put on our imagination and belief in humankind. Holocaust historiography stands out as one of the towering achievements of the historical profession in the modern period. On the other hand, this reconstruction was constantly accompanied by a sense that adequate explanation is either impossible or limited, and that several features of the period (guards leading children and whole families to Treblinka's gas chambers, for example) do not lend themselves to being captured by normal historical methods.[13] In consequence, it has been believed, the Holocaust diverged, on some level and some form, from normal history. Saul Friedländer's work stands for this duality of a whole cohort of historians belonging to the era of contemporaries, whose experience of the Third Reich, either personally or as members of the second or third generation or as influenced by Holocaust remembrance in public culture, impinged on their historical understanding. He argued that "the 'Final Solution,' like any other historical phenomenon, had to be interpreted *in its historical unfolding* and *within the relevant historical framework*," and out of this understanding he produced his magisterial *Nazi Germany and the Jews*. But he also claimed in a following sentence and in the same breath "but, as we know, this is not the case and, implicitly, for most, this cannot be the case. No one of sound mind would wish to interpret the events from Hitler's viewpoint."[14]

I have reservations about this dual historical understanding, which has been dominant among historians and laypersons alike since 1945 and is now in a process of transformation. It is wrong to assume that the Holocaust is exceptional because the historical discipline cannot fully interpret, explain, and capture it. It burdens history with massive expectations that it cannot possibly fulfill.[15] For, in fact, in its inability to be fully captured, the Holocaust is not unusual. It is not that the Holocaust is unique because the historical discipline cannot capture it, but that the extreme case of the Holocaust lays bare the basic fact that the historical discipline cannot fully capture any past.[16] It is better to argue that the historical discipline can never fully interpret, explain, and capture a past, that all interpretations are incomplete, and that all historical understanding is a work in progress. And that, moreover, the historical discipline itself is crucial but insufficient to understand the past, for some experiences can only be captured by artistic representations such as poetry, sculpture, painting, literature, and film. This is particularly true for extreme historical events—and for the Holocaust, which is the extreme of the extreme—that call into question our cognitive, imaginative, and emotional abilities to comprehend the world. The profundity of human experience in the Holocaust captured by Primo Levi's *Se questo é un uomo* ("If this is a man," horrendously translated into English as *Survival in Auschwitz*) is unrivaled.

The historian, to my mind, has a way through the intractable intellectual labyrinth of the dual sensitivity about the possibility and limits of historical understanding. It is difficult to be isolated from or emotionally removed from the Holocaust, the event that is a moral signifier of our age. (That the Holocaust is *a*, perhaps *the*, signifier in current Judeo-Christian civilization is attested by the fact that its very existence is negated in lectures, publications, and on the Internet. Why is the existence of, say, the First World War, the Russian Revolution, the Ribbentrop-Molotov agreement, or the Berlin Wall never questioned?) And no one should aspire to be detached from the event, if by detachment we understand neutrality where Nazis and Jews are morally equal. The crux of the issue is that detachment is not in itself a good guide for historical insight. Historians should not seek a detached Archimedean point, for it does not exist; they cannot exist outside of their culture. They have to live and manage the issue of involvement with the Holocaust, and with history. What they can do is rely on their discipline to provide a guide to understand the Holocaust. The simplest historical principle is the following: German history, as *res gestae* (the things that happened), was made by human beings and it therefore lies, on a fundamental level and in principle, within historical experience and understanding. But its *historia rerum gestarum* (the narration of the things that happened) is at times represented as beyond historical experience and understanding. This narration should be taken for what it is, namely as a step in our internalization of the Third Reich, in our journey to self-consciousness of an event that calls into question the basic values of Western civilization and the idea of shared humanity. Our problem in telling and understanding what happened does not shed light on the historicity of the years 1933–45, which can be submitted to the basic principles of historical analysis, narration, interpretation, explanation, and understanding.

Once we keep a distinction between *res gestae* and *historia rerum gestarum*, questions of historical understanding fall into place.[17] We need not call for the historicization of the Third Reich, as some scholars did several years ago, for we do not need to historicize what is already history. It is wrong to assume that some approaches possess intrinsic moral qualities that make them either better or worse for the study of the Third Reich, as had been suggested with regard to everyday-life history, because it might prompt us to empathize with the Nazis, for historical approaches are more or less useful in illuminating the past, but it is ultimately the intention of the historian that gives them meaning. And it is limiting to ask only why Germany was radically different—and to take this difference as the center of investigation—instead of recognizing also that modern German history fits well within larger trends of European history and that the main question is how these similarities produced excesses.

To understand the things that happened in German history, we must also interpret the events in part from the Nazis' point of view, and we must capture the recognizably human and moral in the Nazi world as many Germans viewed it by exploring mentalities, motivations, and ethics. Mais est-il vrai que tout comprendre c'est tout pardonner? To my mind this is a non sequitur—one can understand without forgiving and forgive without understanding. "Understanding" does not mean identifying with what one understands; "familiarization" does not mean justification. The imperative of historical understanding must remain the act of familiarizing the past, treated without qualifications with the tools of the historian's craft. Nazism set out to construct a new type of society, based on racial ideas, that posed a historical alternative and challenge to both liberal democracy and communism. It was a destruction of civilization, in the traditional sense of a culture aspiring to moral values and worthy of emulation. But it also constructed an alternative civilization. And to reconstruct Nazism as a civilization seems a task worthy of the historian.

To a post-Auschwitz historical consciousness, the idea of Nazism as a civilization is blasphemy. Let us think about it with the help of an observation of Marc Bloch from *The Historian's Craft*, written during World War II: "We speak also of civilizations in the plural and merely as realities. From this point, we admit that there may be, if I may venture to say so, civilizations of people who are not civilized."[18] Which civilization of uncivilized people did he have in mind? For a Frenchman, a Jew, a refined thinker of the past, and a humanist, the civilization of the uncivilized, in the darkest war years, could only mean Nazism. But for Bloch there was no necessary dissonance in making this statement, because he did not have the full knowledge and perception of the rupture that was the Holocaust. Nazism, for him, was uncivilized but squarely within the territory of the historian. For us, calling Nazism a civilization seems blasphemy because we perceive Auschwitz as a foundational break that imposes enormous strains on our imagination. Consciousness of the enormity of the Holocaust could not but influence historians, for while historians know that the Holocaust is historical, they have resisted applying to it fully the methods of historical understanding. Present-day historians should bring to the understanding of the Holocaust a recognition of its foundational meaning and the rupture it has caused in modern historical consciousness. But this rupture should be assessed as fully historical based on the act of familiarity for the purpose of understanding. "When all is said and done, a single word, 'understanding,' is the beacon light of our studies."[19]

The principle of understanding joins, to my mind, with yet another historical principle to comprise, together, the essence of historical thinking: the notion of contingency. Let this view be expressed in the following two texts. Alexander Herzen put the issue poetically: "If humanity marched straight toward some result, there would be no history, only logic. . . . If history followed a set libretto it would lose all interest, become unnecessary, boring, ludicrous. . . . [H]istory is all improvisation, all will, all extempore—there are no frontiers, no itineraries." More specifically about Germany, the Third Reich, and the Holocaust, Victor Klemperer wrote in his diary on September 29, 1939: "I am just reading the first few pages of the Tocqueville, which Frau Schaps gave me in 1924. No one, not even the most significant and knowledgeable contemporaries, anticipated the course of [the French] Revolution. Every page of the book surprises me with analogies to the present."[20] Whatever happens is not predetermined to happen; it does, as a result of a million events in unanticipated sequence, which the historian needs to reconstruct and explain. It is an inherent paradox of history that while the historian perforce looks at the past backward from his or her temporal location, to understand its meaning he or she must imagine the temporal location of past historical actors and look forward into an unknown future. The historian knows what this future would bring, but for contemporaries the future was still unanticipated with a million possibilities. Capturing people's angst, hopes, and happiness over unknown possibilities is a necessary step toward understanding past experience.

Historians should think twice before they doubt the ability of history to interpret and understand the Holocaust in the same way, which is not without limitations, history can understand and interpret all past events. Of course, any account of the Holocaust, however convincing, will continue to evoke in us a sense of moral inadequacy, for the victims of the Holocaust died in complete innocence; no historical narrative will ever relieve us from the agony of the Holocaust. But it has the potential of making us wiser. Therefore, if a representer and remembrancer of the past in society doubts the ability of his or her craft to interpret and understand the world the Nazis built, then this is grim news indeed: for while the historian is not the only representer of the past in society, he or she does have a vocational obligation to speak truthfully about the past.

The notion of speaking truthfully about the past raises a certain discomfort in a culture that has come to distrust historical truth in the name of a relativism that claims that all truths are simply a result of power relations in a given society. The mistake of historical relativists was to assume that because the historian is always influenced by the point of view of time and place he or she is incapable of gaining historical understanding. As if historical understanding can be gained only under conditions of a pure state of objectivity. But the fact that the historian cannot be totally free from the point of view of his or her culture does not necessarily foreclose historical understanding or establishing historical facts. Historical knowledge is established through a process of collection and classification of sources and of reconstruction of the context that made them. This process is composed of asking the sources questions that cannot be wholly arbitrary, for they are limited by the empirical data and the specific conditions of the sources' period. This process of constant negotiation between the sources, which are limited by their time and place, and the historian's search for knowledge is more or less illuminating based on the ability of the sources to produce possible answers to possible questions. This negotiation is obviously articulated in language, whose meaning shifts, but there is a truth outside of the text precisely because language itself is conditioned by its time and place: historical inquiry can detect its anachronisms, lies, and tendentiousness, much as Lorenzo Valla centuries ago used this strategy to unmask the Donation of Constantine.

To my mind, history is a form of narrative art practiced with tools that permit verification of our knowledge about the past. Differently put, historical writing is an art that uses scientific methods of inquiry. History permits verification because historians are committed to using evidence as the primary material of their craft. With the help of evidence, historians put forward differing interpretations that are weighed against each other. Interpretations differ, but not all interpretations are equal: some clarify the historical world better than others, and some are downright wrong. But in spite of historians' use of evidence history remains simultaneously a form of art: historians can never achieve the precision, say, of mathematicians who work with numbers, where two plus two makes four under any social, political, and cultural circumstances. And they always work with words that are potentially unstable.

Their final product is a story, a narrative that falls squarely in the realm of art, just as the best of history writing is touched by the grace and beauty of art.

Historical relativism confuses evaluation of facts with evaluation of values; the two are related but are not the same. Historians can establish true or false knowledge about the past, while also recognizing that historical understanding is always complex, incomplete, and still under construction. The point of view of the present is unavoidable—our knowledge about the past changes (we know more or we learn that what we had known was wrong), and the significance of it changes—but this does not mean that "when it comes to apprehending the historical record, there are no grounds to be found in the historical record itself for preferring one way of constructing its meaning over another."[21]

Let us consider the extermination of the Jews as a historical case that has undergone tremendous interpretive shifts, which however did not fundamentally question the basic truth of what happened. As noted previously, it is a good event to treat as a case study because, as an extreme historical event, it sharpens professional procedures and moral choices. After the war, understanding the foundational historical meaning of the extermination of the Jews, as well as embracing the point of view of the victims, was rare, even for intellectuals who were Jewish or antifascist. Thus, for example, Primo Levi's *Se questo é un uomo* was rejected in 1947 by Einaudi in Turin and later by five other publishers before it was taken by a small publishing house in Turin. The Einaudi literary reader who rejected the book, claiming it was not "right" for Einaudi's list, was the young and talented novelist Natalia Ginzburg, a member of an exemplary antifascist family and the wife of resistance fighter Leone Ginzburg who was murdered by the Germans in Rome in 1944.[22] Raul Hilberg's monumental *The Destruction of European Jews* was rejected in 1959 by Princeton University Press because, as the outside reader noted, the manuscript did not "constitute a sufficiently important contribution," and "readily available" books on the subject existed "in sufficient detail." That critic was Hannah Arendt.[23] And West German historians, if they considered the extermination at all, saw it as a German not a Jewish tragedy. Martin Broszat, whose distinguished career was dedicated to exploring National Socialism, rejected in the 1950s the work of Joseph Wulf, a German-Polish writer and an Auschwitz survivor, who focused on the extermination of the Jews as inherent in Nazi ideas, motivations, and regime. Broszat rejected this approach as polemical and nonprofessional and, above all, questioned the professional distance of Wulf from the subject matter by implying that a "scientific-historical" description of the extermination of the Jews could not and should not be left to Jews and survivors.[24] Holocaust survivors were not objective and Jewish historians of the Holocaust were emotionally unable to study the topic scientifically.

Now, of course, we have a radically different sensitivity to these issues. Many react to such examples with moral outrage. The extermination has now been transformed into The Holocaust or The Shoah. Holocaust scholarship has been in part the producer and in part the product of this new consciousness. The historian's work has been influenced by the point of view of present-day public, artistic, and political representations of the Holocaust. The enormous contribution of this scholarship to our historical understanding of the Holocaust—in terms of method, scope, interpretation, and sheer new knowledge—is undeniable. We know today infinitely more about the comprehensive nature of the Nazi racial state, worldview, implementation, terror, and extermination than people did in the 1950s. We know that the extermination originated and was planned by Germans, but was a European project in scale and participation. We know that the main interpretative topic is not whether Nazism was a form of totalitarianism, fascism, or antimodernism (as was commonly debated in the 1950s and 1960s), but how the Nazi utopian racial vision—as part of broader European trends of life and thought—was justified, internalized, and murderously executed. And by focusing on memory, the victims' point of view has become prominent in the way we narrate the years 1933–45, be they Jews, Gypsies, mentally ill patients, slave laborers, homosexuals and lesbians, or others.

In short, historical knowledge and interpretations of the Holocaust have dramatically changed in the past half century. But these changes do not question the basic facts about what happened in the Holocaust. We now know more about the extermination than ever before, and this knowledge is irrefutable. The historian cannot avoid the culture of the present, but historical understanding is not the prisoner of that culture. Certain knowledge can be acquired in spite of, against, and independently of the point of view of the present. Had the Nazis won the war, let us think with a counterfactual, Hitler's often-repeated lie—that the Jews had been responsible for the Second World War—would have become common knowledge and official truth. But the historian who seeks to represent the past accurately would still be able to refute this claim about Jewish aggression by examining the sources: there are grounds to be found in the historical record itself for preferring a different interpretation than Hitler's way of constructing meaning. A historical event is not only made by words, texts, and narratives, but also by the procedure of historical analysis and by the moral conscience of the historian. Ultimately, if historical reconstruction is only texts and narratives, Hitler's argument may just have the upper hand.

If the historian is not quite a helpless prisoner of his or her culture, he or she still operates under its enormous influence, which tends to conflate history with identity and scholarship with political leanings in ways that prejudge historical stories. Some of the political leanings are justified and humane, and some of the identity building is long overdue, but the ultimate result of these histories is to obscure the past.

The "special path" interpretation to German history (the *Sonderweg* approach) dominant in the 1960s and 1970s is a case in point. In this approach, German history was written within the specific moral economies and political conditions of West Germany. Articulated by German historians who were mostly young during the Third Reich and came of age after 1945 in the Federal Republic of Germany, the special path interpretation argued that modern German history had diverged from the "normal" history of the "West" in its inability to produce a liberal democracy before 1933. Methodologically, as later critiques showed, this interpretation was flawed: it constructed a sugar-coated, ideal-type "West"; it assumed that history has a "normal," modernizing, democratic direction and thereby ended up proposing a teleological explanation to Germany's inability to proceed "normally" before 1945; and it overemphasized impersonal social-economic processes and undervalued contingency and agency. Regardless, it remains a fundamental contribution to postwar German society and historiography. The eminent historian Hans-Ulrich Wehler, one of the interpretation's originators, recently reflected on its meaning: "The young Marx called texts, with which he wanted to clarify a problem, starting points to 'self-understanding.' In this sense . . . [the *Sonderweg* interpretation] can be understood as an attempt at an intensive 'self-understanding.'" It was about giving the "darkest problem of our past a rational, argumentative clarification," as much as it was about participating in the period's political debates by arguing for a democratic, liberal, historically responsible West Germany.[25] It was a laudable cause, if a flawed historical interpretation: a case of well-intentioned historians who attempted to correct in historiography what was wrong in history.

Closer to the present, the recent scholarly emphasis on Holocaust memory and morality, which has offered some important interpretative advances, is also a case where history, identity, and public consciousness blend intimately. By viewing the Holocaust primarily as a morality tale, this approach runs the danger of creating a grand narrative whereby history is propelled by moral considerations; however edifying this narrative is, like all grand narratives it fails to capture the complexity of history. Historical understanding must take morality into consideration, but cannot be reduced to it. Differently put, we run the danger of telling the Holocaust in a narrative that moralizes and pontificates, as a presentist story that too closely reflects present-day perceptions, projecting too starkly the present onto the past. The historian thus becomes so identified with the causes, themes, and concerns of contemporary culture and memory about National Socialism that the delicate balance is broken between being a critical observer of the past and being part of one's own culture. In short, a moral narrative of the Holocaust often has a voice that consciously attempts to master the past, or to master a historical voice that speaks about mastering the past. This voice tells a story that is determined by the knowledge of what happened at the end; it thus cannot escape the libretto of history, and of the present.

At this point, an interpretative shift is likely to take place thanks to historians who ask new questions. For the important thing is not that the historian cannot disentangle himself or herself from the point of view of time and place, but that the historian is conscious of this point of view and of its influence on professional choices of method, subject matter, and inquiry. If the point of view of the present is unavoidable, much depends on how the historian uses this point of view to enhance historical understanding by questioning the past critically.

Historians, then, describe not simply a rendition of what happened but also what happens. Their stories reflect the present. But they are not fables, for they are based on firmer foundations, more reasonable thought, and a self-critical way of thinking, and they aim, sometimes, at a measured dispassion. Just why this state of things—the historian as a person who is always inside his or her culture *and* the historian using methods to verify, establish, and reject knowledge about the past—seems to some people as contradictory is not quite clear to me. Knowledge about the past is not airtight, but not all knowledge is the same; some is more accurate than others. Interpretations are unstable, but not all have the same claim to fairness, evidence, firmer foundations, and reasonable historical thought. When historians write the histories of the past they simultaneously write the histories of their present, but this does not make either of them untrue, though it does make both permanently incomplete, under construction, guaranteed to be revised in mankind's ongoing process of self-awareness of where we came from and how we arrived here.

The essays assembled here reflect the shift of the past twenty years in the way historians represent the past: from society to memory, identity, and culture. In the mid-1980s, the metaphor to describe the historian's profession and working space was still very much the "atelier of history," to use François Furet's metaphor, which he must have taken from Bloch, who also was captured by it.[26] There is something charming about this metaphor, describing the historian as a craftsman and an artist molding in a workshop various methods, theories, facts, numbers, and discourses into historical accounts. There seems to be congruence between choosing the metaphor of the atelier and the cultural and historiographical context of Furet and his generation. The atelier or workshop associates the world of labor, of manual work, of social conditions. In his work, Furet constantly engaged with the ideological and historiographical domination of (various shades of) Marxism. He, of course, demolished the Marxist-influenced social history interpretation of the French Revolution. But my point is that the power that he needed to reckon with professionally and personally (he had been a communist as a young man) was Marxism and social history. The atelier was thus part of the language of the period.

The atelier of history is still a valid metaphor for describing the historian's craft and working space, but not quite in the same way. Much has changed in the way historians think about and practice their discipline. The end of great explanatory models, combined with the rise of interpretative terms like multiplicity, hybridity, invention, negotiation, and interdependence, has made the historian more like a juggler of narratives and concepts than a steady artisan. The emphasis on the historian as a craftsman has turned into an emphasis on the historian as a representer of the past. Nor does the metaphor of the atelier quite capture the tools and spatial working space of the historian in the age of the computer, overlapping Windows environments, and the wireless link to the Internet. The historian can now set up an atelier anywhere. Archives are still crucial, but this has changed, too. "I have my archive in my pocket," a historian of India who is writing an intellectual biography of Gandhi told me, for Gandhi's writings are now available on a CD-ROM.[27]

The present collection of essays explores the hybrid links between two powerful notions that have stood at the center of the shift from society to culture: nationhood and memory. The collection presents a view of German nationhood in particular and of nationhood in general as a culture of remembrance, as a product of collective negotiation and exchange between the many memories that exist in the nation. Nationhood and memory appear as modern sensibilities that give meaning to values and beliefs such as collectivity, selfhood, territoriality, and the past. The notion of memory is used as a means of questioning long-existing boundaries in German culture and historiography, as well as in current historical methods and narratives. A general question of historical interpretation has been central to this work, namely the tendency to interpret the meaning of nationhood and of memory by placing the text within the context. This is a valid approach, and in some respect we have no other. But I am unconvinced by the somewhat self-explanatory and lazy way in which it is often applied. I have therefore attempted to destabilize common interpretative boundaries between text and context by exploring the relations between localness and nationalism and between memory and culture.

Rather than taking nationhood itself as the hard and set context within which memory and localness operate, I attempt to knock off balance the boundaries among these categories and to elucidate their hybrid relations. I call attention to the way localness and memory have been emplotted in stories of nationalism, and to the danger of reducing the local to the national and cultures of remembrance to the hegemony of the nation. Common understanding of the relations between the local and the national has viewed localness as subordinated to nationhood, and the local as not so much a shaper of nationalism but a repository of national belonging created elsewhere. Instead of understanding local identity as part of national identity and localness against the background of nationhood, I view local identity as a constituent of national identity and localness as the symbolic representation of the nation.

Similarly, rather than taking culture as the context within which memory operates, I try to undermine the distinctions between memory as representation and memory as social action. In doing this, I explore whether and in what way the presence of memory is not so much a manifestation of the culture around it, but its shaper. The way we place memory (the text: a museum, novel, monument) within a larger cultural context has interpretative and explanatory consequences. When a memory is placed within a broader cultural context, it is difficult to see in what way it is a shaper, rather than a reflection, of that context. If individual memory, identity, and motivation are only reflections of outside forces (the broader context), then this view stands in opposition to a cherished tenet of cultural history and memory studies: the idea that culture and memory not only reflect the social world but shape it as well. I think that this tenet is tenable. But I also think that it has recently been accepted uncritically as self-evident truth. How *does* the presence of memory act as a shaper of culture?

When I consider the topics of this book, memory and nationhood, and its principles of historical outlook, the notions of understanding and contingency, I can trace some of their origins to my youth in Jerusalem in the 1960s and 1970s. The Nazis and what they had wrought had obviously been all around me in some explicit ways, such as school commemorations, and in some subterranean ways, such as the sense of mystery and taboo that emerged from grown-ups' discussions over what happened "there," as the experience of the Holocaust was referred to. This background could and did produce different attitudes toward the study of modern German history. For me, a certain clarity of mind emerged from the plain moral storyline of the Third Reich, regarding who were the victims and who the perpetrators. I did not find it necessary, interesting, or illuminating to reiterate what was obvious by taking on a condemning, blaming, or pontificating historiographical voice. It was far more illuminating to tell the story of how and why human beings made it happen. Nor was I tempted to try to punish through historiography wrongs committed in history.

As a youngster, I understood human action within a grand narrative of Zionism that saw Jewish history as leading from the Diaspora to historical redemption in Israel. There are still elements of this narrative that are part of me, but what was important was that, as I looked around at my family, neighborhood, city, and larger society, I began to question an interpretation of the world that emphasized "unity and symmetry at the expense of experience," to borrow from Isaiah Berlin's marvelous essay "Historical Inevitability."[28] What impressed me was not the perceived onward movement toward a predetermined historical destination, but instead the unexpected turns, unpredictable outcomes, and malleable narratives that governed people's action and thought. In front of me I had the story of my maternal grandparents who grew up in bourgeois Jewish Roman families only to leave everything behind in the name of Zionism. In their early twenties—they were so young, come to think of it—they exchanged the comfortable accommodation of Via Cavour, just off the Foro Romano, for a leaking tent in a newly founded kibbutz. But there was nothing predetermined about it: my grandfather's older brother joined liberal Italian antifascist groups, while his younger brother turned to communism, becoming one of the leaders of the Italian Communist Party and an anti-Zionist. So much for a single, inevitable historical destination.

And I had in front of me Yona, the owner of the small neighborhood grocery store, who came from Kurdistan to the new state of Israel. I sensed the strong differences of background, class, and status between us; he was religious, I was secular; he joined the Zionist project after 1948, I symbolically owned it through my grandparents' activity. But I had no doubt that, in spite of all the differences, we shared a national history and fate. This was my first lesson in the making of a national "imagined community"—of uniting people who in fact have little, very little, in common—years before the term "imagined community" was coined. Now I know to interpret this as a process of construction of national identity, of making unity out of diversity, by ways of inventing national narratives, symbols, and memories.

As I grew up, I also began to be aware that my peaceful and happy Jerusalem childhood was built not only in the shadow of the Holocaust but also over the tragedy of uprooted Palestinians. It is difficult to think of a more compound modern historical case: the commingled history of the national traumas of two collectivities that claim one small piece of land as their homeland. One could see that that history indeed has no set libretto, for it shows that people are able to change in an amazingly short time. One could also see that the past is not always what it seems, and collectivities, nations, and historians do not always mean what they think they mean, and they do not always tell only the stories they think they tell. And that the historian should stand for justice that is recognizably human, a justice for both sides, that does not strive for a zero-sum-game solution in the name of some absolute, eternal—that is, nonhistorical—entity.

Someone else's book was never far from my mind when I wrote this text. Marc Bloch's *The Historian's Craft* had justifiably achieved canonical status as a meditation on the ways historians construct their object of study. Bloch began his book in 1941, as Europe seemed to enter a new, long-term historical epoch of dictatorships, racism, and extermination. Nazism was victorious on all fronts; doubts about the efficacy of human rationality and goodness were unavoidable. The opening line of the book is therefore understandable: "Tell me, Daddy. What is the use of history?" The book is an attempted answer by describing how and why a historian practices his or her trade.

"What is the use of history?" is always a pertinent question, also today, albeit for different reasons. History is assaulted by the acceleration of time as a result of the global market economy, by the rapid change of social and cultural ways of life and thought, and by technology's annihilation of space and time. But the past is relevant, today perhaps even more than yesterday, precisely because it disappears so quickly. I asked myself what we can learn by thinking about the historian's craft today in association with Bloch's book, and by thinking about modern German history in association with a classic that was written in the midst of the events that will forever define this history. It is a query that can only be briefly sketched, by way of conclusion.

Compared with the historical consciousness that informed *The Historian's Craft*, two present-day factors seem to be different and pertinent to the present book. The first is the rupture that the Holocaust brought to post-1945 historical sensibilities. Bloch understood the severity of the Nazi assault on truth and morality, but he could not have known or foreseen the severity of this assault or the magnitude of its consequences. One of these consequences has been the view, to various degrees also held by historians, that there are limits to our interpretation of the Holocaust as opposed to other events that face no such limits. Perhaps Bloch would have also expressed such doubts had he been faced with the Holocaust. Perhaps not, for he was a rationalist historian who was confident, too confident I would say, about the ability of the historical discipline to explain and interpret. Thinking about Bloch, the historian par excellence, puts the Holocaust in slightly clearer focus. The Holocaust can, like all historical events, be narrated and interpreted. It cannot be fully captured by the historical discipline, again like all historical events. The rupture that was the Holocaust is the ultimate case in showing that some understanding of the past is reserved for nonhistorical representations.

In terms of the historical discipline, therefore, it is not tenable anymore for historians to doubt in any way the possibility to narrate, explain, and interpret the Holocaust. There are elements in the extermination of the Jews, in the motivations and mind-set of the perpetrators, that are mysterious and irrational—similar to such elements in the history of, say, witchcraft—but instead of submitting to them, they should be submitted to investigation as historical mentalities. The problem of Holocaust thinking is that issues such as Nazi fears, redemptive ideas, collective mentalities and memories, and irrational, cosmological and theological views are all too often considered beyond the realm of history, instead of being studied as history. Everything is human, also inhumanity, and all is game for the historian. Bloch, who interpreted at times human experience too rationally, sensed precisely that in front of the Nazi assault on humanity. "Does anyone consider that the oppressive moral atmosphere in which we are currently plunged comes only from the rational part of our minds? We should seriously misrepresent the problem of causes in history if we are always and everywhere reducing them to a problem of motive," wrote Bloch during the war.[29] The way to understand this event historically is to explore the fact that, as Blaise Pascal observed in a different context, "Le coeur a ses raisons que la raison ne connaît pas."[30]

A second factor of present historical consciousness that is different from the early 1940s is the pervasiveness of the view that the truth is a metaphoric and rhetorical construct, thus undermining the notion of historical proof and blurring the distance between historical knowledge and fiction. This view has intellectual roots that reach well before 1945, but it has received in the half century after the Second World War wide public and scholarly attention and has, as we all know, become a major debate among scholars. It is interesting to think how Bloch would have reacted to this: he may have been surprised that an assault on truth that he associated with the Nazis became so widespread after the victory over the Nazis (and coming often from the left). In its extreme position of denying a possibility of verifiable historical knowledge, this view, to my mind, is closely connected to the Second World War, a sort of a paradoxical counterreaction to its horrors: the negation of the possibility of truthful accounts in order not to admit the terrible truth about what humans can do to each other. This extreme position, as I have discussed earlier, seems to me wrong on grounds of the procedures of data collection and evaluation of historical evidence as well as on moral grounds. The milder position—regarding the inherent bias of the historian who cannot be freed from his or her culture—reaffirms a well-known fact, which in itself does not undermine the basics of history as a method and technique. What do we do with this insight is something I have attempted to discuss in this text. At any event, it appears advisable to keep in mind the Third Reich and its horrors when arguing that all constructions of historical meaning are equal.

Ultimately, the historian's craft is to negotiate between articulating the beliefs, representations, and actions of historical actors and identifying the conditions that often unconsciously both shape and constrain the choices of these actors. And this, in a sense, is also the condition of the historian, who acts according to the rules of the discipline in attempting to craft a truthful, enlightening narrative about the past, while being constrained by the culture of his or her time and place.

PART I

THE LOCAL LIFE OF NATIONHOOD
GERMANY AS HEIMAT, 1871–1990

Several years ago I was asked to give a lecture on the "local turn" in the study of nationhood. The term left me pensive. It was exaggerated as far as it associates grand shifts in the humanities such as the linguistic or cultural turn. But it was not inappropriate to describe a grand shift in the study of nationhood, and the use of the term itself was significant. Who would have thought two decades ago that it would make no sense—in terms of method, theory, and empirical research—to understand the national without the local? I would like to articulate briefly this shift in the study of nationhood and of German nationhood, and to place my own work within that context.

The historiography of nationalism has been organized in the past two decades or so according to a three-tiered explanatory model: from the global— often expressed in terms of modernity—via the national, down to the local. How has the local been treated, as an explanatory device of nationalism, in these three levels? The first level is that of theoretical studies, such as the path-breaking works of Ernest Gellner and Benedict Anderson, that attempt to explain nationalism as a global historical phenomenon, as a social and cultural result of modernity.[1] For Gellner, nationalism is a result of industrial social organization; for Anderson, of print capitalism and widespread literacy. As modernity spreads around the globe, it spreads nationalism as well, though how this is exactly done we are never told. For these and other theoretical studies are interested, understandably, in the macro. They mention individual national cases only by way of example and by focusing on official and elite nationalism. As a result, they are uninterested in the ways modernity shaped, as well as was shaped by, the local. In short, for them the local can never be explanatory in any significant way: it is only the background, the context, for the national idea.

The second level is that of research on nationalism in specific nations. Scholars have explored the symbolism and social engineering of nationalism and the relations between old and new pasts in the making of nations. They have analyzed how people invented the nation through monuments, celebrations, museums, images, and other artifacts. But a dominant approach in these studies has viewed the locality only as a test case of a given territory where the nation fulfills itself. Already, with Eugen Weber's outstanding *Peasants into Frenchmen*, the question was posed in these terms: How did peasants (the local) become Frenchmen (that is, the national)? How the locality and the concept of localness altered, even forged, national belonging was an issue left largely unexplored.[2] In short, in terms of the scale of explanation, these studies are not fundamentally different from the perspective of Anderson and Gellner: they are simply doing on the national level what Anderson and Gellner had done on a global level.

Studies of the third, local level only took the invention of the nation onto a narrower spatial category, namely the locality and the region. The aim has been to show the nationalization of the locality and the region, and how the nation penetrated the local level, thus introducing mass politics, industrialization, and modernity. In the most extreme interpretation, influenced by modernization theory, local identity was seen as obliterated by national identity. Thus, in the 1970s and 1980s, two distinguished historians, Jürgen Kocka and Eugen Weber, made this argument for Germany and for France.[3] Again, in terms of the scale of explanation, this approach was simply doing on the local level what other studies did on the national and global level; the scale of observation was the local, but the local was not explanatory in any significant way.

A much more complex view of matters has now evolved.[4] We insist that the national did not simply erase or write over the local. We emphasize instead how the local appropriates the national, how the nation acquires different local meanings, how the local is celebrated in nationalist thought as the national home, and how the nation claims to actually be the local. We appreciate that no modern national identity could ignore or do without ideas of localness and regional identity. The old shibboleth about the relations of localness and nationhood was turned on its head: nationhood did not obliterate local and regional identity but instead invented, revived, and breathed new life into them.[5] The locality was not a bedrock of provincial backwardness but was interconnected with modernity. And nationalism and state building were constructed on the foundation of old regional, particularist states. This was the case in Germany, for example, where governments of territorial states (such as Bavaria and Württemberg) fostered particularism by building on policies and representations of German nationalism, which in turn were used after the unification in 1871 to sustain the new nation-state.[6] Overall, this new treatment of the local reflects the important shift from functional and structural analysis of nationalism toward analysis in terms of negotiations, mediation, culture, representation, memory, and agency.[7] The result of this approach, which has startlingly transformed the study of nationalism in terms of method, sophistication, and empirical knowledge, has been to view localness as part of, not as contradictory to, nationhood.

My work on the Heimat idea has been indebted to this distinguished body of work. From Anderson I took the idea of the nation as an imagined community that should be treated not as an ideology but in an anthropological spirit as religion and kinship; from Gellner, the idea that nationalism is not the awakening of nations to their deep historical essence but rather serves to invent nations where these do not exist; from Chatterjee, the process of appropriation, reception, imitation, rejection, and reinvention of the national idea by different groups within the nation; from Weber, the magnificent historical reconstruction of how ways of life and thought altered when nationhood met localness. And I have shared with other scholars of the new approach the view that negotiations and memory are fundamental to the meaning of localness and nationhood.

Still, it has been my sense that the challenge posed by localness to the understanding of nationhood—that is, to make the local the stage of the national plot, the shaper of nationhood imagination, and one of the explanations for the success of the national idea—has not been quite met. The locality has not been treated to a sufficient degree as an experimental variable. This has been true also for the new approach that views the relations between localness and nationhood in terms of mediation and negotiation, and which has a clear advantage over the model that saw the local as only the background of the national historical plot. For this new approach did not automatically change the basic perspective under which the meaning of the local was subordinate to the national. Some sophisticated treatments of the relations between national and regional identities, influenced by cultural history, have viewed the local as a significant part within the national plot, but they have not changed the explanatory relations whereby the nation acts as a context within which the region can be intelligibly understood and without which it has no meaning.

The point can be illustrated by using the following analogy, where the relations between nationhood and localness are viewed in terms of the relations between text and context. National identity often functions in studies of nationalism much like a necessary context that describes and analyzes the general conditions within which a particular local reality evolves. The national plot functions as a foundation story that, while complex and multifaceted, still provides a single context within which and in relation to which people make choices about local and national identity. It constructs one social reality within which local identity must make sense. But what happens when we reject this separation between localness and nationhood, when we break down the dichotomy of text and context? This is an invitation to reject the historian's common approach to place and explain the text in relation to a context. To reject the separation of localness and nationhood assumes that historical actors participate in various processes at the same time, that localness and nationhood simultaneously and reciprocally interact. To accept that none of these identities has primacy and yet to understand the meaning of national identity, we need to understand all of them as intertwined — the nation as a whole that is bigger than the sum of its parts. This serves as a reminder of what is declared more often than practiced—namely, the multiplicity of social experiences and representations, in part contradictory and ambiguous, in terms of which people construct the world and their actions.[8]

I attempted this kind of conceptualization in my own work on the Heimat idea in modern Germany.[9] My point of departure has been that there is no meaning to the national without the local, and that the question to ask is how did localness mold nationhood. Instead of understanding local identity as part of national identity, and localness against the background of nationhood, I viewed local identity as a constituent of national identity and localness as a shaper of nationhood. In contrast to the view of local, regional, and national sentiments as contradictory or overlapping, I viewed the Heimat idea as representing interchangeably the locality, the region, and the nation through an interlocking network of symbols and representations in which the nation appeared local and the locality national. Germans thus imagined nationhood as a form of localness. We have come full circle from the days when the local was the background and context of nationhood and could never be explanatory in any significant way: it has instead become the maker of national imagination and one of the explanations for the success of the national idea.

This way of using the notion of the local was useful to destabilize long-existing boundaries in current historical methods and narratives. One main problem in the study of nationhood is how to pose questions and at what level or scale. The three levels in the historiography of nationalism—the global, the national, and the local—are analytically neat and well organized; but they also create a tautology of narration within prearranged categories.

By looking at the Heimat idea, we challenge the boundaries and the hierarchy between these levels and scales of explanation. Rather than taking nationhood as the hard and set context within which localness operates, the attempt is to elucidate their hybrid relations and interdependent influences. We thus learn that nationhood is not primarily experienced and enacted on the abstract national level, but instead that it comes into being on the local level, in everyday life, in people's multiple decisions to become national and to embrace its past (invented or not). As a result the local appears as a shaper of nationhood: it is not merely symbolic of some deeper and more real national reality; it is a national reality (but not *the* national reality, for there are many others). It is not simply a place where the local and national meet in social practices; it is a place where one is made by the other. There is no pure space where the local remains immaculately local and the national immaculately national; they are in constant configurations as one shapes the other.

In German historiography, the pioneering study of Celia Applegate, *A Nation of Provincials: The German Idea of Heimat*, signaled a new evaluation of the role of the local within the national. Tracing the Heimat idea in the Palatinate from the 1850s to the 1950s, Applegate shed new light on its cultural invention and social origins and on the reformulations of the concept that placed the Palatinate and its inhabitants within the context of the nation for more than a century of political upheavals. Viewing the Heimat idea as a mediating concept between the immediate local life and the abstract nation, Applegate successfully showed the different ways in which Pfälzers used it "to rest finally on what both region and nation have in common."[10]

After being excoriated for decades, the Heimat idea has thus enjoyed in recent years a historiographical revival. Before the current interpretative change, the Heimat idea was usually seen either as a mythic German concept or as a human state-of-mind that longs for stability and human relations.[11] It was viewed as hopelessly antimodern, a reactionary escape from modernity, and a desperate nostalgic longing for a bucolic past.[12] Manufactured by conservatives in nineteenth-century Germany, the Heimat idea fostered, so the argument went, fundamentally anti-industrial and antitechnological ideas about a return to a primeval and pure state of society. From here the road was short and one-directional to the Nazi use of Heimat as an ideology of race, blood, and soil (*Blut und Boden*). Reactionary, provincial, antimodern, and manipulative—the Heimat idea epitomized all that was wrong with German nationhood.

In contrast, the Heimat idea is now considered a sophisticated cultural artifact engineered anew in the wake of the 1871 national unification as a way to reconcile local, regional, and national identities. Compared with two decades ago the number of new studies today is considerable and continues to grow.[13] Based on novel approaches to culture, nationalism, and memory, new studies have argued that Heimatlers took traditional ways of thinking about, and modes of representation of, the local and regional community and gave them a whole new meaning by connecting them to the nation in ways that were unpredictable before 1871. Far from being antimodern, Heimatlers expressed the ambiguity of modernity itself by simultaneously mourning the past while applauding the material progress and cultural opportunities promised by modernity. They commonly attempted to strike a modus vivendi between the preservation of national roots and the continuation of modernity and the prosperity it promised. Moreover, Heimat, far from being an exclusively reactionary idea, was widely popular in German society as a shared idiom of localness and nationhood. It has been appropriated by every group and ideology since 1871, from the bourgeoisie in imperial Germany, to the Nazis, to postwar West German Heimat films and East German authorities.[14] A flexible, dynamic, and malleable notion, Heimat was appropriated for different political and cultural ends; no one had exclusive copyrights on the Heimat idea, as it had been appropriated by very different hands in unpredictable ways.

What, then, was the significance of this diversity of meanings that constituted the Heimat idea? Was there at all a common denominator to this idea that steered such different emotions, represented different ideologies, and served different spatial and political masters? If we wish to understand the Heimat idea in terms of ideology, we miss the point. The ideological element of the Heimat idea is important if we wish to uncover aspects of political legitimacy and cultural representation. But the meaning of the Heimat idea was precisely its ability to go beyond ideological difference by providing a national lexicon to think and talk about Germanness regardless of who was in power. It would, I think, make things easier if one treated the Heimat idea as a historical mentality that gave Germans a cultural backbone to the modern changes in polity and society. It had a portable, symbolic manual that represented one ideology after another and gave Germans a sense of identity over time, regardless of the frequent political changes and opposing ideologies. Still, why this symbolic manual and not another? Which symbolic ingredients made it a success, and why? The following chapters tell the story of the invention, attributes, and working of the Heimat symbolic manual from the unification in 1871 to the unification in 1990.

1

THE NATION AS A LOCAL METAPHOR

Heimat, National Memory, and the German Empire, 1871–1918

The essence of a nation is that all individuals have
many things in common, and also that they have forgotten many things.
—*Ernest Renan*, What Is a Nation? *(1882)*

THINKING THE NATION

In the past two decades the most influential way of making sense of the sense of national belonging has been to regard the nation as a cultural artifact, as a product of invention and social engineering.[1] This "cultural turn" in the study of nationalism displaced the modernization theory, prevalent during the 1960s and 1970s, that argued that nationhood was a necessary concomitant of modernity, a form of belief produced by the cultural, economic, and technological transformation into and of modernity.[2] But in spite of the now flourishing interest in nationalism, the sense of national belonging remains a puzzling problem. This is due, in part, to the paucity of studies exploring the ways in which theories of nationalism have worked in practice in distinct countries. Perhaps more important is the failure of theory to encompass the malleability of nationhood. Scholars have usually emphasized one aspect of nationalism, such as economy and industrialization (Karl Deutsch, Ernest Gellner), ethnicity (Anthony Smith), or invention of the past (Eric Hobsbawm).[3] But nationhood defies these definitions. Although they are part of it, none fully embraces its ambiguous and often contradictory meanings. The multifariousness of nationhood is indeed striking: while it represents attachment to a defined territory, the *inter*national spread of nationalism appears to be its essence; while it is a new historical phenomenon, it is believed to be ancient; while it is part of modernity, it obsessively looks back to the past; while it yearns for the past, it simultaneously rejects the past by seeking to construct an improved version of it; while it represents the uniform nation, it tolerates a host of identities within the nation.

In order to understand the multifaceted character of nationhood and how it works, we should take note, I believe, of two features. The first is the process by which people internalize the nation. The modernization theory has been unsuccessful in providing an answer because by viewing nationhood as an inevitable product of modernization it has made national identity an inescapable progression from traditional to modern identity, whereas in reality nationhood is an irregular and uneven process in which people simultaneously embrace and repudiate the past. Scholars of the new cultural approaches to nationalism have not been more helpful. Although Eugen Weber, employing Deutsch's approach, has shown us in his study *Peasants into Frenchmen* how people pull themselves from local affairs into national affairs, we still lack a similar study that incorporates the new cultural and anthropological approaches to nationalism, delineating how people internalize the abstract world of the nation to create an imagined community.[4]

Indeed, the state of the research can be illuminated by the following example. Since 1983 Anderson's fascinating notion of the nation as an imagined community has become a household term in the way we conceive nationalism; but we still await a study that explores the process—social, political, and cultural—by which people come to imagine a distinct nation. Nationhood is a metaphor for social relations among millions of people:[5] we need a method that can tell us about the way people devise a common denominator between their intimate, immediate, and real local place and the distant, abstract, and not-less-real national world. Such a method must also be a remedy to the artificial dichotomy between nationalism from above and from below by exploring nationhood as a process by which people from all walks of life redefine concepts of space, time, and kin.

The second feature of national identity is its ability to represent the nation without excluding a host of other identities. Because it rejects other nations, national identity has often been regarded by scholars and laypersons as exclusive. The striking potential of nationhood to integrate diverse and frequently hostile groups within the nation is forgotten too easily. The full force of this fact becomes clear when we consider nationalism not as an ideology, like liberalism, fascism, or communism, but as a religion.[6] Nationalism, like religion, is a common denominator that defies gender, regional, social, and political divisions, relegating these categories to secondary position. Both are capable of representing the oneness of something, God or the nation, and simultaneously the particularity of other identities; their representation is more than the sum of the identities that coexist in them. We need a method of analyzing national society and culture that embraces both nationhood and other identities that exist in the nation.[7]

How, then, are we to look at nationhood? I suggest viewing it from the perspective of collective memory, as a product of collective negotiation and exchange between the many memories that exist in a nation. This is a developmental approach to the history of nationhood, emphasizing the contingencies in its construction. By stressing the interaction between national memory and other memories, this approach explores nationhood through the metaphor of whole and parts, taking cognizance of national identity and national society as a global entity where peculiar component parts interact.

Furthermore, I suggest expanding the notion of national memory to embrace also the notion of imagined community, so that memory can tell us not only what people remembered of the past, but also how they internalized an impersonal world by putting it in familiar and intelligible categories. Anderson described a similar process: the nation "is imagined because the members of even the smallest nation will never know most of their fellow members . . . yet in the minds of each lives the image of their communion," or, we may say, the image of their national memory.[8] By combining the notions of national memory and imagined community, we can understand how people construct a common denominator between local and national memory.

In this chapter, I recount how Germans constructed a collective image of the nation, and how conceptions of localness and nationhood altered in the process. My point of departure is the deep fractures—mainly regional, but also social, political, and religious—that characterized German society during the Second Empire (1871–1918), and the logical question that follows: how did Germans construct across the lines that divided them a certain idea of German society and Germanness that represented them all, so that in August 1914 they marched united in the name of the nation?

COLLECTIVE MEMORY

The notion of collective memory has been used in the past two decades, with uneven degrees of success and sophistication, to explore how a social group, be it a family, a class, or a nation, constructs a past through a process of invention and appropriation and what it means to the relationship of power within society. The notion of memory has been a latecomer in historical studies.[9] Historians were preceded by psychoanalysts (Sigmund Freud), philosophers (Henri Bergson), and writers (such as Marcel Proust), who, unlike historians, regarded memory as a faculty of the individual mind; by anthropologists, who found memory a more suitable concept than history to understanding illiterate societies (Jack Goody); and by sociologists (Maurice Halbwachs and Roger Bastide).[10] The first to have used the concept systematically was Halbwachs, whose fundamental contribution was to establish the connection between a social group and collective memory. In a series of studies, Halbwachs argued that every memory is carried by a specific social group limited in space and time.[11]

Of course, social groups cannot remember, for this is only a faculty of the individual.[12] And, certainly, people cannot remember events in which they did not take part. Yet you do not need to have stormed the Bastille in order to celebrate July 14 as a symbol of national identity. One's memory, like one's most intimate dreams, originates from the symbols, landscape, and past that are shared by a given society. Because the making and the reception of memories, personal and collective, are embedded in a specific cultural, social, and political context, we can explore how people construct a past in which they did not take part individually, but which they share with other members of their group as a formative sense of cultural knowledge, tradition, and singularity.[13]

I use collective memory as a tool to get at a component of the historical mentality of Germans in the past, namely that which concerned local-national memory. I view memory as a symbolic representation of tradition and of the past embedded in the context of social action. Differently put, the study of collective memory explores the experiential history of people's perceptions of the past where social action and symbolic representation commingle. The notion of collective memory is interesting and useful in that it can tell us not only about how the past is represented in a single museum or commemoration but about the role of the past in the life of a social group. In the study of collective memory we should look not only at the representation of the past but also at its rejection and reception. Every society sets up imaginary pasts. But to make a difference in a society, it is not enough for a certain past to be selected. It must steer emotions, motivate people to act, and be received; in short, it must become a sociocultural mode of action. Why is it that some pasts triumph while others fail? Why do people prefer one invented past over another? The answers to these questions lead us to formulate hypotheses and perhaps draw conclusions about historical mentality. I attempt to answer these questions with regard to the symbolic representation of the German nation in the Heimat idea after the unification in 1871.

What, then, was the matrix of German memory in the new nation-state?

Germany's modern national memory began in 1871. Before 1871 there was a history of the Germans and German history, but no history of Germany; only thereafter did German history proceed as a single development. As James Sheehan has aptly said, before 1871 "'Germany' did not exist. . . . [T]here was no clear and readily acceptable answer to the question of Germany's political, social, and cultural identity. German history, therefore, [was] not the single story of a fixed entity . . . [but] many different histories that co-existed."[14] The unification of 1871, therefore, joining the German nation, German society, and a German state within a single territory, redefined the spatial and historical dimensions of the nation and the ways Germans remembered their pasts. To be sure, Germans had national recollections before 1871, but the foundation of the nation-state conditioned a reevaluation of old memories as never before. To suppose otherwise is to view German history and German national memory as predetermined; but, on the contrary, before the Prussian-Austrian War in 1866, the exclusion of Austrian history, the hegemony of Prussian history, and the superiority of Protestant to Catholic memories, to mention only a few notable examples, were not inevitable for German nationhood.[15]

At the same time, in spite of the unification of the nation-state, German nationhood continued to exist as a patchwork of regions and states, a mosaic of divergent historical and cultural heritages sanctioned by the nation-state's federal system. While the regional states lost their sovereignty, they maintained their preunification structure including a head of state, symbols, a Landtag (regional parliament), a government, a bureaucracy, and peculiar laws. Of course, slowly in the 1870s and more effectively from the 1880s, institutions were developed on the Reich level that introduced standardization throughout the empire. One can think of the standardization of currency, weights, and measures put into effect in 1873, or of the more complex and gradual uniformity of law and the court system. But, in general, standardization in important fields such as education, social policy, economic policy, national symbols, and also courts and jurisdiction proceeded little by little; the constitution of 1871 left policy in these and other matters largely to the choice of the states.[16] Perhaps the most revealing element of this principle of German nationhood was the multitude of political systems in the empire. In Germany, as in the United States, the empire had one political system, while every region kept its own traditional one. As a consequence, the empire had an authoritarian political system based on free male suffrage and a Reichstag that had little real power to influence the government and the emperor; Prussia had a conservative and antidemocratic three-class suffrage system designed to keep the Junkers in power; and Württemberg enjoyed a more liberal and democratic political system. This high level of regional fragmentation reflected the diversity of regional identities and their autonomy with respect to national identity.[17]

Among the many peculiarities that have been attributed to German history, this was a genuinely distinctive feature—for no European people set up a nation-state as a conglomeration of regional *states*.[18] Regional diversity, of course, has been a common feature in the European nation-states, and overlapping regional and national allegiances were not at all unusual. An obvious case was Italy, unified between 1860 and 1870 from as many regions as Germany, which had to cope with a tremendous level of regional fragmentation between North and South. But even nineteenth-century Britain, which is often viewed as enjoying a progressive integration, knew a similar phenomenon. Victorians strongly perceived national diversity between the North and South of England, between London and the provinces, and between the distinct national identities of Scotland, Wales, and England.[19] In Germany, however, regional diversity was institutionalized in regional states. Maintaining such a level of regional variegation and autonomy within the nation was more than simply acknowledging regional differences, which were also acknowledged in countries that did not have the German form of nationhood. It was rather a reflection of the essence of the nation as a whole, composed of regional identities and, by extension, of the locality and the region as the cradle of German nationhood.[20]

The notion of collective memory enables us to reinterpret the unification of 1871 and the regional fragmentation of Germany within the context of consciousness of national belonging. What Ferdinando Martini, secretary of education, declared during the patriotic outburst following the humiliating Italian defeat at Adua in 1896—"We have made Italy: now we must make Italians"—applied after 1871 to regional Germans: they had made Germany; now they had to make Germans from the multitude of regional identities, Germans who would be attached to the region as well as to the nation-state, not ceasing to be local patriots but acknowledging the supremacy of national patriotism.[21] The problem was, then, how to construct a national memory that would reconcile the peculiarities of the region and the totality of the nation? And, more generally, how to construct a memory that would reconcile Germanness and the multitude of identities within the nation?

Historians must therefore seek an idea of Germanness in the Second Empire that was a national framework for symbolic diversity, a representation of German nationhood based on the metaphor of whole and parts, a concept for understanding the German way of life as comprising the various ways of life that existed in the nation. Such a concept may not be immediately visible in the common sources of nationalism, such as documents of national associations, history books, and even symbolic representations of the nation like national holidays. For the essence of this idea is its indistinctness, its capacity to mean different things to different people: in order to work as a national common denominator, the meanings of this idea had to be interchangeable. We have to look for such an idea, therefore, not in the social and cultural meeting points where nationalism was explicit and its meaning palpably manipulated, but rather in the realm of collective mentality where things were implied rather than said, and blurred rather than clear. Such an idea of Germanness, or of any nationhood for that matter, which crossed regional, political, class, confessional, and gender lines, had to be abstract enough to collapse differences into similarities.

This mode of proceeding has led me to the idea of Heimat, which represented after the 1880s the ultimate German community—real and imagined, tangible and symbolic, local and national—of people who had a particular relationship to one another, sharing a past and a future. Germans constructed Heimat as an interchangeable representation of the local, the regional, and the national community. In the minds of Germans, the Heimat idea allowed Catholics and Protestants, liberals and socialists, Prussians and Bavarians to remain themselves, yet to form together a transcendent national community.

Although the meaning of Heimat memory was, as we shall see, fluid, Heimat was—as a collective memory—an organized and structured social reality. Composed of three elements—history, nature, and folklore or ethnography—the Heimat idea was carried in German society by diverse vehicles of memory. Some of the most important were the Heimat books (*Heimatbücher*), published by communities to make public to natives and foreigners alike their singularity in national and local history; the Heimat studies (*Heimatkunde*) that entered the school curriculum in the 1890s; the 371 Heimat museums that were founded between 1890 and 1918 across Germany, in locales ranging from the metropolis of Berlin to provincial small towns; and a host of associations that cultivated and propagated the Heimat idea, thus giving to memory a social continuity and regularity, such as local beautification societies (*Verschönerungsvereine*) and historical associations (*Geschichtsvereine*), regional Heimat associations, and, from 1904, the national German League for Heimat Protection (Deutscher Bund Heimatschutz).

These vehicles of memory and others demonstrate the extent of Heimat's diffusion and popular origins in German society. The social origin of the Heimat idea was the German bourgeoisie in its wider definition, including diverse groups such as the intellectual and economic upper bourgeoisie (*Bildungsbürgertum*) and bourgeoisie of the lower middle class (*Kleinbürgertum*). The composition of Heimat associations exemplified the social diversity of the Heimat idea. Heimat associations, strictly speaking, such as the German League for Heimat Protection or the League for Heimat Protection in Württemberg and Hohenzollern (Bund für Heimatschutz in Württemberg and Hohenzollern), the flagships of the Heimat idea, comprised the upper classes and *Bildungsbürgertum*. Their membership was selective; the league in Württemberg and Hohenzollern numbered in 1911 only 3,500 members.[22] The social composition of associations such as the beautification societies or historical associations varied, however, according to a locality's size and importance. In a small community, with few or no members of the upper classes and *Bildungsbürgertum*, lower-middle-class notables played a central role. Thus, in 1885, when Heimat memory began to develop, there was little in common socially, economically, and culturally between the distinguished *Bildungsbürgertum* members of Stuttgart's Beautification Society and the members (a local teacher, a pharmacist, and the like) of the society of Eningen in Württemberg, which had 3,405 inhabitants.[23]

Thus, the diverse geographical origins of Heimat memory in cities, towns, and small towns demonstrated its diverse social origins. Although the difference in wealth and social status between Heimatlers from Eningen and Berlin was enormous, they produced together the Heimat idea. The production and reception of the Heimat idea, therefore, like that of the national idea itself, question the notion that cultural cleavages and cultural common denominators are necessarily organized according to social divisions constructed beforehand. The idea of Heimat defies an attempt to explain cultural originations in social structures. Instead, it was a popular representation of the nation, not in the sense that it was from below instead of from above—a dichotomy that should be avoided—but in the sense that it was produced, carried, and received by diverse social groups, both from below and from above. Heimat stemmed from *l'Allemagne profonde*, from dozens of provincial localities and big cities that boasted a Heimat museum or a historical association.

The production of Heimat memory after the 1880s reflected social and political changes in imperial Germany, namely, the enlargement of the public realm that entailed the gradual loss of control by the notables over provincial life, and the ascension of new social groups such as the petty bourgeoisie and middle classes who demanded a domestic place in the sun. Heimat associations, such as historical associations, again exemplified these changes. The associations had existed before the 1880s and, composed solely of notables, reflected their control of the public interpretation of the past, local and national. After the 1880s the number of associations grew rapidly and their social composition and message changed. The middle classes and petty bourgeoisie of provincial towns, not only *Bildungsbürgertum* notables from political and cultural centers, were members of the associations. Moreover, economic progress elevated a new group of merchants, businessmen, and industrialists who had a modern idea, determined by commercial considerations, about the role of the past in the growing public realm. A new mode of communication and display of the past developed, which was public, visible, and accessible to all, thus changing the social destination of the associations' message and turning the Heimat idea into a collective experience through lectures, newspaper inserts, popular publications, and school activities. The Heimat museum, which will be discussed later, epitomized the popularization of the new representation of Germany's local and national pasts. The public representation of the nation, once a territory reserved for the scholarly elite, was now popularized, appropriated, simplified, and packaged for mass consumption.

Neither peasants nor workers took part in the production of the Heimat idea, and while aristocrats were members of associations in, say, Berlin, their overall influence was moderate. The origins of Heimat memory were overwhelmingly in provincial Germany, and, after all, how many aristocrats were there in Eningen? The notable and nonnotable members of the bourgeoisie who originated the Heimat idea were city and town dwellers, who, being often leaders of the community, stood at the crossroads of the great developments of German society after 1871: modernity and nation building. In Heimat memory they found a way to reconcile local with national identity, and local and national pasts with modernity. To understand how it worked, let us focus on the south German state of Württemberg and its people, the Swabians.

HEIMAT: A COMMON DENOMINATOR OF VARIOUSNESS

One of the most striking phenomena in the study of nationalism is the discrepancy between people's willingness to believe in their nation, to identify with it, and even to die for it and scholars' belittlement of nationalism's depth of meaning (most common under the ubiquitous manipulation idea). Even scholars who have taken nationalism seriously have too often explained it by concentrating on one variable such as ethnicity or economic progress. For most, if not all people, however, nationhood includes the whole of life, and what makes the Heimat idea so interesting for scholars of nationalism is that it reveals the depth of meaning, intellect, and feeling of the national idea. Through Heimat, Germans made sense of their local and national nature, history, and old—and vanishing—ways of life and thought; gave apposite answer to modernity; and interpreted social and political relations in imperial Germany.

Heimat memory was, first of all, a framework for interpreting national history and the multitude of histories that coexisted in Germany. Heimat history wove the past, present, even the future, of Swabia and Germany into a coherent history, which highlighted both the distinctiveness of the part, Swabia, and the oneness of the whole, Germany. The Heimatlers' aim was to show not Württemberg's glory but Württemberg's distinctiveness in an age of national standardization and the place of this distinctiveness within the fatherland. The subjects of Heimat history embodied the essence of Swabianness and Germanness. Herwarth von Bittenfeld, a mercenary from a distinguished Swabian family, joined the Prussian army of Friedrich the Great, thus symbolizing Swabian courage, good judgment, love for the fatherland, and the converging histories of north and south Germany.

But there was more than history in Heimat history. Wilhelm Seytter, an author of a Heimat book about Stuttgart, explained the difference: "Heimat studies . . . enter affectionately into people's simple and daily life, down from the ivory tower of scholarship into the valleys and meadows of civil, family, and even personal life. . . . Heimat is not a prosaic system of concepts, and Heimat studies are not a logical theory. Heimat has been given to us by the disposition of our ancestors." [24] Heimat was not a system of concepts but rather a system of sentiments that combined knowledge and sensibilities. Heimat history did not lend itself to historical scientific rigor because it attempted to evoke empathy and identity with its subject matter, rather than an understanding of it. The detachment demanded from historians for an objective evaluation was the antithesis to Heimat history, which was personal and direct. That is why the Heimat was usually addressed in the second-person singular: "o you [Du] my Heimat, you my native land / How my heart has turned to you full of love!"[25] Anthropomorphizing Heimat was seen as neither ridiculous nor preposterous: it elicited an intimate relationship with Heimat. A reader of a Heimat book was not an outside observer to an unfolding of facts, but always an integral part of the narrative, the landscape, and the history. "It is a bright May morning," opens a Heimat book for Kirchheim unter Teck, "I would like to take you by the hand, dear reader, and lead you into the quiet splendor of the valley's spring."[26]

Like every history, Heimat history appreciated the past for what it bestowed on the present. With its mixture of facts and literary narrative, Heimat history provided roots in an ever-changing world. In particular, Heimat history looked in the past for reassurances of local uniqueness in times of homogenization of national politics, economy, and culture. The program of the Committee for Nature Conservation and Heimat Protection (Landesausschuss für Natur- and Heimatschutz), founded in 1909, declared that its tasks were "to emphasize and to stress the peculiarities of local character of the various areas of Württemberg . . . which constitute the diversity of the Heimat."[27] Armed with hometown patriotism, every locality wrote its own Heimat history, emphasizing its own historical importance and inheritance: the people of the small town of Tuttlingen took care of the ruins of Honburg Castle, destroyed in 1642, and those of Kirchheim renovated the Reussenstein ruins. At the same time, this local activity showed the boundaries within which Heimat history was meaningful, namely, a national context that made sense of the present, the German Empire. For although Seytter argued that Heimat history was not a logical theory, it had in fact an innate and distinct logic. Local peculiarities had to contribute to national similarities and were not to stand out as digressions in the Heimat idea. Therefore, several episodes in Württemberg history were eradicated, notably the wars in 1813, when Württemberg fought on Napoleon's side in the Battle of the Nations against fellow Germans, and in 1866, when Württemberg fought with Austria against the unification of Germany under Prussia's hegemony.

Every notion of territoriality, such as nationhood, has to provide a reading of the relations between humankind and nature. Through poems, stories, travels, and conservation activity, Heimatlers cherished and cultivated a poetic view of nature, which was fundamental to Heimat sensibilities because it connected the local community with the national community and endowed the national community with a sense of homeyness that became the hallmark of the Heimat idea. Tangible, visible, and therefore easier to identify with than history, Heimat nature attached coziness to the hometown, Württemberg, and the fatherland. The language of poeticized nature lent itself easily to sentimental and gushy descriptions: "o you, my Heimat, valleys and hills / In my soul you will always be."[28] Used in local and national contexts, Heimat nature underscored the affinity between man, nature, roots, region, and fatherland.

Associating the locality or the nation with nature was commonplace in German poetry and literature before the 1880s. The novelty of Heimat nature, however, was that it enlarged the territory of sentimental belonging from a local to a national one. It created a base for Württembergers to feel "o you, my Heimat, valleys and hills" for landscapes they had never seen or visited, such as Thuringia or Pomerania. The foundation in 1904 of the German League for Heimat Protection and in 1909 in Württemberg of the League for Heimat Protection and the Committee for Nature Conservation and Heimat Protection merely confirmed the changes in the perception of nature that had taken place since the 1880s. So the League for Heimat Protection in Württemberg vowed to "protect the natural and historical peculiarity of the *German Heimat*."[29] The language of Heimat nature fostered an abstract image, beyond the physical and concrete nature of locality, a stereotypization of national imagery, as we shall see in the discussion of the iconography of Heimat.

Having embraced local history and nature, Württembergers set out to infuse Heimat with life, and particularly with the Württemberger way of life, by cultivating a local ethnographic consciousness—Heimat folklore. A project to collect all the popular traditions in Württemberg organized in 1899 by the state's Royal Statistical Office and the Württemberger Folklore Association included the whole of life: food, clothing, habitation, law and administration, rituals, festivities, songs, legends, dialects, beliefs and superstitions, customs at home and work, and many others—a genuine field questionnaire of anthropologists.[30]

Folklore was used and understood in German society in various ways. Some ethnographic studies followed well-known and established academic methods based on the principle of telling what the past really looked like. But creativity and invention were integral to the cultivation of ethnographic consciousness. For Heimat as a "system of sentiments" Truth was never a goal. Traditions could be invented, providing they conformed to contemporary notions of ancientness, peasant culture, and Swabianness and that they would not stand out awkwardly among real historical traditions. Swabian *Tracht*, or traditional folk costume, was a case in point.

After the decline and disappearance of traditional costumes in the course of the nineteenth century, Württemberg's Heimatlers from towns and cities, in their search for origins, counterresponded to monotonous modern apparel by dusting off the traditional colorful peasant dresses. They called the traditional costume *Tracht*, a word that originated among the urban bourgeoisie and that no peasant could understand.[31] Heimatlers simplified the myriad and elaborate traditional costumes (unlike modern costumes, villagers had special apparel and articles of clothing designed for weekdays, social purposes, celebrations, and the like), constructed a few prototypes, and packaged them for mass consumption: what was important was the colors of the costume, not its historical accuracy. The invented tradition of *Tracht* was very popular: sections on local *Tracht* became a staple of Heimat books;[32] a *Tracht* association was founded; and Heimat museums displayed it. Soon the commercialization of *Tracht*, that is, of tradition, was in full swing. Villagers understood that selling at town markets in traditional dress associated freshness and health with their products. Others sold for high prices the old costumes from grandmother's chest. And photographers sold pictures, taken some weeks before, of authentic *Tracht* from the good old days. Heimat folklore thus integrated many single local traditions into a whole—Württemberger ethnographic consciousness—that was more than the sum of its parts. Local *Tracht*, therefore, gave rise to *schwäbische Tracht*, pure historical invention.[33]

Most important, Heimat ethnographic consciousness represented the nation as a three-tier construction of local, regional, and national ways of life. A classic case was the study of Swabian dialect, *Mundart*. Language embodied Swabian distinctiveness: "The language of our people offers one of the most important means to know its peculiarity. . . . [Our language] still streams in the localities of our Heimat with its blend of power, originality, nativeness, and simplicity."[34] The first tome of the Swabian dictionary published in 1904 symbolized this uniqueness. At the same time, language embodied Germanness. The editor of the dictionary, Hermann Fischer, declared in the introduction that the history of Swabian dialect was part of the history of German philology.[35] The nation resembled the Russian Matryoshka doll, as it accommodated and integrated smaller versions of itself: areas in Württemberg had different dialects; together they formed the Swabian dialect; and all the regional dialects constituted the German language. Similar constructions occurred with regard to food, dance, and the like. Heimat folklore linked generations by emphasizing the longevity of traditions, real or invented, thus connecting the past and present. In times of technological change, finding one's roots meant making sense of modernity.

Through the Heimat idea, Heimatlers transformed the localness of history, nature, and folklore into a concept of nationhood. In particular, it was the task of the Heimat museums—which, existing across Germany, represented the single community, yet in their totality were a representation of the entire nation—to mold the image of the nation and transform localness into nationhood. What was the image of the nation that Heimatlers constructed from local existence?

HEIMAT MUSEUMS:
A NATIONAL HISTORY OF LOCAL AND EVERYDAY LIFE

Between 1890 and 1918, 371 Heimat museums were founded in cities, towns, and small towns across the German homeland, which amounted to a popular assault on the representation of the local and the national pasts.[36] A direct outcome of the production of Heimat memory, Heimat museums embodied, first of all, the uniqueness of the locality. The past of even the smallest community was worthy of collection and exhibition, as museum activists in Oettingen (Bavaria) explained in 1908: "Although some may think that in the Ries there are no historical objects to collect, we are nonetheless convinced that even here there are plenty of interesting historical objects to find and to preserve."[37] As Heimat museums became the symbol of local identity, how could a community live without one? Th. Bruss, a Heimat activist, gave in 1913 the reasons for the foundation of a museum in his hometown: "Reinfeld [Holstein] belongs to a category of localities that cannot be denied the foundation of a Heimat museum, for Reinfeld has had, as everybody knows, a long history."[38] Every community in Germany had had, as everybody knew, a long history, and Heimat museums therefore proliferated rapidly, endowing the local past with significance in times of national standardization.

Heimat museums displayed the past in its entirety, from prehistory to the present, as a story of origins and everyday-life experience. The museum activists in Oettingen were true to their words and collected "plenty of interesting historical objects": heraldic figures, documents, drawings, objects of guilds, pottery and kitchenware, *Trachten*, furniture, genealogical albums, "miscellaneous such as" locks, shoe buckles, spoons, knives, rings, and many other items.[39] These objects, which filled Heimat museums across Germany, emanated from people's lives in the community—the private and the public spheres, home, work, and family.

The aim of Heimat museums, however, was not simply to represent local communities but to give meaning to the national whole. Museum activists claimed that national identity sprang from local identity. The Heimat museum in Jever in Friesland (founded in 1887) was established in order to "advance the local archaeology and through this activity the love for Heimat and for the German fatherland."[40] By founding Heimat museums that represented the local German past, Heimatlers constructed a typology of the national past. Although every local history was particular, it was displayed by means of similar objects. Together Heimat museums across Germany constructed a national narrative that depicted "small people" instead of the elites, everyday life instead of major historical events, and the locality as the location of the origins of the nation. Heimat activists not only exhibited everyday-life objects but also set out to record popular historical memories. In Vilsbiburg (Bavaria) the museum committee collected people's memories of "interesting, historical, or local events, for example, from the Napoleonic Wars," a project that today we call oral history.[41] The habitat of common people was reconstructed, as in the open-air Heimat museum of Scheeßel in Lower Saxony (founded in 1913), which had a fully equipped peasants' house of 1830.[42] This comprehensive approach to everyday life included peasants, *Bürger*, and members of the guilds, the majority of small-town inhabitants before industrialization. As a national phenomenon, Heimat museums thus endowed the abstract nation with the tangibility of local experience.

The Heimatlers' conception of local and national history sheds light on the relation between memory and social change in Germany. Heimat museums were part of the enlargement of both the public sphere and the social boundaries of the nation that included after the 1880s the petty bourgeoisie and the middle classes. A comparison between historical museums founded before the unification and Heimat museums is revealing and permits an understanding of the changes in German society around 1890. The big historical museums founded in Germany before 1871 (the Museum rheinisch-westfälischer Altertümer, founded in Bonn in 1829, the Germanisches Nationalmuseum in Nuremberg and the Römisch germanisches Zentralmuseum in Mainz, both founded in 1852) were established in central cities and displayed a national history. The diverse social and geographical character of Heimat museums attests to their new reading of German history. Whereas the national museums were established by the upper classes for the educated public, forming public spaces dominated by strict and elitist social manners, local Heimat museums were established for the general public, as expressed in their humble location, simple exhibition, and nonscholarly representation of the past. While national museums were located in cities that were cultural and political centers, Heimat museums were located also in small localities, in the periphery; national museums pertained to urban Germany, Heimat museums also to German hometowns. Heimat museums thus reflected a popular and inclusive conception of culture.[43] That is why museum activists set open hours on Sundays, which permitted working people to visit the museum on the day of repose, and entrance was free or fees were minimal (twenty pfennigs, for example). Heimat museums, therefore, presented an alternative to an elitist, educated, and centralist image of the nation that excluded the social and the geographical periphery of the nation.

The Heimat idea, transforming local Heimat history, nature, and ethnography into a concept of nationhood, thus bridged diverse social groups within the German bourgeoisie. It also bridged the local Heimat and the national one and became a definition of both. After the 1880s new Heimats seemed to spring up daily in the German homeland. Heimat meant Germany, as in the German League for Heimat Protection. Heimat also meant region, as in the League for Heimat Protection in Württemberg and Hohenzollern and other organizations for almost every German province and region. Heimat meant district, as in the Heimat book *Heimat Studies of the Göppingen District*.[44] Heimat meant city, as in Wilhelm Seytter's *Our Stuttgart*. It meant town, as in *Heimat Book of Reutlingen*. And it meant small town, as in a Fellbach Heimat book.[45] Everywhere one looked in Germany, there lay a Heimat, which became the ultimate metaphor in German society for roots, for feeling at home wherever Heimat was—the homeland, the region, the hometown. Thus, one's Heimats were simultaneously, say, Reutlingen, Swabia, and Germany. How many Heimats were there in the German Empire? One, two, three . . . a thousand?

By allowing localities and regions to emphasize their historical, natural, and ethnographic uniqueness and, at the same time, by integrating them all, the Heimat idea was a common denominator of variousness. It balanced the plurality of local identities and the restrictions imposed by the imperatives of a single national identity. A thousand Heimats dotted Germany, each claiming uniqueness and particularity. And yet, together, the Heimats informed the ideal of a single, transcendent nationality. It is to this generic Heimat, therefore, that we now turn.

THE NATION IN THE MIND

All Heimats were both different and similar, but one was more different from and more similar to all the others. The German Heimat comprised all the Heimats, but was more than the sum of its parts. It was, in the words of the founding declaration of the German League for Heimat Protection in 1904, "the Heimat itself, our German land, the fertile soil of German civilization." [46] As the German imagined community, the national Heimat was the ultimate expression of the Heimat idea and the ultimate symbolic representation of the German nation and of its histories, memories, and sentiments.

The period of the First World War proves especially fruitful for exploring the Heimat idea as an imagined national community and its reception in German society. In the crucible of the war, Germans embraced the symbols, values, and ideals that united and represented them most. If Heimat had become part of the collective memory of German society before 1914, then, logically, Germans would employ it during the war.

Two privileged sources of *l'histoire des mentalités* are used in this exploration. Literary sources have been regarded by scholars as a fundamental representation and vehicle of collective memory. A model of this genre is Paul Fussell's *The Great War and Modern Memory*, which is based solely on British literary sources. Typically, the war gave rise to a flood of literary works by people from all walks of life, soldiers at the front and civilians at the rear. The most popular literary genre—by far—was poems published for mass consumption, in small, cheap booklets made of inexpensive paper. Their diffusion was widespread, and booklets by the tens of thousands were printed and sold in Germany and at the front. Even the names of the booklets indicated the status of the Heimat idea in the public mind. One booklet was entitled *Around the Heimat: Pictures from the World War*, another was named simply *The Heimat: New War Poems*.[47] Obviously, in these booklets Heimat meant Germany. The second source of this investigation are images where the Heimat idea was defined and codified as a collective representation of the nation.

In the patriotic, military, and unstable environment of the war, the idea of Heimat represented, as before 1914, the eternal German community. In the Heimat idea, the nation was associated with an ideal, small community, a village or a hometown, which personified intimacy. A poem entitled "Heimat" described the idea with precision:[48]

> Is this not the Heimat?—September's meadows.
> Over there, clear golden rays pierce the air.
> Mowed fields. The strong scent of the harvest.
> And a chain of hills, like bowed giants,
> On the horizon. With round, red knob
> Rises dignified the Heimat's church tower.
> The trees hang satiated and loaded with fruits.
> The peasants' wheat accumulates in golden swaths.
> This is the Heimat!

We do not know whether Julius Berstl, the poet, indeed lived in a village or whether the village's church tower had a round, red knob, but this is of course irrelevant. What is important is the description of warmth and familiarity, a description that arouses immediate recognition.

Heimat always depicted the nation as a community within nature and in harmony with nature. Trees, fruits, gardens, brooks, hills, and the earth were made part of the representation of the nation.[49] This landscape had human dimensions and suggested companionship between man and nature. Nature that inspired awe and challenged—or seemed to defy—men and women, such as big mountains and rivers, was left out. With descriptions of brooks and hills, nature in the Heimat idea was, to use an expression from our own days, user-friendly. This depiction of nature was never attached to a specific place or time. It was an aggregation of the most appealing elements of nature that informed a generic Heimat.

Descriptions of the village or hometown also avoided reference to specific buildings, institutions, and places in the locality, such as school, market, and town hall. Even the church tower, which became a leading symbol of Heimat, was never described in detail, so as not to resemble a specific one.[50] The church tower was the symbol of the manageable and intimate community. Every German could easily think of his or her locality's church tower, for every German locality had one. Before skyscrapers dotted the urban landscape, church towers were the dominant architectural feature in the German skyline. Returning to the locality, one saw the church tower from afar and sighed with happiness; leaving it, one looked back to see the tower and cherish the memories. The church tower evoked the sound of bells, which was a traditional symbol of a community.[51] Bells rang to summon the community, on Sundays and holidays, and to announce important news; theirs was the sound of human activity and human society. The church tower, there-fore, symbolized not only a locality, but also its people. It was a center of com-munal life, a pivotal location for one's relations to man and God. In the idea of national Heimat, the church tower evoked human community. Although it was a dominant feature, the church tower was never too imposing. It was noticeable enough to emphasize human community and modest enough to express the harmonious relations between nature and man. Perhaps more important, the church tower, historically old, represented history itself, the roots and immemorial times of the community.

The emphasis on indeterminate nature and locality in these poems and elsewhere led to the representation of the nation as a generic Heimat. This was crucial to the reception of Heimat in German society as an imagined na-tional community that embraced the individual Heimats. To fit every Heimat in Germany, the German Heimat had to fit no specific one. To enable every German to imagine his or her own individual Heimat, the German Heimat had to fit any place and no place, thus becoming applicable to every local and regional identity in Germany. A clearly defined national Heimat would have been unable to convey the meaning of unity *and* diversity and to harmonize the indivisible nation with the multitude of local and regional identities.

The embodiment of the collective image of the nation was expressed in the iconography of Heimat. Heimat images were diffused across the length and breadth of Germany through newspapers, journals, publications of Hei-mat associations, school textbooks, Heimat books, Heimat museums, and the like. The diffusion of Heimat images reached its peak when associa-tions for the advancement of tourism (*Fremdenverkehrsvereine*) adopted and propagated the Heimat idea as an image of the nation: Heimat images be-came a necessary part of local, regional, and national travel guides, and posters of Heimat were placed in all German train stations and public places.

As part of the advancement of tourism and the growing commercializa-tion at the turn of the century, German localities published postcards, self-promoting images, that represented the locality. These postcards, which often appeared in the "Gruss aus . . ." (Greetings from) series, displayed a typical Heimat image such as that of Reutlingen in Württemberg (figure 1). It included the principal Heimat elements: a small community, in harmony with nature, and a church tower as a leading symbol. At the turn of the cen-tury, however, Reutlingen was far from being *this* kind of a community, but was instead a developing town with 25,000 inhabitants, factories, and so-cial conflicts emanating from rapid industrialization. The image showed the adoption of the idea of Heimat as a representation of German communities.

This kind of Heimat image soon became a stereotype of all German communities. A local newspaper published in 1913 "A Heimat image"—note the nonspecific "a," meaning an image of every Heimat—consisting of a small community with a church tower (figure 2). Renningen, where the image was produced, had at the time only 2,116 inhabitants, which did not prevent its Heimat image from resembling Reutlingen's. Indeed, although the Heimat images of Reutlingen and Renningen were intended to represent these communities, they were general enough to apply to others as well.

The First World War epitomized, again, the Heimatization of Germany and the construction of a collective image of the homeland. The Heimat image of the nation appeared, among others, on posters of the campaigns for war loans, campaigns that appealed to the most common, familiar, and uniting German national symbols. The poster in figure 3, proclaiming "Protect your Heimat," presents an image of a Germany of small villages, and two factories, in harmonious relationship with nature. It was an image of tranquil, and very local, national existence. Similar motifs appear in the poster in figure 4. The image of the national Heimat was the ultimate stereotypization of Germany, its nature, its people, and its communities, as figures 3 and 4 could fit almost every area in Germany. Because nothing ever happened in the images of the national Heimat, they became a stage on which every German could direct the action in his or her mind. The images were powerful because they were, in a sense, empty. Paradoxically, therefore, the image that was the epitome of German national memory was the most abstract of all; indeed, it elevated national forgetfulness to its highest level. Imprinting the idea of Heimat in their minds, Germans ceased to associate the nation with real social and political processes and viewed it as immemorial.

The images of Heimat existed in German iconography long before the 1880s to represent a community or an area. During the Second Empire, however, Germans redefined the meaning of the old images and made them a representation of the nation as a whole. This tells us about the creativity of people when it came to making sense of the national idea, as they took old notions that were not connected to the nation and endowed them with new significance that gave the nation the appearance of ancientness. Most important, it tells us that after the 1880s Germans could grasp the abstract image of the nation, and that this was not simply an isolated phenomenon of a few Germans but a popular social reality. Is not this an answer to the question, When did Germans internalize the nation?

The idea of the Heimat national community was very specific, however, in pursuing symbols of unity and coziness, the very symbols that were easily applicable to every Heimat. The Heimat idea informed a structure of sentiments and images with which people could grasp the nation; in order to be effective this structure had to include personal, recognizable experiences, which were immediately familiar and capable of being projected onto larger entities. The community was the core symbol; it led to the related symbols of home and family, both evoking togetherness. There were good reasons why the home became a leading metaphor for the nation. The origins of the ideas of home and of Heimat had much in common, as had their function and effect in society. Like the invention of Heimat, the invention of the home in the nineteenth century as an intimate point of orientation was a response to the expansion of time and space and to growing individual mobility.[52] Home, as the community of family, and Heimat, as the national community, were sites of unity, of a shared past and future and of a collective memory, which distinguished themselves from all other homes and nations. And in the minds of Germans, the values of home and family and the sentiments they aroused were inextricably associated with women.

The connection between home and Heimat transformed women, always accompanied by children, into the human protagonists of the imagined Heimat. Usually they inhabited the Heimat: "[The soldiers] thought of Heimat, wife, and home," was a common description of Heimat, as was the combination "Heimat, wife, and child."[53] The connection went beyond the specific conditions of the war, when men were at the front and women at the rear. Sentiments and images of harmony were best expressed in the private spheres of home and family, assigned to and dominated by women and associated with feminine sensibilities.[54] The connection of Heimat, home, coziness, and women was, therefore, a logical one. Just as the home and the family were women's domain, so was Heimat. At home women represented a point of orientation for all the members of the family. While men worked during the day and were absent from home, women stayed home to care for the family nest. While men were on the move, women were fixed to one place. In a changing world, home, family, and women were symbols of stability. The Heimat idea used these symbols in the same way and projected their meaning onto the nation as a whole. By embracing women and home, Heimat became the favored site of fond memories, sweet dreams, and ideal relationships.[55] The memory of the family, home, and community was powerful because it was uneventful: a memory of the simple things one took for granted, of kinship, commitment, and continuity.

Like nature and localities, people in the Heimat representation of the nation were anonymous; they had roles—mother, father, wife, child—but no name, address, or face. To be sure, there were Heimat poems and stories that identified their heroes. But the effectiveness of the Heimat idea increased when it remained undefined in as many areas as possible. The important message was that these people were Germans; whether they were from Reutlingen or Tübingen, Swabia or Saxony, was irrelevant to the national Heimat idea. Indeed, there were no real people in the four Heimat images we have seen in figures 1–4.

With no specific nature, locality, and inhabitants, the Heimat national community became an eternal community beyond time, thus creating a chain between the German past, present, and future. The ellipsis opening Julius Berstl's poem "Heimat"—". . . Is this not the Heimat? September's meadows"—suggests that Heimat had a long history before he or the reader encountered it. Heimat conveyed the feeling of having always been there. Figures 1, 2, and 4 were general enough to fit the present and the past. Perhaps the best example is figure 3, where two factories point to the modern era. At the same time, the armored person protecting Germany was certainly not a contemporary. The image, therefore, flattened the past and the present, obscuring the chasm between them.

In spite of being timeless and therefore, strictly speaking, without history, Heimat interwove local, regional, and national histories in a manner that endowed the nation with continuity and causality. While the national Heimat enjoyed eternity, the local Heimats pursued Heimat history and founded Heimat museums. After 1871 this was the best of all possible worlds for the nation because it solved the problem of German nationhood by combining the mundane local Heimat with the symbolic national one.

The attributes of the national Heimat raise the question whether there was a difference between *Heimat*, on the one hand, and *Vaterland* and *Nation* on the other. These three words described the German people and the territory of Germany, but their meaning was not identical. The words differed in what they represented, how they represented it, and their effect on German society. While fatherland and nation represented Germany as one and indivisible, Heimat represented Germany as the one and the many. While fatherland and nation had, therefore, univocal meaning, Heimat's meaning was multifaceted and interchangeable between local, regional, and national levels. Fatherland and nation, although potentially ambiguous, did not share Heimat's depth of meaning. They do not seem to have matched the richness of metaphor and imagery of the Heimat imagined national community. Fatherland and nation, which brought to mind Germany's borders, territorial integrity, political system, or military, represented Germany as something fixed. Heimat, which brought to mind history, traditions, and land-scapes, was, in contrast, infinitely malleable. Heimat was, therefore, easier to understand and to identify with than fatherland and nation. As Ernst Jünger wrote in "The Battle as Inner Experience," a book about his participation in the First World War, "State and nation are unclear concepts, but what Hei-mat means, this you know. Heimat, it is a feeling." [56]

The fields where Heimat, on the one hand, and fatherland and nation, on the other, played out their differences most clearly were war and gender. Hei-mat was a representation of the nation informed by feminine sensibilities. Fatherland and nation, in contrast, conveyed masculine qualities such as courage, combativeness, and competitiveness. Fatherland and nation, there-fore, could go to war, while Heimat could never do that. Thus, one could say "the fatherland (or the nation) declared war on France," but to say "the Hei-mat declared war on France" made no sense. Similar to values such as family and community, Heimat was something one fought for, never something that participated in battle. The images demonstrated this clearly by placing war outside the Heimat: the sword (figure 4) and the person (figure 3) pro-tect the Heimat, but they are not part of it. [57] Heimat was the antithesis of war and all that war represents: havoc, suffering, disorientation. At the same time, war underlined the identity between Heimat and women: both stayed away from battle, in the rear—objects of dreams and fantasies, personifying the home to which men yearned to return and the just cause for which men fought. Heimat and fatherland were as incongruous as Heimat and war, as women and war. [58]

These contradictory representations of the nation were nonetheless com-plementary. Nations, like people, have more than one face. Heimat and fa-therland described Germany in different conditions and situations. Father-land presented it at war, as an empire, as an energetic and expanding society, whereas Heimat presented it as a peaceful community.

THE APOLITICAL NATION

German society before and during the First World War was not, of course, a small community at peace with nature and itself, but a burgeoning industrial state rife with social and political tensions. What, then, was the meaning of the Heimat idea in this society?

If nations were made aware of their inner conflicts and differences all day long, they would never hold together. The Heimat idea functioned success-fully as an integrative symbol because it was an ideal that kept reality at bay in order to collapse differences into similarities, thereby resolving on the symbolic level the regional, class, political, and gender differences in German society. The imagined national Heimat gave a respite from everyday social and political conflicts. The Germans' symbolic solution to their inner conflicts was to displace the meaning of the nation into the imagined Heimat beyond the recognizable here and now, into the past and the future.[59] In this way Germans during the German Empire, in spite of inner conflicts, stuck together and kept their nation together.

Heimat's integrative force is illustrated in the relations between politics and memory in imperial Germany. The Heimat idea took shape during the 1890s in the context of the multiple effects of Bismarck's resignation, the end of the Socialists' Law and the *Kulturkampf*, the orchestrated campaigns to marginalize the socialists and Catholics, the political mobilization from below of peasants and the middle classes, and the foundation of political pressure groups. Together these amounted to the replacement of the old-style liberal and conservative political culture by politics in a new key, as Carl Schorske described Viennese politics in the same period.[60] The new political culture was volatile, unpredictable, and dominated by mass movements. The intense politicization of German society made politics a synonym for national disunion.

Looking for a national common denominator that would prevail over the reality of mass politics, the German bourgeoisie displaced the meaning of the nation beyond the conflicts of the political realm: Heimat provided a never-never land, where Germans found a second Germany, impervious to politics, one of harmonious relationships, to compensate for the deficiencies and conflicts of the first, and real, Germany. The Heimat idea depicted the nation as a small and classless community, at peace with itself and with nature. Heimat was associated with home and family, social spheres that embodied unity and were antithetical to the political sphere, and with women, whose disposition was regarded as unsuited to political thought and action. Without male political protagonists, Heimat also lacked political faculties, such as making war. The distinction between *Vaterland* and Heimat was, therefore, also a distinction between a political and an apolitical representation of the nation.

Nonetheless, Heimat was not, of course, without a political meaning. The political effect of the Heimat idea depended on the ability of social and political groups to appropriate it, to become its only authoritative interpreters, and to connect it to a specific political worldview. What makes Heimat so interesting as a collective memory was its reception in German society across

religious, social, and political lines. We cannot analyze here in detail the production and consumption of Heimat memory among the various groups in
German society. Let us raise, therefore, only a few general points.

Catholics and Protestants found in the Heimat idea an integrative representation of Germany because it reconciled the particularity of their
religious beliefs with the unity of the nation. Every locality—Catholic and
Protestant—espoused its religious uniqueness (in Heimat books, for example), but the nation was represented as neither Catholic nor Protestant. The
divisions between Catholics and Protestants in German society were not
expressed in Heimat ideas and organizations. Moreover, while Catholics
founded their own gymnastic, singing, and cycling associations, constituting
a Catholic culture distinguished from working-class and Protestant cultures,
they never founded separate Heimat associations. Obviously, Catholics did
not feel the need to affirm a Catholic German Heimat in opposition to a Protestant one. Heimat seemed indeed to have collapsed this eternal religious
division in Germany.

More difficult was to find a common denominator between socialists and
bourgeois because the apolitical representation of Heimat accorded with the
bourgeois refusal to sanction political differences as a means of resolving the
problems of equality and democracy in German society. The Social Democratic Party found ideological difficulty in appropriating the Heimat idea because of its commitment, in theory at least, to the international working-
class movement, which ran counter to Heimat's classless representation of
the nation. Socialists, however, less compelled to follow the doctrine and
more inclined to identify with socialism *and* Germany, regarded Heimat as
a German, not a bourgeois, idea and identified with it on their own terms.[61]
Thus, while socialists, like Catholics, founded their own gymnastic, singing,
and cycling associations to affirm their identity against similar bourgeois associations, they refrained from establishing working-class Heimat associations.[62] By considering it unnecessary to oppose the bourgeois Heimat associations with a socialist German Heimat, socialists implicitly confirmed that
there was only one Heimat for all Germans. Although it may be argued that
socialists refrained from founding such associations because they were in-
different or even hostile to the idea, the sources point to another direction:
socialists actively demonstrated their Heimat sensibilities in their associations such as The Friends of Nature (Die Naturfreunde), and an analysis of
reading patterns in workers' public libraries reveals that workers read Heimat literature more than any other literary genre.[63]

One of the perennial questions about the German labor movement is why socialists adhered to the nation. Scholars have asked how socialists explained and justified this attitude and how they reconciled it with the authoritarian regime of imperial Germany. We should explore whether part of the answer to these questions lies in the socialists' reception of the Heimat idea as a representation of the German nation. The Heimat idea was not inherently antisocialist and bourgeois, but rather emphasized themes, such as nature and the centrality of the local community, that could be attached to everyone in German society. The malleable Heimat idea thus lent itself to appropriation by conservatives and socialists alike. Indeed, socialists saw Heimat as a particularly suitable idea for imagining the nation precisely because it appeared apolitical: while it disarmed socialists by excluding classes, it at the same time disarmed antisocialists by eliminating the very weapons with which they attacked socialism, namely militarism and authoritarianism, thus allowing socialists to embrace the nation without condoning antisocialist ideas. The discrimination socialists suffered in the real Germany disappeared in the apolitical second Germany because all were equal in the Heimat. Paradoxically, therefore, when bourgeois Germans extracted Heimat from the here and now, they made it accessible to everyone, including socialists in imperial Germany and communists in East Germany, as we shall see in chapter 4.

In this analysis of the relations between politics and the Heimat idea, it is not my intention either to negate or to minimize the religious and political conflicts of German society. On the contrary, my point of departure has been the deep fractures that characterized imperial Germany and the logical question that follows: which collective image of the nation united Germans? If in August 1914 the German working-class movement felt German first and socialist second—despite socialist ideology and constant repression by the German authorities—this was, perhaps, also thanks to Heimat national memory. At the same time, while different social groups identified with the Heimat idea, it was not monolithic, understood similarly by all, but rather resembled a mirror that reflected the beholder, be this a German Catholic or Protestant, conservative or socialist, Swabian or Prussian. This was the reason why the Heimat idea was successfully and rapidly diffused throughout German society.

Heimat remained a collective German memory across political lines even after the First World War. In a booklet distributed in 1918 to homecoming prisoners of war, Emperor Wilhelm II conceived Heimat as the Germans' solace: "The Heimat will heal again, with God's will, the wounds of the long period of captivity."[64] Similarly, Ernst Jünger saw Heimat as a profound German "feeling." And Kurt Tucholsky, in a 1929 essay entitled "Heimat," defined the Germanness of Heimat to be beyond political conflicts: "Germany is a divided land. One part of it is us [the communists, the other part is the bourgeoisie]. And in the midst of all the contrasts exists—unshakable, with no flag, no sentimentality, and no drawn swords—the quiet love for our Heimat."[65] Wilhelm II, Tucholsky, and Jünger, men of diametrically opposed political persuasions and very different personalities, had little in common, but the idea of Heimat was one thing they shared as Germans.

THE GERMAN LOCAL METAPHOR

Germans like to think of the word Heimat as unfathomable, mysterious, and, above all, peculiarly German. But that it should have come to seem to Germans all that is indeed the very core of the meaning of the Heimat idea, which was not an inherent attribute of the German nation, but came to appear as such after the 1880s, representing the permanent identity of the local and the national communities, the immutable in the ups and downs of German history. Heimat became immemorial because memory is short; a timeless national memory invented in the second half of the nineteenth century, for a timeless nation, unified in 1871.

The birth of the Heimat idea was a result of a conjuncture of German and international conditions. The first matrix of the idea was national integration; while 1871 mapped the temporal and spatial dimensions of the German homeland, Heimat endowed the territorial nation a particular symbolic meaning across the lines that divided German society. Moreover, Germans manufactured Heimat as a set of collective ideas about the immemorial heritage of the nation as part of a European and North American response to modernity's transformation of the landscape and liquidation of the past.[66] Heimat, therefore, like nationalism, originated from modernity, which produced the condition of being mentally and physically extraneous to old ways of life and thought. In an essay about his hometown, "Heimat. Calw," Hermann Hesse painfully and perceptively recognized that "I would not have had to write about Calw, had I stayed in this beautiful town. But to stay was not my destiny."[67] It was also not the destiny of fellow Germans who experienced in the modern age the disappearance of the traditional community, only to reinstate it intact, and at times improved, in the Heimat imagination.

Originating from modernity, nationalism changed concepts of space, time, and kin, which brings us back to the question posed at the outset of this chapter: how did Germans internalize the nation? Theories of nationalism often present people's internalization of the nation as a progression from the small to the big, from the locality to the nation, from the tangible to the abstract. In reality, however, people conceive the world in a spasmodic and unmethodical fashion. In these pages we have seen the construction in a few years of a new idea of Germanness that has been generally regarded as originating at a far earlier date. We have seen the one score years before the Great War as determinant in the formation of German national memory, a later and far shorter period than most accounts of German nationalism suggest. And we have seen that the articulation of the nation in images, organizations, and the topics of history, nature, and folklore emerged through a *reciprocal* and *simultaneous* changing of perceptions about abstract national life and an immediate local one, as Heimat became a symbolic depiction of the locality, the territorial state, and the nation at one and the same time.

The Heimat idea takes us beyond the reiteration of the by-now classic definition of the nation as an imagined community by telling us *what was the image* of people's imagination of the nation. People imagine the nation in different ways, but all people imagine their nation as a local metaphor. The idea of Heimat was the local metaphor of nationhood imagined by Germans.

2

A CENTURY OF LOCAL NATIONHOOD

Edgar Reitz's *Heimat*, Memory, and Understandings
of the Past, 1871–1990

The invention of the Heimat idea in imperial Germany marked the beginning of a great career. Heimat remained a symbolic representation of the locality, the region, and the nation throughout the twentieth century, possessing different combinations, meanings, and ideologies. This diverse symbolic career is demonstrated in one of Heimat's masterful representations in the last generation: Edgar Reitz's television series *Heimat*.

Reitz's *Heimat* was first shown in 1984 and has since been rightly regarded as a milestone in the history of cinema. A series of fifteen hours and thirty-six minutes in eleven parts, *Heimat* tells the story of the Simon family from 1919 to 1982 in Schabbach, a small village in the Hunsrück region near the Rhine. Yet *Heimat*'s breadth of vision is anything but parochial. It is a film about the identity of Germans in the twentieth century: where did they come from, where are they going to, what have they lost and accomplished on the way? As such, it is one of the most intriguing interpretations of German history in recent years, a bold attempt to set the rules as to who is permitted to talk about German history and what is permitted to be said.

The motivation to make *Heimat* emerged from *Holocaust*, the NBC series that was shown in Germany in 1979, and engendered tremendous public interest. Reitz, a West German, was appalled by his fellow countrymen's reaction to *Holocaust*, by the "crocodile tears of the nation, where the morality was to be sure correct, but the rest kitsch."[1] Made in Hollywood, *Holocaust* presented a stereotype of German society instead of genuine human relations.[2] In contrast to the kitsch representation of German history, Reitz made clear his understanding of the past with the first image shown on the screen: the words "Made in Germany" are chiseled in stone in English.

This chapter uses the film as a vehicle to explore a century of Heimat tradition. To understand *Heimat* and its phenomenal success among the German public we should analyze it in the context of the role of the Heimat idea in German society and culture since its invention in the 1880s as a representation of the nation. And we should explore the sources of symbolic authority that rendered the film "authentic," that is, familiar and "German," for the German public. *Heimat*, I argue, is ultimately an uncritical reproduction of the Heimat myth, for Reitz does not critically explore the origins and functions of the myth, and is instead absorbed by it.

To make sense of the symbolic authority of *Heimat* as a rendition of twentieth-century German history, I focus on Reitz's conception of history based on memory, experience, and storytelling, and on its consequences for our understanding of the past. Relying on the notions of memory and experience, *Heimat* lays claim to a specific mode of "knowing" and "connecting" with the past. What were the cultural origins and meanings of this conception of history? Why was it so successful in claiming the right to define German identity? To answer these questions I place the notions of history and experience within the symbolic capital of the Heimat idea.

I then seek to articulate further the relations between Heimat, memory, and history. "Memory" and "experience" seem to have become mandatory terms in any representation of identity and the past in contemporary society, be it among scholars or the public. In this respect, Reitz represents larger trends in our society by sanctifying memory and experience as modes of connecting with the past, while assuming a dismissive attitude toward history. I explore, via *Heimat*, the consequences of memory for German historical narrative and representation and examine how it relates to another representation of the past—no less important, some would argue—namely, history.

The full force of this approach becomes clear when we consider the critiques of *Heimat* shortly after the release of the film that, given the marginal treatment of the Holocaust in the film, have either blamed the film for sins of omission or focused incessantly, even obsessively, on whether it came to terms with the Nazi past.

HEIMAT AND ITS CRITICS: FOCUSING ON THE SINS OF OMISSION

Heimat centers around the character of Maria, from the years of her marriage to Paul Simon after the First World War until her death in 1982 at the age of eighty-two. The film opens when Paul comes back from the war, and the first episodes describe the evolving relationship between him and Maria. Then, one day in 1928, Paul suddenly leaves the village and disappears. As the story of the daily life of the inhabitants of Schabbach unfolds, the sequence of important historical events, such as the 1918 Revolution, and Weimar's hyperinflation, the Depression, and the rise of Nazism, are mentioned only secondarily, if at all. In the thirties, as Maria raises her two sons, Anton and Ernst, alone, Nazism arrives in the village as the symbol of technology, with the *Autobahn*, electrification, and telephones. Eduard, Paul's likeable but simple-minded brother, becomes the Nazi mayor of the district, not for any ideological reasons but to move up the social ladder. Things look as good as they can be, and at Christmas 1935 Eduard wishes that history would stop. It does not, of course. Just before the Second World War breaks out, Paul suddenly appears for a short visit, now a rich, insensitive Detroit businessman. During the war Maria falls in love with Otto Wohlleben, an engineer stationed in the village. As a result of their love affair Maria bears a child, Hermann; Otto, however, is killed in a mining accident. Maria's sons by Paul survive the war—Anton in a film unit on the eastern front, and Ernst as a fighter pilot.

The second part of the film tells the story of post-1945 Germany. It opens with a black soldier chewing gum—the Americans have arrived. Eduard and other former Nazis quietly begin a new life; some resent the occupiers, others find America a model of technology and prosperity. Following the American victory, Paul visits Schabbach, wearing a large cowboy hat and carrying a load of food parcels. But his is not a generous soul; he represents America as the antithesis to Heimat: a consumerist and soulless society. In the episodes about the 1950s and 1960s, Anton establishes an optical instrument factory that is threatened with takeover by a multinational, and Hermann grows up to be a musician. In the last episode Maria dies, and a surrealistic party takes place with participants from the early episodes, many by now dead, while contemporary Schabbach is the site of a loud drinking festival.

Heimat is a masterpiece of a film. Reitz and Peter Steinbach, who together wrote the script, lived for a year in the Hunsrück and collected oral testimonies and material objects from the past. The apparent authenticity of the film was enhanced by the participation of local people who were not professional actors. *Heimat* captivates because it presents everyday life not as a backdrop to a more significant plot of historical events, but as the plot. As a work of narrative art, *Heimat* resembles a book, more than a film, for it challenges the traditional ninety-minute length, and it requires attention that spans several days. It calls for reflection between showings. Second and third viewings are surprisingly rewarding. Reitz is an admirable storyteller who depicts human relations and emotions with sensitivity. Like the Arabian tales that went on and on for a thousand and one nights, I wished *Heimat* would go beyond sixteen hours.

The film resulted in a high-level debate. While almost all the critics praised the film, they also attacked what they viewed as Reitz's revisionism of German history. Much of this discussion was centered on the post-1945 period and the role of America in the foundation of West Germany. Americans are represented, as Kenneth Barkin put it, as "shallow, rootless, money-grabbing materialists. They lack any sense of Heimat."[3] The Germany allegedly created by America after 1945 is depicted far less favorably than the Heimat before the defeat, although, as Timothy Garton Ash observed, "Americanized Germany is actually better than the old *Germania intacta*. For example, in having democracy."[4]

What drew most criticism, however, was one part of German history that is not represented in the film, the Holocaust. The story of Heimat, critics argued, allowed Reitz to omit the Holocaust and give a sugarcoated depiction of National Socialism. Not surprisingly, this issue, intensified in the context of the Historians' Dispute (Historikerstreit, the mid-1980s debate in West Germany over the uniqueness of the Holocaust and the Third Reich), and by President Ronald Reagan's controversial visit to Bitburg in 1985, had become the center of the debate on *Heimat*. Gertrud Koch, one of the most severe critics of the film, expressed an opinion that has been shared by most of Reitz's critics, namely that the Heimat idea and the Holocaust are mutually exclusive, and that "in order to tell the myth of 'Heimat' the trauma of Auschwitz has to be bracketed from German history. Thus Reitz has to revise history."[5]

This incisive and detailed critique has exposed some of the great problems with *Heimat*. I am in basic agreement with all these points. And yet I find this critique to be unsatisfactory. One reason is the shift of the discussion about the film from what actually happens in it, to what should have happened, but did not. A major yardstick to evaluate the film has been the treatment of the Holocaust, an event that is not an integral part of the plot. My point here is not that the role of National Socialism and of the Holocaust is irrelevant to understanding *Heimat*, but that most of the criticism of the film has become an exercise in assessing how and whether it came to terms with the past.[6] The critics have faulted the film for sins of omission, at times at the expense of paying attention to plot and action. And by concentrating on what does not take place in the film, we risk losing the meaning of what does. In truth, the obsessive concentration on *Heimat*'s representation of National Socialism explains very little of the larger cultural and political significance of the film. We misconstrue the film and its reception when we ignore *Heimat*'s larger context: its symbolic link to the Heimat idea. For since the 1880s the Heimat idea's symbolic capital enabled Germans to construct mythic pasts that were only secondarily governed by rules of historical factuality. *Heimat* is significant when we place it as a myth within history, rather than blame it for sins of historical omission.[7]

The main problem in the critical analysis of the film has been the failure to analyze the central concept of the film—the concept of Heimat. The film's critics accepted without question the common-wisdom view about the role of the Heimat idea in German society and culture. Anton Kaes stands for *Heimat*'s body of criticism when he writes in his elegant study that, as an "antimodern, antiurban movement, Heimat was precisely that which was abandoned on the way into the cities; from then on [the 1890s] the word 'Heimat' began to connote 'region,' 'province,' and 'country,'" but not nation.[8] Kaes states that for Reitz "Germany as a nation or a state cannot be a Heimat," and, as he leaves unexplored the cultural sources, political implications, and historical accuracy of this statement, it appears that he holds the same view.[9] But is this view of the Heimat idea correct? Why should we take Reitz's notion of Heimat at face value? Is there not something oversimplified in arguing that the meaning of Heimat had remained unchanged since the 1890s? Instead of accepting a fixed definition of the idea and its social and cultural role, it seems more fruitful to place the film and its director in the century-long reception and interpretation of the Heimat idea as a symbolic representation of the nation-state. In this way, we can learn via the Heimat idea about changing conceptions of nationhood in German society.

Moreover, because Reitz and his critics all agree that Heimat is an allegory of German history (or else what is the big fuss? There must have been at least one village in Germany whose inhabitants knew next to nothing about the Holocaust), should we not be curious about the relationship between Heimat as an allegory of the nation and Heimat as a local concept? Are Heimat and nation really contradictory, or perhaps symbolically complementary? In short, Reitz's use and understanding of the Heimat idea have not been systematically explored and, as a result, the symbolic authority of Heimat has been either ignored or misunderstood. We know very little indeed about the ways the film borrowed from, diverged from, and gave new meanings to the symbolic capital of the Heimat idea.

My analysis of the film, therefore, begins with its most venerated concept —Heimat.

For Reitz, Heimat is the local, tangible territory, the home, the village, and its surroundings. Heimat represents intimate and immediate spaces and relationships and is closely connected to the everyday life of ordinary people. As such, the idea of Heimat is the antithesis of the idea of the nation, the abstract idea that has organized life and thought in the modern world. Reitz is unequivocal: "Heimat and nation . . . are contradictory terms."[10] They are contradictory, according to Reitz, because while the idea of nation is associated with conflict, that of Heimat is associated with harmony; while the nation is a conglomeration of diverse and opposing groups, Heimat stands for tightly knit community; while perceiving the nation requires a process of generalization and stereotypization, the Heimat embodies face-to-face human relations. The local meaning of the Heimat idea enables Reitz to disavow the notion of national history and to fragment the larger processes of German history into numerous histories of local Heimats.

Here lies an ambiguity: although Reitz sets out against the concept of national history, the underlying assumption of *Heimat* is that Schabbach is a metonymy of German history. *Heimat* does claim to be an interpretation of German history, and is, according to Reitz, an interpretation "made in Germany," by which he means, one presumes, a Germany that is a social, cultural, and political entity. Or does he use the term "Germany," following Metternich, as a geographical idea? If Heimat and nation are contradictory, why not begin the film with the inscription "Made by a German"? Or at least "Made in West Germany"? However provincial and hillbilly Schabbach may have been, if its inhabitants lived beyond the national pale, unable to comprehend, unwilling to participate, and uninterested in national affairs, then their story becomes an exception, and is interesting precisely because it was eccentric and out of place in a national history that was in fact quite different. But the truth is, of course, that Schabbach and its people captivate us because they tell us something about German history as a whole.

In fact, the very Heimat idea that Reitz viewed as merely local was the best representation he could find among German cultural artifacts to connect the locality to the nation. Since its origin in the 1880s, the Heimat idea has provided Germans with a set of images and symbols to negotiate the relations between localness and nationhood. *Heimat* was indebted to the symbolic capital of the Heimat idea, although Reitz gave new meanings to old symbolic forms. Let us place the film within the development of the Heimat idea as a local-national representation.

In the wake of unification in 1871, as we have seen in the previous chapter, bourgeois Germans devised the Heimat idea to reconcile local and national identities. Far from being a concept of localism, as Reitz has it, the Heimat idea represented simultaneously the locality, the region, and the nation. Through the Heimat idea, Germans underscored their regional peculiarities while placing these peculiarities within the context of German national identity. The Heimat idea connected local identity to regional and national identities by emphasizing German nationhood as a symbolic diversity of regional identities, and the local place and the region as the cradle of German nationhood.

The Heimat idea was not simply a mediator between local and national identity, but became an actual representation of the nation. Together, the Heimats made up the ideal of a unique nationality. The German Heimat comprised all the Heimats, but was more than the sum of its parts. This was symbolically represented, for example, in the three-tiered organizational structure of the Heimat idea in imperial Germany that fitted perfectly the symbolic representation of the nation as a composition of local, regional, and national Heimats. From the local to the regional to the national level, associations merged to form bigger organizations that informed new kinds of Heimats and brought together more Germans. Local associations, such as historical and folklore associations, were organized in regional bodies, such as the League for Heimat Protection in Württemberg and Hohenzollern. These in turn were organized into national bodies, notably the German League for Heimat Protection established in 1904. With the creation of the German League for Heimat Protection, the idea of making the nation one's symbolic habitat received an organizational affirmation. The statute of the organization opened with a declaration that "the aim of the association is to protect the evolving natural and historical uniqueness of *the German Heimat.*"[11] The national Heimat became the ultimate symbolic representation of the German nation and of its local and regional histories, memories, and sentiments. The network of local, regional, and national Heimat associations thus corresponded to the constitutive metaphor of the Heimat idea—the metaphor of the whole and its parts—and was consciously perceived as such by Heimatlers.[12] The interlocking structure of national and regional associations represented the relationship between the oneness of the German Heimat and the multitude of local Heimats.[13]

From the symbolic capital of the Heimat idea that originated in imperial Germany, the Nazis maintained the notion of the German community of shared past, present, and future, but they altered the definition of community in fundamental ways. They now defined Heimat in terms of race, blood, and soil, as stated by a member of the Nazi Association of Teachers: "Yes, blood is a substance, but not in the false, materialist sense, rather in the sense of Heimat, soil, and racial property."[14] A vast literature disseminated the idea of the racially pure Heimat in poems, novels, and plays.[15] The race and the nation demanded loyalty over all other German identities. Therefore, while the Heimat idea in the German Empire celebrated local distinctiveness within the greater national whole, the Nazis underplayed the distinctiveness of local identity at the expanse of a racially homogeneous national community.

After 1945, as a counterreaction to the Third Reich, the idea "Heimat equals nation" became associated solely with racism, nationalism, and imperialism.[16] The multiple meanings of the Heimat idea as local and national metaphors were largely forgotten. Now, Heimat as a representation of local identity came to define German identity, with a significant payoff, for it made it possible for West Germans to feel the pride of being Germans without associating it with the militarist, state-led nationalism of the Third Reich.[17] From the 1960s the local meaning of the Heimat idea was reinforced from a different ideological and cultural direction, when the German New Left developed the Heimat idea as a countersymbol to West German political culture. An antithesis to nationalism, Americanization, and consumerism, Heimat came to symbolize local roots and authentic German ways of life. It made it possible for many on the New Left to cultivate a new, positive sense of Germanness that opposed fascism and the shallowness and materialism of Americanism.[18] Closely connected was a powerful movement by historians and laypersons from this milieu to recover the experience of the "little people" by using oral history and history of everyday life. Reitz's most immediate notion of Heimat derived from the New Left.

For more than a century, then, the Heimat idea served as a metaphor for the changing relationship between localness and nationhood in German society: from the time of Heimat's national meaning in imperial Germany, to the racial national community in the Third Reich, and thence to the representation in West Germany of suppressed national sentiments via the symbol of the local Heimat. *Heimat* is the latest, though certainly not the last, interpretation of German local-national relations using the Heimat symbolic manual. By "Heimat symbolic manual" I mean a set of Heimat images and symbols that together constitute a kind of handbook of ideas. This manual has proved to be an invention on which it is impossible to secure exclusive rights. It became available for appropriation by widely different hands. Reitz's use of the Heimat idea to decouple local and national existence is really an additional interpretation of German local-national relations expressed in the Heimat idiom. His representation of Heimat as an antithesis to nation is interesting because it is so different from previous meanings of the Heimat idea—and it is insightful when weighed against them.

Studies of *Heimat* have given various explanations for the success of the film, but one fundamental explanation is the origins of *Heimat*'s symbolic authority to lay claim to speak for German nationhood. In spite of Reitz's emphatic declaration that Heimat and nation are contradictory, the Heimat metaphor in fact serves historically and culturally as a means of negotiating between local and national identity, not least in the film itself, whose symbolic authority derives from the tradition of the Heimat idea as a local-national metaphor. And thus, paradoxically, the symbolic origins of Reitz's perception of Heimat as a contradiction to nation lie in the symbolic capital of the Heimat idea that originated in imperial Germany as a representation of the nation as a whole. For more than a century the Heimat symbolic manual provided ideas of localness and nationhood that represented the essence of Germanness; *Heimat* struck a cord among Germans because it appropriated this culturally familiar symbolic manual.

THE HEIMAT SYMBOLIC MANUAL II:
HEIMAT AND HISTORY

Heimat and the Heimat idea provided not only a symbolic manual to imagine the nation but also one to imagine the past. How does Reitz's approach to understanding the past contrast with the kitsch representation of German history made in Hollywood? Reitz's understanding of the past is based on three notions: experience (*Erfahrung*), storytelling (*Erzählung*), and memory (*Erinnerung*). Germans must first cultivate their past by remembering their experience. Reitz distinguished between a genuine scene and one that is made up for commercial reason, such as the scenes in *Holocaust*. The difference is similar to that between "experience" and "judgment." Judgments over experience can be misused, manipulated, and taken out of context; experience, on the other hand, belongs to the people and their ability to remember it.[19] By "experience" Reitz means the life of the little people, an approach that reflected the flourishing of everyday life and oral history in West

Germany in the period the film was conceived. Telling the multitude of personal histories enables Germans to get the real sense of their past. "There are thousands of stories among our people that would be worthwhile to film," wrote Reitz. "We should not prohibit ourselves any more from taking our personal lives seriously." [20] Telling the stories of past experiences is made possible only by remembering the past. "The most profound expropriation that exists is the expropriation of people from their own history," stated Reitz in response to *Holocaust*.[21] To reappropriate history Germans need to remember. And unlike the "German memories" produced artificially in Hollywood, "The images in my memory are German; I produce German memories because you cannot invent memories." [22]

Hollywood producers were not the only ones to expropriate the German past, however. Reitz set his approach to understanding the past against that of another group that distorts German history—historians: "Over the years I have increasingly come to use film as a vehicle for memory work. History, as we learn it in school, or as is practiced by historians, attempts to generalize, to order events, to disclose cause and effect . . . To counter this abstract system that confronts us . . . we have to defend ourselves with a powerful weapon. This weapon from time immemorial has been art, especially narrative art: literature, poesy, film." [23] As an approach to understanding the past, according to Reitz, history is the direct opposite of Heimat history: while history is detached from the concerns of the little people, Heimat history is empathetic; while history explores impersonal trends, Heimat history focuses on everyday life; while history is a science, Heimat history is an art; while history is an artificial construct, Heimat history is an authentic, popular discourse. Heimat, then, stands in opposition to nation and to history, and this explains Reitz's objection to *Holocaust* that, to borrow Reitz's appraisal of history, "attempts to generalize, to order events, to disclose cause and effect."

Reitz uses household terms in modern discourse about identity: memory, experience, authenticity, popular history. But what are the symbolic origins of his perception of the past? From its inception in imperial Germany, the Heimat idea was considered in German society and culture as an authentic historical discourse that defined national character, national origins, and Germanness. Wilhelm Seytter, the author of a Heimat book about Stuttgart whom we met in the previous chapter, explained in 1904 the meaning of Heimat history in words that are strikingly similar to Reitz's:[24]

As a Heimat study, this book imparts not only bare historical knowledge, but aims at animating the Heimat by enlivening its history. . . . By looking at Heimat's simple and daily life, Heimat history is being stripped of learned academic scholarship, and becomes vivid, conceivable, and therefore popular. . . . While history rushes to generalize from concrete facts and surveys at a glance mountains and valleys only to get a general impression of the landscape, Heimat studies enter affectionately into people's simple and daily life.

Both Seytter and Reitz expressed deep reservation about the capacity of the discipline of history to capture the historical experience of people. For both, the legitimacy of Heimat history emanated from its allegedly popular origin. Also Seytter expressed the idea that understanding the past demanded art, not science. Heimat history was then a system of knowledge and sensibilities that connected Germans with their past during the unprecedented changes of modernity. Obviously, for Heimatlers such as Seytter, exact relations of cause and effect, or the general patterns of national development, were secondary.

Take Heimat museums, for example, that displayed the history of a community by creating a narrative of origins based on the notion of experience. Local history began with the Germanic tribes, such as the Franks and the Alemanni, represented in archaeological exhibits, advancing to the Middle Ages, with displays of weapons, coats of arms, and heraldic figures, progressing to the life of hometown inhabitants in the early modern period, and finally to the recent past. The aim of the museums was not to be historically comprehensive but to enlighten; they educated by being entertaining, not academic. Ultimately, the aim of Heimatlers was to overcome the inherent strangeness between the past and present and to connect the visitor intimately with the German past. That is why Heimatlers described the representation of the past in the museums as "theatrical," aimed at "bringing closer the spirit of the past in an emotional way."[25] The museum in Lübeck was considered successful because it let the visitor "experience the state of mind of old times."[26] Historical accuracy thus gave way to a representation of an aestheticized past.

The notion of experience and the notion of the past as a form of art remained a mainstay of the Heimat idea after the fall of imperial Germany. Whether appropriated by Weimar's loyalists or by right-wing opponents, the Heimat idea was viewed as "an experienced and experienceable total bond with the soil," as "spiritual sentiments of roots." These words were expressed by Eduard Spranger, a Berlin educator, psychologist, and philosopher, who was considered a Heimat expert and whose Heimat publications were adopted in school curricula. Typically, he believed that Heimat studies were an "educational tool for a deeper and richer Heimat experience."[27] The Nazis, whose worldview glorified instinct and will over rationalism, found especially appealing the aestheticized conception of history that valued spirit and intention over facts and strict causality. The term "experience," indicating the perfect blending of thought and action, was essential for them, and they appropriated the idea of Heimat to mean a racial national community.[28] Hanns Johst, president of the Reich Chamber of Literature (*Reichsschrifttumskammer*) and first winner of the NSDAP Prize for Art and Science, which he received at the 1935 Nuremberg party rally, described Nazism as a form of experience in his play *Schlageter*.[29]

> AUGUST: You will not believe this, Daddy, but that's how things are: among the youth, these slogans carry no weight any more . . . they die out . . . class struggle dies out.
> SCHNEIDER: So . . . and what replaces it?
> AUGUST: The national community!
> SCHNEIDER: And this is not a slogan . . . ?
> AUGUST: No!! It is an experience!

The Nazis continued to base their Heimat history and Heimat studies on the fundamental principle of "knowing, experiencing, and loving the Heimat"—yet predictably they gave Heimat, as a metaphor of German nationhood, a racial spin. Heimat history and Heimat studies blended "Heimat, kin, race, Volk, and Führer" in a mixture of fact and fiction about the history of the German racial community. For when it came to questions of ideology, the Nazis, similarly to other Heimat believers before and after, never let themselves be confused by facts. Heimat studies in schools thus began with Hitler as "Führer and master" and continued with the "Nordic race" as "creator and carrier of mankind's culture." Ultimately, Heimat education aimed, as one Heimat textbook put it in 1936, to make "every German youth . . . a follower of the Führer."[30]

Always capable of adapting symbolically to historical circumstance, the Heimat idea survived the 1945 bankruptcy of German nationalism. From the rubble of defeat, West Germans resurrected Heimat as a leading image to imagine German nationhood precisely because it ignored strict historical causality and was capable of reconciling the (selectively chosen) German past with post-1945 West Germany. They now associated the Heimat idea not with the Nazi regime, but with its victims, and construed it as the locus of tradition and stability, and as the essential German community that could renew the nation.[31] Historical representation in Heimat films, the most popular film genre in West Germany in the 1950s, continued the Heimat tradition of molding the past at will: in Heimat films "'the war,' 'the Third Reich,' 'the flight' [of Germans from eastern Europe] have neither causes nor effects, neither perpetrators nor victims, are just caused by 'fate.'"[32]

What were the symbolic origins of Reitz's perception of the past, to return to the question that opened this discussion? *Heimat* appears to be the most recent reading of German nationhood using the Heimat-history symbolic manual. This manual included a representation of the past based on the notion of experience, on an aestheticized understanding of history, and on creating fabricated historical links between the past and the present disregarding historical causality. Again, the symbolic manual proved to be an invention on which it was impossible to secure exclusive rights. But for more than a century the Heimat symbolic manual provided a set of images of the past that represented the essence of Germanness. *Heimat*'s success in claiming to speak for German identity can be understood, I maintain, by placing the film within a century of Heimat symbolic representation of the nation, rather than by focusing on sins of historical omission. Heimat history has never been about getting the facts of German history right, such as establishing some sort of a causality between Schabbach's residents and Nazism. On the contrary, it is about getting the story crooked, about inventing a causality in Heimat museums between the Germanic tribes and imperial Germany, or obscuring a causality in Heimat films between the crimes of the Third Reich and West Germany. That is why Reitz chose, partly consciously and partly not, as we shall see, to recount German history through the Heimat metaphor. And for historians, the true story is often boring: it is when people choose to get the story crooked that it becomes truly interesting to the matter of understanding perceptions of identity and of the past.

Let us turn, then, to Reitz's perceptions of the past and to its consequences for telling about German history.

REPRESENTING THE PAST:
ARE GERMAN MEMORIES INVENTABLE?

In *Heimat*, as we have seen, Reitz appropriated the Heimat discourse about the past whose legitimacy was based on the belief that memory is immutable: "I produce German memories because you cannot invent memories." Unlike Hollywood films, the Heimat discourse, according to Reitz, did not manufacture the past, it reflected it genuinely. And yet, alongside this notion Reitz developed an acute awareness of the ways reality is constructed, rather than simply reflected, in films: "Many people in our profession make the mistake of confusing film images with reality. . . . The entire lot of terrible television programs and commercial offerings in cinemas is in reality the revenge of the camera on those stupid abusers who think they are reproducing reality."[33] *Heimat* includes sensitive scenes of the ways in which the camera and technical instruments reproduce reality, whether by Paul and his radio, Eduard and the camera, Anton and cinema, Hermann and electronic music. The film calls upon viewers to be conscious of the deceptiveness of the camera.

An ambiguity thus appears in *Heimat*. On one level, Reitz professes that the film is an accurate representation of German history ("I cannot invent memories"). To be sure, adds Reitz, "A movie must always be a little bit stronger than life. On the other hand, *I cannot add things that wouldn't have happened.*"[34] On a second level, he firmly states that "only stupid abusers" believe the camera reproduces reality. We should not view this ambiguity as contradictory, but rather as complementary. This duality does seem fundamental to Reitz's life as an artist and as a German, for it enables him to hold on to artistic standards while at the same time formulating a national identity. The duality may reveal Reitz's true opposition to *Holocaust*, and its logic is as follows.

If the camera produces a malleable and unreliable representation of the past, of reality, then there is no way to determine whether *Heimat* is truer to the German experience than *Holocaust*: our judgment of the films must be based solely on aesthetic grounds. This view of the relations between film and the representation of the past, however, qualifies both Germans and Americans in Hollywood to talk and think about German history in equitable measure because, faced with the basic impossibility of representing the past in film images, the argument that America expropriates German history becomes irrelevant. But if memories cannot be invented, if experience is the yardstick to knowing the past, then Reitz can claim that America misunderstands and misrepresents German history. Thus, *Heimat* originated as a project of national identity, seeking, like every national identity, to claim an authentic national voice that differentiated what Germans know about themselves from what others know about them. With all his artistic arguments about the artificiality of Hollywood, Reitz's opposition to *Holocaust* comes down to a matter of national identity; Americans in Hollywood, and by extension anyone else, did not experience and therefore cannot know German history.

The discrepancy between the claim to recover in *Heimat* genuine German memories and the inherent impossibility of representing reality on film creates a fascinating tension in *Heimat*. On the one hand, *Heimat* feels like a documentary that records life accurately through the use of black and white, the depiction of everyday life, and the centrality of quotidian material objects. Watching the film, we want to believe, and no doubt many do, that this *was* the way things really were. On the other hand, Reitz always alerts the viewer to the need to distrust the camera by showing how reality is reproduced and constructed by technical instruments. In fact, Reitz seems to tell us that while memories are cultural artifacts, they are at the same time genuinely ours. But as a project of national identity, *Heimat* gives priority to the ability of memory and experience to capture the past over the constructedness of film images. Although film cannot reproduce reality, Reitz appears to be saying, the memories reflected in it are closer to the truth when they stem from "real" experiences. Thus, *Heimat* implies, the experience and memory of Reitz and the people of Schabbach go a long way toward overcoming the obstacles of technology; if Reitz produces cinematic memories that are likely to be corrupted by technology, they cannot be totally fake because they are based on "real" experience.

THE CONSEQUENCES OF MEMORY
AS AN ARBITER OF THE PAST

Experience and memory are key words in contemporary discourse about identity. A common manifestation of this position is the idea that since "I personally experienced the landing at Normandy or the fall of the Berlin Wall, I can therefore make sense of it better than historians who explore events after the fact." Differently put: I experienced the past, therefore I understand it. I remember the past, therefore I know it. *Heimat*'s success among the public is no doubt due to this perception that people's recollection of their experience is a reliable guide to understanding the past. We should be fully aware, however, of the consequences of this perception of the past. The elements of Reitz's conception of history—memory, experience, and storytelling—have been identified and discussed by his critics, but the significance of his ideas to the understanding of the past has not been systematically analyzed.[35] What sort of German past does Reitz's conception produce?

Reitz's approach to understanding the past blends myth and reality, experience and imagination. Heimat history has never claimed to verify the evidence and we should therefore not measure Reitz by the standard of professional historians who must tell a story based on the available evidence. But what are the underlying assumptions behind the faith in memory and experience as guides to the past? In what way do they affect historical narrative and representation? Because Reitz is not constrained by verifiable evidence, does anything go in Heimat history? Of course not. As a metaphor of German nationhood, the Heimat idea can be applied with discrimination, a kind of symbolic ax that defines Germanness by exclusion. By basing his understanding of the past on memory, Reitz excludes non-Germans from evaluating German history because they, by definition, cannot remember it. Similarly, by basing his understanding of the past on experience, Reitz again limits a "true" understanding of German history to Germans. The implications of this view are disturbing. For Reitz, in effect, delegitimizes the opinion of foreigners, historians, and nonhistorians regarding German history and espouses a notion of "German history to the Germans." Yet few national histories in this century share a universal meaning as does German history. This is not simply a question of hermeneutics: Germans did not visit Paris, Warsaw, Prague, Copenhagen, Amsterdam, Athens, Rome, and Kiev as tourists in the early 1940s.

Moreover, the idea that German history belongs to the Germans is the corollary of Reitz's belief that memory is fixed, immutable, and indestructible: "You cannot invent German memories." This view flies in the face of the very quality of memories, personal and collective, as malleable, prone to manipulation, appropriation, and fabrication. Reitz's view remains a naive conception, even though he qualifies it by stating that film cannot reproduce the past. Whether from the Hunsrück or Hollywood, memories about Germany are the least reliable guide to understanding the past. And, in fact, Reitz's reliance on memory is predictably selective: there is no oral history in *Heimat* among Germany's victims, such as forced laborers in rural areas similar to Schabbach, although their experience is part of German history too.

Perhaps more important, the logical corollary of the idea that our understanding of the past is determined by memory and experience is that we cannot seek insights to pasts that cannot be remembered. Reitz spent a year in the Hunsrück conducting oral-history research and used his own family and childhood memories to write *Heimat*. If this mode of operation forms the foundation of our understanding of the past, how can we understand the history of the region during, say, the French Revolution and the Napoleonic

Wars? Reitz's approach undermines any social understanding of the past, by historians and nonhistorians, by rejecting the intellectual possibility of explaining and integrating into our culture events that we have not experienced. Is it really necessary to storm the Winter Palace in order to explain the Russian Revolution? In fact, we have the benefit of hindsight over contemporaries in analyzing the revolution's long-term historical significance.

The consequences of elevating memory to act as an arbiter of historical truth are clear when we consider the place of the Holocaust in *Heimat*. Gertrud Koch and Anton Kaes argue that Auschwitz can have no place in Reitz's conception of Heimat. This is not entirely correct. In a past that is determined by experience, everyday life, and personal recollections, there is no reason why Reitz cannot film *Ordinary Men*, with Christopher Browning as historical adviser, about the experience of a group of lower-middle-class folks from Hamburg who, as members of Police Battalion 101 in Poland in the Second World War, shot to death 38,000 Jews and helped deport to Treblinka an additional 45,200.[36] The symbolic manual of the Heimat idea, in itself, does not prohibit the inclusion of Auschwitz in *Heimat*; think of Seytter who defined the Heimat idea as "people's simple and daily life." Indeed, Reitz argues that it is important to maintain a sphere where people can "encounter their own lives, their own world of experience."[37] Auschwitz, too, was a German world of experience, not only Schabbach.

But in a past that is determined by personal memory, the chances that Germans would prefer to remember Auschwitz are slim, while the chances that they would prefer to repress it are infinitely greater. The issue of excluding the Holocaust from *Heimat* thus comes down to using "memory" for the purpose of repression and has little to do with Reitz's alleged argument about *Heimat* as a corrective to the expropriation of German history by *Holocaust*. Memory liberates because it permits us to lie to ourselves about the past. Reitz admitted that "It is almost impossible to show how some ss officers could do what they did and be as sympathetic within their families as they were. It is really too much for our eyes. Sometimes it is too much for our mind."[38] He sets out to tell the story of some ordinary Germans, but not others. There is nothing wrong in telling the story of Germans who were not ss officers, but the problem begins when their story remains the only one. It is interesting to know about the people of Schabbach, although, judging from *Heimat*, they faced few of the moral dilemmas that have shaped the last century. It is certainly as interesting to know about people who were murderers from nine till five and "sympathetic within their families" at dinnertime. Reitz's masterpiece is a historical film based on a moral decision to conceal parts of history and to highlight others so that they will not be "too much for our mind." But perhaps it is incumbent on historians and film makers to make sure unpleasant stories are also told. One can only hope that this great film maker will enrich our world with these stories as well.

The sanctified status of memory and experience is the flip side of Reitz's prejudices against historians. Reitz's view of the historical profession says more about the myths he lives by than about historians: they do (fortunately) explore general trends and relations of cause and effect, but why ignore new and innovative fields of study that place "little people" at the center of our culture, such as microhistory, social history, history from below, women's history, and the history of everyday life? [39] More significant is Reitz's distinction between historians' scientific and therefore detached understanding of the past, on the one hand, and, on the other, his empathetic approach based on people's "real" experience. Few historians would willingly accept Reitz's definition of history as science these days, for they have grappled in the past three decades or so with the epistemological status of their discipline so intensely (it is enough to mention the work of Paul Veyne and Hayden White) that some are referring to the "crisis of history." But for Reitz the dichotomy is clear: while he views Heimat history as an art, he sees history in an uncomplicated manner as a science.

To put it differently, he views memory as an art and history as a science. It is a neat division, but in reality things are not that simple. The relation between history and memory is fundamental to every representation of the past, whether by historians or film makers. It is ironic that some scholars who had an excessive belief in the power of scientific history shared Reitz's view of the neat division between history and memory, while giving it a positive spin. I am referring, of course, to the pioneering work on memory of Maurice Halbwachs. Halbwachs sharply distinguished between history as a scientific rendition of the past and memory as a malleable one.[40] His basic argument was that memory belonged to a premodern society where tradition was strong, memory was a social practice, and historiography was at its precritical stage, whereas the discipline of history, emerging in the nineteenth century, belonged to modern society where tradition declined and history became part of the social sciences. Although Reitz and Halbwachs shared the view of history as a scientific discipline and of the consequent sharp division between history and memory, they used this view to legitimize diametrically opposed agendas. For Halbwachs, this view served to legitimize the claim of history as the science of the past. For Reitz, it served to undermine the legitimacy of history and in its place to construct the "authentic" authority of memory as a discourse about the past.

Almost no historian would subscribe today to Halbwachs's view of history as a scientific discipline and to the consequent separation between history and memory. Collective memory, to my mind, both differs from and converges with history. Memory is a malleable understanding of the past that is different from history because its construction is not bounded by a set of limiting disciplinary rules. Invented pasts are characterized by features that historians attempt to avoid in their studies: anachronism, parochialism, presentism. Of course, history is also a malleable understanding of the past, but it is governed, with varying degrees of success and problems, by rules of evidence and verification. Memory and history converge because the historian conceives of his or her story within the general image of the past shared by society. The historian's task is to reveal the connections between memory and history without obscuring their differences.

Unlike Reitz and Halbwachs, I think that history is a form of narrative art practiced with tools that permit verification of our knowledge about the past. History permits verification because historians are committed to use evidence as the primary material of their craft. With the help of evidence, historians put forward differing interpretations that are weighted against each other using critical analysis of sources, rules of cause and effect, and extrapolation. Interpretations differ, but not all interpretations are equal: some explain better than others, and some are downright wrong. But in spite of historians' use of evidence and rules of verification, history remains simultaneously a form of art: historians can never achieve the precision of mathematicians who work with numbers, where two plus two makes four under any social, political, and cultural circumstances. Historians can never reach a cultural Archimedean point from which one can interpret the world from the outside. They are always inside culture; they are products of the intellectual tradition and historical mentality of their society, while attempting at the same time to explain and criticize it. And they always work with words that are ambiguous. Their final product is a story, a narrative, that falls squarely in the realm of art, just as the best of history writing is touched by the grace and beauty of art.

History and memory, then, are not identical, but cannot be separated either. Yet given Reitz's ranking of memory and history, this evaluation rests on desanctifying the values of memory while recognizing the uses of history.

Like every national memory, *Heimat*'s representation of German history is selective: it collapses the differences between past and present by linking the 1919 inhabitants of Schabbach to some undefined, pure past; it is parochial in concentrating on a few episodes while ignoring concepts of continuity and change. And it stems entirely from the obsessions of the present: Reitz's aim is not to deconstruct Heimat memory but to immerse himself in it; not to understand German history critically but to rewrite it, then embrace, justify, and identify with it. Consequently, Reitz's historical horizons are as wide as his reminiscences and personal experience. He constructs the image of twentieth-century German history in the image of his own experience. It is an image rooted in presentism.

The Heimat symbolic capital consists roughly of three major stages: the pre-1933 period, the Third Reich, and the post-1945 era. But Reitz never engages in and negotiates with the three periods equally. We can explain how Reitz selectively shapes his image of twentieth-century German history by examining what he explicitly and (as far as we can determine) consciously uses, as well as what he rejects or ignores from the Heimat symbolic capital.

It is quite clear that although the national meaning of the Heimat idea in imperial Germany contradicts the basic supposition of the film—that Heimat represents the separate community, detached from and opposed to the nation—Reitz does not engage *Heimat* in a discussion about this previous symbolic meaning. It is not entirely clear, in fact, whether he was aware of it. *Heimat*'s coproducer, Joachim von Mengershausen, was surprised to learn of the national image of Heimat and of the existence of the German League for Heimat Protection.[41]

Born in 1932, Reitz informed his ideas about Heimat under the influence of and in opposition to the Nazi propaganda and the Adenauer-era economic miracle. Taking 1984 as a departure point, I see three concentric circles of identity that shaped Reitz's view. The first and farthest in time from the film's production is connected to the Third Reich, which Reitz counteracted by emphasizing Heimat's local meaning as a symbol against racism and nationalism. The third circle of identity, which is closest in time to the making of *Heimat*, concerns Reitz's involvement in the New Left in the 1960s and 1970s.

The second circle of identity, covering the 1950s, is also the most important in cinematic terms. Reitz was influenced by the Heimat-film genre that reached its zenith in the 1950s, when more than 300 films were produced.

PLATE 1. Brinkmann, "Nur eine starke Frauenvertretung im Parlament sichert den Frieden!" (Only a strong representation of women in parliament protects the peace!), 1946, poster. (Courtesy of the Deutsches Historisches Museum Berlin—Bildarchiv)

PLATE 2.
Haberichter, "DFD in jedem Ort" (Democratic Women's League of Germany in every community), after March 8, 1947, poster. (Courtesy of the Deutsches Historisches Museum Berlin— Bildarchiv)

PLATE 3.
Werner Meier, "Die Kraft der 5 Millionen" (The strength of 5 million), 1949, poster. (Courtesy of the Deutsches Historisches Museum Berlin—Bildarchiv)

PLATE 4. Boehner, "Enteignung der Betriebe der Kriegs- und Naziverbrecher.
Volksentscheid zum Schutz von Haus und Hof, von Vieh und Ernte!" (Expropriation of
companies owned by Nazis and war criminals. Plebiscite to protect home and hearth,
cattle and harvest), 1946, poster. (Courtesy of the Deutsches Historisches Museum
Berlin—Bildarchiv)

PLATE 5. Wolgram, "Jugend, die Heimat ruft Dich!" (Youth, the Heimat calls you!), 1946, poster. (Courtesy of the Deutsches Historisches Museum Berlin—Bildarchiv)

WER DIE HEIMAT LIEBT

gibt seine Stimme am 23. Juni den Kandidaten der Nationalen Front

PLATE 6. *"Wer die Heimat liebt" (One who loves the Heimat), 1957, poster.*
(Courtesy of the Deutsches Historisches Museum Berlin—Bildarchiv)

PLATE 7. *"Deutschland das schöne Reiseland" (Germany the beautiful traveling land), in* Deutsche Werbung *(June 1935): 1076. (Courtesy of the Historisches Archiv zum Tourismus am Willi Scharnow-Institut für Tourismus der Freien Universität Berlin)*

PLATE 8. *"Teutoburger Wald. Freizeitgenuss à la carte"* (Teutoburg forest. *Leisure fun à la carte), 1993. (Courtesy of the Ostwestfalen Lippe Marketing GmbH. Teutoburger Wald Tourismusmarketing)*

PLATE 9. *Ludwig Hohlwein,* "*Deutsches Reisemerkbuch*" *(German travel bookmarks), in* Deutsche Werbung *(March 1939): 323. (Courtesy of VG Bild-Kunst, Bonn 2005)*

PLATE 10. *Rudolf Koch,* "*Kampf dem Atomtod. Wählt die Kandidaten der Nationalen Front—Für Frieden, Wohlstand und Glück!*" *(Fight nuclear death. Vote for the candidates of the National Front—for peace, prosperity, and happiness!), 1958, poster. (Courtesy of the Deutsches Historisches Museum Berlin—Bildarchiv)*

The genre communicated a world of "little people" in villages between tradition and modernity. It conservatively emphasized stability of human relations, conformity to common values, and security in a familiar environment.[42] Heimat films made it possible for people to "dream" of marriage and a happy family, prosperity, leisure, and, for the refugees from Eastern Europe and East Germany, of a new Heimat. The genre came under attack in the Oberhausen Manifesto in 1962, in which twenty-six young German directors, including Reitz, opposed the conventional German cinema and the primacy of commercial considerations. Vowing to create "a new language of film," the new German cinema developed the "anti-Heimat film," which critically raised social, political, and ecological issues and demonstrated keen awareness of conflicts and injustices in German society. The first critical Heimat film was *Hunting Scenes from Lower Bavaria (Jagdszenen aus Niederbayern)*, made in 1969 by Peter Fleischmann, about a village community riven with conflict and narrow-mindedness. This was a conscious attempt to use an indigenous genre by changing the meaning of its cherished narrative patterns.

Heimat does not fit in easily with the development of the Heimat-film genre. On one level, *Heimat* is an archetypal Heimat film of the classic era to the extent that it uses the genre's basic cinematic motifs and narrative patterns. In Heimat films, "landscapes and regional mentalities are visualized in picturesque images that transform into vacation landscapes that constitute the stage for an exotic display of traditional dresses, customs, festivals, and local cuisine." This motif is easily recognizable in *Heimat*, which was popular because it offered the viewer the opportunity to be a sort of tourist in a journey into the German local past. A second motif in the post-1945 Heimat films portrayed the tension between tradition and modernity, and everyday life situations such as love, marriage, problems between parents and children, and conflicts between natives and newcomers. This motif characterizes *Heimat* as well. Finally, Heimat films represented history according to the Heimat idea's symbolic manual, ignoring strict relations of cause and effect between the Nazi regime and postwar conditions while emphasizing "just . . . 'fate.'" Reitz reminds the audience of the long tradition of the Heimat-film genre in a scene in which Maria and her sister-in-law Pauline watch Carl Froelich's 1938 film *Heimat*; he thus makes sure the audience sees his *Heimat* as part of this tradition. (Significantly, Reitz does not mention previous traditions of the Heimat idea in imperial Germany.) On a second level, however, while Reitz, as a member of the Oberhausen group, shared the values and ideology of the New Left that gave rise to the critical Heimat film, *Heimat* is not an anti-Heimat film because it largely avoids a critical approach to social and political issues. It is principally about identity and, as such, is full of nostalgic craving for a lost world—a nostalgia that is alien to the anti-Heimat film, yet so much a part of the classic Heimat film.

Heimat thus belongs neither to the classic Heimat films nor to the anti-Heimat films, but instead is, as one scholar put it, a "highly ambivalent adoption of the genre."[43] Reitz's motivation was to counter the made-in-Hollywood rendition of German history by using an indigenous genre that represents and defines German identity. He created a unique Heimat film. From the classic Heimat films he adopted cinematic motifs and narrative patterns that had been considered traditional and conservative, while infusing them with New Left meanings from the 1960s and 1970s, such as rejecting the embellishment of reality and highlighting the experience of "little people" through oral history. From the anti-Heimat films he adopted the depiction of real life (Schabbach is composed of hard-working people, of messy living conditions, and of jealousy), although he departed from it by not passing judgment and by keeping a nostalgic longing for a putatively lost Heimat. By selecting elements from Heimat films and anti-Heimat films, Reitz seems to tell us that the genre is neither inherently conservative nor inherently progressive, but—if properly used through memory, experience, and storytelling—can be a mirror of the German ways of life.

To return to the starting point of this discussion, while Reitz's aim is to represent German history, his key to the past is his memory. The history of the Heimat idea before the Third Reich disappears from his story, and the understanding of German history is dependent on his personal experience. This point becomes clear when we consider that the social and cultural topics that have preoccupied Germans since the nineteenth century are presented in *Heimat* as problems created by post-1945 West German Americanisms, the period when Reitz grew up and made up his mind about the world.

Let me give one brief example. One of Reitz's most powerful arguments in *Heimat* is the way West German society lost touch with its past and identity by selling itself short to materialism. This is best exemplified by Ernst, the son of Maria and Paul. In the 1960s Ernst sets up a business to renovate old peasant furniture that is sold to city dwellers. The pieces are not authentic, however, because Ernst's workers make three pieces of furniture out of two in order to augment the profits. To ensure the apparent authenticity of the furniture, Ernst has a special spray made for him, which gives the furniture the "smell of 1865."[44] Ernst symbolizes the transformation of post-1945 German society: having lost Heimat artifacts to consumerism, he sells Heimat sentiments as a commodity for mass consumption. (It is worthwhile to pause for a minute and consider that Ernst's commercial activity is to invent German memories.)

For Reitz, the past was an organic part of reality before the foundation of West Germany and became a commodity thereafter. But this view has more to do with Reitz's deep antipathy to West Germany than to any complex understanding of the modern perception of the past in general, and of Germans' perceptions of the past in particular. The connection between consumer culture and perceptions of the past was common long before the foundation of West Germany. Heimatlers in imperial Germany saw in the Heimat idea not only a source of local and national identity, but also a source of profit. The two were united by the development of tourism. Heimat museums exemplified the connection because they attempted to attract tourists by marketing their past as worthy of a visit. But Reitz believes in a dichotomy of unconditional totalities between German national society dominated by consumerism and rootlessness after 1949 and a national society of authentic relations to the past, while refusing to consider that both elements can intermix. Often (perhaps always) nations construct an idea that there once existed a pure, homogeneous national identity, uncorrupted by modernity and its offspring, consumer culture. This idea exists as an ideology, a belief, and a propaganda. But the coexistence of consumer culture with notions of roots and authenticity, that is, making authenticity a commodity for mass consumption, is what really happens. Here Reitz's description of German identity is unsatisfactory not because he fails to include the Holocaust, but because he fails to embrace the complexity of modernity.

LONG CAREER AND SHORT MEMORY

Heimat has often been compared with Bernardo Bertolucci's *1900*, but the analogy, I believe, is misleading. *1900* is a film about the role of political ideology in Italian history; it breathes politics, and as such is the antithesis to *Heimat*. Reitz, unlike Bertolucci, is obsessed with memory, with the passing of community ties, with nostalgia. As such it brings to mind another oeuvre d'art whose task was to immortalize national identity and whose feeling is of deep loss. I mean *Les lieux de memoire*, the grand and now classic work on France's national memory edited by Pierre Nora.[45] Like *Heimat* among films, this work is unique among historical studies, seven volumes dedicated to exploring French nationhood throughout history. Like *Heimat*, its obsession is with national identity. Like *Heimat*, it places the roots of the nation ahistorically somewhere in the remote past. And like *Heimat*, it bemoans the "acceleration of history," the disappearance of "real environments of memory."[46] It is a measure of the need to reaffirm national identities in our age that two of the oldest European societies produced major introspective works; it is a measure of the indiscreet charm of nostalgia that both works embraced the concept of the nation uncritically; and it is the pleasure of basking in the past that makes these works fascinating.

Memory is captivating because we can convince ourselves in a remarkably short time that certain newly constructed images of the past have been a permanent part of our identity. But memory is perceived as immemorial, definitive, and representing reality because, ultimately, memory is short. Memory can have empowering consequences, as when history of everyday life finds its way to the mainstream of historical discourse via oral history. But, at the same time, it can also provide individuals and societies with a vehicle to ignore the moral responsibilities of their past. It is no accident that in order to obscure the Holocaust, Reitz chooses to hide behind the mantle of "memory." For memory's presumed authenticity is, of course, deceiving; it distorts the past, and this (among other things) accounts, I believe, for its sanctified status in contemporary popular discourse. It is this ambiguity of memory, as a vehicle of empowerment and self-deception, that makes it so fascinating—and worthy of critical study.

3

HEIMAT AND MEMORIES OF WAR IN WEST GERMANY, 1945–1960

Traveling through Germany . . . this lovely country you will never forget.
—*Promotion by the German Central Tourist Association, 1952*

Nineteen-forty-five was an end with two beginnings for German nationhood, one communist the other liberal-democratic. But what could possibly be salvaged from the wreckage of German nationhood? Not the idea of the German nation, but perhaps the idea of the German Heimat.

By 1945 the Heimat idea had already had a distinguished career in German culture. Germans had considered it since 1871 as a way to reconcile local, regional, and national identities through an interlocking network of symbols and representations in which the nation appeared local and the locality national. They thus imagined nationhood as a form of localness by taking traditional ways of thinking about, and modes of representation of, the local and regional community and giving them a whole new meaning by connecting them to the nation in ways that were unpredictable before 1871. And far from being antimodern, Heimatlers expressed the ambiguity of modernity itself by simultaneously mourning the past while applauding the material progress and cultural opportunities promised by modernity. Significantly, as a widely popular idiom of localness and nationhood, the Heimat idea had been appropriated by different groups and ideologies; it was not exclusively bourgeois or socialist, fascist or Marxist, left or right wing.[1] A flexible, dynamic, and malleable notion, no one had exclusive copyrights on the Heimat idea.

What a fitting concept, then, to represent the homeland following the total bankruptcy of German nationhood in 1945. Always capable of adapting symbolically to historical circumstance, the Heimat idea did not simply survive the Third Reich; it helped define postwar German nationhood in the German Democratic Republic (GDR) and the Federal Republic of Germany (FRG). This chapter explores aspects of the Heimat idea in the FRG, while the next one focuses on the GDR.

By talking about Heimat, West Germans found a way to discuss that which was so problematic to talk about, namely national identity. Through the Heimat idea they articulated sentiments of victimhood and guilt, of the lost territories in Eastern Europe, as well as of the new Heimat in the making, namely West Germany. Heimat was not a backward concept representing false harmony and repression of the Nazi past. On the contrary, while Heimat was an integrative symbol, it also exposed social tensions in West German society, as well as the built-in contradictions of German national identity following the Third Reich. It was a vehicle not to repress but to remember selectively the Third Reich, while placing this remembrance within the new postwar European conditions.

This text explores the uses of the Heimat idea in postwar West Germany through various sources, but I particularly focus on the link between Heimat and traveling. This link was evident from the end of the nineteenth century, when modern tourism and the Heimat idea emerged.[2] In 1955 *Der Fremdenverkehr* (Tourism), the main journal of the German Central Tourist Association (Deutsche Zentrale für Fremdenverkehr, or ZFV) founded in 1948 as West Germany's national tourist organization, stated clearly: "The relations between Heimat studies and tourism are as wide reaching as the notion of Heimat itself. Tourism uses the historical facts [of Heimat studies] in order to keep alive the memory of great events." In the wake of the war—of the need to rebuild German identity—continued the journal, it is especially important to connect Heimat studies with tourism, to use tourism as a vehicle to embrace local, regional, and national history, and to familiarize oneself with the natural and human peculiarities of the German people.[3]

POSTWAR HEIMAT:
THE HOMELAND AS AN INNOCENT VICTIM

What was, then, the image of the German Heimat in travel literature after the war? On first sight, the shibboleth that Germans totally repressed the Nazi past after the war seems to be supported by ample evidence.[4] Germany, according to the German Central Tourist Association, was an assemblage of "music and theater, art, folk costumes and festivals, entertainment (Carnival) exhibitions and fairs, spas, and gastronomy of all sorts."[5] This selective list of cultural and historical accomplishments, propagated after 1945 in brochures, travel guides, and tourist images, represented a Germany devoid of the Third Reich. The *Deutschland Revue*, a colorful, popular magazine published by the German Central Tourist Association simultaneously in German and English, invited foreign tourists to visit "this lovely country you will never forget" that is "imbued with the spirit of freedom [and] open-hearted friendliness. World renowned healing powers, flowing from our soil, are again serving suffering humanity."[6] The moral dissonance embedded in this description is striking: in the name of racial healing, Germans made millions suffer, only to claim now the German soil as a healer "serving suffering humanity." At the same time, this kind of tourist publicity is, in a sense, to be expected. Countries usually don't publicize their shameful past and disreputable history as tourist attractions.

But this is only part of the story. When we read the sources (travel publications, Heimat literature, and documents of tourist and Heimat associations) more closely, sensitive to silences, gaps, and ellipses, a very different picture emerges. The image of the German Heimat was used, first, to distance Germany from the Third Reich. The anniversary of Goethe's birth in 1949 gave a good occasion to equate the great writer with "the true Germany," since Goethe's "spirit and thoughts were not forgotten by most Germans even under the Nazi regime."[7] The aim of promoting Germany's cultural heritage was not to show the transformation from the brutalities of the Nazi regime to the civil society of West Germany but to negate the connections between the two historical periods. As it was put shortly after the "First German Tourism Day" (Erster Deutscher Fremdenverkehrstag) in 1950, "It all depends on convincing the world that a Germany of violence and inhumanity does not exist any more, that this un-German Germany was something temporary and that every guest from abroad meets again [in Germany] a hospitality in its classic meaning."[8] One can certainly believe that some foreign tourists were welcome in Germany in 1950, but it can be safely assumed that, for most Germans, Jews, blacks, Poles, and Russians were not among them. By referring to National Socialism as "this un-German Germany" (*jenes un-deutsches Deutschland*), tourist rhetoric extracted it from German history, as if a magical time machine had stopped German history in 1933 and resumed it in 1945.[9]

Perceiving the Third Reich as "un-German" led Germans to the extreme of blaming foreigners who did link National Socialism with postwar German history as naive and ignorant. "The ignorance about Germany is often terrifying, and also the judgment on German conditions, without knowledge of the precise conditions, is of amazing naivety. Germany must be active enlightening the entire world, today more than ever."[10] Like other countries who conduct immoral policies and who refuse to own up to them, also in Germany a prevalent idea was that the problem was one of public relations. The idea that Germany's image problems were a result of the history of racial domination and extermination was not readily internalized. Moreover, behind the argument that foreigners did not understand the complexity of German conditions was the idea that condemning Germany for the war did not take into consideration German suffering. Foreigners' "ignorance about Germany and its conditions" was a code phrase for German victimhood.

Indeed, Heimat was used not only as an idiom to distance the Third Reich from postwar Germany but, in fact, as an idiom that combined removal with victimhood. It was common to talk in the postwar period about Germany as the "unfortunate fatherland." There were good reasons to feel that way, be they material, political, national, or moral; German individual and collective self-respect was in a miserable state. The problem is not with viewing Germany in the year 1946 as the "unfortunate fatherland," but with the silence over why Germany was miserable and who was responsible for that. Thus, A. D. Ochs, who convened a meeting in June 1946 to prepare the foundation of the German League of Tourist and Spa Associations (Bund deutscher Verkehrsverbände und Bäder), noted that he hoped that tourism would "bring about equality and friendship among nations and re-create for our unfortunate fatherland respect and prestige in the world." [11]

Perhaps the celebratory meeting of tourist officials in June 1946 was not the right occasion to reflect on the reasons for Germany's misery. Perhaps we should not expect, as some scholars and laypersons do, that every German reference to the Nazi past would include an expression of guilt and of owning up to it. But the truth is that other occasions rarely include these expressions either. Indeed, if there was rhetoric on the Nazi past that emerged in postwar West Germany, it was one of suffering. And as an idiom of suffering, the Heimat idea often represented Germans as twice victims: of the Hitler regime and of the Allies, especially the Russians and other East Europeans. Local and regional members of the Associations for German Heimat, Travel, and Nature Protection (Deutsche Heimat-, Wander- und Naturschutzbünde) met for the first postwar meeting in March 1954 in the Bundesrat hall. Among the well-wishers and speakers was the Federal Republic's president, Theodor Heuß. The prime minister of North Rhine–Westphalia, Karl Arnold, conveyed a common belief on Heimat and German suffering: "We saw how the rulers of the Hitler Reich—those who could not have enough folk costumes and midsummer festivals, who raised to their lips the blood and soil and traditions—did not hesitate to deny in cold blood the right of Heimat to the inhabitants of South Tyrol, and to expel them purposefully into foreign land. We have since experienced one of the most horrible recidivisms into barbarity that humanity has ever seen in the expulsion of millions from their hereditary Heimat. That our sisters and brothers from the east and southeast honor the memory of their Heimat is not a result of obstinacy or revanchism. For their Heimat is a part of their essence. . . . Their Heimat, their native land, is however also a part of our Heimat."[12] The crimes of National Socialism and of East Europeans who expelled Germans were equal, as both violated the innocent Heimat. National Socialism was reduced to a phenomenon of several "rulers" who imposed their terror on an innocent German people. And while the German expellee victims were clearly identified in the speech, the victims of National Socialism were not mentioned.

The memory of German expellees shows that it would be a mistake to view Heimat as a metaphor that only distanced Germany from the Third Reich. The Third Reich was alive in postwar memory, only selectively alive, assigning Germans the roles of victims and conveying overall moral indifference to the victims of Nazism. Some 12 million expellees from Czechoslovakia, eastern Prussia, and parts of eastern Germany ceded to postwar Poland survived the end of the war. They were Germans who had left or were driven out of Eastern Europe by the Red Army as the war wound down. In 1950 about two-thirds of them lived in West Germany (16 percent of all inhabitants). Divided among regional organizations, hundred of thousands of these Germans in traditional costumes commemorated annually the lost Heimats, keeping alive the memory of a lost world. In postwar West Germany, the lost Heimats of the East served as a powerful idiom of national victimhood and suffering.

This idiom soon led to equating Germans with Jews. Similar to Arnold, Hans Christoph Seebohm, minister of transportation, expressed a common sentiment when he wrote in May 1952 that the concept of German reparations to the Jews was acceptable because it would lead to reparations to expellees: "I am ready to acknowledge at any time the moral reparation duty toward Judaism, but I can do it only when others in the world are also ready to fulfill their moral reparation duty toward the German Heimat expellees. The methods that were used by the National Socialists against the Jews and that we all fiercely condemn are equal to the methods used against the German Heimat expellees."[13] Jews and Germans, then, had experienced the same kind of persecution and were thus morally equal. Although he condemned "the methods" used against the Jews, Seebohm, by denying relations of cause and effect, displayed a basic resistance and moral inability to grasp the essence of the Nazi regime—and of the agency of Germans, not of "methods," who actualized it: the Jews were innocent victims, while the expulsion of Germans from the East was a result of Hitler's murderous war.

The Heimat idea came to symbolize the suffering of an innocent Germany. Heimat memories of expellees tended to construct an ideal and nostalgic image of the past, while describing in detail the suffering of women and children, the rapes, and the act of expulsion. In these stories the Heimat was not a participant in the war but a victim of it. This Heimat representation in postwar West Germany agreed with the representation of Heimat in imperial Germany, which we have seen in chapter 1: in both periods Heimat was something one fought for, not something that participated in battle. Heimat was the direct opposite of war and its associated brutality, bloodshed, and destruction. The Heimat could, of course, suffer, but it could not cause suffering. It could be wronged, but could do no wrong. In war, it needed to be protected, but could not attack or destroy. Heimat images from imperial Germany placed war outside the Heimat; postwar expellees' memories represented the Heimat and its Germans as victims of the war, less as agents whose actions, motivations, and crimes participated in it.

Moreover, the relations between Heimat, war, and gender highlighted the link between Heimat and (what was perceived as) feminine sensibilities. Women narrated many of expellees' stories, and the reason lay not only in the fact that most men in 1944–45 in Eastern European German communities were at the front. Women were always viewed as authentic authorities on Heimat matters. In the case of the expulsions from Eastern Europe, the reality of expellees agreed with key topics, metaphors, and narrative devices that were used to describe a Heimat, and which were closely connected in the mind of contemporaries with feminine sensibilities: family, children, and home.[14] The stories of children's suffering, family dispersion, and burnt homes represented the violated Heimat. The rape of German women was the reality as well as the powerful metaphor par excellence of the violated lost Heimat. At the same time, war underlined the identity between Heimat and women: both ideally stayed away from battle, representing an image of normality and home to which men longed to return. When war reached women and the Heimat, as happened in the years of total war and defeat, the result was violation, rape, and changing of what was viewed as the natural order. The violation of German women stood for the violation of Heimat and nation. This link between gender and Heimat, which emerged already in imperial Germany, was embraced by postwar West Germans, as old Heimat motifs articulated the post-1945 new national conditions.

But Heimat has never been a fixed concept. It was not a local concept opposing the nation, or simply a mediator between localness and nationhood. Instead, the interchangeability of Heimat as local, regional, and national image underscored the malleability of the idea. In the same speech mentioned in the previous section, Karl Arnold, the prime minister of North Rhine–Westphalia, put it this way: "The feeling for Heimat and nationhood is not a self-evident and indestructible mental property. Also the Heimat feeling can suffer from a disease and ultimately lose meaning and content."[15] And he went on to give the example of the Nazis, who corrupted the Heimat idea. But if a Heimat can be lost and a Heimat feeling can "suffer from a disease," then it can also be found and revived anew. Heimat, as spatial and historical identity, can be about past memories of where you had belonged, but it can also be about present memories of where you belong now. A "new Heimat" is not an oxymoron. In West Germany, the Heimat idea provided old and new roots that coexisted in tension. It was not only about well-defined local space that survived National Socialism but, in particular, about fluid national space. On one level, the national Heimat was now, politically speaking, West Germany. But Heimat was never a photocopy of political sovereignty. In the wake of war, where and what was Heimat was a contested, ambiguous spatial idea.

There were (at least) two German territorial Heimats that challenged the clear boundaries of postwar West German Heimat: East Germany and the lost territories in Eastern Europe. The longing for these Heimats, politically divided now among four sovereign states (East Germany, Czechoslovakia, Poland, and Russia), represented a homeland whose boundaries were unstable and unclear. The sentiment of a homeland in flux was expressed in various ways. Konrad Adenauer could insist in a 1950 meeting of Silesian expellees that one day Silesia would again be German.[16] Although his specific political aim was to win expellee electorate votes, his statement also reflected the open-endedness of public discourse with regard to Germany's eastern borders.[17] On the occasion of the fiftieth anniversary of the Tourist Association of the Harz (Harzer Verkehrsverband) in 1954, the chairman of the association wrote that the Harz "reflects the great misfortune that befell Germany in the year 1945." (This "misfortune" [Unglück], again, had no agency, no name, and no address. It simply "befell" Germany.) The pride over the achievements of the association in the west, he continued, mixed with sadness over the loss of the Harz territory in the east (the German-German border ran through the Harz region).[18] And a picture book published in English by the German Central Tourist Association, entitled *Deutschland*, felt the need to explain what is meant by "Germany": "This postscript makes clear that, when speaking of Germany, we mean west [*sic*] Germany, that is to say, the Federal Republic of Germany. The freedom of travel unfortunately does not apply to the German provinces behind the Iron Curtain, regions equally rich in natural and cultural beauties."[19]

Heimat, therefore, did not represent simply a cozy, local place, bounded within well-defined territory. On the contrary, it represented in these cases a homeland in flux. The greater national Heimat, the regional Silesian Heimat, and the West German Heimat were linked in a web of Heimat sentiments of national belonging and shared past. They coexisted, but in tension. The idea to make Silesia German again, or to possess again the "provinces behind the Iron Curtain," contained a utopian desire that went beyond and undermined the current political order, be it the domestic prosperity and stability of West German society or the international Cold War order that made Adenauer's Germany part of the West. Heimat sentiments toward territories in the East stood in contradiction to political stability and practical consideration of foreign policy. In this respect, the Heimat idea possessed a destabilizing potential in the Federal Republic.

The crux of the issue, in a sense, was this: If West Germany was a temporary Heimat, then just how temporary was "temporary"? Ten years? Fifty? One hundred? Forever? Should the expellees refuse to set roots in West Germany in anticipation of their future relocation to their old Heimat? The expellees themselves appreciated the complexity of this dilemma. They lobbied the government in Bonn to make sure their "Right for Heimat" in the lost territories in Eastern Europe stayed on West Germany's foreign policy agenda, while at the same time expellees' organizations pressured the national and regional governments to act decisively to enable expellees to start over. The utopian desire to return to the lost home coexisted with the practical solutions to get integrated within West German society. Expellees wanted to keep the memory of past lives alive, but much of the reconstruction and economic miracle in West Germany was about leaving the war behind, about a return to normality.[20] It is often remarked how hopelessly nostalgic expellees were with regard to their lost territories. This is certainly true.[21] But their efforts to set new roots in West Germany should not be forgotten either. The integration, prosperity, and ultimate satisfaction of expellees were crucial for the success of German domestic peace as well as European and international peace.[22]

Heimat films captured successfully in the 1950s this duality of the Heimat idea, as a longing for a lost home as well as an anchor in a new, though incomplete, Heimat. The Heimat-film genre reached its zenith in the 1950s, as has been discussed in chapter 2, representing a world of everyman in villages and hometowns, and focusing on the solidity of, and conformity to, social relations and values. This conservative message was attacked in the Oberhausen Manifesto, which promised to create a new German cinema that would be politically and socially engaged. The Oberhausen Manifesto set the tone for a whole generation of film makers, critics, and scholars who were satisfied to condemn the Heimat-film genre as bucolic escapism and conservative longing to a utopian past. But, in fact, Heimat films reflected important sentiments in postwar West Germany. While the genre did represent a world of simple people in villages and hometowns, it also stressed and problematized the tensions between tradition and modernity. Heimat films made it possible for people—in the wake of a destructive war and in the midst of a changing society—to dream of marriage and a happy family, prosperity, and leisure, and, for the refugees from Eastern Europe and East Germany, to dream of a new Heimat.

Heimat films such as *Grün ist die Heide* (Green Is the Heath, 1951), about a Pomeranian expellee now living in the Lüneberger Heide, and *Waldwinter: Glocken der Heimat* (Forest in Winter: The Bells of Heimat, 1956), about Silesians who made a new home in Bavaria, told about the preserving power of the world expellees left behind, while placing this world in the new home in the West. *Waldwinter*, especially, emphasized not only the problems of expellees to integrate into the new society, but also their Heimat values and beliefs that contributed to building the new Heimat. In the film, the Heimat values of Silesians—their mystics, poets, and storytellers, their intelligence and memory, as one reviewer of the film put it—became a foundation of the 1950s prosperity and economic miracle. Silesians are portrayed not as stuck in the world of yesterday but as ready to use past values to embrace modernity.[23] A similar sentiment is evident in *Schwarzwaldmädel* (A Black Forest Girl, 1950), the first big postwar Heimat film, made by Hans Deppe, who also directed *Grün ist die Heide*. In one of the more evocative scenes of the film, a raffle ticket wins the heroine Bärbel the party's grand prize: a shiny red Ford Taunus.[24] The Heimat idea, therefore, was neither a one-dimensional local identity nor an appeal to return to nostalgic village life, nor simply a reactionary, irredentist political cry. While it conveyed expellees' longing for their lost homes, as well as a moral blindness to the historical reasons of their expulsion, it also helped them integrate within West German society; while it honored the perceived values of Heimat regional identity, it also praised the ability to apply these values to a changing, modern world. While it preached the integrity of the eternal Heimat of the East, it also built a new (and obviously eternal as well) Heimat in West Germany.

THE HEIMAT AT HOME AND ABROAD

If Heimat served as a multiple idiom to remember lost territories and to set up new roots, it also represented the new, postwar German national identity placed within a new Western Europe. Here traveling was viewed as fundamental: tourism after 1945, apart from being a source of joy, was viewed as a national pedagogical project aimed at transmitting to Germans the values of a new Germany. It enabled Germans to cultivate, for themselves as well as for foreigners, a sense of national identity in a period when this concept was totally bankrupt. As an assemblage of culture, art festivals, and spas, Germany, according to the German Central Tourist Association, was devoid, as we have seen, of the National Socialist crimes. Tourism thus made it possible to speak about national identity in times when it was considered taboo. "It should be clear to anybody, whether a German or a member of another nation, that one should get to know *first* one's own Heimat," wrote Matthias Thömmes, director of the German League of Tourist Associations (Bund Deutscher Verkehrsverbände). A trendy habit developed in Germany, continued Thömmes, whereby youths take organized trips abroad before they "first set roots in the Heimat soil." And he did not fail to cite Goethe, the ubiquitous post-1945 moral German authority, who said "One who does not know the Heimat has no yardstick to understand foreign lands." [25]

Alongside this national education project there was a second one that placed Germany squarely within Europe. This project aimed at impregnating Germans with sensitivity commensurate to the new emerging Western Europe. This sensitivity was already expressed to a degree by Thömmes, who was not so much against youth trips abroad as he was against taking them instead of trips at home: "For how should a united Europe come into being when one does not know and understand oneself in one's own land!" [26] But traveling abroad was not enough. Following a war of domination and extermination, Germans needed to be instructed on how to behave abroad. A concerted effort was aimed at educating Germans traveling to neighboring countries that were occupied by Germany in the war. In the 1950s, stories abounded of Germans' insensitivity. The *Frankfurt Allgemeine Zeitung* carried a story in 1953 of a German couple on a trip to Amsterdam. The man rang the bell of a beautiful villa, and to the question, What do they wish? answered that he wanted to show his wife where he had lived during the war. This kind of behavior was unacceptable, suggested the newspaper. The tourist was essential to the image of Germany abroad. The Germans thus needed to learn "manners for tourists": "Every German who crosses the Dutch border as a tourist should be well aware that he—significantly more than the politicians and the businessmen who arrive in the Netherlands as partners for practical discussions—influences through his behavior the opinion of the Dutch people about Germany."[27]

The combined tourist pedagogical projects—one emphasizing national identity, the second placing it within a European context—were complementary. They reflected the new post-1945 conditions in Western Europe, where a group of nation-states increasingly coordinated policies and interests. The love of one's Heimat was not viewed anymore as necessarily contradictory to love of thy neighbor's Heimat.

The Heimat idea, then, elastic, flexible, and interchangeable, provided after 1945 a whole set of rhetorical possibilities to talk about nationhood without breaking taboos. It was an idiom that distanced as well as embraced the Third Reich, and that presented Germany as a victim, not a perpetrator. In the moral morass that was West Germany after the war, it was a concept made in heaven: it allowed one to link to a selective personal and collective experience of the Third Reich, while sidestepping moral questions.

HEIMAT, EAST GERMAN IMAGINATION, AND AN EXCESS OF REALITY

Our Heimat, it is not only the cities and villages,
Our Heimat is also all the trees in the forest,
Our Heimat is the grass in the meadow, the grain in the field
And the fish in the stream are the Heimat.
And we love our Heimat, the beautiful.
And we protect her, because she belongs to the people,
Because she belongs to our people.
—East German youth song[1]

POST-1945 GERMAN COMMUNISM AND THE HEIMAT IDEA

There are good reasons to think that German communists would reject the Heimat idea after 1945 as ideologically objectionable and symbolically impractical. Ideologically, the Heimat idea was viewed by communists in the Soviet Occupation Zone (Sowjetische Besatzungszone, or SBZ) and later in the German Democratic Republic (GDR) as a vestige of bourgeois culture and Nazi imperialism. Politically and administratively, the emphasis on regional autonomy and identity opposed the idea of democratic centralism. Culturally, the Stalinism of the new power elite in the SBZ was set on demolishing precisely the kind of traditional, bourgeois, and Nazi mental structures that the Heimat idea represented, while in the GDR regional identities fit in uncomfortably with the state ideology of class consciousness determined by the means of production.[2]

It is not surprising, then, that Helmut Holtzhauer, Saxony's minister for public education, explained in October 1948 in the following words the reasons for bringing to an end the independent existence of the Saxon Regional Association for Heimat Protection (Landesverein Sächsischer Heimatschutz, founded in 1908): "The ministry of public education is not interested in reviving the association, especially when we take into account that a remarkably large number of its former 62,000 members come from petty-bourgeois, antiprogressive elements."[3] The Saxon Association was thus forced to integrate within the Cultural League for the Democratic Renewal of Germany (Kulturbund zur demokratischen Erneuerung Deutschlands), an umbrella organization of antifascist artists, writers, scientists, and intellectuals founded on July 3, 1945. The Cultural League was initially a home to people of different antifascist persuasions, but it soon came under the control of the Socialist Unity Party of Germany (Sozialistische Einheitspartei Deutschlands, or SED), the ruling party from its foundation in April 1946 to 1990.[4] The Heimat idea seemed destined either to go the way of traditional relics such as private property and Junker estates, or simply to wither away in the new revolutionary state.

But could German communists really jettison the Heimat idea? It was Karl Marx, after all, who noted that people make their own history but not under conditions of their own choosing. The Heimat idea was a symbolic representation of the local, regional, and national since the beginning of the nation-state in 1871; it provided a system of knowledge and sensibilities with which Germans gave meaning to their past, present, and future. By 1945, to jettison the Heimat idea meant to jettison Germanness itself. Communists had little choice but to integrate it into their new ideas about Germany's destiny. This sentiment was indeed expressed by Holtzhauer, a long-time member of the German Communist Party (KPD) and later the SED, in the letter mentioned previously: "The positive ideas of Heimat protection will obviously be promoted by the ministry for public education in the most active way." The question, then, was not whether to integrate the Heimat idea within a new East German identity, but how and which kind of Heimat idea.

Differently put, whatever East German ideologues thought about the Heimat idea, they thought it within a framework of post-1871 Heimat images and rhetoric. If they wanted to abolish it, they had to reckon with its persistent hold on the German imagination. If they wanted to use it to bolster their rule, they had to take into account its tradition of symbols and meanings. The Heimat idea, as we have seen, was a concept that could be used by any regime, any ideology. But it was endowed with a symbolic manual that imposed certain limits: it represented the nation as a local metaphor; it was more effective when iconographically subtle and politically silent; it linked the Germans of the present to immemorial notional ancestry in the past. How, then, did the first socialist state on German soil, as the GDR proudly called itself, engage with this symbolic manual? How did East German communists handle the tension between the notions of class and nation, thus attempting to reshape long-term Heimat symbols to fit immediate ideological needs?

To answer these questions historians must seek a set of sources that reveal the relations between direct ideological intentions and long-term cultural sensibilities, between conscious political use of the Heimat idea and unintended consequences of operating within the symbolic manual of it. Written documents that reveal the expressed ideological goals of the regime are not necessarily sufficient guides in this exploration. They can show the ideological use and function of the Heimat idea: but this is the starting point of our investigation, not the end result. We need a set of sources that goes beyond the literal meaning of expressed ideology, that tracks down silences and contradictions that exist underneath, and in opposition to, ideological positions. These sources should capture how the German communists combined Heimat sensibilities with Marxist ideology.

We turn again to Heimat images as a source for capturing mentalities, that which cannot quite be said but is present nonetheless. This chapter explores Heimat images in the official iconographic production of the SED from 1945 to 1970. The posters were produced for election purposes, to mobilize for programs such as the Two and Five Year Plans, or to extol social organizations controlled by the SED such as the Free German Youth (Freie Deutsche Jugend, or FDJ), the Free German Trade Union Association (Freier Deutscher Gewerkschaftsbund, or FDGB), and the Society for Sport and Technology (Gesellschaft für Sport und Technik, or GST). They were produced by the regional or national levels of the SED for the purpose of representing what distinguished the new communist Germany from the past and depicting how it would look in the future. For purpose of comparison, I discuss also Heimat images produced by organizations other than the SED and relate the images to policies and expressed ideology based on documents of state ministries, newspapers, youth organizations, and various publications.

The focus is on the communist elite in the SBZ and the GDR, the most committed ideological group and one that had, in theory at least, the most reservations about the Heimat idea. The aim is to explore whether the tradition of the Heimat idea existed in the place it was least likely to exist, in the place we least expect to find it: at the heart of German communism's representation of itself. Whatever the findings of this investigation are, they add to our understanding of German identity and political ideology. With its emphasis on class, the GDR presented the local-national Heimat idea its most severe symbolic challenge. But if the Heimat symbolic manual existed in East Germany—and it did—then we are able to identify one of the mainstays of modern German national identity and, more generally, a revealing historical case of national identity. The Heimat symbolic manual thus becomes more than just a case of one of those isolated objects that—voilà!—are declared by scholars as "German identity"; rather, it was a case of a system of representation without which it was impossible for Germans—since the beginning of the nation-state, under any political regime—to imagine their localness and nationhood.

How did I sift meaning from East German Heimat images? How can I know what I am arguing? My interpretative mode of procedure was to put in relation the GDR's iconography of and commentary on Heimat posters, as well as expressed Heimat ideology, on the one hand, with the long-term iconographic symbolic manual of the Heimat idea, on the other. I interpret the East German Heimat images within two contextual circles: the immediate post-1945 context of the foundation and history of the GDR, and the long-term post-1871 context of the imagining and history of the Heimat idea. The iconographic tensions, agreements, and negotiations between these two contexts are the backbone of our story.[5] Heimat iconography, as we have seen in chapter 1, presented an image of a Germany of small villages, a hometown, and some industrial symbols such as factories, in harmonious relationship with nature (figures 1–4). It was an image of tranquil, and very local, national existence. The image of the national Heimat was a stereotypization of Germany, its nature, its people, and its communities; images could fit almost every area in Germany. Nothing much happened in the images of the national Heimat, which were powerful precisely because they were, as stated above, empty. Imprinting the idea of Heimat in their minds, Germans ceased to associate the nation with real social and political processes and viewed it as immemorial. This tradition serves as a point of departure and as a basis of comparison with the East German idea of Heimat because it served this function for East German communists themselves.

1945–1949: THE PERSISTENCE AND CHANGE OF THE OLD HEIMAT REGIME

Following the defeat of the Third Reich in May 1945, all Germans faced the problem of finding new ways to talk and think about their discredited nationhood. As a central representation of localness and nationhood before 1945, the Heimat idea offered one possible alternative.[6] But its career in the SBZ seemed tenuous, and its activities were severely curtailed, either by the Soviet administration's decision to terminate all independent associational life or by the ideological suspicion of the KPD and later the SED. While the newly established Social Democratic Party (SPD), Christian Democratic Union

(CDU), and Liberal Democratic Party (LDPD) supported resuming Heimat activities, German communists viewed regional traditions as demonstration of political obsession with particularism and revanchism.[7] They strove for a unified national culture without fascist-bourgeois deviation.[8]

But individuals and societies do not change overnight just because history takes a new direction and new ideology is empowered. Collective representations and mentalities cannot shift suddenly because the Third Reich was defeated, Germany was occupied, and East Germany was founded: their changes are often gradual; there are continuities that persist. Some are noticeable, others subterranean; new modes of representing reality emerge that, however radical they are, must have roots in previous habits of mind. The meaning of Heimat in German culture was more than a set of facts about regional history and concerned more than overt political use by this alleged class or that alleged race. It was a set of mental representations that endowed the abstract national territory with intimacy, familiarity, and a sense of home, and these representations could not have been so easily discarded by communists in 1945.

The iconography of the period provides evidence that Germans, regardless of political persuasion, continued to imagine the nation as a local metaphor. Let us look first at political posters from the important local and regional elections of September–October 1946, the first postwar elections and the only (relatively) free elections in East Germany until 1990. All parties represented themselves in contradistinction to Nazism by appealing to what was perceived as the most positive, common, German, and authentic national symbols. It is not surprising that the CDU, a new nationwide party representing former members of the Catholic Center Party as well as conservative and nationalists Protestants, portrayed the nation in the classic Heimat image (figure 5).[9] It is more significant that an SED poster in Thuringia proclaiming "For peace, justice, and Heimat" presented an image, including the ubiquitous folk costume, that was indistinguishable from Heimat representation since the 1880s (figure 6).[10] This was not an iconographic aberration. An election poster in Bautzen (Saxony) presented the town's past, present, and future in three Heimat images (figure 7): the town destroyed in 1945, presently reconstructed in 1946, and flourishing in 1948. The representation of a town's identity with postcard-like images was a familiar trope of Heimat iconography since imperial Germany and was viewed as such by Germans.[11] The SED in Erfurt (Thuringia), to give another example, provided a different version of this short local history with national-historical morale (figure 8): it presented on top a classic Heimat image with the label "So looked Erfurt when the Nazis took it over"; the consequences appeared in the second image "In ruins they left us the town"; and an image of reconstructed Erfurt provided the political conclusion "SED . . . therefore your vote to the party of reconstruction."[12] By using established Heimat symbols of local identity, folk costume, and landscape, the SED linked itself to a Heimat tradition.

Also the peaceful generic Heimat landscape with scattered villages, hometowns, and smoking factory chimneys appeared on SED images. This was the case in a poster of the Women's Committees (Frauenausschüsse) from the 1946 Dresden election (figure 9; the committees joined women of various antifascist parties and persuasions, and enjoyed certain autonomy, but were controlled by the SED) and of its successor, the Democratic Women's League of Germany (Demokratischer Frauenbund Deutschland, or DFD), founded on March 8, 1947, and serving as a mouthpiece of the SED (figure 10; see the similarity to figures 3–4 from the First World War). These images used in addition the symbolic link between Heimat and (perceived) peaceful feminine sensibilities, thus placing the SED within another Heimat iconographic tradition.[13]

What was the meaning of the communists' use of Heimat iconography? There was an element of political manipulation in using these images, as the SED attached itself to a common cultural representation in order to gain legitimacy. The case of figure 9 is instructive. The SED leadership insisted on the participation of the Women's Committees (and other mass organizations such as the Free German Trade Union Association) in Saxony's local elections against reservations of party members and outright opposition of the CDU and the LDPD, whose voters came from the liberal middle classes. The electoral participation of an organization that was not a political party was targeted to attract nonsocialist voters; the middle-class woman in figure 9, superimposed on a Heimat landscape, was aimed to appeal to bourgeois women. This form of political deception used the Heimat image and the middle-class woman to provide a kinder, gentler representation of the SED and of future communist rule. The iconographic tradition of the working-class movement emphasized muscular and female workers, not bourgeois women professionals; when bourgeois professionals were used in socialist iconography, as in the Soviet Union in the 1950s for the first time, they always appeared together with workers, but not alone.[14] Therefore, in immediate postwar politics, the KPD first and SED later, not having yet secured a power monopoly, appropriated the Heimat image as a popular representation with broad appeal. This explains the representation of serene landscapes where CDU and SED were indistinguishable (compare figures 5, 6, 9, and 10).

This is part of the story, but it is not the whole story. It should be asked whether the meaning of the Heimat idea can be reduced to politics and whether the crucial explanation for SED Heimat representation was power manipulation. The assumption that a Heimat image, a site of identity that represented localness and nationhood, reflects only a narrow political reality is misplaced. Identities are meaningful not because they provide an accurate representation of reality (political or otherwise), but often precisely because they enable people to articulate relations beyond it. The result of understanding the representation of Heimat images only in terms of strict power politics is that the subjective meaning attached to the images is largely lost, while concepts like subterfuge and manipulation take center stage as explanatory devices.

The simple argument is this: whatever German communists said or did about the Heimat idea, they still imagined localness and nationhood in its idiom. They did not favor the eradication of the Heimat idea *tout court*, but the eradication of the (perceived) bourgeois, fascist political use of the Heimat idea. From this perspective, the communists' actions to limit (what they considered) reactionary Heimat activities fit perfectly with the adoption of a generic Heimat iconography, which they considered a common representation of the intimate, tangible nation.

This explains figure 11, made for the second SED party convention in 1947, that used a Heimat landscape to represent Germany in a time of national disunity and uncertainty, thus providing a similar function to the use of the Heimat idea in the western part, as we have seen in the previous chapter. Figure 11 represents two workers reaching to each other from west and east over Germany's landscape. The political agenda was there: the SED supported in September 1947, following Stalin's policy, a unified, socialist, neutral Germany, thus opposing the construction of a Western-oriented, capitalist second Germany. But the message was portrayed in a nonconflictual way, through a generic German landscape: as a local space that represented the national space, Heimat was suitable to describe the division of postwar Germany, the sort of spacelessness of the nation in flux between 1945 and 1949, its past eastern territories lost, its present sovereignty suspended, its future boundaries and political arrangement unclear. Without a distinct spatial and political look, it was not quite clear how to represent this Germany. But Heimat was an available, shared representation used successfully in the past. And, indeed, it is quite striking to note how similar the Heimat images of this period were to pre-1945 Heimat images.

The ubiquity of Heimat images in this period, as well as its conformity to iconographic tradition, shows that Heimat was meaningfully used not so much as a vehicle for manipulation but as a national imagination. The posters made for the fall 1946 elections fit within a widespread production of Heimat images in the SBZ by the SED and others. "The dead admonish: reconstruct!" (figure 12) cries a poster of a war-devastated Heimat with two townscape silhouettes of houses and church towers. A peaceful Heimat emerged from a poster of the Union of those Persecuted by the Nazi Regime (Vereinigung der Verfolgten des Naziregimes, or VVN), founded in January 1948 as the moral conscience of the SED to represent the interests of victims of Nazism (figure 13).[15] And a 1948 Dresden exhibition, New Heimat, New Life, targeted at expellees from former German territories in Eastern Europe portrayed the familiar symbols of a generic Heimat (figure 14).[16] The exhibition was set up by church groups and by the regional authorities of Saxony organized in the Block Parties (the forced cooperation under the domination of the SED of the smaller parties CDU, LDPD, and DBD, or Democratic Farmers' Party of Germany, and the major mass organizations the Free German Youth, the Free German Trade Union Association, the Women's League of Germany, and the Cultural League).

The images we have seen so far have a local feel to them, representing through few simple motives a German space that radiates security and stability. These images received their meaning within the context of Heimat iconography that goes back to imperial Germany. The townscape, landscape, and folk costume, the mixture of rural and industrial elements, were all banal enough, were they not connected to the sensibilities associated with the Heimat idea that linked the local, regional, and national in German culture by representing a transcendental community, here, there, and everywhere. They were mostly generic, empty images. Who could tell which precise Heimat was represented in figures 9–12 and 14? Who could tell without reading the caption whether figure 6 represented Thuringia, Saxony, or perhaps Württemberg? And the images are also mostly empty of people (figures 5, 7, 8, 10, 13, 14).

But this Heimat tradition was not left undisturbed by the communists. Figures 9 and 11 identified Heimat with explicit SED contemporary politics: the middle-class woman was used to attract bourgeois votes in Dresden local elections, while the two workers symbolizing a united Germany corresponded to the politics of the Soviet Union in 1947. The old and the new were

mixed. But we need to acknowledge the persistence of the Heimat iconographic tradition in order to explain the transformation of this iconography
in the SBZ and the GDR in a more communist, ideological direction.

For if East German communists embraced Heimat iconography they did
so on their own terms. While working within the Heimat idiom, their aim was
to redefine it, to fit socialism to the Heimat system of knowledge and sensibilities. A political poster of the 1946 elections with the caption "For a successful reconstruction of our Heimat! Therefore vote SED" (figure 15) shows
a view of a hometown dominated by factory chimneys that indicate the way
of the future. Factories, industries, and other signs of modernity have been
integral to Heimat images from imperial Germany (figures 3, 9, 10, 14). But
industry looms very large in this specific image, especially since landscape
is not represented. The predominance of communist symbols in representing the workers' and peasants' Heimat is evident in two 1949 images: one,
announcing an exhibition of the Free German Trade Union Association, portrays the Heimat as a mixture of rural and industrial landscape dominated
by a muscular worker (figure 16), while the second, mobilizing citizens for
the Two Year Plan, has a land worker superimposed over a Heimat iconographic mixture (figure 17).[17]

This last image reveals the SED's aim of molding Heimat images. Peasants
appeared at times (though not often) in Heimat images, as, for example, part
of a serene and ideal landscape in a First World War poster calling upon Germans to donate to the war loan campaign.[18] The SED followed this tradition
in, for instance, a poster used in the June 30, 1946, plebiscite in Saxony over
the expropriation of companies owned by former Nazis and war criminals
(figure 18). The initiative for the plebiscite came from the Saxon branch of the
KPD, and while all parties joined in, the CDU and LDPD had clear reservations
because their voters had the most to lose. The SED ran a campaign that hid
more than it revealed its true intentions, avoiding words such as "socialism"
and emphasizing a vague "justice to war criminals."[19] Although the main
issue of the plebiscite was expropriation of industry, the main representation
in figure 18 was of a rural Heimat, which the plebiscite was supposed to "protect" as indicated at the bottom of the poster. The dominant female landworker stood for security, for "home and hearth." She, the landscape, and the
overall feel of the image have more in common with past Heimat pictorial
trends, which we have seen in chapter 1, than with the rough landworker of
figure 17, a tough activist whose main task was to raise production quotas.

This Heimat of communist productivity reached an extreme in figure 19,
a poster that propagated the Five Year Plan. A worker stood in front of hills,

a river, some villages, and a mostly urban landscape. The area of the river at the back was similar to figures 3 and 4. But what distinguished this image from the First World War posters in figures 3 and 4, where a similar set of modern and landscape elements existed, was that Heimat became synonymous with industry and production, and came to represent explicitly a particular social and ideological system.

We have seen, then, two iconographic trends among communists in the years following 1945. One trend highlighted traditional Heimat features, another attempted to reshape Heimat in a socialist way. Let us compare one image from each trend, figures 6 and 19; these are extreme representations, but extremes are sometime helpful to expose hidden meanings. Both images linked the SED with Heimat iconographic tradition, but not in the same way. The Heimat idea was most powerful when empty, as in figure 6, when it let the viewer's imagination do the work. The emptier it was, the more effective it became. By "empty," I mean that the politicalness of the message did not shine through and that the message was tied to sentiments and associations that conveyed loyalty and identification. Figure 19 was explicit and didactic, and had less of a local feel; it almost reminded one of a lecture, with the copious text and the graph comparing production levels in 1936 and 1955. Production and standard of living were thus designated to forge loyalty to the new regime; the SED, similar to all countries of the communist bloc, would live to regret this choice of loyalty. Through the poster depicted in figure 19, the SED tried then to bolster its legitimacy by linking its policies to the Heimat idea. But this move cut both ways. The party might have gained legitimacy, but linking the idea of Heimat to a contested policy of a contested dictatorship could also subvert authority by pointing out the dissonance between promises and reality.

It might be argued that the difference between the posters in figures 6 and 19 represented the ideological hardening of the SED and its concerted move, after the foundation of East Germany, to remodel society along Stalinist ways. This is correct, but only partially. East German Heimat iconography did not proceed in a one-directional way; the communists used at one and the same time the intimate Heimat image and the more ideological one. The two trends coexisted: Heimat was about sensibilities that enabled one to love home, region, and nation; it was only natural to apply these sensibilities to the new breed of German Heimat, the socialist state. If there was one ideological communist direction to Heimat iconography, how could the poster from the immediate postfoundation period of the GDR in figure 20 be explained? "We are building him a new Heimat . . . a Berlin of work, peace, and progress!" announces the poster showing industrial reconstruction and a typical small-town Heimat silhouette. Why portray *this* silhouette when the issue at hand is the reconstruction of the big city? Because this iconography associated sensibilities of security, hominess, peace, and progress. No more needed to be said in this poster devoid of direct political representations.[20]

The two iconographic trends tensely coexisted between 1945 and 1949. The traditional trend represented local and more rarely regional identities. The new, socialist trend reflected the SED ideological belief in the collectivity and its means of production, and its opposition to Heimat as a local idea. All this took place in a German territory under occupation that was not a state and certainly not a nation. But the foundation of East Germany in 1949 created a defined, bounded political space. How was this space to be represented? Could East German communists reconcile the two trends of Heimat iconography by creating love for the "socialist Heimat"?

EAST GERMAN HEIMAT, 1949–1961:
A SOCIALIST NATION OR A SOCIALIST STATE?

The hallmark of the Heimat idea was not representing the locality or the region, but the nation as a whole. The real challenge for East German communists was to use Heimat as a representation of the new state. Let us trace this representation by looking at posters that identified the SBZ and the GDR as Heimat.

We begin with a series of three images: a 1946 poster of the Free German Youth proclaiming "Youth, the Heimat calls you!" (figure 21); a 1952 poster with a message against West Germany's army buildup "Remilitarization means loss of the Heimat" (figure 22); and a 1957 poster, "One who loves the Heimat," which calls for support of the Unified List of the National Front in the June 23, 1957, local and district elections (figure 23). The National Front of Democratic Germany, founded together with the GDR, forcibly united all the political and social organizations in the state, thus ensuring the power monopoly of the SED. In a practice that was undemocratic, the list of the National Front was presented in elections for voters' approval or rejection.

The important point that emerges from these posters is this: they represented the SBZ and the GDR as a German Heimat that only happened to be socialist, and they conveyed intimate feelings of localness and nationhood that are symbolically independent of socialism, thus giving priority to Germanness (and Heimatness) over socialism. If we take away the words that identify the posters chronologically, the images could have easily represented other regimes. Who could tell the 1930s from the 1940s if one replaced the "FDJ" in figure 21 with "HJ and BDM" (Hitler Jugend, or Hitler Youth, and Bund Deutsche Mädel, or League of German Girls, the Nazi youth movements)? Who could tell whether figure 23 was from 1917, 1927, or 1937, or 1957 West Germany?

There is an interpretative danger of brushing these posters aside as pure ideological manipulation; we have already addressed this topic. Ideology is not culture but part of it. Given what we know of the longevity of the iconographic tradition of the Heimat idea, and its potential of being appropriated by different ideological hands, it must be considered a poor explanation to view these images only as ideological manipulation. Instead, we have to take these posters seriously as a demonstration of genuine cultural sentiment about Germanness. Heimat images persisted even at the heart of SED fanaticism precisely because it was difficult, if not impossible, to talk, think, and draw Germanness without considering the Heimat traditions. And herein lay the conundrum for the SED regime: these images made sense symbolically independent of socialism because they represented nationhood and Germanness. The challenge for East German communists was to make the Heimat socialist. Was it possible to reconcile socialism and nationhood in Heimat iconography?

We continue with a second series of images: three images produced by the Free German Youth in 1952 that call for the "protection" and "defense" of the Heimat (figures 24–26); and an image of the Society for Sport and Technology from 1956 with the charge "Learn to protect the Heimat" (figure 27). These images should be understood within the context of East Germany's attempts in the 1950s to build a military force whose task, it was now explicitly articulated, was the defense of the Heimat and the "building of socialism" proclaimed by Walter Ulbricht in 1952. The Free German Youth had a role in the militarization of society and of the Heimat idea, as did its related organization, the Society for Sport and Technology, which was founded in 1952 to provide premilitary training to youths older than fourteen, especially to male youths between the ages of sixteen and eighteen. Developing in the 1950s into an organization with hundreds of thousand of members, the society was under the authority of the Defense Ministry, while its high functionaries were members of the National People's Army (Nationale Volksarmee, or NVA). The People's Army was officially announced in 1956, emerging from the People's

Police in Barracks (Kasernierte Volkspolizei, or KVP), which was founded in July 1952 as East Germany's army in all but name. The name disguised the violation of the Allies' agreement on the demilitarization of Germany.

Under the circumstances of securing Germany's first "workers and peasants' state," the Heimat idea became a topic of a lively debate. What should be its meaning under the conditions of socialism? It could mean, as it had in the past, love of the locality and the surrounding nature, but there was nothing particularly socialist about this. The response was that Heimat in socialist Germany should be defined in terms of class, not of geography and birthplace, basing it not on birth at a given locality but on ownership of the means of production.[21] The idea of Heimat, according to official pronunciations, enabled the individual to feel at home in socialist Germany (not simply in Germany, as was the credo of the classic Heimat idea). If for the classic Heimat idea the individual was defined as any German, for the GDR it was defined as a worker by virtue of his or her relations to the means of production. In this respect, the posters in figures 24–27 make sense in the context of the GDR's attempt to generate support for the development of its armed forces and for its idea of a socialist Heimat; the two are related, as we have already seen in previous chapters, because the Heimat must be protected while the army's reason for being is to safeguard the intimate territory of the nation.

The explicit intentions of the regime can be gauged from a text by Karl Kneschke, a leader of the Cultural League and the editor of its journal *Nation und Heimat*. In 1950 he described the idea of Heimat in words that seem like a commentary on the images depicted in figures 24–27: "The roots of every people lie in the space where it lives, lie in the nature and in its Heimat. . . . After the political transformation, after the expropriation of the Junkers and the war criminals, of the big economic companies and the monopoly-capitalists, our Heimat has passed with all its preciousness and beauty into the ownership of the entire people. . . . Heimat history, Heimat protection is therefore closely related to the most important political questions."[22] These Heimat images thus became an overt political tool of East German Cold War policies. Similarly, the 1950s exhibited an additional case were Heimat images explicitly expressed the regimes' ideological intentions, namely in the de-Christianization of the images. Only rarely did they include church towers, which had been beforehand a common Heimat symbol.[23] This fits the aggressive antichurch policies of the regime in the early 1950s and the overall attempt during this decade to de-Christianize East German society.

Let us compare this series of images that call to protect the socialist Heimat with images in figures 3 and 4 that sought to protect the Heimat in the

First World War. Both series were produced by the state, linked to causes that were clearly political. But the effectiveness of Heimat as a symbol of belonging was precisely its ability to hide political issues. In this sense, the images in figures 3 and 4 were more successful. What was the Heimat that one was asked to protect? In the First World War this was the nation, the entire Germany, about whose legitimacy and loyalty there was no disagreement. In 1956 this was a state that was a contested part of the nation. In the First World War Heimat and nation were congruent. In East Germany, they were incongruent: protecting the socialist Heimat meant taking up arms against other Germans. The East German idea of Heimat cut against the idea of the nation. The socialist Heimat, based on the idea of historical materialism, class relations, and the international victory of proletariat, was contradictory, not complementary, to the idea of German nationhood.

What kind of larger community was generated by Heimat imagination? In imperial Germany, Heimat was used to imagine the nation. In East Germany, it was used to imagine a state whose self-perceived historical essence was a specific mode of production. A 1954 booklet of travel and history for the youth explained: "Traveling through our German Heimat teaches [us] to love our republic and its government, to love and appreciate the working people and their party, the Socialist Unity Party of Germany."[24] By imagining Heimat, East Germans were called upon to associate the nation with real social and political processes that by definition were historical and therefore temporal but not national and immemorial. The Heimat idea was most powerful when abstract, while the East German Heimat idea posited an excess of reality. The youth travel booklet continued: "Above all, the traveling youth learn to get to know and to love their Heimat. They feel what it means when all these beauties and accomplishments of the working people are being threatened with extermination by American robbers. In this way, their readiness and preparedness grow to defend the Heimat against all those who stretch their dirty hand toward it."[25] This explains the active and masculine air of the images in figures 24–27, which convey alertness, strength, and the fighting spirit that was linked, as has been noted, to the foundation of the GDR's armed forces. It stood in contradistinction to the feminine image of Heimat in the past. It fit the revolutionary ideology of a society on the march to its destined meeting with history, but it gave little respite, and offered the viewer little to imagine and dream.

Consequently, there was a tension between the historicity of socialism and the immemorial roots of Heimat, of Germany.[26] The idea of Heimat as immemorial German territory was replaced by the idea of Heimat as historical socialism. Communists substituted the transcendent ideas of Heimat with a transitory political meaning about a government, a party, and a state. But these come and go, while the German Heimat, at least in theory, is eternal. The power of the Heimat idea was that it gave meaning to being German under any political regime: one does not stop feeling German because Bismarck, William II, Stresemann, Hitler, Adenauer, or Ulbricht assumed power. But if Heimat is explicitly identified with a highly contested specific government, state, and social system, then it undercuts the elements of national roots.

As a result, the GDR used Heimat to gain legitimacy, but the tradition of the Heimat idea also undermined the state because it was used to legitimize the GDR not as a nation but as a socialist state. This was a "state, young and wholly different from any past German state," as a GDR children's song proclaimed.[27] There were advantages to legitimizing the GDR as a revolutionary creation of social and political justice. But being "wholly different" carried a price: the consequence of identifying Heimat with socialism was that the GDR could use only with difficulty the tradition of the Heimat idea, the popular belief of national roots, continuity, and character, and the political mantle of previous German states.

It is interesting that the images in figures 24–27 offer no representation of the Heimat; they show the action that needs to be done (protecting the Heimat), not the Heimat that needs to be protected. They lack the mystery that comes with evasion and illusion. Perhaps it was unavoidable because real existing socialism wanted to provide in art a social depiction of reality, while Heimat was all about imagination, about misrepresenting reality. It is not that East German Heimat did not represent a set of illusions and fantasies, of Heimat as an integrative symbol that went beyond the here and now in the name of some transcendental redemption: of course it did, and with abundance, but these were fantasies about socialism, not about the German nation. The Heimat idea always offered redemption of some sort, whether national in imperial Germany, racial in the Third Reich, or socialist in East Germany. The socialist Heimat was a transcendental idea about socioeconomic historical development that one day, in a sort of miracle, would reach its final destination, thus bringing about a worldwide communist society and an end to classes, nations, states, and conflicts. But this transcendental idea—unlike the Heimat national and racial redemptive ideas—existed independent of Germanness and of the German Heimat, which in fact was also bound to disappear in this final stage of historical development. As a principle, the universal communist revolution undermined the sentiment of Germany's national uniqueness; in the reality of things, it was undermined by it.

The meaning of the two East German Heimat trends we encountered (figures 21–23 and 24–27) is now clearer. There was one GDR Heimat representation possessing mystery and poetics that came with iconographic minimalism, subtlety, and the value of what we have called the emptiness of Heimat images, and there was another possessing ideology, politics, and an excess of reality. Yet the two trends did not seem to converge: when images represented the imaginary Heimat (figures 21–23), it was not socialist; when they represented East Germany, it was too socialist and political. The problem of the East German Heimat idea in the 1950s was not that it was too ideological, but that it did not find a way for politicalness and poeticalness, socialist ideology and long-term Heimat traditions, class and nation to coexist.

These problems become evident when we think of West Germany in this period. Of course, West German notions of Heimat were as ideological. And any Heimat idea in the postwar period was destined to be incongruent with the nation as it had existed before 1945. But there are important differences between the use of Heimat and nation in the two states that throw into sharp focus the East German predicament. Heimatlers in West Germany resumed activities with the support of the state; the Heimat idea, as we have seen in the preceding chapter, was embraced as a leading metaphor to understand the postwar condition. Heimat organizations were active on the local and regional level, and a sense of the lost Heimat of the eastern territories was publicly cultivated with official consent. Overall, the adoption of the Heimat idea in West Germany was rather unproblematic compared with that in the SBZ and GDR. Historians thus face different problems in explaining the careers of the Heimat idea in West and East Germany: in the Federal Republic of Germany (FRG), the problem is how West Germans selectively remembered the Heimat idea in order to link their society to a wide range of past German national traditions and experiences (from democratic traditions to the war experience); in the GDR, the problem is how the regime selectively used the Heimat tradition, in spite of some ideological reservations, to create a new society whose Marxist-Leninist essence ran against the same German national and Heimat tradition.

The careers were different indeed. While communists' instincts were to view the Heimat idea as reactionary, abolish its organization, oppose regional identities, and sever it from past traditions, the Heimat idea in West Germany cultivated a sense of national continuity with the past (only the "good" past, of course). While the GDR could not use, ideologically, the tradition of the bourgeois Heimat idea, Heimatlers and the state in the FRG viewed themselves as heirs to this tradition. While the Heimat idea in the GDR claimed to speak in the name of the socialist mode of production, the Heimat in the FRG spoke in the name of the nation (not of capitalism). It declared itself a part of immemorial German identity, claiming to speak for the nation as a whole even if this nation was, at the moment, dismembered. Both regimes used Heimat for their political ends but with different results: claiming to speak in the name of the nation gave Heimat in West Germany a traditional, apolitical image that could not be achieved in East Germany, which claimed to speak in the name of the socialist mode of production. The West German claim could not have been effective without a legitimacy that came with democracy. Its claim to represent the "true Germany" was politically and ideologically tendentious, but its citizens at no point attempted to leave the state to live in the other Germany.

In this respect, 1961 provided new risks and opportunities when the construction of the Berlin Wall sealed East Germany hermetically from West Germany: a risk, because the tense relations between the ideology of class and the sentiment of nationhood could have reached a breaking point; an opportunity, because East German communists could regenerate their efforts to construct a new German identity in the socialist Heimat.

THE SOCIALIST HEIMAT AS A SOURCE OF LOVE AND HATE

If in the 1950s the idea of Heimat was used with various degrees of official self-confidence and self-consciousness, in the 1960s the notion of a socialist Heimat was systematically constructed by the regime in order to foster loyalty and love among the citizens who were now, for all intents and purposes, its prisoners.

In a way, the identity bequeathed by East German Heimat concerned not so much the past as the future. This was a young state with a self-perceived novel historical role. Here was a vital purpose of East German Heimat education: to transmit the values of the socialist Heimat to future generations. Activities and images therefore directed their efforts to the children and the youths whose identities and personalities were still in a sense a *tabula rasa*. The socialist Heimat was a pedagogical project aimed at impregnating the spirit of the GDR.

I would like to explore this pedagogical project by looking at two sources describing youth activities: the *Junge Welt*, the magazine of the communist youth movement Free German Youth, and documents of the Committee for

Tourism and Traveling (Komitee für Touristik und Wandern, or KTW). Starting from the late 1950s and continuing energetically in the 1960s, these organizations sponsored a range of activities to get to know the Heimat. A 1964 national game "We love our socialist Heimat" is a case in point. Modeled on similar games played between 1961 and 1963, it was entitled a *Suchfahrt*, or "a hunting trip," akin to the children's game treasure hunt. In this case, the hunt was for the identity treasures of the socialist Heimat. Participants had to follow clues and specific tasks that led to a final prize. The "touristic hunting trip," according to the Committee for Tourism and Traveling, drew in the past four years ninety thousand participants on foot, bicycles, scooters, or cars. The major newspapers printed announcements and information about the games, which were mostly played in the summer when the weather was good and people had time on their hands and fun on their minds. "What do we want to achieve? The aim is to have our citizens be intimately familiar with the beauty and the reconstruction of our socialist Heimat, to strengthen our love for it and to deepen our knowledge of it in the general education. [This will be achieved] through the search for many worthwhile tasks, cultural-historical towns, centers of the struggle of the German working class as well as striking landscapes and significant industrial areas." [28]

East Germany thus used the venerable Heimat tradition of imparting identity through traveling, history, and nature. [29] It combined fun, sport, recreation, and the pedagogic project of fostering loyalty to the GDR. These kinds of identity games were very common. Celebrating the twentieth anniversary of the GDR in 1969, a competition entitled "Join in — the beauty of our cities and communities" was based on fulfilling certain tasks, such as a visit to a site of working-class history, or taking part in a sport, tourist, or local beautification activity. Participation was free and open to all citizens. It was enough to fulfill three tasks in order to enter the competition; among the prizes was a plane ticket to Warsaw and Prague, and a holiday in a state-run vacation retreat. [30] Other games included the 1966 "Discovery tour through the GDR" and the famous Urlaubstombola, or Vacation Tombola, a summer game that was similar in principle to the hunting-trip game. [31]

These initiatives emphasized the poetic side of the socialist Heimat. The *Junge Welt*, suggesting to its readers in 1962 to take "traveling tours in the beautiful Heimat," proposed a route of eleven days that took the traveler through the Saaletal and the Schwartztal in the area of Jena (Thuringia) on a trip that was much more about local nature and history than about working-class ideology. The intimate Heimat language we encountered in chapter 1 about imperial Germany—"I would like to take you by the hand, dear reader, and lead you into the quiet splendor of the valley's spring," as a Heimat book for Kirchheim unter Teck opened—is evident in East Germany as well: "On the eleventh day [of our trip] it is time to bid farewell to this beautiful, small patch of our socialist Heimat."[32] This is the tender side of GDR's Heimat idea, continuing a tradition of Heimat sensibilities. And it must have had some success in creating among East Germans a sense of belonging to the local and the natural, as well as to a certain way of life.

But the Heimat idea in the GDR always possessed a crude ideological element as well. As a pedagogical project, the socialist Heimat imprinted on the impressionable personalities of children the reason for the existence of the new state: "To love the party of the working class; to love the socialist Heimat, our workers' and peasants' state; to hate the imperialism in West Germany; to promote friendship among peoples, especially friendship with the Soviet Union."[33] Hate and rage and a certain begrudging sentiment were part of East German official rhetoric.[34] And even when the rhetoric was not extreme, Heimat education was replete with endless working-class ideology, duties to serve the collectivity, lists of socialist achievements, and an obligation to note the wonderful life-style generously given by the party to the people—all of which seemed more vacuous and patronizing as the years went by. As early as 1964 the central committee of the Committee for Tourism and Traveling observed that the hunting-trip games, in spite of official attempts at providing a relaxed, fun atmosphere, were still dominated by a sense of productivity and obligation.[35]

The tense coexistence of the two faces of the East German Heimat idea is evident in the youth song cited at the beginning of this chapter. It starts poetically by noting Heimat cities, villages, and nature. The last line of this description sums up this sentiment: "And we love our Heimat, the beautiful." But then comes the ideological dissonance: "And we protect her, because she belongs to the people." The sentence changes the tone of the song. Isn't it clear that the Heimat belongs to the people, as it has always since time immemorial? Not quite, apparently, for one protects the Heimat not because she is German, but because she is socialist and because socialism made her —in the land with no private property—the property of the people as a whole. The last line of the song repeats this rationale—"Because she belongs to the people"—in a tone that betrays anxiety as to whether this message has been properly internalized by the people. And perhaps it had not. For, surely, the cities, trees, and meadows were part of East Germans' identity not because they were socialist but because they were German.

The socialist Heimat educational project commingled love for one Germany and hate for another. But the meaning of the Heimat idea since imperial Germany was about being German, not about being socialist or bourgeois. East Germany could not reconcile the fundamental contradiction between being part of the German nation and fostering an ideology that, in theory at least, claimed to supersede the nation. A constant tension existed between the intimate representation of Heimat as potential integrative force linking localness and nationhood and its representation as an instrument of class ideology against the idea of nation.

Ultimately, the poetics of nationhood and the ideology of class could not be reconciled. A meeting of the Committee for Tourism and Traveling on May 4, 1957, announced the importance of tourism, Heimat, and education: "As a result of their love for the Heimat and of the respect for the great ideas of humanity, the tourists, travelers, and mountain climbers of the GDR are resolute opponents of the war politics of the Adenauer regime, of the nuclear armament of the Federal Republic, and of the domination of the imperialists and militarists in West Germany, all of which bring about a threat of civil war and the complete extermination of our Heimat." The meeting took place as the committee was preparing for the local and district elections of June 23, 1957.[36] These were the same elections for which the poster in figure 23—a classic Heimat image if ever there was one—was made. The image and the rhetoric of the elections were incongruent. The rhetoric divided the nation by using the Heimat idea as a source of socialist loyalty to one part of the German nation and as a source of opposition to another, while the image placed the East German present within a timeless German nation. For the East German regime to succeed, it required either the adoption of communism in both Germanys or the decline of the idea of the nation. Neither was about to happen in the modern world as we know it.

POST-1989: THE LONGING FOR A CERTAIN GDR HEIMAT

East Germany began in 1949 a process of identity building more audacious than the one begun in 1871. The aim of the Heimat idea after 1871 was to reconcile local, regional, and national histories, landscapes, memories, and loyalties, to link between the immemorial past and the invented tradition of the present. The East German regime, in contrast, built a new identity by repudiating much of existing loyalties, memories, and histories. The attempt to reconcile the poetic and ideological side of Heimat failed, but this dialectic may provide us with a key to understanding one of the most puzzling post-1989 phenomena among former East Germans, namely a longing for the past.[37]

The classic Heimat idea created Germany as an immemorial nation with an unlimited future. The socialist Heimat idea created not as much of a past for the GDR's citizens, for the past of the working-class movement was historical, not immemorial, and the GDR could not link itself to most of the national past. And it did not create as much of a future either: while the *Junge Welt* stated confidently in 1961 that "the United States will be [economically] surpassed by 1970," this date came and went and East Germans' hopes and their standard of living sunk further with every passing year.[38]

But it did create a present, suspended in history without much of a past or a future. Not the ideological present, which predictably failed when Heimat was attached symbolically to immediate and transitory political fights (such as in the images in figures 24–27). And not a political present, which could not instill long-term Heimat belonging to the GDR "government, republic, and state" that owed their meaning instead to the presentist, specific historical conditions of the postwar Cold War. And also not the material present, which, predictably, also failed, although there were good reasons for the socialist Heimat to construct the material present. The regime was dependent on the achievements of the everyday: its essence of being was the fulfillment of better moral and material life compared with that offered by capitalism. For that reason the TV news hour focused on the production successes of a shoe factory or the harvest activity on the farms. (Imagine the ratings of a news hour in the West covering these items.) There was a never-ending emphasis on socialist tasks and socialist achievements; every new quota, new product, and new crop of potatoes that made it to the grocery shelves was a small step in the victory of socialism. Not much has remained of this sense of the present either. Heimat as socialist ideology failed.

But the poetic side of Heimat in the GDR may have survived the demise of the state in 1989. A sense of the present, of a special GDR way of life, or *Lebensgefühl*, was created during the lifetime of East Germany, and was missed thereafter. If Heimat museums collected the past, in the GDR the Heimat idea seemed at times to collect the present. For years, the everyday present received iconographic representation in black-and-white postcards that were designed, conceived, and produced through a state-run company. The price was an unchanging twenty pfennig. They showed "socialist accomplishments" according to themes such as vacation and campground locations (vacationing with a tent was a mainstay of GDR vacation habits and, for a time, an achievement), landscapes, new buildings, modern beautifications, art, architecture, domestic design, and cars. Appropriately, the name of the publishing company, which produced 90 percent of all postcards in the GDR, was Bild und Heimat (Image and Heimat).[39] The postcards were a familiar mix of Heimat elements of history, nature, and everyday life objects, not very different from images and objects in Heimat museums in imperial Germany.

The image and experience of this socialist Heimat present was not without success, albeit of a very particular kind. The GDR had its own distinct way of life. One becomes attached to where one is born; has shared language, dialect, and slang; and has intimate relations to surroundings, friends, and everyday life objects. Not all Heimat memories are good, but all are ours. The citizens of the GDR rejected the communist political and economic repressions, the ideological Heimat. But at the same time some shared after 1989 a sense of nostalgia, even affection, for life in the GDR that was represented in the poetical Heimat, in the sense of belonging to a certain way of life that identified and made one proud and made sense to the people who experienced it. Ultimately, this way of life was jettisoned, but not without a sense of nostalgia and tenderness, which has, after all, been from its beginning the hallmark of the Heimat idea.

But memory is short, as we have already seen. This is why we can convince ourselves in a remarkably short time that certain newly constructed images of the past have been a permanent part of our identity. And this is also why certain images of the past cannot outlive the generation that actually experienced them. The nostalgia for the GDR is generation-specific. Economic and social differences between the western and eastern parts of united Germany will remain for decades, as will cultural and identity divides. But the East German Heimat—whether constructed by the regime or by its people—will not survive its own historical and chronological boundaries.

5

A NATIONAL LEXICON FOR ALL SEASONS

We began this extended essay by noting that every society sets up imaginary pasts. But to make a difference in a society, it is not enough for a certain past to be selected. The Heimat idea steered emotions, motivated people to act, and was viewed by every ideological regime as the bedrock of political legitimacy; in short, it was received, was internalized, and became a socio-cultural mode of action. In a poll taken in Germany toward the end of the millennium, 90 percent declared themselves sympathetic to the idea of Heimat (whatever they meant by it).[1]

It is true, but in these pages we have also seen how different were the emotions steered by the Heimat idea, the actions taken in its name, the crimes and good deeds made in its defense. What was the common denominator of it all, we asked at the beginning of this book? What was the meaning of this diversity? The Heimat idea was a historical mentality that gave Germans a cultural backbone, an identity through time, regarding modern changes in polity and society. For more than a century after 1871, as we have seen, the Heimat idea had been used for different ideological purposes. Heimatlers in imperial Germany infused it with nationalism, Nazis with race, East German communists with socialism, and West Germans with dreams of victimhood, lost territories, and local-democratic renewal. The ideological element of the Heimat idea illuminates issues of political legitimacy and cultural representation. But it is only partially illuminating to understand the meaning of localness and nationhood. The meaning of the Heimat idea was precisely its ability to transcend ideological differences, to allow Germans to feel German regardless of who was in power, to provide a national lexicon to think and talk about Germanness under all political seasons.

Heimat, like the national idea itself, cannot be reduced to ideology. This is its true meaning, the secret of its effectiveness and appeal to inhabit people's mind. The full force of this fact becomes clear when we remember that nationhood itself is not a form of ideology, like liberalism, fascism, or communism, but a form of a community that imagines itself through unlimited time and bounded space. This was, to my mind, Benedict Anderson's long-lasting contribution, namely to argue that precisely because nations come in different ideological forms their meaning cannot be defined by these forms. Similarly, as we have seen, no ideology had a copyright on the Heimat idea; it could be appropriated by different hands for different purposes. The meaning of Heimat and of German nationhood lies in cultural common denominators believed by Germans to be shared regardless of their ideology. It had a symbolic manual that was transferable from one ideology to another, that gave Germans a sense of continuity over time. How was it possible to continue feeling German under such different renditions of Germanness as Weimar democracy, National Socialism, communism, and liberal democracy? The fact that this question seems absurd to us and to Germans is precisely because there were (real or imagined) cultural common denominators that made sense of nationhood across time. The Heimat idea was one such common denominator, and I would like to draw in these pages some of its fundamental shared attributes.

"GET TO KNOW GERMANY!"

Similarities over time in Heimat language and images do not tell us about different values and beliefs; similarity of formal attributes cannot be taken as a proof of similarity of meaning, for similar words and images can mean different things in different contexts. In a century of radically different ideologies, the Heimat idea provided a national lexicon, a shared representation, to articulate differences. The nexus of Heimat, tourism, and identity is a case in point.

Let us take as a starting point the East German extreme ideological position represented in the 1954 booklet of youth travel mentioned in the preceding chapter: "Above all the traveling youth learn to get to know and to love their Heimat. They feel what it means when all these beauties and accomplishments of the working people are being threatened with extermination by American robbers. In this way, their readiness and preparedness grow to defend the Heimat against all those who stretch their dirty hand toward it."[2] "Lernt die Heimat kennen" (Get to know the Heimat) was the exhortation of East German ideologues.

If the ideological use by a socialist state was new, the general meaning was just stock-in-trade of the Heimat idea. The idea of socialism gave new meaning to the familiar and traditional axiom of Heimat and tourism "Lernt Deutschland kennen!" (Get to know Germany!) that encouraged locals to search for their historical roots, national identity, and essential group characteristics in the physical traits of their locality, region, and nation. As such, the revolutionary idea of socialist Heimat fit within the boundaries of the genre: it was new, but not as new as it proclaimed itself to be.[3]

After the unification in 1871, getting to know Germany, or Württemberg, or Göppingen was used to invent a past that linked the old locality and region to the new nation-state and to German historical roots. This was the meaning of merchant Herbst's observation at the closing ceremony of the 1912 Swabian Exhibition for Travel and Tourism (Schwäbische Landesausstellung für Reise- und Fremdenverkehr), when he stated that the exhibition allowed people "to get to know one's own Heimat and to appreciate its worth."[4] The exhibition, organized by the Association for Tourism in Württemberg and Hohenzollern (Württembergisch-Hohenzollerische Vereinigung für Fremdenverkehr), featured, among other displays, a black forest tavern, folk costumes, and folk art. The exhibition catalog, which included sections about history, landscape, art, wines, and cuisine, was a handsome booklet of 100 pages that read like a guide to "how to become a Swabian in several easy steps." The exhibition attracted 70,000 people, and thousands more read the catalog (published in 60,000 copies).

Tourism was viewed as a cultural vehicle for national integration and raising national identity. Gustav Ströhmfeld, a leader of the tourist associations of Stuttgart and Württemberg, an organizer of the Swabian exhibition, and editor of its catalog, articulated in 1910 the widely accepted views that tourism is a matter of culture, "and one cannot create culture, for it is the outcome of a glorious development . . . the sum of world-shaking events, it is history. . . . [People travel] because [in traveling] they find a link to the past. . . . In this sense, tourism is a problem of culture."[5] And he further wrote in *The Tasks and Duties of the Cultivation of Tourism*: "We therefore look forward to the increase of tourism not only from the point of view of economic advantage, for we are entitled to hope for a national advantage: as the Germans actively embrace Heimat feelings and national belonging, so will our German Empire grow stronger from within."[6]

The Nazis took this framework of tourism-Heimat-identity and infused it with racial ideology. The aim of Nazi tourism was to build a utopian racial community where race would replace class as the organizing principle: "The community Strength through Joy [Kraft durch Freude, or KDF, the Nazi tourism and leisure agency] has tackled the most decisive tasks of our time: the stamping of a new German person and the production of new social forms. It should above all contribute to eliminating forever the inferiority feeling of the German worker. It should form self-confident Germans with their heads held high and with looks of pride, for National Socialism wishes to breed a master race in all strata of our people. . . . The blood is the bond of our new community."[7] This was the Nazi racial revolution in tourism.

But, again, the revolutionary idea of race fit within the boundaries of the genre; again, it was new, but it was also articulated in familiar rhetoric, and therefore not as new as it proclaimed itself to be. "Get to know your Heimat —travel with Strength through Joy!" announced one publication. "Strength through Joy's traveling means to search for the Heimat . . . in order to bestow upon the productive Germans an enduring experience. . . . Traveling . . . is bringing together ideas with the aim of understanding the Heimat as a gift from heaven."[8] The nexus of race, traveling, and identity was thus based on appropriating familiar language about Heimat, experience, and even God. Baden's Federation of Regional Tourism (Landesfremdenverkehrsverband Baden) combined in its 1935–36 annual report the call to "get to know the Heimat" with the duty for the Nazi national community (*Volksgemeinschaft*). It argued for the transformation of tourism from an economic activity into being a "German essence according to tourist culture."[9] Ströhmfeld could easily identify with this claim about tourism and culture—not because he was a Nazi *avant la lettre*, but because the Nazis used a familiar discourse that had already linked Heimat, tourism, and identity.

After the war, to return to the 1950s where this discussion began, in the same years that East Germany viewed Heimat as an anti-Western weapon of sorts, West Germany constructed its own idea of "Get to know Germany!" It became a catchphrase that made it possible to speak about national identity in terms that otherwise were unacceptable, and to represent a German iden- tity devoid of the Third Reich. "Lernt Deutschland Kennen!" wrote Matthias Thömmes director of the German League of Tourist Associations (Bund Deutscher Verkehrsverbände), as we have seen in chapter 3: "It should be clear to anybody, whether a German or a member of another nation, that one should get to know *first* one's own Heimat. . . . [Therefore,] the league [calls to the Germans]: 'Get to know Germany first!'" This national educa- tion project went hand in hand with a second project that placed Germany within the new emerging Western Europe. Thömmes did not oppose youth trips abroad; he wanted them to take place in the context of trips at home: "For how should a united Europe come into being when one does not know and understand oneself in one's own land!"[10]

The point of this discussion is not to diminish the importance of the ideas of race, socialism, and democracy in Nazi, East, and West Germany. Rather, it is that "Get to know Germany!"—and more generally the Heimat idea—became a necessary idiom within which to articulate ideas of race, socialism, and democracy. These ideas were thus represented and understood within, and as part of, familiar cultural patterns that began before the onset of a given regime and continued after it. And they were internalized or rejected partly, as we have seen in these chapters, because of the way they fit within the Heimat tradition.

AN ICONOGRAPHIC COMMON
DENOMINATOR OF VARIOUSNESS

But the challenge for the Heimat tradition was to represent the nation in Germans' minds in times when the nation itself was unstable, changing its borders several times after 1871, shrinking on some occasions and expanding on others. Under these conditions, the Heimat idea provided an iconographic common denominator of variousness.

Let us look at a map (figure 28). Every map is a symbolic representation, but some are more symbolic than others. This is not a map that delineates simple political boundaries, but rather one designed to attract tourists. I would like to call this map—published in 1935 by the Central Reich Railway for German Tourism (Reichsbahn Zentrale für den deutschen Reiseverkehr) and entitled "Germany, the beautiful traveling land"—an identity map. According to *Deutsche Werbung*, a leading journal of advertising and tourism in the Third Reich, the map was "truly a vivid compendium of the political and cultural history of the German lands and the German people, as well as of their customs."[11] It represented German "traditions and character" in small decorative designs of Heimat attributes such as architectural sites, historical events, monuments, landscapes, and folk costume. Potsdam, for example, is dominated by Frederick the Great, Bayreuth by Richard Wagner. Heavy industry represents the Ruhr, whereas the agricultural life-style symbolizes Pomerania. The romanticism of Heidelberg exists alongside the mundane Baden-Baden. The style is cartoonish, more than a real-life depiction; the atmosphere is, while not idyllic, pleasant and joyful.

Representation of the nation in tourist images during National Socialism continued a genre that can be found in the first half of the nineteenth century, and perhaps even before.[12] In the second half of the nineteenth century, and particularly after the turn of the century, following the development of tourism, maps became very popular. The tourist identity maps continued to function as a vehicle to represent German nationhood after the Third Reich.

In West Germany, the 1953 Great German Transportation Exhibition (Große Deutsche Verkehrsausstellung) in Munich presented a huge mural identity map of Germany with similar decorative designs (figure 29).[13] And the regional tourist associations of Baden-Württemberg issued a popular identity map in the 1950s (figure 30). West German identity maps represented the nation in terms of culture, not in terms of capitalism, although some maps may have shown consumer goods as a defining postwar West German identity. (I have not found these kinds of identity maps, but I have reason to believe they exist.) The GDR's identity maps oscillated between a representation of German culture (that is, nationhood) and of industrial production (that is, historical materialism). The genre was appropriated by the SED to promote socialist production policies, as can be seen from a 1959 poster of the Seven Year Plan (figure 31). A slightly different map appeared in the summer of 1962 as part of the season's treasure-hunt identity game. The second leg of the game, "Do you know the GDR?," was illustrated by an identity map showing cultural icons (the statue of Goethe and Schiller in Weimar, the Brandenburg Gate) as well as industrial and economic symbols (figure 32).[14]

The minimalist, empty quality of identity maps allowed different ideological regimes to represent their particular sense of nationhood. In the case of the Nazis, this was a representation of murderous policies. A 1942 book entitled *German East—Land of the Future: A Call of the East to the Heimat!* presented an identity map that incorporated the Polish areas under German control (General Gouvernement) as part of German culture and inheritance (figure 33): "Here precisely must the circulation of our national blood become more animated and accelerated."[15] It kept silent about the crimes perpetrated in the name of this vision. Edited by Heinrich Hoffmann, Hitler's photographer, the book had a print run of 310,000 copies.

The Nazis applied Heimat sensibilities to areas in Eastern Europe they included in their racial empire. A typical Heimat picture book was produced in 1940 for the Polish Vistula River area, to which the Germans now "return . . . in order to create a Heimat and thereby serve the people."[16] The majority of the inhabitants in the area were Poles and Jews, who, while mentioned briefly and derogatively in the text, were nonexistent in the images that showed landscape, hometowns, churches, and economic activity. There was no iconographic mentioning of the Jews of Lodz, who numbered 202,497 in 1939 (33 percent of the total population). They were eradicated in images and imagination before being annihilated in real life.

In postwar East Germany, identity maps were used to promote friendship among the same people Germans persecuted only years before. Figure 34 showed a 1955 identity map of the GDR, Poland, and Czechoslovakia. The legend included items of industrial production, not cultural identity. This was partly because of the communist common denominator among the three states, but surely also because economic production was represented dispassionately, while cultural identity could have aroused from the grave unpleasant historical ghosts. It is instructive that East Germany's identity map turned eastward to its socialist sister-states, while excluding the other part of the German nation. West Germany is represented as a shadowed, indiscrete area, the state of Adenauer, Nazis, and capitalists who flee the socialist prosperity. The GDR's difficulty in reconciling the socialist Heimat with German nationhood is thus iconographically represented.

Postwar West Germany had fewer scruples in reconciling Heimat and nationhood. The 1953 mural identity map (figure 29) in Munich thus portrayed Germany in its 1937 borders. It was not uncommon for Heimat books, representing Germany's art, architecture, landscapes, and the like, to include territories in East Germany, Poland, and Czechoslovakia, as, for example, *The Beautiful Heimat: Pictures from Germany*, published in 1961.[17] As late as 1989 (before the Wall came down), a board game "Travel in Germany" included both Germanys. Players started and ended the game in Munich, going through a host of historical, economic, social, and natural German-identity items.[18] The game was similar to the East German summer treasure hunt, only the boundaries of the Heimat were not. Extending the idea of Heimat to the other German state reinforced in West Germany the idea of nationhood upon which the state was built. In East Germany, in contrast, the socialist Heimat ended at the border because extending the traditional idea of Heimat to the other German state undermined the GDR, just as East Germans' freedom of travel to the FRG was considered subversive by the regime.

Identity maps continue to represent German nationhood to our day. The tourist association of North Pomerania (former GDR) issued such a map in 1997 depicting the Baltic Sea.[19] But, by now, a new self-consciousness of the constructedness of national identity has developed, which has contributed to acknowledging the element of cliché in Heimat images. A tourist image from the 1950s, which invited English-speaking people to visit Bavaria, effectively epitomized the components of the tourist representation of German nationhood: the identity map, the folk costume, and the German community (figure 35). This image was reprinted in a 1990 Bavarian journal celebrating a century of regional tourism as an example of "all the current clichés" of German identity.[20] Acknowledging clichés is part of a new understanding in which Germans take seriously their terrible past and critically their national identity of the present. Present-day identity maps thus illustrate the continuity as well as the different meanings of the iconography of German nationhood. Figure 36, presenting the Teutoburg Forest in western Germany, is entitled "Leisure fun à la carte." (The German "Freizeitgenuss à la carte" contains a pun on "carte" as a menu and as a map.) Published in 1993 by the local tourist association, the poster shows at the center the monument for Arminius, Herman the Cheruskian, the warrior who led the Germanic tribes to victory against the Romans in the year A.D. 9 and who was an important and very serious symbol of German identity for decades. The iconographic patterns and motifs have not changed, but the meaning has. For this image is anything but serious: it is devised in the ironic mode, indeed, in the self-ironic mode. And when national identity is taken with a grain of self-irony, and not with pompous seriousness, this surely is an improvement.

Whether elaborate like the one depicted in figure 28 or stylistically poorer like that in figure 30, identity maps maintain essential iconographic patterns and motifs—architectural sites, folk costumes, historical events, monuments, landscapes, and symbols of economic and material progress—and define them as German. There is something utterly banal, even trivial about these identity maps. But the real issue with trivial images is not that they are banal, but how they became so common, and why? Tourist Heimat images appear to us trivial precisely because they have been so common in German society, everywhere, part of what we associate with Germanness. To articulate this idea with an oxymoron, these images are important because they are trivial. In trivial Heimat images, people and ideological regimes reveal about themselves more than they might have wished. But the important question is not whether the iconography of Heimat images was trivial, but what it meant, and how and why it came to represent Germanness. This has been one story we have followed in these pages.

THE NATION IN THE MIND

The importance of the Heimat idea was its capacity to represent what was otherwise unrepresentable, namely the nation, and to forge bonds of affection and loyalty to that abstract territory. It made it possible to carry an image of the nation in one's mind. The representation of the German community—local, regional, or national—maintained throughout the twentieth century the iconographic formula constructed in the German Empire (figures 1–4). After 1918, the generic representation of the German Heimat remained the same. The opening image of the 1926 book *German Heimat: Pictures from City and Countryside* (figure 37) looks similar to figures 2, 3, and 4, while the introduction begins with the familiar words "Since I got to know Germany from one end to the other . . ."[21] The generic images of the local, regional, and national became standard and appeared in different contexts. Thus a 1930 political poster of the right-of-center German People's Party, "Elect my party," featured Weimar's late foreign minister Gustav Stresemann over the Rhine River.[22] The image does bear a relation to real landscape, although by 1930 and thereafter this Heimat landscape with a river was used to represent a generic Heimat that had nothing to do with the specific Rhine (such as figures 3, 4, and 39, and from East Germany figures 10, 13, and 19).

The Nazis, being children of their time like anyone else in history, were not far behind in using the Heimat image. The interpretative point is not that the Heimat idea before 1933 was racist, anti-Semitic, and nationalistic because the Nazis used it between 1933 and 1945 (although this was one of its meanings, if a marginal one). Rather, it is that the Nazis used the Heimat idea because this had been the available symbolic representation for localness and nationhood. To lay claim to represent the "true Germany," the Nazis, similar to all modern German regimes, appropriated the Heimat idea. In doing this, they succeeded much more than the other German dictatorship, for two reasons. First, National Socialism was a mass movement, guided by a charismatic leader, that was, until the very end, significantly more popular than communism and the SED ever were. Second, it was easier to reconcile race and nation than class and nation, and more Germans could conceive of themselves and of the nation as having a historical racial identity than as having a historical identity through time based on class. The Nazis thus represented during the final years of Weimar the revival of Germany in images of Heimat localness. "Germany awaken!" showed a sun rising over small Scheidegg (in Allgäu, Bavaria; figure 38), while "The alarm will sound just one last time!" had a swastika rising over a Heimat image of Germany (figure 39). The postcards juxtaposed the future promised in Nazi victory with the authentic German past embedded in the Heimat.

After the war, East Germany appropriated the Heimat idea, albeit with the difficulties we have discussed in the preceding chapter, while West Germany seemed to have less problems in negotiating selectively with the Heimat tradition of the past. This can be seen in figures 40 and 41, the latter of which we have encountered in chapter 3 as the image that provided the epigraph that described Germany as "this lovely country you will never forget."[23]

Since the unification in 1871, Germans have imagined nationhood as a form of localness. When we look at the images of Reutlingen at around 1900 (figure 1), Renningen in 1913 (figure 2), an unknown city in 1939 (figure 42), Heidelberg in 1955 (figure 43), an unknown East German town in 1957 (figure 23), and Bingen in 1965 (figure 44), we can see that the Heimat image became the ultimate representation of the German community.[24] The 1939 Nazi poster articulates this meaning clearly. It was made by Ludwig Hohlwein (1874–1949), perhaps the greatest of German posterists. A master of color, interlocking lines, and tonal contrast, he depicted consumer goods, status symbols, places such as the Munich zoo, and events such as the 1910 Brussels World Exhibition, the 1913 Great Berlin Art Exhibition, and the 1936 Winter Olympics. His style was simple and minimal: one or two figures in the foreground against a background that emphasized them.[25] From the early 1930s he made many tourist posters, some of rare elegance; the arrival of Nazism did not change his style, though his posters depicted more athletes and soldiers. Figure 42 was part of a series called "German travel bookmarks." In the mid-1930s the bookmarks portrayed German sites; in 1939 they included also the new incorporated Heimat, Austria, of which figure 42 is a representation: "The thought of Greater Germany was crucial for the choice of the image," explained *Deutsche Werbung*, ". . . up to the elevated high mountains [of Austria] rises now the German landscape."[26] In other words: if it is part of Germany (Reutlingen or Lodz, Austria or the Polish General Gouvernement), it must be—and must be represented in terms of—Heimat.

But ultimately, the Heimat iconography came to represent in German culture not simply a German sense of belonging within a familiar, intimate space. It became exceedingly difficult, perhaps even impossible, to imagine any space of belonging without the Heimat representation. And so it came to represent a metaphor for a universal sense of togetherness and shared humanity. The evidence for this meaning comes from a rather unexpected quarter, which only enhances its significance. Figure 45 is a 1958 poster produced by the GDR, the regime that had the most difficulties among modern German ideologies in reconciling with the Heimat idea; its use of Heimat iconography is therefore most revealing. The election poster instructed "Fight nuclear death. Vote for the candidates of the National Front—for peace, prosperity, and happiness!" It included the usual propaganda that viewed the danger of nuclear weapons as a Western-capitalist threat to humanity but never as a Soviet-communist one; this had the unavoidable air of ideological presentism. But the image of the community threatened by nuclear weapons —in East Germany and all over the world as atomic bombs know no borders —was not presentist at all and had nothing to do, strictly speaking, with the Cold War, communism, or capitalism: it was the Heimat image—the tranquil and harmonious hometown, with a few houses and a church tower, invented in imperial Germany (compare figure 2) and since used by Germans to represent relations of space and belonging. The local has thus come full circle, representing the regional, national, and finally the global.

Heimat was a concept that gave meaning to Germans' best and worst intentions and dreams. And while I reject the tendentious use of Heimat in this poster, the idea of feeling at home in the world, of using Heimat as a notion of human solidarity, rights, equality, and justice, is something I can identify with.

This has been a long journey that began with Heimatlers in small-town Württemberg attempting more than a hundred years ago to find a common denominator between their small world and the abstract nation—a long journey, but one with a persistent theme of finding a common denominator between the immediate local life and an abstract territory. If for Württemberg's Heimatlers the main challenge was to reconcile the local with the national via the regional, our own challenge today is to reconcile the local with the global via the national. The local and the national are complementary and not contradictory, and so are the national and the global. The local should serve as a metaphor for the global, much as it serves one for the national. In the end, it is our moral decision whether we want to feel at home in the world, in a just world. And for this task, the Heimat idea is ready for proper use and may find its lasting call.

FIGURE 1. *A postcard of Reutlingen around 1900 displayed a typical Heimat image including a small community in harmony with nature and a church tower as a leading symbol. (Courtesy of the Württembergische Landesbibliothek Stuttgart)*

FIGURE 2. *O. Elsässer, "Ein Heimatbild" (A Heimat image), in* Heimatklänge aus der Gemeinde Bempflingen und Kleinbettlingen *(March 1913): 3. A representation of the generic local German Heimat. (Courtesy of the Württembergische Landesbibliothek Stuttgart)*

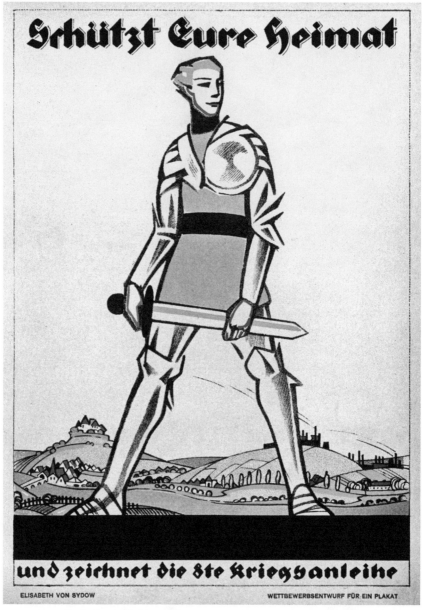

FIGURE 3. *Elisabeth von Sydow, "Schützt eure Heimat" (Protect your Heimat), 1914–18, poster, in* Das Plakat *10 (March 1919): table 29. The Heimatization of Germany: the Heimat image commingled features of modernity, such as the factories on the right, and of the German past, such as the knight defending the Heimat. By dissolving the distinction between past and present, the Heimat image represented the nation as immemorial. (Courtesy of the Württembergische Landesbibliothek Stuttgart)*

FIGURE 4. *Hugo Frank, "Leiht euer Geld für der Heimat Schutz und Wehr!" (Loan your money for the protection and defense of the Heimat!), 1914–18, poster, in* Das Plakat *9 (September–November 1918): 248. The Heimatization of Germany: the German Heimat as an ensemble of small hometowns in harmonious relationship with nature. The national Heimat became a rallying collective image to mobilize the financial and emotional resources of Germans in the First World War. (Courtesy of the Württembergische Landesbibliothek Stuttgart)*

(left top)

FIGURE 5. *Fritz Deutschendorf, "Keiner fehle—jeder wähle! CDU Christlich-Demokratische Union. Auch Du trägst die Verantwortung mit für das Schicksal Deiner Heimat"* (No one misses out—everyone votes! CDU Christian-Democratic Union. You too carry the responsibility for the fate of your Heimat), 1946, poster. The postwar continuation of Heimat iconography: the CDU image of Germany. (Courtesy of the Deutsches Historisches Museum Berlin—Bildarchiv)

(above)

FIGURE 6. *"Für Frieden Recht und Heimat. Thüringen wählt SED"* (For peace, justice, and Heimat. Thuringia votes SED), 1946, poster. The postwar continuation of Heimat iconography: the SED image of Germany was similar to Heimat representations since the 1880s. (Courtesy of the Deutsches Historisches Museum Berlin—Bildarchiv)

(left bottom)

FIGURE 7. *Gerhard Benzig, "Bautzen im Aufbau. SED hilft mit"* (Bautzen in reconstruction. The SED lends a hand), 1946, poster. An SED election poster of Bautzen (Saxony) represented in postcard-like images that were a familiar trope of Heimat iconography. (Courtesy of the Deutsches Historisches Museum Berlin—Bildarchiv)

FIGURE 8. *K. Dingelstedt, "*SED *... Darum Deine Stimme der Partei des Aufbaues"* (SED *... therefore your vote to the party of reconstruction), 1946, poster. A local history with national-historical moral in three easy steps: how the policies of the Nazis destroyed Erfurt (Thuringia), and how the* SED *rebuilt it. (Courtesy of the Deutsches Historisches Museum Berlin—Bildarchiv)*

FIGURE 9. Brinkmann, "Nur eine starke Frauenvertretung im Parlament sichert den Frieden!" (Only a strong representation of women in parliament protects the peace!), 1946, poster. The peaceful generic Heimat image with scattered villages, hometowns, and smoking factory chimneys was used by the SED, which appropriated it as a popular representation with broad appeal. (Courtesy of the Deutsches Historisches Museum Berlin—Bildarchiv) (Reproduced in color as Plate 1)

FIGURE 10. Haberichter, "DFD in jedem Ort" (Democratic Women's League of Germany in every community), after March 8, 1947, poster. The SED used the generic Heimat image to represent its Germany, this time in a poster made for the party's organization for women. (Courtesy of the Deutsches Historisches Museum Berlin—Bildarchiv) (Reproduced in color as Plate 2)

FIGURE 11. *"Für die einheitliche demokratische deutsche Republik" (For the united democratic German republic), 1947, poster. The SED used a Heimat landscape to call for a united Germany. As a local space representing the national, Heimat was suitable between 1945 and 1949 to depict a German nation that lacked a distinct spatial and political look. (Courtesy of the Deutsches Historisches Museum Berlin—Bildarchiv)*

FIGURE 12. *Flim, "Die Toten mahnen: baut auf!" (The dead admonish: reconstruct!), 1946, poster. The ubiquity of Heimat images in the immediate postwar period, as well as their conformity to iconographic tradition, shows that Heimat was meaningfully used not so much as a vehicle for political manipulation but as a national imagination. An antifascist poster of a war-devastated Germany represented as two Heimat townscape silhouettes of houses and church towers. (Courtesy of the Deutsches Historisches Museum Berlin—Bildarchiv)*

(left top)

FIGURE 13. Fliegel, "VVN [Vereinigung der Verfolgten des Naziregime]. 1. Kreis-Treffen" (Union of Those Persecuted by the Nazi Regime. First district meeting), 1949, poster. (Courtesy of the Deutsches Historisches Museum Berlin — Bildarchiv)

(above)

FIGURE 14. Albert Jahn, "Neue Heimat, Neues Leben" (New Heimat, new life), 1948, poster. (Courtesy of the Deutsches Historisches Museum Berlin — Bildarchiv)

(left bottom)

FIGURE 15. Aman, "Für erfolgreichen Neuaufbau unserer Heimat! Darum wählt SED" (For a successful reconstruction of our Heimat! Therefore vote SED), 1946, poster. East German communists embraced Heimat iconography on their own terms: their aim was to fit socialism to the Heimat system of knowledge and sensibilities. The poster shows a hometown dominated by factory chimneys that indicate the way of the future. (Courtesy of the Deutsches Historisches Museum Berlin — Bildarchiv)

FIGURE 16. *Werner Meier, "Die Kraft der 5 Millionen" (The strength of 5 million), 1949, poster. Communist symbols predominate in a representation of the workers' and peasants' Heimat: a poster of the Free German Trade Union Association portrays the Heimat as a mixture of rural and industrial landscapes dominated by a muscular worker. (Courtesy of the Deutsches Historisches Museum Berlin—Bildarchiv) (Reproduced in color as Plate 3)*

FIGURE 17. *Harras, "Alles für den 2 Jahr-Plan!" (Everything for the Two Year Plan!), after October 1949, poster. Communist symbols predominate in a representation of the workers' and peasants' Heimat: a land worker is superimposed over a Heimat iconographic mixture in a poster mobilizing citizens for the Two Year Plan. (Courtesy of the Deutsches Historisches Museum Berlin—Bildarchiv)*

FIGURE 18. *Boehner, "Enteignung der Betriebe der Kriegs- und Naziverbrecher. Volksentscheid zum Schutz von Haus und Hof, von Vieh und Ernte!" (Expropriation of companies owned by Nazis and war criminals. Plebiscite to protect home and hearth, cattle and harvest), 1946, poster. This image, which shares a Heimat pictorial tradition that goes back to imperial Germany, puts in sharp focus the changes introduced to Heimat iconography by communist symbols in figures 16 and 17. (Courtesy of the Deutsches Historisches Museum Berlin—Bildarchiv) (Reproduced in color as Plate 4)*

FIGURE 19. Eva Hinze, "Die Zeit der Erfolge" (The time of successes), 1950, poster. The Heimat as a German community of communist productivity is depicted in a poster propagating the Five Year Plan. The Heimat idea thus became synonymous with a specific mode of production—not immemorial nationhood—which defined its essence. (Courtesy of the Deutsches Historisches Museum Berlin—Bildarchiv)

FIGURE 20. Pewas, "Wir bauen ihm eine neue Heimat . . . ein Berlin der Arbeit, des Friedens und des Fortschritts!" (We are building him a new Heimat . . . a Berlin of work, peace, and progress!), after October 1949, poster. East German Heimat iconography attempted to use simultaneously the intimate Heimat image and the more ideological one. The poster represents the reconstruction of the metropolis of Berlin by a typical small-town Heimat silhouette, an iconography that associated security and hominess. (Courtesy of the Deutsches Historisches Museum Berlin—Bildarchiv)

Jugend, die Heimat ruft Dich!

FIGURE 21. *Wolgram, "Jugend, die Heimat ruft Dich!" (Youth, the Heimat calls you!), 1946, poster of the Free German Youth. Figures 21–23 represent the SBZ and the GDR as a German Heimat that only happened to be socialist. Giving symbolic priority to Germanness and Heimatness, they convey intimate feelings of localness and nationhood that are symbolically independent of socialism. They are powerful because they are empty, letting the viewer's imagination do the work, and connecting the GDR to an immemorial German nation. (Courtesy of the Deutsches Historisches Museum Berlin—Bildarchiv) (Reproduced in color as Plate 5)*

(above)

FIGURE 22. *"Remilitarisierung bedeutet verlust der Heimat" (Remilitarization means loss of the Heimat), 1952, poster against the military buildup in West Germany. (Courtesy of the Deutsches Historisches Museum Berlin— Bildarchiv)*

(left)

FIGURE 23. *"Wer die Heimat liebt" (One who loves the Heimat), 1957, poster calling for votes for the Unified List of the National Front, dominated by the SED, in the June 23, 1957, local and district elections. (Courtesy of the Deutsches Historisches Museum Berlin—Bildarchiv) (Reproduced in color as Plate 6)*

BEREIT ZUR VERTEIDIGUNG DES FRIEDENS
UND ZUM SCHUTZ DER HEIMAT

FIGURE 24. *"Bereit zur Verteidigung des Friedens und zum Schutz der Heimat" (Ready to defend the peace and protect the Heimat), 1952, poster of the Free German Youth. In figures 24–27, the notion of Heimat becomes an overt political tool of East German Cold War policies in defense of the communist mode of production. But the effectiveness of Heimat as a symbol of belonging was precisely its ability to hide political issues, to represent the nation as self-evident and uncontested. The socialist Heimat, based on the idea of historical materialism, class relations, and the international victory of the proletariat, runs contrary to the idea of the nation. (Courtesy of the Deutsches Historisches Museum Berlin— Bildarchiv)*

BEREIT ZUR VERTEIDIGUNG DER HEIMAT
Wiedersehenstreffen der Teilnehmer der Friedensdemonstration am 15.8.51 in Westberlin
vom 16.-17. August 1952 in Halle

FIGURE 25. *"Bereit zur Verteidigung der Heimat" (Ready to defend the Heimat), 1952, poster. (Courtesy of the Deutsches Historisches Museum Berlin—Bildarchiv)*

FIGURE 26. *Garloff and Richter, "Erhöht die Bereitschaft zur Verteidigung der Heimat und zum Schutze unserer demokratischen Errungenschaften" (Raise the readiness for defending the Heimat and protecting our democratic achievements), 1952, poster of the Free German Youth. (Courtesy of the Deutsches Historisches Museum Berlin—Bildarchiv)*

FIGURE 27. *Joachim Bredow, "Lernt die Heimat schützen kommt zur GST" (Learn to protect the Heimat. Join the Society for Sport and Technology), 1956, poster. (Courtesy of the Deutsches Historisches Museum Berlin—Bildarchiv)*

FIGURE 28. *"Deutschland das schöne Reiseland" (Germany the beautiful traveling land), in* Deutsche Werbung *(June 1935): 1076. This identity map, published by the Central Reich Railway for German Tourism, represented German nationhood in small decorative designs of Heimat attributes such as architectural sites, historical events, monuments, landscapes, and folk costumes. It provided an iconographic common denominator of variousness to be used in all ideological regimes. (Courtesy of the Historisches Archiv zum Tourismus am Willi Scharnow-Institut für Tourismus der Freien Universität Berlin) (Reproduced in color as Plate 7)*

FIGURE 29. *"Reiseland Deutschland" (Traveling land Germany), in* Der Fremdenverkehr *5, nos. 13–14 (1953): 9. A mural identity map in the Great German Transportation Exhibition in postwar Munich. (Courtesy of the Historisches Archiv zum Tourismus am Willi Scharnow-Institut für Tourismus der Freien Universität Berlin)*

FIGURE 30. *A popular identity map issued by the regional tourist association of Baden-Württemberg in the early 1950s, in* Der Fremdenverkehr 6, nos. 17–18 (1954): 31. *(Courtesy of the Historisches Archiv zum Tourismus am Willi Scharnow-Institut für Tourismus der Freien Universität Berlin)*

FIGURE 31. *Unknown [Arno Fleischer?], "Berliner, es liegt in unseren Händen den Sieg des Sozialismus zu vollenden" (Berliners, it depends on us to complete the victory of socialism), 1959, poster. An* SED *identity map promotes socialist production policies for the Seven Year Plan. (Courtesy of the Deutsches Historisches Museum Berlin—Bildarchiv)*

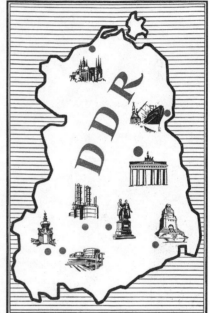

FIGURE 32. *An East German identity map in* Junge Welt, *August 4–5, 1962, mixed the common ingredients of cultural icons and economic symbols as part of the nationwide summer game that sent people on the trail of the state's new identity. (Courtesy of the Universitäts- und Landesbibliothek Sachsen-Anhalt in Halle [Salle])*

FIGURE 33. *"Das General Gouvernement" (General Gouvernement), in Heinrich Hoffmann, ed.,* Deutscher Osten—Land der Zukunft. Ein Ruf des Ostens an die Heimat! *(Munich, 1942), 136. Identity maps allowed different ideological regimes to represent their particular sense of nationhood. The Nazis presented an identity map of the Polish area under their control as part of German culture and inheritance. The silence of the map about Jews and Poles was deadly.*

FIGURE 34. *"Drei Völker—drei Freunde—ein Wille zum Frieden!"* (Three people—three friends—a will for peace!), 1955, poster. An East German identity map represented the state's new orientation by including Poland and Czechoslovakia. (Courtesy of the Deutsches Historisches Museum Berlin—Bildarchiv)

FIGURE 35. *"Here Is Bavaria." This early 1950s tourist image was evaluated self-consciously in 1990 by a leading Bavarian cultural journal as having all the clichés of German identity: the identity map, folk costume, and Heimat community. In* Charivari: Die Zeitschrift für Kunst, Kultur und Leben in Bayern 16, no. 5 (May 1990): 61. *(Courtesy of Dr. Walter Stelzle, Das Kommunikationskontor, Gräfelfing)*

FIGURE 36. *"Teutoburger Wald. Freizeitgenuss à la carte" (Teutoburg forest. Leisure fun à la carte), 1993. An identity map devised in the ironic mode: a local tourist association represented the Teutoburg forest and Herman the Cheruskian, the warrior who led the Germanic tribes to victory against the Romans in the year A.D. 9, as harmless identity pawns. It represented a new self-consciousness of the constructedness of national identity. (Courtesy of the Ostwestfalen Lippe Marketing GmbH, Teutoburger Wald Tourismusmarketing) (Reproduced in color as Plate 8)*

FIGURE 37. *This image in M. Paul Block and Werner Linder,* Deutsche Heimat. Bilder aus Stadt u. Land *(Berlin, 1926), 1, looks similar to figures 2, 3, and 4 produced in imperial Germany. The generic image of the local, regional, and national became standard and appeared in different contexts throughout the twentieth century, regardless of ideology. It became an iconographic formula to carry the abstract nation in the mind.*

FIGURE 38. *"Deutschland erwache! Heilgruss aus Scheidegg (Allgäu)" (Germany awaken! Heil [Hitler] Greetings from Scheidegg in Allgäu), 1932. The nation as a locality: to lay claim to represent the true Germany, the Nazis, similar to all modern German regimes, had to use the Heimat iconography, the authentic and available symbolic representation for localness and nationhood. (Courtesy of R. James Bender Publishing)*

ZUM LETZTEN MAL
WIRD NUN ALARM
GEBLASEN !

FIGURE 39. *"Zum letzen mal wird nun Alarm Geblasen!" (The alarm will sound just one last time!), 1932. An SA man awakens Germany—depicted as a small hometown Heimat—to a new morning. (Courtesy of R. James Bender Publishing)*

FIGURE 40. *H. Berann, "Deutschland" (Germany), in* Der Fremdenverkehr *11, no. 10 (1959): 30, poster produced by the German Central Tourist Association. (Courtesy of the Historisches Archiv zum Tourismus am Willi Scharnow-Institut für Tourismus der Freien Universität Berlin)*

FIGURE 41. *"Travelling through Germany gives you genuine impressions," in* German Review, *September 1952, promotion by the German Central Tourist Association. (Courtesy of the Historisches Archiv zum Tourismus am Willi Scharnow-Institut für Tourismus der Freien Universität Berlin)*

FIGURE 42. *Ludwig Hohlwein, "Deutsches Reisemerkbuch" (German travel bookmarks), in* Deutsche Werbung *(March 1939): 323. (Courtesy of VG Bild-Kunst, Bonn 2005) (Reproduced in color as Plate 9)*

FIGURE 43. *Alex Meysen, "Heidelberg Heidelberg," in* Der Fremdenverkehr *17, nos. 3–4 (1955): 11, poster produced by the city transportation and tourism bureau. (Courtesy of the Historisches Archiv zum Tourismus am Willi Scharnow-Institut für Tourismus der Freien Universität Berlin)*

FIGURE 44. *Otto Müller, "Bingen," in* Der Fremdenverkehr *6 (1965): 42, poster produced by the city transportation and tourism bureau. (Courtesy of the Historisches Archiv zum Tourismus am Willi Scharnow-Institut für Tourismus der Freien Universität Berlin)*

Wählt die Kandidaten der Nationalen Front — Für Frieden, Wohlstand und Glück!

FIGURE 45. *Rudolf Koch, "Kampf dem Atomtod. Wählt die Kandidaten der Nationalen Front—Für Frieden, Wohlstand und Glück!" (Fight nuclear death. Vote for the candidates of the National Front—for peace, prosperity, and happiness!), 1958, poster. The apotheosis of the local: the Heimat image appears as a representation of humanity in a GDR poster against the proliferation of nuclear weapons. (Courtesy of the Deutsches Historisches Museum Berlin—Bildarchiv) (Reproduced in color as Plate 10)*

PART II
MEMORY AS HISTORICAL NARRATIVE AND METHOD

A shift from "society" to "memory" has occurred in historical studies in the past two decades or so. It began in the early 1980s as a shift that was not brisk or revolutionary but gradual and measured.[1] By the 1990s, however, the notion of "society"—as it had been practiced by social historians along the twentieth century and particularly after 1945—was swept away by the interpretative onslaught of memory and cultural studies. The notion of society, broadly speaking, was often based on a linear concept of history developing forward along one temporal timeline and privileging social and economic topics interpreted in terms of their function and structure. The notion of memory, in contrast, is based on a multitemporal concept of history where past and present commingle and coalesce, capturing simultaneously different and opposing narratives and privileging topics of representation interpreted in terms of experience, negotiation, agency, and shifting relationship. "Memory" now governs questions of historical interpretation, explanation, and method in such a way that it seems appropriate to speak of a paradigm shift in historical studies from "society" to "memory."

This paradigm shift in historical studies has been part of a larger cultural shift in historical consciousness that has made memory a concept for and of our time. Several reasons for this transformation can be mentioned. The metaphor of memory is linked to the acknowledgment of the foundational meaning of the Holocaust to European and North American Judeo-Christian civilization, and of the epistemic challenge it poses. It is also linked to the end of the Cold War, which set free in Europe all sorts of claims about the past, many of them conflicting and disparate: they included renewed anti-Semitism and Holocaust denial as well as greater awareness of the Holocaust; ethnic, religious, and national rivalries as well as a political and economic vision of Europe as a peaceful federation of states. In Germany, the unification posed the challenge of constructing a new German nation from old opposing ideological regimes and of confronting a new problem of coming to terms with the past, this time the East German past. And the notion of memory has also been a nexus of morality, legal proceedings, and international relations in the creation of the United Nations International Criminal Tribunal, which made genocide a punishable offense for rulers and their helpers, and which constituted the International Criminal Tribunals for the former Yugoslavia (ICTY) established on May 1993 and for Rwanda (ICTR) established on November 1994.

There are other, completely different, reasons why at the end of the twentieth century memory has become a fundamental creed of group and individual identity. We are interested in memory because, as a result of the capitalist economy, history moves forward at such a speed that the past of even twenty years ago seems distant and alien. Because the commercialization and commodification of every aspect of our lives produce, with the help of the mass media, an ever growing number of memories, "old," new, and instantaneous. And because, as John Gillis put it, "Today the past has been democratized and we all must have our own history. What was once a luxury has become a necessity. What was once a privilege is now a right."[2] None of these elements in itself is sufficient to explain the current interest in memory. Nineteen-eighty-five is not any more distant and alien from us than 1935 was in 1955, or than 1905 was in 1925. It is a combination of elements—the experience of the Second World War and the acknowledgment of the Holocaust, the development of human rights, the commercialization of the past, and the transformation of historical methods and theories, among others—that brought about the shift toward memory.

The reasons for the transformation of memory into the signifier of our time are multiple, and its meaning, consequences, and history are still to be chronicled and fully understood. The chapters that follow explore these topics with respect to the memory paradigm shift in historical studies. Two current views about memory and history seem to me unwarranted. The first is the view of memory as self-explanatorily important. Using the notion of memory to understand how people remembered this or that event is potentially beneficial. But memory studies risk becoming predictable, following a familiar and routine formula, as yet another event, its memory, and its appropriation are investigated. Memories are described, following current professional and public parlance, as "contested," "multiple," and "negotiated." It is correct, of course, but it also sounds trite by now. The details of the plot are different in each case, but the formula is the same. We know that a study of memory undertakes to explore how people imagine the past, not how the past actually happened, although this in itself is not a new undertaking, nor is it an insight limited to historians. Thus the frequent contention that the past is constructed not as fact but as a cultural artifact to serve the interest of a particular community may still be considered by some a *dernier cri*, but one cannot possibly present it anymore *pour épater les historiens*.

The second is the view that memory studies are a fashion and a fad. As one historian recently put it, "Everyone is doing memory work these days. . . . Perhaps 'memory' is simply what a generation of scholars calls what used to be known as 'history.' . . . The concern with memory in recent years reflects an egocentric obsession with the past-in-the-present in the guise of preparing for a 'better' future."[3] I don't know whether everyone is writing on memory, but many certainly are. It has taken its place now as the leading term in historical analysis, replacing the previously dominant terms of class, race, and gender. But through their interest in memory, historians reflect more than shape contemporary engagement with the past evident in all levels of society, in popular culture, government initiatives, heritage and tourist industry, family and genealogical history, reparation claims, and repentance declarations. It follows that ironically to dismiss memory as fashionable will not do. The reason to take it seriously is precisely because everyone *is* doing memory work these days: be they individuals engaged in family history, the Vatican in releasing its documents on the persecution of the Jews "We Remember" (1994), descendents of African American slaves who seek compensation, German financial and industrial companies who employed slave labor in the Second World War, or "truth commissions" in democratizing Latin America, Eastern Europe, and South Africa. The list goes on. Memory is a fad, but it has also developed into a fundamental term with which individuals and collectivities define their identity. It deserves serious, though critical, consideration.

For historians the question is not whether to explore memory, but how. Given the primacy of memory in historical studies, there is little critical thinking about the meaning and consequences of studying memory for historical method, theory, and explanation.[4] In the essays that follow, I explore memory as a problem of historical narrative and method. The main interest is not in how a specific event was remembered and commemorated. The aim, rather, is to view how historians and the public use and understand the concept of memory to make sense of the past. It is tempting to assign the notion of memory an explanatory weight it cannot possibly carry. Scholars do it when they reduce social, cultural, and political relations to "identities" and "memories," thus making our understanding of the past impressionistic and presentist. Laypersons do it when they believe that memory is an unmediated road to understanding the past and to building an authentic, wholesome identity. I therefore ask in these essays, how do historians and laypersons think about memory and how do they construct the object of their thinking? What are the explanatory and narrative potentials and dangers of the notion of memory?

Like no other concept, perhaps, memory confers in our culture legitimacy, roots, authenticity, and a sense of identity. Historians could not avoid this cultural baggage. How could they? It was to be expected that they also would find memory an apt metaphor to describe the ills or redeeming qualities of their discipline. Pierre Nora, whose remarkable essay "Between Memory and History" has become a classic in memory studies, viewed memory as "life . . . in permanent evolution . . . affective and magical." There existed once a "real memory—social and unviolated, exemplified in but also retained as the secret of so-called primitive or archaic societies." But now, in the modern era, memory as a social practice, as "a milieu of memory," has been replaced by voluntary and deliberate memory. His distinction between premodern real memory and modern voluntary memory is wrong, for all memory is voluntary, and all is carried by social practice. But his essay should be read as a poetic elegy by a historian who embraces the past nostalgically.[5] Others look at memory as a notion that can either reaffirm or regenerate the discipline in new directions. Joyce Appleby, Lynn Hunt, and Margaret Jacob (the first two, former presidents of the American Historical Association) approach memory as a form of knowledge that can rescue history from the postmodernist critics of historical objectivity,[6] while others find in memory a diametrically opposed meaning, namely a vehicle to understand the discipline of history as a personal pursuit, like autobiography, thus asking, "Can we talk about historians as writers—leaving veracity in the sources as well as in the historical text?"[7]

I happen to think, as becomes clear from the following chapters, that the notion of memory can neither undermine nor redeem the discipline of history. But a more important issue is at stake. I bring these cases not out of any desire to criticize but to point out the protean power memory holds for historians—not simply as an analytical tool but as a meaningful metaphor to describe the state, development, and changes of the discipline. This in itself has a long history, for the relations between history and memory are as old as the discipline. Herodotus, the father of history, set out his purpose in the opening of his work to preserve the memory of the "marvelous deeds"

of the Greeks and the barbarians, so that "human achievements may not become forgotten in time."[8] The purpose of history—to remind and remember
—has remained to our days. The Holocaust, a barbarism produced by Western civilization, provides the signature memory event for contemporaries.
On December 8, 1941, the Jewish historian Simon Dubnow, eighty-one years
old, who had taught in Vilna, Kovno, and Berlin, was murdered during the
Nazi evacuation of the ghetto of Riga. The story is told that his last words to
his fellow Jews were: "Write and record!" (in Yiddish: *Shreibt un farshreibt*).
"The story is told . . ."—note that we don't have secure evidence that Dubnow
actually said this sentence. Memory works here as a surrogate to history. But
whether Dubnow really made this statement is perhaps secondary: what is
revealing is that those who told this story expected a historian to say this
sentence in this situation. As the foregoing cases show, the discussion of the
relations between history and memory goes on, with its varied present-day
inflections, such as the importance of postmodernism, the end of the Cold
War, the commercialization of the past, and genocide and the role of the witness to evil.

Historians have a duty to continue this discussion that opens the door for
a new field of vision about what history is today. It possesses immense possibilities, but it also has dangers. Historians, we have said, should explore
memory precisely because it is morally, politically, and legally relevant well
beyond the walls of academia. But herein lies also a risk, for historians use
memory as a critical concept to understand the past, while they are at the
same time part of the historical mentality of their age that sanctifies memory. Contemporaneity carries its risks. Memory is at times linked to the past
less by a series of questions and problems than by the historian's desire to
recapture a distant world, to link with the emotions, traditions, and beliefs
of people in the past, to redress a tragic and traumatic past, or to connect
with and personalize the historian's craft. There is nothing wrong in doing
all this; it can foster an identity, build self-confidence, and assuage the difficulties of life. But it is not what is required of the historian qua historian.
This is a classic, unavoidable case of the Archimedean predicament of the
historian, which we have encountered several times thus far: historians can
never reach a cultural Archimedean point from which one can interpret the
world from the outside. They are always inside culture; they are a product of
the intellectual tradition and historical mentality of their society, while attempting at the same time to explain and criticize it.

This is not a soluble problem; rather it is the condition of the historian. It
is not a reason to despair or to proclaim the crisis of history or the death of

the discipline in favor of a view that all stories of the past are fictions. On the contrary. This Archimedean condition can be the historian's source of moral authority when addressing the wider public on contemporary issues, as well as a source of interpretative insight when conducting research about the past—providing one approaches this duality with sufficient self-awareness.

6

FREUD, MOSES, AND NATIONAL MEMORY

Moses and Monotheism has been treated in the decades following its publication within the framework of biblical studies, of the history and anthropology of religion, and of Sigmund Freud's own inner psychology.[1] More recently, it has been explored with enormous erudition within the framework of Jewish history, of Western memory of Moses the Egyptian, and of the writing of history.[2] I would like to understand the book within a different, though related, context: that of the modern discourse of nationhood. Toward the end of *Moses and Monotheism* Freud explains what this book, among others, is about: "an investigation into what determined the character of the Jewish people."[3] A story of nationhood, then, and a narrative, however fragmented, of national character. But what kind of a dialogue existed between Freud, who defined himself as one "who cannot participate in nationalist ideas," and European notions of nationhood?[4] My aim is to explore the analogies, affiliations, and parallels between the representation of national character and nationhood in *Moses and Monotheism*, and the way people talked and thought about these subjects during Freud's lifetime and beyond.

My own fascination with the book, as a historian of Germany, of nationalism, and of collective memory, arises out of a profound interest in the way people in the modern world compose historical accounts of nationhood and memory that are a fantasy and a fable, and how they internalize them, believe in them, and are ready to die for them. The book has a phantasmagoric quality, a fable made into a sequence of historical arguments. What happens, then, when we link the historical fable of Moses narrative with the historical fable of national narrative?

Freud's concept of nationhood in *Moses and Monotheism* was both similar to and different from contemporary notions of nationhood. A shared sentiment among commentators of *Moses and Monotheism* is that the narrative of the book is "shocking," "pure fiction or phantasy," and "situated between history and fiction."[5] I share this sentiment. While the most immediate shock was that Moses was not a Hebrew and that monotheism was an Egyptian creation, Freud's concept of nationhood also raised eyebrows. What was this concept, and why was it seen as shocking?

For Freud, national character is linked to the historical origins of the nation. Once formed, national character seems to have a life of its own in national consciousness, presented as tradition, and in the national unconscious, presented as memory.[6] Thus, "a sort of memory of [Moses' religion] has survived, obscured and distorted, [exerting] its effect from the background, it slowly attained more and more power over the minds of the people."[7] This is a story of national reawakening, as the return of the repressed reveals the true national destiny.

The key to deciphering the character of national collectivity, according to Freud, is applying the insights of individual psychology. "I hold that the concordance between the individual and the mass is in this point almost complete. The masses, too, retain an impression of the past in unconscious memory traces. . . . if we accept the continued existence of such memory traces in our archaic inheritance, then we have bridged the gap between individual and mass psychology and can treat people as we do the individual neurotic."[8] What an extravagant, imaginative, even hallucinatory passage! Some scholars have responded to it in disbelief. Peter Gay was perplexed by this "single-minded Lamarckianism, according to which historical events are transmitted in the unconscious from generation to generation."[9] Yerushalmi viewed Freud's "Lamarckian predilections" as an "audacious step . . . [that] makes the most difficult demands on fantasy itself," and linked it to Freud's "Jewishness."[10] And Bernstein, in a spirited response to Yerushalmi, goes to great length to defend Freud.[11]

But this way of describing nationhood happens to fit very well within European ideas of the nation in Freud's lifetime. These ideas presumed kinship between present and past and saw national identity as based on some form of hereditary characteristics. These hereditary characteristics were not necessarily racial or biological, but they were always historical. They assumed a historical continuity of national character and tradition over centuries. In 1882, before Freud invented psychoanalysis, Ernest Renan gave his famous "What Is a Nation?" lecture at the Sorbonne. His answer was that a nation "is a soul, a spiritual principle . . . [based on] the possession in common of a rich legacy of memories. . . . The nation, like the individual, is the culmination of a long past of endeavours, sacrifice, and devotion. Of all cults, that of ancestors is the most legitimate, for our ancestors have made us what we are."[12] We can find here the basic elements of Freud's view of the Jewish nation as they appear in *Moses and Monotheism*: the search for origins; the nation as an organic entity endowed with soul, spirit, or psyche; the parallel between the life of the individual and that of the collective; and the importance of memory and the transmission of this legacy over many centuries. These were the fundamental ingredients of national identity in the period, and Freud's *Moses and Monotheism* should be seen within this context.

Thus, in France, to give one example, the period of Renan and Freud was replete with stories about "nos ancêtres les Gaulois." The myth of national origins began in the Second Empire of Napoleon III (1851–70) and continued under the Third Republic (1870–1940) and Vichy (1940–44). The myth was, according to one historian, an "invocation of an alleged community of ancestors, identified in this instance with the Gauls, [which had] the effect of presenting the French as people of a common blood, members of a single family and thus different from people unable to claim such ancestry."[13] Connecting the present to the most remote past was also the function of the many historical museums founded at that time. A museum of French monuments, wrote one activist, will provide "irrefutable evidence of the ancient splendor of France."[14] And in 1942, only three years after the publication of *Moses and Monotheism*, a ceremony took place in Gergovie, in which Marshal Petain linked the founding of Vichy with the awakening of national identity among the Gauls twenty centuries earlier.[15]

Like every concept of origins, Freud's "national character" is based on a presumed continuity between past and present. There are in the book two kinds of continuities at play. The first is the continuity of Jewish character: "[T]he Jewish character . . . even then [in the remote past] was what it is now."[16] This basic assumption provides the justification for Freud's research: namely, Freud explores the origins of monotheism in order to illuminate Jewish identity and hatred of Jews in his own period. The second continuity is linked to the story of Moses, namely the continuity in the national unconscious of Moses' murder, and the return of the repressed many generations later. Both continuities are fundamental to the narrative, although they are somewhat vague and never fully defined. Both continuities are represented by Freud in the language of evidence and scholarship. But Freud is also aware of his anachronism.

This vision of continuity was common in national representations of the period. In Germany, Heimat, or homeland, museums exemplified this vision after the national unification in 1871. Answering the questions of who we are and where we came from, bourgeois Heimat activists defined in Heimat museums an idea of the nation, its origins, and its members. Whether Germans were represented as the descendants of the ancient Germanic tribes or of hometowns' people from the Middle Ages, Heimat museums endowed the new nation-state with the mark of time immemorial by collecting objects of everyday life from the community's past. Connecting the German present with the German past called on the visitors to use their imagination as travelers to the past. Thus, the museum in Weinheim was described approvingly as a "fantasy."[17] Given this approach to the past, Heimatlers often interpreted quite generously the task of displaying history in the museum. The museum activists in the island of Föhr, whose museum was considered after its foundation in 1908 to be representative of "the principle of a Heimat museum in all its purity and rigorousness," had the museum built as a characteristic North Friesland peasant house. "An accurate copy of a peasant house was not recommended, however, since such a house was hardly suitable for exhibition purposes."[18] The peasant house was thus remodeled to fit modern standards of exhibition. This anachronism diluted the notion of time in the past and connected Germans in the post-1871 unification period with their ancestors.

Freud thus shared an important affinity with national scholars and activists of his age. Like them, Freud searched for historical, scientific proofs of national identity. Historians, ethnographers, archaeologists, geographers, and museum activists labored to provide nationhood with scientific evidence or, to put it more accurately, with scientific representation. Thus, establishing a museum of ancient history, as we have seen, was a way of providing "irrefutable evidence" of ancient splendor. But just as Freud did not really have proof for the murder of Moses, so national historians did not really have proof for, say, the archaic French identity among the Gauls. The making of nationhood at the period was thus expressed in the rhetoric of positivism, science, and evidence, but it was constructed by poetic invention and imagination. And Freud's *Moses and Monotheism* was no different: it is strenuously conveyed in the language of evidence, but is dominated by the language of fantasy.

The national project of the period was a genealogical project. And because the nation was believed to have a soul and a character, it also had agency, wishes, and motivations. In short, it acted in the world as an individual. The Italian historian Gioacchino Volpe, a distinguished scholar during his lifetime, described in 1925 the course of Italian history in words that could have been taken from Freud's narrative of Moses. His book *Moments of Italian History* describes in a language that tends to blend past and present how the Italian nation "affirms its national personality [*personalità nazionale*]."

Speaking about "the dawn of our history," Volpe recounts how the nation in the following centuries "restored something of the ancient past, or reacted unconsciously [*inconsapevolmente*], to the invasions of the barbarians. . . . In reality, this restoration is a new and original construction because new and original is the spirit that first agitates the massive, weary, and slow unconscious . . . then [acts] more energetically and consciously: the spirit of a new agent of history, the spirit of a people that is born from all this unconscious work and begins to reveal itself."[19]

A most revealing case for the affinities between Freud's narrative of ancient Israel and modern narratives of nationhood was the case of Zionism. Stripped to its basic essentials, Freud's narrative told of a nation that had repressed its essential historical character for centuries, only to retrieve it later. Memory was awakened, repression overcome, historical destiny revealed. A fundamental narrative of Zionism (though not the only one) proposed a similar theme, namely that during the period of the Diaspora, Jews had repressed their real national character, which could be revealed only by a return to the land of Israel and by reviving the national home. In Freud's narrative Jews rejected their centuries-old repression to connect anew to Moses' monotheism, while in the Zionist story Jews rejected their centuries-old exile to connect anew to their national sovereignty in Eretz Israel. In Freud's narrative, the return of the repressed linked two historical events that were centuries apart (the murder of Moses and the return to monotheism), while in the Zionist story the return to Zion and to history linked two distant periods of past and present national independence, in effect canceling out the intervening centuries of exile. In Freud's narrative national awakening was achieved when the repressed had been overcome, while in the Zionist story national awakening was achieved when exile had been overcome. In terms of the logic of the stories, overcoming the repression of Moses was functionally equivalent to overcoming exile. The similarities seem uncanny, for Freud's *Moses* does look at times like a variation of the leading narrative of Zionism.

In Europe around 1900 there was a paradigm by which nationhood was represented. As a narrative on the making of a nation, *Moses and Monotheism* uses metaphors, rhetoric, and modes of argumentation that belong squarely within this common European paradigm. Certainly, Freud owed his story also to his preoccupation with Jewish identity, to the memory of Egypt in the West, and to his psychoanalytic approach. But he also owed it, I would like to suggest, to a common language about how nations were made. Some of his narrative choices owed more than we usually think to the model within which Europeans described the making of nationhood.

Freud described himself, as we have noted, as a person "who cannot participate in nationalist ideas." By personal and professional disposition, he was usually not supportive of national and religious movements. And although he wrote about nationhood, it was not a fundamental topic in his oeuvre, unlike religion, for example. What is intriguing, then, is that this kind of a scholar, who could not accept national ideas, nonetheless composed a Moses narrative that remarkably fit contemporary beliefs in, and representations of, nationhood. It may remind us of a theme that dominates this book from the outset, namely that intellectuals can never reach a cultural Archimedean point from which they can interpret the world from the outside. They are always inside culture; they are a product of the intellectual tradition and historical mentality of their society, while attempting at the same time to explain and criticize it.

And yet, if Freud could not be outside his culture, he could be ahead of it. Freud did write within the model of nationhood representation, but he did it in such a way as to go beyond its boundaries. Freud did not simply write the history of the Jewish people from a national perspective. He was not another national historian whose aim was to use evidence selectively to prove the preconceived idea of national redemption. For Freud posited a new set of relations between national past and present, between national history and memory. This demands elucidation. For the essence of the modern nationhood project has been precisely the commingling of past and present to forge a new historical collective identity. What exactly, then, was Freud's innovation from the viewpoint of nationhood?

Freud emphasized the importance of memory and its concomitant forgetting in the making of nations. But this, after all, was commonplace in the European notion of nationhood. Renan observed that "the essence of a nation is that all individuals have many things in common, and that they have forgotten many things." The foundation of the Heimat museum in Föhr, to give another example, "was a cultural necessity to save that which is still savable from the material and spiritual historical property of the island. The purpose of the museum is to preserve the memory that has been irretrievably lost."[20] Nationhood was about memory, about retrieving old traces of national character and linking the past to the present. In this, again, Freud worked within the dominant representation of nationhood.

Freud went beyond this dominant representation, first of all, by being aware of the intricate interplay of science and poetics in his presentation of

Moses. Freud, like national activists of his age, worked within the paradigm of history; they all looked for proof of immemorial national character. But unlike most national activists, Freud knew that he lacked historical proof at the same time that he attempted to furnish it. *Moses and Monotheism* vacillates between being a historical novel, which Freud initially intended to write, and being a historical essay based on evidence. Jan Assmann has observed that Freud's "conscious anachronism is the unmistakable sign that we are moving in the space of memory rather than history."[21] This can be said also of the historians and scholars who made nationhood. All of them, Freud and the nationals, moved in the space of nationhood, which are spaces of memory *and* of history. Unlike Freud, however, the nationals were, on the whole, unaware of, or unperturbed by, this ambiguity.

An ambiguity, then, comprises an ambivalence that opens the door for further subversive skepticism with regard to the paradigm of nationhood. This awareness of the historicity as well as of the fictionality of nationhood, combined with the paradigm of psychoanalysis, all served Freud to understand nationhood. The result was to open new possibilities to understand the memory of nations. Nationals looked at the past to find links with the present and "to preserve the memory that has been irretrievably lost." Freud was interested in what had happened—that is, the murder of Moses—but also in how what happened was remembered and forgotten. This sets him apart from those who wrote about nationhood to solidify its myth. It is this tension between writing a history of the genealogy of nationhood, on the one hand, and writing about the memory of nationhood as complex, ambiguous, and changeable, on the other, that makes *Moses and Monotheism* such a riveting book.

This approach has provided new possibilities for understanding nationhood, and it shows how Freud, while working within the paradigm of nationhood, helped to expand its boundaries. And yet, if we read with fascination *Moses and Monotheism* these days, it is also because Freud not only complicated the story of how we remember the past, but introduced into it moral and ethical dimensions. The Moses story, as I read it, is not simply a complex, ambiguous, and changeable past, leading to some historical result capable of being verified by evidence. The power of the book lies not so much in its historical narrative, but rather in the representation of remembrance and forgetting as an intermingling of historical, ethical, and moral implications. The book tells about a past of a crime that cannot go away, that may be repressed for centuries, but is bound to return. The ways people remember the past—the killing of the father and of Moses—has moral, ethical, and histori-cal consequences for the character of the Jewish people. These consequences are most apparent in the last pages of the book, where Freud describes the causes of anti-Semitism in terms of the different ways in which the Son Reli-gion and the Father Religion remember the primeval crime.[22]

Looking at *Moses and Monotheism* from a present-day perspective, what is most striking is the book's grappling with the predicament of a hidden past. Ours is an era of memory, and of repentance over repressed pasts. The great convulsion that was the Second World War is often at the center of such memories, although it is not the only historical focus. Apology for the persecution of the Jews was heard from the Evangelical Lutheran Church in America (1994), the Vatican's halfhearted "We Remember" (1994), and the French bishops' "Declaration of Repentance" (1997). "Truth commissions" to investigate past regimes and crimes were established in democratizing Latin America, Eastern Europe, and South Africa. The United States govern-ment apologized to Japanese Americans interned in the war, while a debate takes place over whether former slaves are owed an apology and reparations. The similarity in all these cases is the return of a disreputable past that was hidden, forgotten, or repressed, that now demands its rightful place in the national and historical narrative. This, in one sense, is the story Freud tells in *Moses and Monotheism*.

As such, *Moses and Monotheism* is a book about coming to terms with the past (the murder of the Father and of Moses), before the term received any of its present-day implication and weight. Our civilization, particularly after 1945, is now based on the assumption that nations have a hidden, repressed past; that the idea of nation includes national traumas and guilt; that the past comes back to haunt national collectivities; and that therefore this re-pressed consciousness must be recognized and addressed. The involvement of Germans as well as of other Europeans in the Holocaust is, of course, the twentieth century's paradigmatic example. The intricacies of the debates on Germany's coming to terms with the Holocaust past is irrelevant here; what is important is that these debates take place at all, that our civilization be-lieves that nations—like individuals—have to own up to their pasts and can-not escape them. This is a wholly novel, very modern idea, and it has Freud's marks all over it—although not only Freud's, of course.

In this respect, Freud's ideas of history and nationhood in the book have survived longer and aged better than other such ideas in twentieth-century

Europe. In *Moses and Monotheism* Freud outlines a conception of history: "Early trauma—defense—latency—outbreak of the neurosis—partial return of the repressed material: this was the formula we drew up for the development of a neurosis. Now I will invite the reader to take a step forward and assume that in the history of the human species something happened similar to the events in the life of the individual. That is to say, mankind as a whole also passed through conflicts of a sexual-aggressive nature that left permanent traces, but which were for the most part warded off and forgotten; later, after a long period of latency, they came to life again and created phenomena similar in structure and tendency to neurotic symptoms."[23] Yerushalmi's astute observation about the Moses narrative is valid here as well: the text requires a "suspension of disbelief."[24] It reads like a fantasy about human history from the workshop of the twentieth century.

But then, the 1930s experienced other implausible fantasies about human history. In the name of Marxism-Leninism, a society was envisaged in the Soviet Union in which by an act of transcendence the state would disappear and all alienation cease. One class would assume power, it was believed, and this would bring an end to class society, an end to history, and a future of changeless, perfect society. In the name of Aryan racism, a regime was founded in Germany based on biological hereditary ideas espousing the predetermined, changeless, immemorial character of individuals and groups. Translating these ideas into actions, Germans proceeded to select humanity into those fit and unfit to live. The Freudian, Marxian, and racial conceptions of history share some similarities. They all believed in their scientific credentials, in presenting a universal truth, and in discovering the essential element of history, be it class, biological heredity, or the psychic repetition in human history of father-son relations.[25] Above all, the fictions of class, race, and psychology—as well as the current fiction of free-market economy as universal panacea—have demanded a great suspension of disbelief.

But, of course, there are also the most fundamental differences among these conceptions of history. Race and class were state ideologies in whose name millions were murdered. Their fiction was paved by an all-too-real human suffering. At the dawn of a new century, these fantasies about human history are discredited beyond repair as projects for ameliorating the collectivity and the individual. Freud's creation, on the other hand, is still with us. The "self," "memory," and "repression" are beliefs that do not enjoy the support of military divisions, of a state and secret police, of ministries of propaganda and of official ideology, but they have become pillars of civilization.

Whether Freud's creation is a fiction of the twentieth century, a science, or both is perhaps irrelevant. For it brought individuals and collectivities the wisdom and moral probing that comes with seeking self-consciousness.

Let me tie the threads of this essay together. I have argued that far from being shocking, Freud's narrative of nationhood was part of a general European paradigm. At the same time, he broke free of this paradigm, opening new ways to understand national remembrance. Freud straddled two worlds. He was a man of his time by thinking of nationhood as genealogy, and by attempting to provide national identity with scientific supporting historical evidence. He posited a metaphysical continuity across centuries, and he looked for origins that extended over millennia. But he was also a man of our times, that is, of the post-1945 period when nationhood has been viewed as a culture of remembrance, for he posited that a national community was the sum of its memories and forgetting, that guilt and repression were integral to national identity, and that memory had moral and ethical, as well as historical, consequences. Memory is now the fundamental way we conceive of nationhood. And in this sense, we have all become somewhat Freudian.

I do not think that Freud's legacy and influence in the post-1945 period would have been possible without his prior adoption of the paradigm of nationhood. To inspire new thinking about nationhood, he had to work within its framework. For nationhood, needless to say, is still with us. True, there is a more doubtful, ironic, view of nationhood, and many creeds of the paradigm have fallen into disrepute. But it is still a fundamental creed by which people organize and understand the world.

What makes *Moses and Monotheism* a great book, among other reasons, is that is it a national fantasy in search of historical self-awareness. Written by a "Godless Jew," as Freud described himself, the book combines a history of, and a fantasy about, the Jewish people. In this, it is like nationhood itself, which offers a history of, and a fantasy about, a given people. The trouble begins when people attempt to realize their utopian national fantasy in history. The most dangerous fantasy these days is the mixture of nationhood and religion. I am not certain Freud foresaw this. Certainly, the land to which Moses led his people has had its own share of suffering as a result of this dangerous fantasy. At this particular historical moment, Palestinian suicide bombers have lost all moral concern for the sanctity of human lives, their own included, in the name of nationalism and religion. In Israel, there is a rendition of Jewish nationhood, based on messianic territorial expansion, that in the name of Moses and his Jewish God practices inhumanities against others. This is a far cry from Freud's belief that the most profound achievement of Mosaic monotheism is the "progress of spirituality."[26] Rejecting the fantasy of an imperial Jewish nationhood in favor of a modest Jewish existence within bounded history will endow a moral, ethical, and human dimension to Jewish nationhood. Paradoxically, comparing the Jewish ideology of expansive territoriality to Mosaic spirituality leads us to question Freud's assumption about the existence of "*the* character of the Jewish people."[27] But if the Jewish people lack *a* character, it certainly has a history. And it is the historical task of Jewishness these days to renounce national, inhuman territorial expansion and revert back to humanism. In doing so, it may just happen that Godless Jews will save Jewishness. And this, too, will be a legacy of Moses.

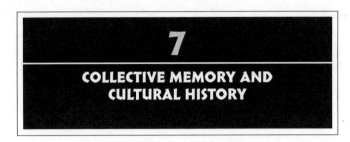

7

COLLECTIVE MEMORY AND CULTURAL HISTORY

Problems of Method

The concept of "culture" has become for historians a compass of a sort that governs questions of interpretation, explanation, and method. And the notion of "memory" has taken its place now as a leading term, recently perhaps the leading term, in cultural history. Used with various degrees of sophistication, the notion of memory, more practiced than theorized, has been used to denote very different things, which nonetheless share a topical common denominator: the ways in which people construct a sense of the past.[1] It has been used to explore, first, the memory of people who actually experienced a given event, such as the memory of Holocaust survivors.[2] In addition, it has come to denote the representation of the past and the making of it into a shared cultural knowledge by successive generations in "vehicles of memory" such as books, films, museums, commemorations, and others.[3] The richness of memory studies is undeniable. Perhaps collective memory has been so useful to think about how people construct pasts because of its open-endedness, because it is applicable to historical situations and human conditions in diverse societies and periods.

But the benefit of richness cannot overcome a sense that the term "memory" has been depreciated by surplus use, while memory studies lack a clear focus and have become somewhat predictable. The often-made contention that the past is constructed not as fact but as myth to serve the interest of a particular community may still sound radical to some, but it cannot (and should not) stupefy most historians. The history of memory, in fact, has developed into a fragmented field. It lacks critical reflection on method and theory, as well as a systematic evaluation of the field's problems, approaches, and objects of study. It is largely defined now in terms of topics of inquiry. Repressed memory. Monuments. Films. Museums. Mickey Mouse. Memory of the American South. Of the Holocaust. The French Revolution. Memory of recent events, of current events, and instant memory of yesterday's news.[4]

One cannot avoid a sense that the choice of subjects is all too often governed by the fashion of the day. The history of memory defined topically becomes a field with neither a center nor connections among topics. It runs the danger of becoming an assemblage of distinct topics that describe in a predictable way how people construct the past.[5]

Of course, everything is a memory case; memory is everywhere. We construct a sense of the past from the most mundane, everyday-life objects (postcards), as well as from the most sacred totems (the Christian cross). But, then, not everything is a memory case in the same way. Beyond proposing new topics for memory investigation, we need to question the methods of memory studies, by way of refining our approaches and proposing new connections. This essay is an occasion for critical reflection on memory studies and on the field that defines it: cultural history. It is not necessary to state here the advantages of cultural history, but it is perhaps beneficial to remind ourselves of the risks and problems it includes in terms of evidence and in relating the cultural to the social and the political. There is too often a facile mode of doing cultural history, whereby one picks a historical event or a vehicle of memory, analyzes its representation or how people perceived it over time, and draws conclusions about "memory" (or "collective memory"). Memory is a new field of research, but this is not sufficient to make of it a novelty. As a field of study, memory has a label more than a content; that is, though the label is an attractive one, in itself memory does not offer any true additional explanatory power. Only when linked to historical questions and problems, via methods and theories, can memory be illuminating. The aim of this essay is not to propose an alternative strategy, for there is no one, correct way to "do" memory. It is, rather, to think through how it is effective to think with memory. At the center of the essay is the problem of how the term "memory" can be useful in articulating the connections between the cultural, the social, and the political, between representation and social experience.

I think about the study of memory by associating it with two bodies of work: the history of *mentalités* and the work of a European scholar who in the 1920s was among the first to use the concept of collective memory. I mean Aby Warburg, the great art and cultural historian. I do not suggest that we follow on the heels of these works. Not at all. I view them rather as inspiring us to think about the notion of memory, to establish new relations, to suggest new strategies. Certainly, there are other bodies of work that can illuminate the history of memory; but, for the purpose of this essay, I found these two useful in articulating several problems of method that exist in memory studies. I therefore begin this essay by discussing the connections between the history of memory, of *mentalités*, and Warburg, before I analyze questions of method.

The study of memory and the history of *mentalités* appear to share a common purpose and agenda, as well as a sense of fashionableness and crisis. If we replace "mentalité" with "memory," then Jacques Le Goff's opening paragraph to a 1974 article, "Mentalities: A History of Ambiguities," could just as well have been the beginning of this essay: "For the historian today, the term mentality is still a novelty and already devalued by excessive use. There is much talk of the history of mentalities, but convincing examples of such history are rare. It represents a new area of research, a trail to be blazed, and yet, at the same time, doubts are raised as to its scientific, conceptual, and epistemological validity. Fashion has seized upon it, and yet it seems already to have gone out of fashion. Should we revive or bury the history of mentalities?"[6] Familiar music. Similar to the study of memory, the history of *mentalités* was denounced as a "semantic prestidigitation."[7] Like the history of *mentalités*, a great appeal of the history of memory appears to be its vagueness.[8] And both histories have by themselves no additional explanatory value; their value depends on the problems posed and methods used.[9]

But the history of *mentalités* is useful not only in order to outline the dangers faced by the new history of memory. There is also a great advantage in thinking of the history of memory as the history of collective mentality. This way of reasoning resists the topical definition of the field and, conversely, uses memory to explore broader questions about the role of the past in society. The history of memory is useful and interesting not only for thinking about how the past is represented in, say, a single museum but also about, more extensively, the historical mentality of people in the past, about the intermingled beliefs, practices, and symbolic representations that make people's perceptions of the past. This kind of history of memory should aim at "reconstructing the patterns of behavior, expressive forms and modes of silence into which worldviews and collective sensibilities are translated. The basic elements of this research are representations and images, myths and values recognized or tolerated by groups or the entire society, and which constitute the content of collective psychologies." These words, which articulate so well an agenda for the history of memory, are Robert Mandrou's analytical description of the history of *mentalités*.[10]

Moreover, memory as a study of collective mentality provides a comprehensive view of culture and society that is often missing in the history of memory, whose fragmentary tendency is to focus on distinct memories. The history of mentality distinguished itself from the history of ideas by looking at the common man. This included both examining objects produced by the common man (popular literature, for example) and studying the reception by the common man of objects of high culture (say, Shakespeare). It attempted, in theory if not in practice, to outline the mental horizons of society as a whole, to link both Shakespeare and popular literature within a single cultural world. This is a useful corrective for the history of memory, a field that is inclined, as we shall see, to isolate memories instead of placing them in relation to one another and to society as a whole. This approach heightens our awareness that collective memory is an exploration of a shared identity that unites a social group, be it a family or a nation, whose members nonetheless have different interests and motivations; and that the crucial issue in the history of memory is not how a past is represented but why it was received or rejected. For every society sets up images of the past. Yet to make a difference in a society, it is not enough for a certain past to be selected. It must steer emotions, motivate people to act, be received; in short, it must become a sociocultural mode of action. Why is it that some pasts triumph whereas others fail? Why do people prefer one image of the past over another? The answers to these questions lead us to formulate hypotheses and perhaps draw conclusions about historical mentality. And to articulate such answers, the work of Aby Warburg is insightful.

Aby Warburg (1866–1929) used but never developed systematically the notion of social memory (*soziales Gedächtnis*).[11] His work focused on the transmission of primitive and ancient motifs to later societies, especially their influence and meaning in Renaissance Florence. All human products, argued Warburg, and artistic work in particular, were expressions of human memory transmitted through symbols from ancient times. He came to believe that the key to deciphering art and culture lay in tracing the collective memory of primitive, primeval beliefs and responses that continued to shape our world through shared symbols.

Warburg's ideas of memory are interesting in themselves. More consequential to this essay is his approach to art and cultural history emphasizing the connection between artistic representation and the social world. Warburg's studies explored what is nowadays called the history of mentality or collective memory. Warburg read widely in anthropology and social psychology. Like a historical anthropologist, he observed the Other to gain insights into his own, modern culture; in 1895 he traveled among the Hopi Indians in New Mexico and recorded their rituals and ceremonies.[12] For Warburg, the historian of artistic production must take cognizance of two intertwining factors. One is the "full spectrum of artifacts" (the context, in other words) in a given culture and the ensuing relationship of artifacts both to one another and to their surroundings.[13] The work of art represents the life of the period and its needs; to interpret it, we need "to reconstruct the connection between artistic representations and the social experiences, taste, and mentality of a specific society."[14] The second is the peculiarity of the individual work of art. Looking at the whole, Warburg attempted to maintain a coherent balance between the way a work of art eventuated in the specific form and quality it did and its connection with the larger culture around it.

This mode of proceeding has enormous potential to the study of memory by reversing a recent trend whereby, as we shall see, a representation of the past (in, say, a museum, a film, or a commemoration) is not placed within the symbolic universe available to the society. The result is studies of memory in symbolic isolation. I would like to view memory as an outcome of the relationship between a distinct representation of the past and the full spectrum of symbolic representations available in a given culture. This view posits the study of memory as the relationship between the whole and its component parts, seeing society as a global entity—social, symbolic, political—where different memories interact. This approach also seeks to reconstruct the meaning of a given collective memory by using an intertwined, double move: placing it within a global historical context and a global symbolic universe, and analyzing the ideas, values, and practices embedded in and symbolized by its particular imagery.

Of special significance is Warburg's approach to the issue of evidence. He rejected the arbitrary selection of evidence by art historians who believed in the autonomy of aesthetic values, which he judged as pure history of ideas that disconnected the individual work of art from the larger politics and society. He also rejected the selection of evidence by proponents of the formalist approach (characterized by Heinrich Wölfflin's 1888 *Renaissance and Baroque*), which explained art history in terms of the development and transmission of shapes, lines, colors, and subjects, for this approach interpreted the symbols and meaning of art too narrowly. To carry out his art-historical method, Warburg used the concept of response, emphasizing the importance of social mediation of images. The theory of response called for a study of those prevailing customs, tastes, and traditions that connected the historical conditions with the artistic representation. When we interpret a work of art, we cannot assume that images are the transparent expressions of political and social values, for in fact artistic style is a most treacherous key for ascertaining political and social developments. In short, the work of art cannot speak for itself; to decipher its meaning, we must examine intermediaries between the social world and the artistic representation.

Warburg's approach is useful in warning us against the danger of assuming that the representation of memory *can* speak for itself, without intermediaries. Studies that focus on the representation of memory, while ignoring social practice and transmission, implicitly make an assumption, as we shall see, that the representation is a transparent expression of a historical mentality, of social and political values. In reality, the crucial issue is not what is represented but how this representation has been interpreted and perceived.

In the 1920s Warburg was not the only one thinking of social memory and the history of mentality. Maurice Halbwachs, the French sociologist, was the first to have used the concept of collective memory systematically. In a series of studies, Halbwachs argued that every memory is carried by a specific social group limited in space and time.[15] His approach was very different from Warburg's. And although Halbwachs' fundamental contribution—establishing the connection between a social group and collective memory—is the starting point for every scholar of memory, Warburg's writings are, I believe, no less suggestive in terms of method. Also active at the same time was, of course, Marc Bloch, who explored in his 1924 classic *Les rois thaumaturges* the "beliefs and fables" around royal healing rites.[16] Bloch and, it appears, also Warburg knew of Halbwachs's work.[17] What kind of an intellectual genealogy existed between a sociologist, a historian, and an art historian who shared the notion of memory and the history of culture is an investigation that still awaits its scholar.

How, exactly, are Warburg and the history of mentality useful to the study of memory? I see three areas of convergence, which have already been alluded to: the connection of the political with the social in the history of memory, the issue of reception and evidence, and the relationship among memories within a given society. I would like to discuss these topics critically by analyzing several excellent studies on memory. In accordance with the principle that one should direct criticism at leading books in the field, I have chosen those books that I found insightful and stimulating. In the short space of this chapter, I cannot possibly claim to do justice to these studies;

I therefore ask the reader to bear in mind the rather limited nature of my investigation. Still, I believe that the characteristics I discuss are representative of the current study of memory.

One of the significant contributions of memory studies has been to explore how the construction of the past, through a process of invention and appropriation, affected the relationship of power within society. The "politics of memory" (at times, "the politics of identity") has emerged as a leading theme in the growing body of literature about memory. Memory is viewed here as a subjective experience of a social group that essentially sustains a relationship of power. Simply stated, it is who wants whom to remember what, and why.[18] This theme is no doubt illuminating to our understanding of the functions and meanings of collective memory. But it seems to me only partially illuminating, for one consequence of it is the tendency to reduce memory, which is fundamentally a concept of culture, to the political.

The problem with memory defined in terms of politics and political use is that it becomes an illustrative reflection of political development and often is relativized to ideology. In *The Past in French History*, Robert Gildea seeks to "explore the relationship between political culture and collective memory," and he views French political cultures as "defined around the main axes of political conflict." Collective memory thus turns out to be the political memory of liberalism, socialism, communism, anarchism, regionalism, Catholicism. Significantly, the political memory described by Gildea is one constructed by party and institutional leaders, among intellectuals, journalists, statesmen, politicians, and publicists. Consequently, when Gildea argues, for example, that "The 'making of the working class' in France did not take place as a result of industrialisation or urbanisation but as a result of the construction of a collective memory, the myth of the Paris Commune . . . as a class war, a proletarian revolution suppressed with unprecedented violence by the French bourgeoisie," one is not sure in what ways "collective memory" is different from ideology.[19]

More important, the result of memory being sacrificed to an analysis of politics and political use is, often, to ignore the category of the social. In this case, representations of the past derive from and are mainly used to explain relationships of political nature, but they are considerably silent about the effect of memory on the organization, hierarchization, and arrangements of social and cultural relationships. An illuminating example of this problem is Henry Rousso's acclaimed book *The Vichy Syndrome*, a study of the memory of Vichy in post-1945 French society.[20] The first and major part of the book,

"Evolution of the Syndrome," is a useful description of the various ways in which the Vichy memory was mobilized for political purposes. Rousso's narrative follows the "unfinished mourning" after liberation, the "repression" of the 1950s and 1960s, the turning point of 1968, the films *The Sorrow and the Pity* (*Le chagrin et la pitié*, 1971) and *Shoah* (1985), and, after 1974, the Jewish and gentile "obsession" with Vichy and the Holocaust. This is an important story, historically, politically, and morally, told with verve and clarity.

But whose memory is it? Similar to Gildea's, this is a memory constructed by politicians and intellectuals: Charles de Gaulle, the Communist Party, *Shoah* film maker Claude Lanzmann, members of the Chamber of Deputies, historians, journalists, or Andre Malraux speaking at the ceremony for Jean Moulin at the Panthéon. *The Vichy Syndrome* shows a very important manifestation of French memory, yet it is a limited one; this is largely a public, often official, and narrowly political memory. The period of repression, 1954–71, for example, is predictably centered on the figure of de Gaulle. But if for Rousso the Vichy memory appears to have been repressed between 1954 and 1971, it is also because the book explores a memory created from above. It ignores the construction of popular memories of Vichy and their links to the everyday level of experience. In the private spheres of family, friends, workplace, and neighborhood, there may have been very different representations of Vichy. Robert Moeller has convincingly argued recently that German society during the 1950s, in contrast to the widely held opinion of scholars and laypersons, did not forget or repress the Nazi era but actively remembered it—selectively and with an inverted meaning of who the victim really was.[21] It is improbable that the mass of French men and women who collaborated with the Nazis, some out of opportunism, others out of ideology, simply forgot it all. *The Vichy Syndrome* thus fails to give a sense of how the Vichy memory made a difference in people's lives, and how it was enacted on the local and private level. Moreover, while Rousso ignores popular Vichy memories that were produced away from the corridors of political, cultural, and entertainment power, he also fails to explore how the memory constructed by the powerful—say, the Moulin commemoration—was received by the people. (We return to this topic below.) Consequently, the Vichy memory from above is isolated from larger patterns of historical mentality in French society. As a study of memory from above, *The Vichy Syndrome* cannot be considered, as it aspires to be, a study of collective memory.

By sanctifying the political while underplaying the social, and by sacrificing the cultural to the political, we transform memory into a "natural" corollary of political development and interests.[22] Consequently, we are the poorer in method and theory to analyze crucial memory issues that cannot be reduced to the political: the relations between modernity (and postmodernity) and memory; the obsession with and/or neglect of memory, forgetting, and conservation in modern and premodern societies. Furthermore, one unfortunate side effect of treating memory as a symptom of politics is the lack of explorations of power in areas that are not politically evident. Thus, we search for memory traces mostly among visible places and familiar names, where memory construction is explicit and its meaning palpably manipulated, whereas we should also look for memory where it is implied rather than said, blurred rather than clear, in the realm of collective mentality. We miss a whole world of human activities that cannot be immediately recognized (and categorized) as political, although they are decisive to the way people construct and contest images of the past. We can think of the family, voluntary association, and workplace but should also include practices such as tourism and consumerism.

Interestingly enough, by sacrificing the cultural to the political, memory studies—and by extension cultural history—have reproduced a model of society that is, in a sense, not dissimilar from that of the social history of the 1960s and 1970s. According to classic social history, cultural cleavages necessarily reflected social differences constructed beforehand; the social structure identified and explained cultural originations that subsequently needed only to be characterized. The underlying assumption was that culture can only be explained by its relation to social structural preconditions; thus changes in the formation of culture are explained by earlier changes in social relations. Cultural history has justifiably demolished the validity of this approach by arguing that culture shapes, as much as it is shaped by, the social structure. But if social history reduced the cultural to the social, cultural history often reduces the cultural to the political. Memory cleavages reflect political differences constructed beforehand. Political differences identify and explain memory origination. Memory thus becomes a prisoner of political reductionism and functionalism.

Another significant consequence to the sacrificing of the cultural to the political is that we tend to ignore the issue of reception, that ogre that awaits every cultural historian. Many studies of memory are content to describe the representation of the past without bothering to explore the transmission, diffusion, and, ultimately, the meaning of this representation. The study of reception is not an issue that simply adds to our knowledge. Rather, it is a necessary one to avoid an arbitrary choice and interpretation of evidence.

Let us look again at *The Vichy Syndrome*, which treats the history of transmission at length. The second part of the book, "Transmission of the Syndrome," focuses on three memory carriers: official commemorations, popular movies, and scholarly works of history. In addition, to gauge "how deep were the roots of the syndrome in French society," Rousso discusses book sales, movie attendance, and polling results.[23] But there is no comprehensive analysis of the diffusion of Vichy representations or a clear rationale for why one piece of evidence is chosen over another.[24] Moreover, however elaborate the polling results are, and however complete the information about box-office sales of *The Sorrow and the Pity* and book sales of Robert Paxton's *Vichy France*, this superficial evidence cannot capture the meaning of the Vichy memory for French men and women. The evidence presented is anecdotal, and the anecdote is presented as proof of reception. The anecdotal approach appears to be confirmed by Rousso's own evaluation of his method as an attempt to "capture the full diversity of 'collective memory' by recording all its *visible* signs."[25] "All the visible signs": one wonders how arbitrary is Rousso's Vichy syndrome.[26] Parallel to the visible representations there were perhaps different Vichy syndromes that can be found among silent and less visible sources. For the Vichy syndrome, like other pathologies, was created to hide as much as to reveal. The book's main metaphors—syndrome, neurosis, repression, obsession, pathology—are taken from psychology. But if we think further with the psychological metaphor, we must wonder whether the historian/psychologist should take the patient's (French society) explicit utterances as a priori important, indeed almost at face value. Should the historian not be suspicious of the visible, explicit narrative offered by public and official French society about Vichy? My argument is not that Rousso interprets the visible evidence naively; on the contrary, he is sensitive to silences, appropriations, lies. It is rather that Rousso interprets *only* the visible evidence: as a result, he interprets the Vichy syndrome within the constraints of public—and, to a large extent, official—narrative. Should we not assume, instead, that the patient would try to conceal the effects and implication of the trauma, that the visible signs of a trauma are at times the least meaningful?[27]

The real problem is one of method: the decision to explain the meaning of the Vichy memory by separating its construction (part 1 of the book) from its reception (part 2). Rousso interprets reception by attempting "not to lose sight of the overall picture" of the syndrome's evolutionary stages established in part 1 (from unfinished mourning to obsession).[28] The result is an interpretation that is closed within itself—because the reception's "overall picture" has already been predetermined. The discussion of reception thus only shows what we have already learned in part 1 and in fact has no bearing on the evolution of the syndrome. This method is an interpretative vicious circle in which Rousso reads into the evidence of reception what he has already learned from other sources and what he wants to "prove."[29] When historians attempt to interpret evidence of memory from a representation of the past, the risk of a circular argumentation through "cultural" reading is high. The overall consequence is an arbitrary interpretation: a conception of the meaning of Vichy memory was formed before exploring the reception of the memory. But in truth, we have no way to evaluate, control, and verify the importance of the evidence without a systematic study of reception, and we end up constructing the history of memory from visible signs whose significance is taken for granted. Although neither Rousso nor scholars of memory and cultural history believe that representations of the past can "speak for themselves," the result of many studies of memory that overlook reception is that representations of the past are used, in effect, as vehicles that explain perceptions of the past without intermediaries.

One result of the separate narratives of evolution and reception, a result certainly unintended by Rousso, is that the evolution of memory stands like a foundational story against which reception is measured. The separate narratives thus assume levels of analysis and explanations: we must first construct the evolution of memory in order to understand its meaning as revealed in reception. But this, of course, is an artificial separation, for the meaning of memory's evolution commingles with, and is dependent on, the story of its reception.

A similar problem of narrative emerges when we attempt to write the history of memory by separating its construction from its contestation. This is the case of Yael Zerubavel's *Recovered Roots*, an excellent, thoughtful study of Zionist collective memory.[30] Zerubavel focuses on three major events in ancient and recent Jewish history: the fall of Masada in A.D. 73, the Bar Kokhba revolt against the Roman Empire in A.D. 132, and the 1920 battle of Tel Hai, in the Upper Galilee, where eight Zionist settlers died defending a small settlement.

The first parts of the book explore the evolution of these events into fundamental myths that shaped meanings of the past in the Jewish society in Palestine. Although the sources are extremely rich, Jewish society is presented as a monolith.[31] There is no differentiation in culture, society, and politics regarding who are the agents of "Zionist collective memory." The term itself takes on a life of its own, as it acts, reconstructs, and produces.[32] The result is a cultural history in a social and political void; the construction of memory here is a story bereft of its sociology and its politics.

Only in the last part of the book, "the politics of commemoration," which explores "the struggle over power and control," does Zerubavel finally discuss how the "different interpretations of those historical events presented competing claims on Israeli collective memory."[33] But are these competing claims not an integral part of the construction of memory? Why assume, even as a heuristic device, that a "Zionist collective memory" existed, when in fact many memories vied for power within Zionism? The result of analyzing the politics of memory as a separate problem from that of the evolution of memory is the omission of a key problem to understanding the construction of Zionist collective memory: how opposing Zionist groups came to believe, in spite of their political and other differences, that they shared a single, transcending national belonging. In other words, how did Zionists construct from their different interpretations of Jewish history a symbolic common denominator? The solution to these questions, in terms of narrative and method, lies in writing the history of memory's construction as commingling with that of memory's contestation, thus emphasizing simultaneously the politics of commemoration *and* how various Zionist groups came to believe they shared a unique national memory, one that overcame symbolically the real differences in Jewish society. The result of the analysis of *Recovered Roots* is a kind of master narrative of an agentless "Zionist collective memory" (described in the first part of the book) against which the different interpretations of Zionist groups are measured (in the second part). The analysis of contestation thus does not influence the story of evolution; it is not so much a part of it as an addition to it. Consequently, the impact of contestation on the construction of memory is reduced, although Zerubavel's intention in separating them was, I assume, the opposite.

One way to reflect about this problem of narratives—the separation of the construction of memory from either its reception or contestation—is in terms of the relations between text and context. The stories of the construction of Vichy and Zionist memories function in the books much like a necessary context, which describes and analyzes the general conditions within which a particular reality evolves. The foundation story is complex and multifaceted, yet it provides a single context within which, and in relation to which, people make choices about reception and contestation. It constructs one social reality within which reception and contestation must make sense.[34] But what happens when we reject this separation of memory's construction from its reception and contestation, when we break down the dichotomy of text and context? This is an invitation to reject the historian's common approach to place and explain the text in relation to a context. The result is, I believe, that we can pursue better the agenda of Rousso and Zerubavel to explore "how members of society remember and interpret [the past] . . . how the meaning of the past is constructed, and how it is modified over time." [35] To reject the separation of narratives assumes that historical actors participate in various processes at the same time, that they simultaneously represent, receive, and contest memory. To accept that none of these processes has primacy and yet to understand the meaning of memory, we need to understand all of them as intertwined—memory as a whole that is bigger than the sum of its parts. This serves as a reminder to realize what is declared more often than practiced, namely the multiplicity of social experiences and representations, in part contradictory and ambiguous, in terms of which people construct the world and their actions. [36]

This argument, in a sense, takes us back to the classic writings of Halbwachs. The fundamental idea of *The Social Formation of Memory* is the "multiplicity of social times," as Halbwachs analyzes the collective memory of, among others, the family, the religious community, and the social class. [37] He writes: "But these various modes by which memories become associated result from the various ways in which people can become associated. We can understand each memory as it occurs in individual thought only if we locate each within the thought of the corresponding group. We cannot properly understand their relative strength and the ways in which they combine within individual thought unless we connect the individual to the *various groups of which he is simultaneously a member.*" [38]

The multiplicity of memory is useful for two reasons: in terms of method, it enables us to write the history of memory as the commingling of reception, representation, and contestation; in terms of subject matter, it makes it possible to avoid artificial distinctions, even as heuristic devices, and to explore how people were, at one and the same time, say, local and national, Zionist and religious, good parents as well as devoted Catholics and Vichy fascists who sent Jewish children to the camps. Furthermore, the multiplicity of memory is also useful in thinking about the place of a given memory within the society as a whole. It is to this topic, then, that I now turn.

I would like to use the idiom of the whole and its parts to illuminate the relationships among memories within a given society. The history of memory should place the articulation of a particular perception of the past within the context of society as a shared symbolic universe. A given memory is subsumed within a culture that is constituted by common practices and representations. National memory, for example, is constituted by different, often opposing, memories that, in spite of their rivalries, construct common denominators that overcome on the symbolic level real social and political differences to create an imagined community. We should stress the interaction between a given memory and other memories in the society and take cognizance of society and culture as global entities, where distinct memories interact.

In contrast, a result of much recent research is that we explore memory in isolation. One approach is to look at the various memories within a society without providing a view of society and identity as a whole. Gildea adopts this approach when he traces French collective memories—socialism, Bonapartism, anarchism, regionalism—and concludes that "there is no single French collective memory but parallel and competing collective memories."[39] This is true, but it is only a partial truth. It is obviously important to avoid essentialism and to reject arguments that impose cultural homogeneity on a heterogeneous society. Conflicts over memory exist. Differences are real. People are sometimes ready to die for their vision of the past, and nations sometimes break because of memory conflicts. But all this only begs the question: How, then, in spite of all these differences and difficulties, do nations hold together? What were the common denominators that bound French men and women across the dividing lines that separated them? Gildea's study is sensitive to the differences in French political culture but fails to capture representations of nationhood that create a sense of oneness among broad and diverse groups in French society. The picture he presents is of a French collective memory splintered into rival political cultures. But this is a one-dimensional picture. Was there no cultural heritage and tradition (real or invented) that united these people together as "French"? Did they not feel a sense of shared destiny?

One danger in exploring the conflicts over national representations, while avoiding the common denominators, is that the historian may read into the symbolic representations what he or she has already learned by other means. Studies of conflict tend to reproduce on the symbolic level the social and political conflicts that are familiar from previous studies. But many a national memory succeeds to represent, for a broad section of the population, a common destiny that overcomes symbolically real social and political conflicts in order to give the illusion of a community to people who in fact have very different interests. People construct representations of the nation that conceal through symbols real friction in their society. These representations should also be studied.

Another approach is to consider the whole while ignoring its component parts. This is, in part, the case of Zerubavel's *Recovered Roots*, where a "Zionist collective memory" becomes a historical agent in its own right. When Zerubavel turns to discuss the contestation of memory, she overwhelmingly focuses on recent decades, although the memories of Masada, Bar Kokhba, and Tel Hai were in the making since the first decades of the century. She argues that the Yishuv society before independence in 1948 was less contested than "Israeli culture today that includes a greater variety of interpretations of the past."[40] As a whole, this argument is correct, but "Zionist collective memory" of the early decades seems to be based on a hegemonic notion of hegemony. It was, according to Zerubavel, hardly contested by non-Zionist Jewish memories and only partially contested from within by different Zionist groups. This seems rather improbable.[41]

If we assume for a minute that Zionist memory in the past was indeed hegemonic and largely uncontested, then Zerubavel needs to reevaluate her argument about the centrality of contestation: for "Zionist collective memory" appears to have been uniquely successful in creating a consensus among gender, political, social, and ethnic groups in the Jewish Yishuv. Yet in order to understand this process, we must explore how Zionists constructed a symbolic common denominator out of different ideological beliefs and how, in essence, "Zionist collective memory" meant different things to different people: to members of the Labor Party, to right-wing Revisionists, to religious Zionists, and to left-wing Marxists. In Zerubavel's narrative, instead, "Zionist collective memory," as understood by Zionists, assumes a rather hegemonic meaning until the 1960s.

A third approach conceives the relationships among memories as dichotomous. This is the picture that emerges from John Bodnar's study of the creation of public memory in twentieth-century America as a product of a power struggle between "vernacular and official memory."[42] Bodnar's underlying assumptions are exemplified in his definition of these memories. On official memory, he writes:

Official culture relies on "dogmatic formalism" and the restatement of reality in ideal rather than complex or ambiguous terms. . . . Cultural leaders [the makers of official memory], usually grounded in institutional and professional structures, envisioned a nation of dutiful and united citizens which undertook only orderly change. These officials saw the past as a device that could help them attain these goals and never tired of using commemoration to restate what they thought the social order and citizen behavior should be . . . By the latter part of the twentieth century public memory remains a product of elite manipulation, symbolic interaction, and contested discourse.[43]

Conversely, vernacular memory is described in the following language:

Defenders of [vernacular] cultures are numerous and intent on protecting values and restating views of reality derived from firsthand experience in small-scale communities rather than the "imagined" communities of a large nation. . . . [N]ormally vernacular expressions convey what social reality feels like rather than what it should be like. Its very existence threatens the sacred and timeless nature of official expressions. . . . [V]ernacular memory was derived from the lived or shared experiences of small groups. Unlike official culture which was grounded in the power of larger, long-lasting institutions . . .[44]

What a neat binary opposition between authentic vernacular culture and manipulative official one! Bodnar idealizes vernacular memory, which he describes in terms—shared experience, protecting values, small-scale communities—that convey in our culture authenticity and intimacy, while he describes official memory in terms—large, impersonal, power-hungry—that are associated with alienation, distrust, and ulterior motivation. Although Bodnar discusses ways in which vernacular and official memory could blend, this dichotomy governs his analysis, method, and conclusions. But, in the real world, things are not as neat. Not only is vernacular memory not as saintly and official memory not as brutal, but they constantly commingle.

Moreover, this inadequate dichotomy also governs Bodnar's analysis of the relations between local and national memories. According to Bodnar, "the central question for public memory will continue to be what it always has been: just how effective will vernacular interests be in containing the cultural offensive of authorities?"[45] This, in a sense, is the wrong question because the challenge is not so much to understand how vernacular and official memories opposed each other but how the nation-state came to be a vernacular memory: how did people internalize the nation and make it in a remarkably short time an everyday mental property—a memory as intimate and authentic as the local, ethnic, and family past?[46]

I have proposed in this chapter a double move: that the history of memory be more rigorous theoretically in articulating the relationship between the social, the political, and the cultural and, at the same time, more anarchical and comprehensive in using the term memory as an explanatory device that links representation and social experience. I have attempted to argue, via the discussion of memory studies, that mine is really a critique of cultural history. A critique of two kinds. There exists in memory studies the danger of reducing culture to politics and ideology, instead of broadening the field from the political to the social and the experiential, to an everyday history of memory. And there exists the danger of reducing culture to some vague notion of memory, whereby memory is separated from other memories in society and from the culture around it. That a given memory exists, that it has a symbolic representation and a political significance is obvious, but in itself it explains little if we do not place this memory within a global network of social transmission and symbolic representations.

Several of my arguments, I am certain, are familiar to some. There is nothing new in pointing out the importance of a history of reception for our understanding of a cultural artifact. And this, indeed, emerges as a lesson we can draw from this chapter: with regard to certain renditions of memory and cultural history, these arguments still need to be made. Certain kinds of cultural history seem to forget bodies of knowledge that one would think had already been internalized, thanks to classic social history.

There are many ways of doing memory, and while my critique raises some problems in current approaches, it simultaneously emphasizes the open-endedness of the notion. The beauty of memory is that it is imprecise enough to be appropriated by unexpected hands, to connect apparently unrelated topics, to explain anew old problems. Among the many roads open for scholars, one, I believe, is especially fruitful in the current state of the field: to write the history of memory. We have to distinguish between memory as a heuristic device and memory as part of the mental equipment of a society, of an age. It is not always clear whether "memory" is used as an imposed methodological tool to analyze how a given society constructed a past (similar to using "class" to understand seventeenth-century Europe) or whether "memory" was indeed a contemporary metaphor to understand the past (like class in twentieth-century Europe). Thus the memory, say, of World War II in a given society cannot be separated from the development after 1945 of the term "memory" itself into a leading concept used by people to understand the past, private and public, personal and national. For if the study of memory focuses creatively on how people construct a past through a process of appropriation and contestation, is the real problem not, perhaps, that people construct the past by using the term "memory" at all?

To write a history of memory, we need to draw the mental horizon of an age. When and why did memory become a habit of mind shared by people to give meaning to the past? One can imagine that it is the kind of historical problem Warburg and Bloch would have been delighted to pose, and perhaps to begin to answer. And so, perhaps the first task of the history of memory is to historicize memory.

8

TELLING ABOUT GERMANY

Narratives of Memory and Culture

Sometime between November 9, 1989, and October 3, 1990, twentieth-century Germany became history. While the century was not over yet, a distinct historical period did terminate. The core of Germany's century—the Third Reich and the Holocaust—did not change, but their place within the century did. The events of 1989 and the unification that followed are a turning point that necessarily also transforms our view of twentieth-century Germany as a whole. It is not surprising that there has been an evident shift in historical interests in the past decade. Before 1990 German historiography was largely preoccupied with the origins of National Socialism.[1] The questions that historians ask today are different. We are now much more interested in the consequences than in the origins of National Socialism: in the development of East and West Germany and in their links to Nazi society, politics, economy, and culture. The growing scholarly interest in the postwar memory of the Third Reich and the Holocaust is part of this trend. The broader question that emerges is, What do we want to know of twentieth-century Germany, if it is no longer the origins of the Third Reich?[2]

While there have been different answers to this question, one approach has recently gained interpretative dominance: the one thing that we seem to want to know now about twentieth-century Germany is linked to memory, identity, and culture. The leading approach in the interpretation of German history has in recent years been cultural history, and the leading topic has been memory. It is not necessary to state here the advantages of cultural history and memory studies, which are adopted now almost reflexively, but it is perhaps good to remind ourselves of the risks they entail and to ask what kinds of questions and problems they have obscured, oversimplified, or simply ignored.

The aim of this chapter is to illuminate some potentials and problems in the way historians use the notions of culture and memory to interpret aspects of Germany in the twentieth century. My main interest is in how historians construct memory and culture as objects of study. I am less interested in what books argue than in how they argue. One strong advantage of cultural history and memory studies has been the possibility of uncovering people's experience. I attempt to explore what kind of "experience" is being revealed in studies of modern German culture and memory, and whose. Looking at the assumptions underlying the cultural and memory approach to modern German history, I ask what this approach explains and how. The danger of circularity is always present in cultural history and memory studies. When historical relations are reduced to "identities" and "memories" the understanding of history is bound to become impressionistic. When culture and identity are seen everywhere, they lose their ability to explain, and we lose our ability to understand change and causation and to identify why things in one country were different from those in another. And because memory is a leading term in present-day culture, there remains for scholars also the danger of anachronism, with our histories of memory and identity reflecting present-day public and scholarly concerns more than they do the lives and beliefs of people in the past.

In accordance with the principle that one should think through such problems by examining leading books in the field, I have chosen those studies that I found particularly insightful and challenging intellectually, studies with which this chapter is often also an argument. This is not a bibliographic survey, but an attempt to articulate, via a discussion of a number of important studies, some new questions, connections, and problems that relate to the ways scholars of Germany use the notions of memory and culture.

I think of the interpretative value of the notions of culture and memory by putting them in relation to narratives of modern German history that I call "fixed" (or "closed") and "open" narratives.[3] Narrative, as an interpretative term that serves heuristic purposes, is useful in reminding us of the style of our own history writing. I am using it here to elucidate problems and formulate questions. Fixed narratives tend to be conceived, organized, and argued in a linear way. They aspire to present the topic under investigation by exhibiting the evidence in a self-contained way to achieve a coherent and commanding argument. Of course, no narrative is totally fixed. Even the most closed narrative must face the uncertainty of language and the possibility that similar evidence will be used to advance different interpretations. And yet these narratives assume that history has a script and that it moves to a specific destiny, which Germany either reached or failed to reach. Ultimately, they look at the past to prove a belief, not to test a hypothesis. In German historiography, a common characteristic of fixed narratives has been to read the modern period from the Third Reich and the Holocaust backward; their interest is in the origins of Nazism, and they view pre-1933 German history as a prelude—sometimes a decade, a century, or ten centuries long—that leads to National Socialism. The *Sonderweg* interpretation dominant in the 1960s and 1970s is a case in point: it argued that German history had diverged (since Luther, since 1848, or since 1871) from the "normal" history of the "West" in its inability to produce a liberal democracy before 1933.[4] For Marxism, studying the past was an exercise of "proving" what had been determined beforehand: the existence of class struggle and the victory of the proletariat.[5] For triumphalist liberal commentators, the fall of communism and the Berlin Wall was a sign of the inevitable historical mission of democracy and the free market.

Typically, fixed narratives present one aspect of history as unchangeable, be it the history of class struggle, of democracy, of German peculiarity, or, as we shall see, of German identity. Fixed narratives carry great explanatory power for some, for they provide the security of an orderly historical movement toward a definable destination. Of course, narratives, as such, have no explanatory power. But paying attention to narratives does help us uncover unproven causal arguments and problems of evidence. Fixed narratives are characterized by claims, which are not supported by evidence, that something in the past caused certain effects. The problem with searching for continuity is that often it becomes an exercise in finding the evidence that one was looking for. It becomes an interpretative vicious circle in which one reads into the evidence the ideas that one has already formed and wants to "prove." Interpretations that see the Third Reich as a result of long-term, built-in German traits face the additional difficulty of explaining how these traits, which continued unabated for decades or centuries, stopped suddenly, somewhat miraculously, in 1945. As a result, these interpretations seem inadequate to explore the consequences of National Socialism and to explain how the dark Germany of the first half of the century changed so dramatically in the second half.

While fixed narratives will no doubt continue to appeal as historical interpretations, the dominant trend in the humanities in the past generation has been toward open narratives. Open narrative self-consciously uncovers the process by which the historian constructs his or her argument, chooses the evidence, and articulates an interpretation. Rather than presenting history as a self-contained, coherent unfolding of facts, open narrative moves toward an analysis that allows memory, ambiguity, negotiations, and contingency. The purpose of open narrative is not to reach a closure when this does not exist; it is, rather, intentionally to leave some tensions unresolved, to embrace contradictions and complexity. Ideally, it should not have the pretension of providing an all-encompassing interpretation. Most history books combine both open and fixed narratives; no book is a pure rendition of one or the other. Even the scholar of the most open-ended narrative ultimately seeks, by choosing the sources and organizing the evidence, coherence of some kind. And even the most fixed narrative must face interpretative uncertainties.

Cultural history and memory studies have exemplified the move toward open narratives.[6] The leading terms in these histories have been "invention" and "construction," thus rejecting the view that social objects, mental perceptions, and political attributes "belong" to a specific social group. In German historiography, studies based on the cultural and memory approach have made important contributions, not least because of their implicit or explicit critique of fixed narratives. Rudy Koshar's *From Monuments to Traces: Artifacts of German Memory, 1870–1990* is an excellent open narrative of German memory.[7] It is the first interpretative synthesis of the large body of work on German memory and monuments from the unification of 1871 to the unification of 1990, breaking new ground by the sheer act of creation of a narrative whole. The book's object of investigation is Germany's "memory landscape," or *Erinnerungslandschaft*, a term that connotes mnemonic qualities not only of architectural landmarks in the narrower sense but also of public squares, street names, historic sites such as concentration camps and Hitler's bunker, and entire natural landscapes. The study focuses on the built environment, monuments, museums, and memorials. As a whole, there emerge the themes of victimhood, resistance, and national decline and rebirth. A key idea in the book is that each political period made different combinations of these and other existing memory elements. The memory landscape united Germans across generations and different political regimes, but Koshar shows convincingly how each generation chose to build its identity on selected themes and symbols within the framework of the developing memory tradition. There were no preordained configurations of memory, no miraculous breaks. Koshar argues further against positing a direct causal link between the Third Reich and earlier forms of German memory and nationalism. By placing German memory within the mainstream of modern European history as having an intermediate position between "West" and "East," Koshar finds Germany to be not peculiar.

Given the primacy of memory studies in German historiography as open narratives, I would like to discuss how successful they have been in overcoming problems of interpretations evident in fixed narratives. Three issues are particularly important: those of historical determinism, of the place of the Holocaust within the century, and of linking the dark Germany of the world wars and genocide with the post-1945 societies. But before beginning that discussion, a peculiarity of German history must be addressed.

Fixed or open, these narratives assume that German history can be meaningfully narrated. But precisely this assumption has been questioned: can the Holocaust, and by extension the Third Reich, be put meaningfully into any kind of narrative?[8] Elie Wiesel took a most radical position when he famously asserted, "The Holocaust? The ultimate event, the ultimate mystery, never to be comprehended or transmitted. Only those who were there know what it was; the others will never know."[9] One identifies with Wiesel the survivor, while at the same time recognizing how hopelessly pessimistic and dangerous is the view about the impossibility of transmitting human values, traditions, and knowledge.[10] Historians, whose métier is to recount the past, face a particular dilemma of how to narrate and explain things that appear to some unnarratable and unexplainable.

The work of Saul Friedländer has been uniquely illuminating on this issue. On the one hand, he wrote, "The 'Final Solution,' like any other historical phenomenon, has to be interpreted *in its historical unfolding* and *within the relevant historical framework*."[11] Friedländer's masterful narrative of the years of Jewish persecution in Nazi Germany between 1933 and 1939—interweaving the experience of victims, persecutors, and bystanders at the levels of everyday life and decision-making policies—attests to the possibility of (some kind of) narration.[12] On the other hand, he believes, there exists with regard to the Holocaust a distinct "unease in historical interpretation." It seems impossible to insert the Holocaust into a large-scale historical interpretation. Friedländer asks: "Does an event like the 'Final Solution' allow for any kind of narrative, or does it foreclose certain narrative modalities? Does it perhaps escape the grasp of a plausible narrative altogether?"[13]

The importance of these questions lies not only in the discussion over possible answers—answers that Friedländer well knows and has worked through in his historical studies—but also in raising them altogether. Friedländer's work captures an undercurrent in popular and scholarly discourse that commingles two opposing, though not contradictory, sentiments: the belief that human events have (or at least may have) a logical historical meaning, and an inner sentiment that the Holocaust displays none.[14] Differently put, while we know now how the Holocaust happened, we are still searching for adequate answers as to why it happened. This search, and the disturbing sense that no answer may be fully justified, or fully satisfying, will accompany humans for a long time, perhaps forever. But the sense that no narrative may be satisfying should not be conflated with the view that no narrative is possible. The Holocaust is not the only event that does not fit within a large-scale historical interpretation. Most of the century's events in Germany and elsewhere do not fit within grand narratives of "modernity," "the triumph of freedom, democracy, and consumption," "the history of class struggle," "a German *Sonderweg*," or "the immutable history of German identity." These are fixed, teleological narratives. Grand narratives are (sometimes) good to think with, but they produce deficient answers that ignore circumstances, contingency, and human agency.[15] The question is not whether the Holocaust can be narrated, but rather which kinds of accounts contribute most to our understanding of it.

One such account in the past generation has been that of memory. It has been used by different groups, for different and at times opposing ends. Survivors, who are identified most closely with the view that the Holocaust cannot be understood, used their memories as a way to give some meaning to what appeared incomprehensible.[16] Many scholars have adopted memory as the leading term to analyze the legacy and representations of the Holocaust.[17] While they have debated the representability of the Holocaust, they have used the notion of memory as an analytical tool that assumes the possibility—or, better, a range of possibilities and limits—of understanding and interpreting the Holocaust. The notion of memory has thus been important for articulating the unease in historical interpretation, as well as the possibilities of overcoming it. The question is, then, how does the notion of memory, as it has been used by scholars, contribute to inserting the Holocaust into a meaningful historical interpretation?

The interpretative value of the notion of memory, to return to where this discussion began, has been a result (among others) of trends in cultural history, German historiography, and Holocaust studies. Memory is now used as a leading term for interpreting twentieth-century German history. This begs the question, How do narratives of modern German memory (at times, modern German identity) attempt to overcome the problems of fixed narratives and Holocaust narrativity? It is to this topic, then, that I would like to turn.

Because the notion of memory is closely tied to the study of the Holocaust, it is worth asking, What is the Holocaust history that memory studies tell? The body of work on German memory has concentrated particularly on the post-1945 memory of the Holocaust and the Third Reich,[18] while exploring memory in the Third Reich has received scant attention.[19] Consequently, the unfolding of the Holocaust as a historical event has remained outside the interpretative framework of memory studies. The links (whatever they may be) between trends in German memory before 1933 and the Holocaust as it unfolded have not been explored, nor has how these links influenced German memory after the war. When we look at the body of work on German memory as a whole, the result is a narrative of twentieth-century German history with the Holocaust (as a historical event, in contradistinction to a remembered event) left out. A case in point is Koshar's *From Monuments to Traces*, which is a useful guide to trends in memory studies. While the memory of the Holocaust naturally dominates the story after 1945, the Holocaust as a historical event is absent from the book. This has interpretative consequences. Koshar analyzes the ways in which German history and, by extension, the Third Reich were one variation within a wider European cultural and political space. But while the book is successful in indicating why Germany was similar to other countries, it is less successful in indicating why Germany was different. When the historical Holocaust is left out of memory studies of Germany, the result is to obscure precisely the historical differences that need explaining.

To be sure, there is no methodological obligation for the notion of memory to shed light on the unfolding of and motivations for the Holocaust; a concept may elucidate one field of German history without elucidating others. We should also avoid the temptation to think that every topic in German history must be connected to the Holocaust. And still, given the prominence of the notion of memory in both German historiography and Holocaust studies, these positions are untenable. It will not do to avoid the central interpretative question of twentieth-century Germany—the making of the Holocaust—while focusing on the representation of the Holocaust and not on its reality. In this respect, memory seems to exhibit problems similar to other interpretations of Nazism. What Friedländer once observed about the place of the Holocaust within interpretations of modern Germany —"the simplest argument is the following: the point is not that such con-

cepts as 'totalitarianism' or 'fascism' seem inadequate for the contextualiza-
tion of the 'final solution,' but, obversely, that these concepts fit much better
the particular phenomena they deal with, once the 'final solution' is not included"—may appear to be the case also with narratives of memory.[20]

One reason for overlooking the historical Holocaust in memory studies
is that "memory" is commonly conceived via historical sites, buildings, museums, monuments, films, or novels with the aim of exploring cultural and
political representations in the public sphere. This mode of proceeding can
successfully explain several historical problems, but is inadequate to carry
the explanatory burden for the extermination of the Jews. It describes the
making of national, collective representations with greater success than it
can describe the psychological, inner world of the killers. It illustrates the
changing representations of the past from one ideological regime to the
next, but not how people changed (or did not change) their habits of mind,
and how the two interacted; it is largely silent over how collective memories were internalized by individuals. In short, it provides a better picture of
the cultural context of the changing representations of the past in the public sphere than of the ways people's mental properties changed and moved
them to act.

How was the Holocaust connected to trends in German memory, and in
what ways can the notion of memory add to our understanding of its causes
and unfolding? Was the notion of memory—understood as a representation
of the past in a given society—important at all to the making of the Holocaust? These questions should be posed. To answer them, we need to think
of a new conceptualization of the notion of memory within cultural history.
I return to this topic at the end of the chapter.

While the unfolding of the Holocaust has not been connected by scholars to previous trends in German memory, the notion of identity has often
been placed at the explanatory center of the Holocaust. It carries unavoidable consequences in terms of method and narrative. In itself, the use of
"identity," a flagship term of open narratives based on the constructedness
of culture, cannot be a guarantee against the kinds of interpretative problems evident in fixed narratives of German history. Indeed, placing (a certain
rendition of the notion of) identity at the center of the Holocaust seems to
result, in spite of scholars' best intentions, in a narrative of unchangeable,
and therefore necessarily anachronistic, history. This has been exemplified
recently in the work of two social scientists. Liah Greenfield's *Nationalism:
Five Roads to Modernity* provides an interpretation of German national identity that, she argues, was born following the defeat of Prussia in 1805-6 as

a romantic nationalism that devalued reason and exalted the irrational and whose social philosophy envisioned a totalitarian society. The denouement of this morality tale is inevitable: "Germany was ready for the Holocaust from the moment German national identity existed [1806]. It is imperative to realize this." [21] Similarly, Daniel Goldhagen has argued that "the eliminationist mind-set that characterized virtually all who spoke out on the 'Jewish Problem' from the end of the eighteenth century onward was another constant in Germans' thinking about Jews. . . . *The eliminationist mind-set tended towards an exterminationist one.* And it did so already at the end of the eighteenth century." [22]

The tension between long-term identity traits and short-term cataclysmic violence is illustrated in the work of Omer Bartov. In a series of influential studies Bartov emphasized the immediate context of Nazi ideology and the barbarization of warfare on the eastern front as the main factors in the making of murderous German soldiers and Holocaust perpetrators. [23] The argument was based on situating the historical actors within the specific conditions of war, Nazi indoctrination, and the development of racial and anti-Semitic ideas; it emphasized a short-term combination of factors in the making of the Holocaust over long-term structural or mental developments. It combined, in a sense, the intentionalist and structuralist views of the Holocaust. [24] It took into account Nazi beliefs and ideology—contra the structuralist view that downplayed these in favor of the dynamics of administrative, institutional, and policy-making processes inherent in the Nazi system of government. And it considered the gradual barbarization of war to be one of the principal factors that turned Nazi beliefs into acts of extermination—contra intentionalists who viewed the expressed ideological, anti-Semitic intentions of the Nazis in the 1920s and 1930s as sufficient to explain the extermination of the 1940s.

But Bartov's new study, *Mirrors of Destruction: War, Genocide, and Modern Identity*, presents an interpretative shift. [25] It puts the Holocaust and the Third Reich at the center of the century's relationship among war, genocide, and modern identity. This passionate book, gracefully written halfway between a scholarly study and an extended essay, attempts to make a case, via an analysis of the Holocaust, for how modern identity has been a product of violence against groups defined as alien to the collectivity. It illuminates the relations between enemies and victims, which are important for understanding modern genocide and the making of national identities. And, by comparing Holocaust representations and notions of victimhood in Germany, France, and Israel, it shows the importance of victimhood to national identity in the twentieth century. But whereas in his previous work Bartov interpreted the Holocaust within the short-term context of war and ideology, in this book he accentuates a longer-term identity factor. He thus argues for a predetermined direct development from Germans' fantasies of violence and destruction in the First World War to the Holocaust and, after 1945, from the Holocaust to a West German sense of victimhood. *Mirrors of Destruction* is not linked to a close examination of the Holocaust's unfolding within the appropriate historical framework so much as it is to Bartov's claim elsewhere that the Holocaust was "the culmination . . . of a process begun in the late eighteenth century and still continuing," [26] a process whereby the utopian idea of perfecting humanity provided collectivities with a justification to eradicate imagined enemies. In themselves, these arguments about identity are viable. Indeed, Bartov's contribution in this book is the attempt to understand the Holocaust beyond its immediate context of war and ideology by considering Germans' long-term habits of mind about violence, enemies, and collectivity that, while changing, existed before and after the Holocaust. But the developments of these habits of mind need to be shown, not assumed teleologically. Adequate evidence should link the interpretative claims made in the name of "identity" with the specific motivations and actions of Germans. A historical narrative linking identity to the Holocaust should thus show how long-term developments of identity affected the behavior of German soldiers under the specific conditions of war and extermination.

The problem with this kind of Holocaust narrative based on identity, to tie the threads of this discussion together, is that it often treats identity as an autonomous force: identity begets identity in a world devoid of cultural transmission and social carriers. It is difficult to see the difference between this history of identity and a history of pure ideas. It leaves little or no space for contingency and agency; identity is not so much made through cultural processes as it "belongs" to Germans. This narrative describes not how identity was made in Nazi Germany, but how preexisting identity was set off in Nazi Germany. The rapidity with which identities were made and remade in the twentieth century becomes secondary to long-term memories. By placing the Holocaust at the narrative and explanatory center of the century, we fail to account for the ways in which people who lead "normal" lives are able in a tremendously short time to commit beastly acts, only to resume "normal" life quickly thereafter. In this sense, this narrative faces the problem of explaining how and why the German identities that produced the Holocaust disappeared so quickly after 1945.[27] At the same time, this kind of Holocaust narrative resonates among scholars and the public alike. It reflects the dominant representation of the Holocaust in contemporary popular culture, a representation that, based on memory and identity, views the Holocaust as a morality tale. It assigns German identity intentionality by telling a story of the moral responsibility of a national identity that went terribly awry. This is an important representation, and an ethically necessary one. But in terms of the historian's craft, the expressed intentions of "identity" have little explanatory power.

Although the literature on German identity is massive, within the historiography of the Holocaust perpetrators "identity" is used to describe, for the most part, Nazi ideology, anti-Semitism, and racial or national ideas. Significantly, cultural history has played a negligible role in this historiography: that is, the investigation of how the perpetrators constructed their worldview is often reduced to acquiescence to the historical circumstances (be they of Nazi society or the war conditions) or to ideological conviction. A whole world of the relations between the disciplinary techniques of the state and the individual habits of mind is excluded. The potential of this topic is indirectly illustrated by the significant book of Robert Gellately, *Backing Hitler: Consent and Coercion in Nazi Germany*.[28] Based on meticulous research, Gellately shows that Hitler was largely successful in getting the backing of most Germans well into the war years. Terror alone can explain neither how the Third Reich came into being nor its staying power. The consensus around Hitler was not uniform, but "pluralistic, differentiated, and at times inconsistent. However . . . the Germans generally turned out to be proud and pleased that Hitler and his henchmen were putting away certain kinds of people who did not fit in. . . . On balance, the coercive practices, the repression, and persecution won far more support for the dictatorship than they lost."[29] One of Gellately's achievements is to show the public dissemination of information about the punitive, repressive side of the regime: far from being hidden, the terror characteristic of Nazi Germany was openly propagated. Exploring the representation of the concentration camps and their prisoners in the media, he concludes that "what is at issue is no longer whether or not Germans knew about the camps, but rather what kind of knowledge they had and how it was conveyed."[30] This finding opens up new avenues of research, which, to be sure, stood beyond Gellately's project: How did Germans internalize the Nazi representations and practices of terror? How did these representations and practices link with previous habits of mind, with notions of everyday life and national belonging? And how did they affect sensibilities such as violence, collectivity, fear, hate, love, killing, and others?

While memory and identity are promising interpretative tools, they also reproduce explanatory problems of fixed narratives and Holocaust narrativity. The real question is what kind of connections we can make between the Holocaust and matters of memory and identity. Obviously, memory and identity are everywhere; they were at the center of the past century. Herein lies not only their importance but also some narrative and explanatory risks. If memory and identity were everywhere in the twentieth century, the result is that they become, by themselves, poor explanatory devices. Jacques Le Goff observed once that the medieval period might best be understood "by its inability to express itself apart from religious references." The Reformation, to take this observation to its chronological limits, happened because of religion, and recourse to this fact should be the first interpretative step in explaining it, not the last. Similarly, if the twentieth century may be understood by its inability to express itself apart from memory and identity references, then memory and identity should be the starting point of our investigation, not its "proof."

One of the most significant contributions of memory studies has been to explore how the memories of the Holocaust and National Socialism were constructed after the war. This body of work has interrogated how struggles over the "right" way to remember shaped political legitimacy, cultural representations, and moral perceptions. The primary mode of proceeding has been to place the representation of the past (be it museums, films, novels, or controversies among historians) in the context of postwar (mostly West) German society, and to show how this representation of the past was used and abused. The benefits of this approach are exemplified in Robert Moeller's major book *War Stories: The Search for a Usable Past in the Federal Republic of Germany*, about the ways West Germans constructed a memory that embraced the war as part of their history while simultaneously distancing themselves from the National Socialist regime.[31] Using sources such as parliamentary debates, Heimat films, and contemporary historical reconstructions of the expulsion of some 12 million Germans from Eastern Europe, Moeller argues convincingly that public memory was dominated by the sentiment of victimhood. He does this with a remarkable, sensitive rhetorical style that never moralizes, while simultaneously letting the reader understand his views of the perpetrators who presented themselves later as a nation of victims. The result is an absorbing and disturbing tale of the ways Germans focused on stories of their suffering and ignored their crimes: "They represented a Germany doubly victimized, first by a Nazi regime run amok, then by communists, and they allowed all West Germans to order the past in mutually exclusive categories in which perpetrators and victims were never the same people."[32]

This mode of proceeding is illuminating to our understanding of the functions and meanings of memory in postwar Germany. But it seems to me only partially illuminating, for one consequence of it is the tendency to sever the representation of the past from the experience of it. The context that gives meaning to these memories is the attempt at constructing a "usable" public German memory following the Nazi regime. But the result of looking for a "usable" memory is that we find a memory that is isolated from the experience of the war and from private memories of this experience because Nazi ideology, occupation of Europe, and extermination were not "usable" to public memory in the 1950s. Consequently, the link between individual memories and public memory is severed, and public memory seems all too often driven by a desire to sanitize the past. Whatever Germans became after 1945 must lie in some measure in their experiences and memories before that period. Whatever postwar memories were, they should be linked with what people during the war thought they were doing, and with what people after the war thought they had been doing during the war.

To capture the full spectrum of emotions and motivations raised by the war, studies of postwar German memory should make the experience of the war an inherent part of the investigation. How did Germans link their sense of postwar victimhood with the memory of their wartime activity as killers and exterminators?[33] On April 8, 1944, the soldier Günther Wiegand wrote from the eastern front: "And what will become of us, if we really endure all this? We become old men, affected with all possible defects and illnesses. We could not enjoy our youth. And we can never make up for it. . . . Our soul and heart became hard through the blood we have seen. And our hands are unclean from the blood they have shed."[34] How did Wiegand reconcile this sentiment ten years later with a sense of victimhood? This topic calls for an exploration that balances public memories, which largely kept silent about "the blood we have shed," with private memories, which in many cases did not. Did Germans sense a dissonance between the experience of killing and the memory of victimhood? Not necessarily. Many Germans did not really think that killing Jews had been wrong. Either way, this line of investigation will bring together the war experience and postwar society, catastrophe and recovery, and Nazi and liberal democratic sensibilities.

Linking the experience of the war with the memory of the war and private memories with public memories is not simply an exercise that adds to our knowledge. Rather, it is a necessary step toward understanding the continuities and ruptures in the transformation from a Nazi society into communist and liberal-democratic societies. Otherwise we end up with an interpretation of postwar memory that is closed within itself because postwar memory becomes dependent on the immediate surrounding context, while ignoring both the experiences that gave rise to it in the first place and the way perceptions of this experience changed.

One limitation of current studies of postwar German memory, therefore, is the tendency to explore the memory of the Second World War but to ignore the effects of the war on memory. These two topics are not quite the same thing. Studying the impact of the war experience on the memory of it is a fundamental contribution of Pieter Lagrou's comparative study, *The Legacy of Nazi Occupation: Patriotic Memory and National Recovery in Western Europe, 1945–1965*.[35] This book, which is about France, Belgium, and the Netherlands, not Germany, provides an interesting contrast to the leading approaches to memory. *The Legacy of Nazi Occupation*, strictly speaking, is not about how France, Belgium, and the Netherlands remembered the war at all: it is about the "social history of the consequences of the Second World War" and how *they* shaped postwar memories of national recovery.[36] In contrast with the prevalent approach to memory that explores the memory of an event, Lagrou is interested in how the war experience of three social groups — resistance veterans, displaced populations, and forced laborers — shaped postwar memories. He argues that members of these groups were "united less as citizens of different states and more by the shared experience" during the war.[37] This approach makes Lagrou's book truly innovative.

Moreover, Lagrou challenges the dominant approach to memory studies influenced by cultural history. He is critical of the "fashionable terminology of 'national memory' [that] might cause its users to forget the metaphorical and probably even inappropriate use of the word 'memory' in this context."[38] Linking his work to the legacy of Marc Bloch, his aim is to integrate collective memories and social history in order to "return to the established methods of the historian's craft."[39] Lagrou's approach is, first, to define social groups as accurately as possible. Influenced by a tradition of French scholarship that insisted on the social foundation of memory, Lagrou provides an important corrective to a facile way of exploring memory in which a film, a novel, or a monument stands for a presumed collective memory.[40] The second element of his approach is to draw a sharp distinction between individual memories and collective representations of the past, as well as between private memory and public discourse. In contrast to most memory studies, which describe but do not explain, Lagrou's approach can in fact explain why the three social groups—based on their experiences in the war—chose to construct certain memories over others. This stands in contrast to many studies on postwar German memory that assume what needs to be explained and interpreted: why is it that some representations of the past in Germany had been adopted while others were rejected?

But, significantly, the final result of Lagrou's different approach is similar to that of Moeller's study based on cultural history: separating individual and collective memories. Lagrou is analytically correct in distinguishing the making of personal and collective memories, but he goes a step further by treating public and private memories as hermetically separated. The individual memories of resisters, labor conscripts, and Nazi victims are not admitted as evidence. The result is a war experience and a collective memory made by the state and by national organizations in a context of impersonal social and political conditions. Consequently, "memory" has a life of its own but very few human beings behind it.

The studies of Moeller and Lagrou illustrate in some ways two historiographical traditions and practices. Lagrou, critical of a certain rendition of cultural history that has little methodological rigor, employs a comparative approach that focuses on relations among social groups, civil society, and the state. It contributes to a kind of history of memory that is only rarely done in the United States today. When social relations are reduced to "identities" and "memories," then the understanding of society risks being reduced to the presumed intentions of ideas and representations. At the same time, it will not do to explore the making of memory by separating it from people's subjective experiences and representations. We hear in *The Legacy of Nazi Occupation* the impersonal voice of the state, of parliament, or of voluntary organizations, but not the voices of people. And should we not, after all, be like the ogre in the fairy tale, who "knows that wherever he catches the scent of human flesh, there his quarry lies."[41] Moeller's approach, in contrast, lies within memory studies and cultural history as they are predominantly practiced in the United States. He is the ogre who looks for German voices, emotions, and personal memories. He captures the haunted image of the war that hovered over German society, the obsession with national victimhood, and the indifference to Germany's victims. But this approach also reflects a certain disinclination among cultural historians to analyze social relations, identify social groups, and link the experience of a past to the memory of it.

Whether memory is explored with a social or a cultural inflection, in both cases there is a danger that the history of the memory of the Second World War will be reduced to its public, collective features. Marc Bloch, after all, who refused to understand "under the name of collective memory the same reality that is understood under the name of individual memory," acknowledged at the same time that the idea that an "individual memory absolutely separated from social memory is a pure abstraction, indeed makes no sense. ... We are free to use the word 'collective memory,' but it is helpful not to forget that one part at least of the phenomenon that we describe by this term is very simply acts of communication among individuals."[42]

Differently put, a topic that is often missing from memory studies is how people's unexpected, remarkable, and weird perceptions of the past shape the memory of events. Beyond exploring the specific remembrance of this event or the function of that memory, the study of memory should investigate how broader perceptions of the past in society shape the memory of a given event. These kinds of perceptions come into sharp focus in Erna Paris's *Long Shadows: Truth, Lies, and History*, which explores how several contemporary societies (such as post-1945 Germany, France, and Japan) face their troubled past.[43] Paris is not a historian, and here lies the value of her book for capturing wide perceptions of memory. These perceptions, which she shares, are ahistorical mystifications; they reveal much more about contemporary values and beliefs than they do about the past. But that is precisely the point: people think in this way about the past.

The first significant perception of memory and history that emerges from the book is that of "experience," which forms the basis for Paris's gathering information and processing knowledge: "In addition to the usual library research, my sources would be my own experience as a writer. ... I had deliberately chosen the most direct path, and the most intimate."[44] No irony is intended or self-consciousness displayed. In her journey, physical objects function as sorts of time machines.[45] The beliefs that one can "experience" the past and that material objects possess a quality that enables us to "understand" it are fundamental creeds of modern memory. This is wishful thinking, of course. But the point is that this perception is important to the ways people construct memory of past events. The second foundation of popular perceptions of the past in Paris's book takes individual psychology, contra Mannheim, Bloch, and Lagrou, as the model for understanding the collectivity. Paris treats the nation as a patient that goes from amnesia and denial to reawakened memory. This approach transforms collective representations into products of psychological reductionism and functionalism. It is a bad method for understanding the past; but to make sense of the ways

memory is constructed, it is important to acknowledge this popular perception that reduces understanding the past to understanding the self.[46]

There is a gap, then, between historians' accounts of how the Second
World War was remembered and popular perceptions of the past that appear more messy and fantastic.[47] Thus, Lagrou sagaciously warns against
the dangers of "psychologising interpretation" of postwar memory and history.[48] At the same time, it would be useful to know how this ahistorical
understanding of the past common in popular memory helped shape postwar memory. And given the centrality of the notion of "experience" to perceptions of the past, how did this notion shape postwar memory? Moeller
tells of a 1955 study by the ethnographer Alfred Karasek-Langer examining
stories of German expellees from Eastern Europe. These stories originated,
noted the ethnographer, "out of the deepest subconscious, legends of the
end of the world; predictions and prophesies, future-oriented dreams, signs
from heaven and appearances of the Virgin Mary, stories of guilt and atonement, punishments by God, curses and blessings, miraculous salvation, the
return of the dead." [49] How did these shape postwar memory? Viewed in this
way, the notion of memory may be helpful precisely in creating a link between individual misperceptions and collective representations.

The relations between individual and collective memories are inescapably
important, for two reasons: because, while memory is inalienably an individual act, groups do have collective images of the past that lead to political actions with moral consequences; and because individual sensibilities in
modern German history had to relate in a remarkably short time to radically
different memory environments created by opposing ideological regimes.
Memory studies should capture the relations, so characteristic of the twentieth century, between, on the one hand, the power of the state, ideology, and
nationhood to regulate behavior and to codify memory, and on the other,
the habits of minds, mental sensibilities, memories, and internalized values
that formed the ways people shaped their lives, thoughts, and actions.[50] The
two are constantly intermingled, but the narratives of the self—how individuals understand their past behavior, place it in a larger context, justify
it; how they tell it to family and friends; how they change it over time; and
how they translate their memories into social and political actions—are not
quite the same as, and certainly not identical with, the narratives of national
memory acted by states and institutions in the public sphere.

Many scholars of memory have either subsumed individual memory
within collective memory or have collapsed the two into an indistinguish-

able cultural entity—or, most conveniently, have disregarded the problem altogether. One tendency has been to focus on the ways narratives of national memory were made in the built environment, monuments, museums, memorials, films, and literary and scholarly controversies, and how they were expressed in ideology, state policies, public rhetoric, and the public sphere. Such conceptions of memory are profoundly insightful and methodologically sophisticated, taking into account contradictions, negotiations, mediations, and human agency. But they are profoundly insightful from a particular kind of perspective, one that remains focused on the public, on usable memory, on the making of narratives of collectivity for the national collectivity. Yet, to use again the words of Bloch, "one part at least of the phenomenon that we describe by this term [collective memory] is very simply acts of communication among individuals." This history of memory, often expressed in quotidian life, should capture, in an anthropological spirit, the subconscious, legends, predictions, prophesies, dreams, the notions of guilt and atonement, punishments and salvation with which people organized their world. How individuals remember, how their memories shape their changing sense of self, and how this sense of self informs as well as is informed by the surrounding memory culture—this cluster of topics has been consigned to the margins of current memory studies.

Some forms of "communicative memory," to use a term of Lutz Niethammer and Jan Assmann, are based on everyday communication—be it a joke, a piece of gossip, a recollection, or a telling of an experience—that takes place in a car ride, at the family dinner table, at a church gathering, or in the local pub.[51] Communicative memory, as Halbwachs showed, is not arbitrary or secondary to memories of states, monuments, or museums. On the contrary, it is socially mediated and relates to a specific group in place and time. Communicative memory is fundamental to putting personal and group experience in a narrative form. It is complementary to the memory of, say, school textbooks and state ceremonies and is, at times, more tangible and immediate than the abstract memory of national representation. To understand the memory culture of a society, all these elements should be captured, as, for example, in the case of the postwar Germanys, where the functional anti-Nazi memory of the West and East German states stood in direct tension with the happy memories of some of the Nazi years by members of the Hitler Youth, League of German Girls, and Wehrmacht soldiers.

These kinds of memories, at times relegated to the margins of mainstream culture and having a certain underground character, can portray successfully volatile aspects of memory. Perceptions of the Holocaust in Israel

are a good example. The postindependence Israeli state memory of the Holocaust was based mainly on heroism. Bartov provides in *Mirror of Destruction*
a fascinating analysis of the writing of Yehiel Dinur, who wrote under the
pen name Ka-Tzetnik. Dinur's novels, representing the Holocaust as a mixture of kitsch, eroticism, and sadism, illustrated (among other things) Israeli
youth's Holocaust imagination in the period from the 1950s to the 1970s. The
story of Israel's heroic memory receives an unpredictable twist as the rigid
state memory encountered the unruly ways in which Israelis remembered
the Holocaust.[52]

Differently put, histories of German memory should be written not so
much in terms of the visible and public collective national memory of Germany—an investigation that methodologically takes the intentions of people to represent memory in public as its point of departure—but in terms
of an overlap, as well as an incongruity, between individual and collective,
public and private, celebratory and everyday, and official and underground
memory. Memory operates in society through a multiplicity of social times,
social experiences, and representations, in part contradictory and ambiguous, in terms of which people construct the world and their actions.[53] The
coexisting diversity of social times means that different beliefs change at
different paces, that the memory time of the state and nation at times converge and at times diverge from the memory time of individuals and their social groups. This is especially important for understanding modern German
history, which knew quick and radical shifts of ideological regimes. Historical studies of German memory are differentiated and complex—but often
within the framework of the nation, collectivity, and public sphere. An opening up of this methodological field would consist of writing the histories of
German memories as a narrative of incongruities between the sensibilities
of the self and the representations of the collectivity in the context of a multiplicity of social times.

The relation among existing works on German memory illustrates this
point. Some two decades ago Lutz Niethammer and a group of collabora-
tors embarked on a pathbreaking exploration, via oral history, of post-1945
personal memories.[54] It is worth noting how little this work has been integrated into standard narratives of memory based on national memory, Holocaust representations, monuments, built environment, and the like. That
the two are kept separate is a testimony to the agenda of memory studies,
which is often satisfied to recount how the past was publicly represented.
After 1945, for example, embracing the experience of National Socialism in
public became a taboo; it did not fit the heroic official narratives of West Ger-

man democratic and East German antifascist reconstructions. But people remembered the Nazi era positively in the private sphere and everyday life. Members of the Hitler Youth and the League of German Girls remembered many of their experiences fondly, and they resented the radical about-face of the adult establishment and political elite who now rejected the past and asked them to disavow their experience.[55] How did these stories link with East and West Germany's useful memory? Was there a memory short circuit between the two? How did the public, useful memory in the two Germanys shape the everyday memory of fond recollection of National Socialism, and vice versa? The multiplicity of social times overcomes a polarity between, on the one hand, the public, official, institutional, and national memory, and, on the other hand, the everyday, communicative memory that linked individuals to specific social groups (a unit of Wehrmacht soldiers, expellees from eastern Prussia, concentration camp prisoners).[56]

These kinds of historical examples are not unknown, although their theoretical potential is not fully developed. Viewing individual and collective memories as overlapping, rather than as isolated or parallel, provides an opportunity to introduce to memory studies two problems of historical analysis. The first considers the range of possibilities for human action and agency within the constraints of historical conditions. At issue is not an attempt to resolve this problem. Historians can only adhere to a commonsense view that people have agency while they think and act within determined historical conditions; those who believe in complete predestination or total human agency can excel as preachers or sellers of far-fetched fantasies, but not as historians. But historians can illuminate this problem by exploring a particularly revealing historical test case, such as the case of modern German memory. What were the relations, in the history of German memory, between, on the one hand, the quick and at times sudden changes of official, ideological, and state memory between 1918 and 1989 and, on the other hand, people's longer-term memories, sensibilities, and habits of mind? The theme, in a sense, has run throughout this essay: What are the relations between individual memories based on experience and collective memories based on constructing a usable past? Between the Holocaust perpetrators' inner world, shaped in part by their early past, and the immediate surrounding conditions of war and Nazi ideology? Between postwar fond memories of the Third Reich and the anti-Nazi state memories in East and West Germany?

A good starting point for this discussion is the observation of Jean Amery that "no one can become what he cannot find in his memories."[57] In spite of the rapid ideological changes in 1918, 1933, and 1945, Germans used past memories and experiences to make up new identities; they adapted to new conditions by using familiar and recognizable forms of life and thought. But on second thought, the phrase appears incomplete: for one thing that German history teaches us is that people can become—as a result of indoctrination, changing cultural conditions, state policy—what they cannot quite find in their memories, that identities are invented in an amazingly short time, and that, monstrously, people can even do things, such as exterminate others, that they themselves could not even imagine possible a short time before. We become, therefore, what we find in our past memories and experience, but, at the same time, our past memories and experiences are malleable and therefore capable of becoming, under certain historical conditions, the foundations for almost any identity. This complex memory arrangement should be studied in its totality.

The second, related problem of historical analysis raised by the preceding discussion is the way scholars use the notion of "cultural context" to ascertain the "experience" of historical actors. A common practice in memory studies is to extrapolate the meaning of individual experience and habits of mind from the surrounding public sphere and commemorative environment, or what is conveniently called "cultural context." The way people remembered and misremembered their experiences is thus subsumed in the public representations of the past that are removed from quotidian social practices and communicative memory. Habits of mind thus become, in effect, mere reflections of the surrounding context rather than elements in the making of this context. But the memory represented in the "culture context" should not simply be viewed as a reflection of the memory and mentality of the individual, for the two shape each other, especially when the construction of national, public memory is incongruent with the way people make sense of their own experience.[58]

Writing the histories of self and collectivity is associated with writing the histories of private and public memories. These histories should be integrated without imposing congruency. Exploring memory in this context of the diversity of social times that made self and collectivity may give memory studies a fresh start. To do this we need a history of memory that is more daring in its ambition and implication.

I have tried to show in this chapter some of the benefits and problems of using the notions of memory and culture to interpret topics of modern German history. The relations between text and context, and between self and collectivity, have served as leading themes throughout. The way we place memory (the text) into a larger context has interpretative and explanatory consequences. When a German memory or identity is placed within a broader cultural context, it is difficult to see in what way it is a reflection, rather than a shaper, of it. If individual memory, identity, and motivation are only reflections of outside forces (the broader context), then this stands in opposition to a cherished tenet of cultural history and memory studies: the idea that culture and memory not only reflect the social world but shape it as well. I think that this notion is tenable. But I also think that it has recently been accepted uncritically as a self-evident truth. How does the presence of memory act not only as a manifestation of the culture around it but also as a shaper of culture, of beliefs and values, of everyday life, institutional settings, and processes of decision making? Lagrou's self-conscious methodological stand is clear: he views remembrance as "an effect rather than a cause."[59] I doubt that many practitioners of cultural history and memory studies in the United States and elsewhere agree with this view. But it is significant that books on memory are more successful in showing how memory and culture reflect the conditions around them than how they shape them. The notion of memory as scholars commonly use it is more successful as a descriptive device than as an explanatory device.

The notion of memory, to my mind, should be neither so open-ended that it could mean anything at all nor so restricted that it can articulate relations only in the public world. It deserves a certain anarchic quality that will take it beyond the sphere of ideas, ideology, and state and public representations and into the ways people acted, shaped, internalized, and changed it: that anarchic quality locates memory not only in monuments and museums but also in the ways people make it part of behavior and of a mental world, of thinking and acting in the world. And the task of memory studies may profitably be to explore not simply how people remember the past after the fact but also how memory structures behavior and thoughts. Memory can contribute to all these issues, but it cannot act alone. In itself, the notion of memory (and of identity) does not offer any additional explanatory power. Only when linked to historical questions and problems, via methods and theories, can it be illuminating. One way to make it useful, I would like to suggest, is to reconceptualize it so that it can be explored as one cultural practice put in relation to other practices that together make up a mental horizon of society. Placing memory within a broader history that takes cognizance of the coexisting diversity of social times makes it possible to study the making of, and reciprocal relations between, a sense of self and collectivity.

Viewing memory as related to other habits of mind has been one fruitful aspect of several memory studies, when memory was linked, as in the studies of Bartov, Koshar, Lagrou, and Moeller, to perceptions such as victimhood, violence, collectivity, and national decline and rebirth. This creative avenue may provide an impetus to writing the history of memory within a history of sensibilities. The term *histoire des sensibilités* was coined by Lucien Fébvre, who wanted to study collective psychology and the reconstitution of emotions and habits of mind.[60] It has since produced original historical studies, although it has also drawn justified criticism; the intricacy of this historiographical debate is not directly related to our current discussion. What is important is the potential of viewing memory within the mental horizon of a twentieth-century German society and its changing configurations of ideological systems of belief and personal habits of minds. By "history of sensibilities" I mean a history of mental and emotional perceptions such as memory, violence, victimhood, pain, prosperity, love, fear, pleasure, sacrifice, suicide, or killing.

Exploring sensibilities has become in a sense part of German cultural history, even if the term is not used and the historiographical pedigree is not known. Perhaps a self-conscious agenda for this kind of history may provide one additional interpretative framework for twentieth-century Germany. A recent important collection of essays, *Pain and Prosperity: Reconsidering Twentieth-Century Europe*, edited by Paul Betts and Greg Eghigian, illuminates the potential inherent in this approach. "The question for us," write the editors, "is not whether Germany is or should be a land identified exclusively with either Auschwitz or the *Autobahn*, but rather how the ideals and values of pain and prosperity reciprocally informed one another. . . . How have they framed German perceptions of belonging and belief, health and history, frustration and future, self and society? In relating the themes of pain and prosperity in tandem, we believe that the histories of German violence and normality are best explored relationally."[61] The book thus explores how the intertwined history of inflicting and enduring pain while promoting and securing affluence framed German conceptions of identity, memory, selfhood, nationhood, violence, and normality.

A history of the mental horizon of society views the coexisting diversity of social times as coming from various directions. Memory and identity obviously represent ideologies and worldviews that are expressed in the public sphere, public rhetoric, and public practices. Such a representation can change very quickly, as one ideological regime is replaced by another. It describes the public social, cultural, and political surrounding within which people move; it elucidates the attributes of a collective (often national) identity. The emphasis is not on vulgar ideological indoctrination from above (although this is certainly part of this history), but on how people make, negotiate, contest, and dismantle symbolic representations of legitimacy, authority, and values. These can range from the construction in East Berlin of the museum of German history, to the making by leading professionals of a teenager's notion of self in 1950s West Germany, to the making of Nazi travel culture.[62]

At the same time, identity is also made of personal sensibilities, memories, education, mental habits, life experience, and the like. This identity changes rather slowly. One's identity is not changed overnight just because Hitler came to power, Nazi Germany was defeated, the Berlin Wall fell, or communism collapsed (although the public representations of memory do). Changes will be gradual; there are continuities that persist. Some are obvious, others subterranean.[63] The experience of the Hitler Youth and the League of German Girls generation determined their perceptions in the history of East and West Germany. Of course, a neat separation between public representation of identity and personal habits of mind does not exist. The two realms are commingled in constantly changing configurations; they overlap in a diffuse and ubiquitous field of cultural interaction. To my mind, what we call identity belongs neither to the first nor to the second realm, but occupies the middle ground between them.

I would like to illustrate this briefly by returning to the interpretative problem of the Holocaust's perpetrators. An evaluation of the historiography of the perpetrators, by which I mean their motivation during the Holocaust, not their memory after it, must begin with the realization that cultural history and memory studies have been absent from it. Two dominant answers to the question of perpetrators' motivation have emerged in recent years. One emphasizes circumstances and is best represented by the work of Christopher Browning, who argued that ordinary men became killers because of the conditions of the war, its barbarization, peer pressure, and the like. The other explanation emphasizes ideology, worldview, and indoctrination as central to making Germans into killers. Obviously, there is no clear-cut distinction between the two views; in most books this is more a matter of nuances, of where one puts the emphasis. The reality of the killing is thus interpreted either through the barbarization of the war or through the indoctrination of the regime.[64] These factors were no doubt fundamental, but neither peer pressure nor Nazi indoctrination tells us much about sentiments and beliefs. These are important approaches, but they ultimately interpret the interior world of the killers as either too close to the level of ideology and official propaganda or as too passive in succumbing to the horrors of war and the pressures of peers.

The notion of memory can be useful if it is placed within a broader framework of the killers' inner beliefs and their society's system of representations. This kind of history views the Third Reich as linked to emotions and to a balance of sensibilities that existed before and changed throughout. It should explore the social conditions, political actions, and values that are connected to the emotions and balance of sensibilities in a given society. The aim is to discover the arrangement of what is "experienced and what cannot be experienced within a culture at a given moment," while realizing that a true history of sensibilities cannot be disassociated from the contingencies of social and political conditions.[65] The point of departure is that sensibilities are not fixed or peaceful, but dynamic and polemical concepts. The ultimate goal is not to replace the analysis of the ideological component, the conditions of the war, and the disciplinary techniques of the state; rather, the goal is to write a history of twentieth-century Germany whereby the disciplinary techniques of the state and the making of the self interact. Placing people's perceptions of the past within this kind of history of sensibilities may give memory studies an innovative agenda.

It brings us, in a sense, to German history's fundamental interrogation—namely, whether the Holocaust resists certain narrative modalities. Perhaps it does; on one level, no historical narrative will relieve us from the agony of the Holocaust. But it seems to me that this proposed approach might be one possible way of narrating it. Saul Friedländer, who looked gallantly at the personal and the collective meanings of the Holocaust, observed that "most interpreters try to avoid the problem posed by the psychology of total extermination by concentrating exclusively on specific ideological motives (i.e., racial anti-Semitism, racial thinking in general, etc.) or on institutional dynamics"—or, I would add, on the context of the brutal war. These are important factors for understanding the motivations of the perpetrators, he continues, but they leave "an independent psychological residue [that] seems to defy the historian." The "core motivation [of the perpetrators] may well be more decisively attributed to a series of elements" that were not strictly ideological but more psychological and emotional.[66] Exploring a whole range of psychological and emotional motivations and sensibilities of the perpetrators—such as memory, love, hate, life, death, values, morality, goodness, justice, evil, pleasure, pain, collectivity, selfhood, and others—would map out the mental horizon that governed German culture in the Third Reich, the world of the perpetrators.

In "identity," "memory," "sensibilities," and "experience" there is some-thing that cannot be reduced either to ideology or to a passive acceptance of the surrounding conditions. They are akin, in a sense, to the way the great Dutch historian Johan Huizinga saw the notion of play in his study *Homo Ludens*: "In play there is something 'at play' which transcends the immediate needs of life and imparts meaning to the action. If we call the active prin-ciple that makes up the essence of play 'instinct,' we explain nothing; if we call it 'mind' or 'will' [or ideology] we say too much." We should, therefore, "take play as the player himself takes it: in its primary significance. We shall observe the action [of images and imagination] in play itself and thus try to understand play as a cultural factor in life."[67] Approaching German history from this direction may go some way toward resolving the problem of circu-larity in cultural history and memory studies, when "identities" and "memo-ries" are viewed as "proof" of individual experience, motivations, and beliefs.

And perhaps it will also be a small step toward overcoming the human and explanatory gap that exists between the following two statements. On March 10, 1933, Josef Goebbels jubilantly announced during the book burn-ing in Berlin's Opernplatz: "Oh, century, it is a joy to live!"[68] Wisława Szym-borska, the Polish poet and Nobel Prize laureate, has a different view, which captures my sentiments well, in "The Century's Decline":[69]

Our twentieth century was going to improve on the others.
It will never prove it now,

. . . .

Too many things have happened
that weren't supposed to happen,
and what was supposed to come about
has not.

Happiness and spring, among other things,
were supposed to be getting closer.

. . . .

"How should we live?" someone asked me in a letter.
I had meant to ask him
the same question.
Again, and as ever,
as may be seen above,
the most pressing questions
are naïve ones.

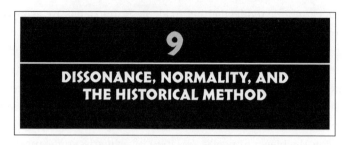

9
DISSONANCE, NORMALITY, AND THE HISTORICAL METHOD

Why Did Some Germans Think of Tourism after May 8, 1945?

Every historical period offers its dissonances: that which actually happened but seems totally incongruent with the conditions of the time and which therefore tests to the limit the interpretative ability of the historian. I would like to present such a dissonance: Germans thinking of tourism following Germany's May 1945 defeat, in the midst of rubble, hunger, and occupation. We think about this period in many terms, but tourism is not one of them. And by denoting the period after May 1945 I do not mean the following years leading to the 1950s, but the following days and weeks. Who dared to think of tourism after May 8, 1945? Is the historian fantasizing? Or is history fantastically unpredictable?

On September 1, 1945, in the city of Emden, a group of tourist activists, soon to be organized into the Regional Tourist Union of East Friesland (Landesverkehrsverband Ostfriesland), asked the Allied occupation authorities for permission to resume activities.[1] Was this a case of Germans who, following the years of war, had become mentally imbalanced? The reverse seems true. On July 20, 1945, five weeks before the Emden case and merely six weeks after Germany's defeat, a meeting took place at Braunschweig's Ministry of State between a senior government official, Dr. Voigt, and the director of a local spa, Mr. Fick, who was also a high official at the Regional Tourist Union of the Harz (Landesfremdenverkehrsverband Harz). On the agenda was the immediate reconstruction of Lower Saxony's tourism industry. The two men asked the British occupying forces for permission to found a tourist association; this was denied, with the argument that the state had more urgent tasks. Tourism activists continued to push their cause through meetings, speeches, and pamphlets. Finally, the British gave in. On March 28, 1946, tourism activists founded the Working Group of Spas and Health Resorts in the Harz (Arbeitsgemeinschaft Harzer Heilbäder and Kurorte).[2]

Obviously, what I term "dissonance" was perceived by some Germans as nothing of the sort.[3] Why did tourism activists revive tourism so quickly after the defeat? This question demands an explanation, for it is simply inconceivable to think that the people who in the summer of 1945 founded the Regional Tourist Union of East Friesland thought only of having fun. There is a familiar historical narrative of West Germany and of travel in the 1950s as an inevitable and rather predictable progress of economic improvement, leading to the development of mass media and consumer culture, and resulting finally in mass tourism. This narrative is true, but it is only half the truth. It can describe the social and economic structures of West Germany and of tourism, but it cannot explain their meanings. And it cannot account for, much less explain, a tourism revival in a devastated society where economic improvement, mass media, and consumer culture belonged to the realm of fantasy more than to the realm of actuality. After all, how many people in Emden could seriously plan and complete a trip in September 1945? Just what, exactly, did these tourism activists think they were doing?

Their evaluations are simultaneously revealing and in need of interpretation. Why did tourism activists use tourism, as we shall see, as a medium to evaluate the Third Reich in terms of progress? What did journalist Anton Luft mean when, following a trip organized by the Nordmark Regional Tourist Union (Landesfremden-Verkehrsverband Nordmark), he said: "It was in June 1948 when we, with DM 40 in our pockets, again began a normal life: we took for the first time [since the war] a press trip to the North Sea."[4] At first blush there is nothing particularly striking about this statement, but on closer reading one realizes that it leaves much to be interpreted. Why did Luft think of tourism as the beginning again of "a normal life"? When exactly was life "normal"? When did it change, and why? What past events or periods did Germans perceive as being not normal?

For the historian, the tourism dissonance is a stroke of luck. First, it enables us to have a glance into a society that often kept its emotions about the recent past under a tight lid. After the defeat, and in some cases already in anticipation of it, there emerged in West Germany a formulaic response as to one's role in and sentiments about National Socialism. Open expression of political and ideological belief in National Socialism was forbidden and, given the denazification policies of the occupying forces, unwise. But it seems improbable that Germans obliterated all traces of the past from pub-

lic and private life. Traces of the past, certainly of one like National Socialism, remained. The question is, where and how to find them? Exploring the
tourism dissonance provides a look beyond what seems at times an impenetrable facade.

Second, the tourism dissonance sharpens our awareness of the procedures by which we attempt to understand the past. There is a gap between
our preconceived assumptions of how Germans should have behaved after
May 8, 1945, on the one hand, and how some of them actually did behave,
on the other. This should make us conscious and critical of our hidden presuppositions, of the attempts to read the past not in its own terms but from
the viewpoint of our concerns in the present, for what I call a dissonance was
perceived differently by some Germans. Tourism activists were levelheaded,
bourgeois professionals who were aware of the gap between talking about
traveling, which associated adventures and exotic places, and the miserable
conditions around them. Still, they and many others, as we shall see, continued to think and talk about tourism. Why? A hidden meaning eludes us.
In fact, thinking about tourism in this period in terms of a dissonance makes
us aware of its limits as an explanatory device. It brings to the fore, paradoxically, the question: Was there really a dissonance? Or better, what, exactly,
constituted this dissonance? Rather than basing our investigation on the expectation that tourism was not congruent with the period, I suggest that we
leave our expectations behind, take seriously Luft's remarks, and think of the
problem not only in terms of dissonance but also in terms of its opposite —
normal life and normality.

It is clear to us what the dissonance is in the tourism case, but how should
we define normality? By "normality" I mean a set of practices and beliefs that
constitute a typical and legitimized pattern of life and code of behavior, for
there is, as we know, nothing normative about normality. What seems normal behavior to one society is rejected as self-evidently absurd or completely
wrong by another. There exists, in a sense, not one single, unified notion of
normality but multiple notions of normalities, for not only among nations
but also within societies there are different ways to conceive of the normal.
The normal is not an appraisal of reality; rather, it is an appraisal of value.
It is based on a process of comparison and analogy with previous experiences as well as with future expectations. For the historian of normality, one
criterion in the selection and interpretation of evidence is the subjective experience and beliefs of contemporaries. In pursuing this approach, I explore
in this chapter the meaning of tourism in West Germany between 1945 and

1960 as a culture of normalities, as a way for Germans to relate to the Nazi period, and to the prewar years (1933–39) in particular, in multiple ways.

I view tourism as the "the exceptional normal," to use the notion of the late Italian microhistorian Edoardo Grendi, when "the smallest dissonances prove to be indicators of meaning that can potentially assume general dimensions."[5] By exploring the dissonance we can get to that which was perceived as normal. This essay is conceived as a thought experiment. Normality and dissonance are taken as experimental variables. These are slippery concepts, but I prefer to try and use them consciously as explanatory devices rather than only as embellished metaphors.

My work is based on an analysis of tourist rhetoric as well as of the tourists' behavior. The methodological problems of getting to the tourist experience are significant. There are many sources on tourist activities, but most are not by tourists. Think about yourself. When you travel, you experience a multitude of emotions, motivations, and fantasies, but you rarely leave behind a trail of written documents. In exploring the tourist experience, the emphasis is on a sensibility that came to be expressed in public action; it calls for a certain mixture of imagination and speculation.

After the war, tourism, as discourse and practice, became a medium with which to think about Germany's recent turbulent past, about that which was normal and exceptional in one's everyday life as well as about national experience. Even before there had been significant actual traveling, there had already been significant tourist rhetoric. And the rhetoric of tourism after 1945, as an image of national belonging, represented several overlapping and at times contrasting attitudes toward National Socialism. The rhetoric was produced by activists in tourist associations and the tourist trade, mostly middle-class men, liberal professionals (writers, lawyers, journalists) and businessmen, who had been connected to the tourist industry for decades, including during the Nazi period. The social composition of German tourism remained unchanged from the 1920s to the 1950s. Most tourists were from the upper and middle classes; some workers traveled, but, overall, workers remained underrepresented. By the mid-1950s, tourism reached the peak levels of the interwar years; the end of the 1950s is considered the beginning of mass tourism in Germany.

Tourist rhetoric depicted the prewar Nazi years as overwhelmingly positive. The fiftieth anniversary of the Tourist Union of the Harz (Harzer Verkehrsverband) in 1954 provided a suitable occasion to draw a historical balance sheet. A special commemorative booklet was published in which members of the tourist union remembered the Nazi period as one of great improvements: "German tourism in general, and with it the tourism in the Harz, experienced strong growth through the decline of unemployment, the general economic activity, and the rapid increase of motor vehicles."[6] The visible symbol of progress was the "Harz highway" project: "In terms of landscape, the highway is one of the most beautiful in northern and central Germany, and will be a particular attraction for motor vehicle tourism in the Harz."[7] The booklet especially mentioned Dr. Fritz Todt, "whose unfailing interest and energy" were invaluable for tourism development.[8] Todt was appointed by Hitler in 1933 as general inspector for German roads and charged with building a new network of motorways, the famous *Autobahnen*. But Todt was not exactly an innocent transportation expert. He joined the Nazi Party as early as 1923 and was Hitler's personal friend. In 1940 he became minister of armaments, becoming the leading force behind the war economy. (Albert Speer replaced him when he died in a plane crash in 1942.) None of this appeared in the Harz association's booklet. The reason lies not, one has the impression, in a premeditated plan to deceive but rather in the perception that there was nothing especially wrong with the *Autobahn* program and, by extension, the regime that supported it.

Indeed, postwar descriptions of tourism in the Third Reich were painted either in the professional language of the trade, which had been in place since the beginning of modern tourism in the nineteenth century, or in a poetic language that is part of tourism discourse everywhere. Either way, the language of tourism was selective and disclosed nothing of several dramatic patterns of German society in those years: accommodation with a murderous system, striving for world domination, and persecution of Jews. For traveling in the Third Reich, similar to every other sphere of life, was an integral part of the period's systematic racial terror. The 1935 Nuremberg Laws forbade most hotels from accommodating Jewish guests.[9] A decree by the Ministry of the Interior from July 24, 1937, set extreme restrictions on the presence of Jews in spas; an additional decree from June 16, 1939, made participation impossible. Given what we know of Nazi ideology, this information is quite predictable. More significant is the evidence of grass-roots activity, before the Nazi legislation, to remove Jews from tourist sites and hotels. Massive discrimination started in the fall of 1934. The case of Neustrelitz stood for many communities in Germany during that period: the owners of the town's hotels and guesthouses together with the local tourist and transportation bureau agreed "to post everywhere the inscription: Jews are unwelcome." In contrast to the silence over this past, postwar descriptions of the conditions of tourism under Allied occupation were dramatic, often expressing self-pity. Thus, one writer in 1954 tells us, conditions for the revival of tourism in the Harz after 1945 were terrible: first, all beds were confiscated by the occupation forces. Then, "the occupying army disposed of 480 percent more than the annual, normal timber production in the Harz forest." The result: "It seems as if fate overtook not only human beings but also nature."[10] West Germans seemed to have felt more affected emotionally by the years of postwar reconstruction than by the prewar years of the Third Reich.[11]

At the same time, tourism rhetoric represented the Nazi period in a commingling of distancing and victimhood; the Nazi Party was thus a foreign entity that imposed a dictatorship and a war on an innocent people. The German Central Tourist Association (Deutsche Zentrale für Fremdenverkehr), founded in 1948 as West Germany's national tourist organization, articulated this creed clearly in the first postwar tourist campaign aimed at foreigners, the "Goethe Year 1949" campaign. The organization complained that the task of bringing tourists to Germany was very difficult

> because the years of the Nazi dominion made Germany the least beloved country in the world. . . . The German Central Tourist Association must show foreign tourists a way that will enable them to meet again the true Germany. To be sure, Goethe's Germany was brutally trampled on and degraded in the years of tyranny. But not all Germans took part in this maltreatment. The true Goethe's Germany was, is, and remains immortal and indestructible. In this Germany we believed in the period of rape [*Vergewaltigung*], in this Germany we believe today.[12]

Significantly, during the same period when "rape" became an accusatory metaphor to describe the Allied occupation of Germany—as well as a harsh reality for many German women, especially in the Soviet zone—the German Central Tourist Association chose this same word to describe the Nazi regime. It thus achieved two aims: it distinguished between the Nazis and the Germans, as if Nazis were not "true" Germans; and it drew a semantic likeness between the Allies and the Nazis.[13] West Germans made tourism a medium to consider the nation an innocent victim of war and occupation.[14] According to this view, National Socialism was an aberration in the normal German history of cultural and artistic accomplishments.[15]

I have described the discourse of tourism after the war as a way to embrace as well as deny the Third Reich. The previously common argument in historical literature that the Germans kept the Nazi past hermetically sealed and silenced does not stand up to historical evidence. We may not like everything that Germans had to say about their experiences during National Socialism, but they were not silent about them. At the same time, they remembered the past selectively because distortions, lies, and evasions are the bases of identity. But what kind of identity? We should not just criticize the distortions as misunderstandings of reality or attempts to repress and conceal, but instead try to illuminate their function and meaning.

Was the meaning of post-1945 tourist revival a flight from reality into a nostalgic past? The problem with this view is that the subjective meaning of the tourist experience is largely lost, whereas concepts such as irrationalism, repression, and manipulation take center stage as explanatory devices. Tourism, like festivals, religious ritual, art, and cinema, is not a flight from reality but a symbolic practice and representation to understand and negotiate with it. Tourists are not social scientists: "The claim that they should understand the world in an objective way fails to appreciate their motivations for and the character of modern traveling."[16] Rather, the question is why did Germans choose tourism as a medium to think about the Third Reich? What kind of emotions and recollections did Third Reich tourism evoke in the post-1945 era? To answer this question we have to go back to the tourist experience in the Nazi era.

After 1933, as a result of the cumulative effects of Nazi policies and the improved world economy, German tourism flourished. The Nazis' tourist activities ranged broadly; more Germans traveled, an experience that stood in stark contradiction to the Depression years. The 1934 Oberammergau Passion Play, for example, attracted 400,000 tourists (including 60,000 from abroad). The 1936 winter and summer Olympic Games in Garmisch-Partenkirchen and Berlin put Germany on the map and attracted, in Garmisch-Partenkirchen alone, more than 1 million tourists.[17] Between the Depression and the early 1960s, 1937 was the best tourist year.

More important, the improvement of tourism between 1933 and 1939 reflected on the ability of the Nazis to improve social, material conditions. For ordinary Germans, "Strength through Joy" (Kraft durch Freude or KdF)—the plan to give every worker a paid vacation—became the most popular program instituted by the regime.[18] This sentiment is well illustrated in the detailed reports of opposition groups that reached the exiled leaders of the Social Democratic Party (SOPADE). The SOPADE reports are, as is well known, an excellent source on life in Nazi Germany, although they have one significant problem: they naturally emphasized prevalent opposition to and discontent with the regime. The reports on the KdF, however, are different in tone and content, which makes them a valuable source to understand the attitudes toward the KdF and, more generally, the link between tourism and the Nazi regime. One report stated that "some KdFlers say: '[N]ever before did we receive such a thing from the state. Never before could we go out from our hole.' Especially women keep telling for months on end about the beautiful trips and thus also excite their friends and companions."[19] Certainly, many longtime socialists refused to be impressed by the "KdF ballyhoo,"[20] but many saw no contradiction in holding both views, namely, that unions were important but that KdF tours were a positive novelty. "It was like a Grimm fairy tale, we were like one big happy family," gushed one KdFler about his trip years after the fact, in the 1980s—when it was not politically correct to praise National Socialism.[21] The KdF program, and the improvement of tourism in general, endowed the Nazi regime with legitimacy and associated the prewar years with improvement.

Traveling raised the expectations for those who traveled, and even more so for those who did not. One important result of the KdF was that by 1939, although most workers still did not travel, vacation was perceived by workers as an established right, an entitlement. Tourism for workers was thus associated with social progress and mobility. "For young and old alike," Mary Nolan has perceptively argued, "perceptions of the 'good' and the 'bad' times were based more on the availability of employment and the prospects of security than on political events."[22] Significantly, KdF travel was not necessarily associated with Nazi ideology. One worker, who was a communist sympathizer until 1933, recalled after the war that the KdF "was a real vacation. It had usually nothing to do with [propaganda and politics]. It was similar to the way one goes on vacation today. People were together, laughing, singing, dancing."[23] Valued as an entitlement, traveling belonged in a realm beyond politics and ideology, as part of modern life.

After 1945, to return to where this discussion began, talking, thinking, and practicing tourism was, among other things, a medium to capture the perceived good years of the Nazi past, the prewar years.[24] The revival of tourist activities after 1945 was often viewed as a return to the good old traveling days of the late 1930s. This is why tourism and the KdF always figure prominently in post-1945 oral histories about personal experiences under National Socialism: they were viewed as a measure of normality and improvement. In a 1951 opinion poll, half of the West Germans questioned viewed the Nazi prewar years as Germany's best years.[25] There was no more talk, according to the Public Opinion Institute (Institut für Demoskopie), "of German re-

birth or of racial awakening. . . . [T]hese bits of Third Reich are antiquated."
Many Germans put what they considered the "politics" of the period aside,
that is, the terror, mass murder, and war, and remembered the prewar years
as positive: "guaranteed pay packet, order, KdF, and the smooth running of
the political machinery. . . . [T]hus 'National Socialism' makes them think
merely of work, adequate nourishment, KdF, and the absence of 'disarray'
in political life."[26] It is therefore not surprising that tourist brochures of the
1950s looked purposefully similar to those of the 1930s to associate a familiar experience; the first postwar production of the Oberammergau Passion
Play in 1950 was directly modeled on the 1934 production, and its poster was
adopted as well.[27]

This was, then, the meaning of Luft's statement that the beginning of
postwar travel was associated with normal travel during the pre-1939 period,
interspersed with years of war and occupation. Viewed in this light, the discourse on tourism appears not so much a dissonance but a link to connect
the present aspiration to normality with what was perceived as the past experience of it.

But why was tourism perceived as a measure of normality? One reason is
that identification with tourism was based on the intimate link between it
and everyday life. Tourism is a refuge from the routine and standardization
of modern everyday life, but at the same time it also is a practice that (sometimes) confirms one's way of life in comparison between oneself and the
other. The cultural process behind tourism, therefore, is similar to the one
behind normality. In traveling, we do not appraise an objective condition of
the other but our own subjective image of it. Traveling is based on a process
of comparison and analogy between our own values and those of the other.
As a result, and as a practice of everyday life, tourism places subjective meanings and experiences of concrete settings within larger contexts and bigger
developments. It places our daily life and practices—of small occurrences,
norms, behaviors, and ways of thinking—within the history of "big events."

Traveling, as a desire or an actuality, reflected in a sense the ways personal
experience shifted with the tide of big historical events and developments
between 1933 and the postwar period. In the normal life of peace, between
1933 and 1939, things improved, one could travel, and more people did travel.
Then came the first years of war, between 1939 and 1941. These were peculiar
years: the war was a source of obvious anxiety, but Germany did win on all
fronts; fewer people traveled, but travel did take place.[28] This period was followed by the years of total war, defeat, and occupation: in the end, there was
no Reich, no sovereign Germany, and certainly no travel. Finally, there came

the economic recovery, political sovereignty, material improvement, and the resumption of travel in the 1950s. Thinking about German history using the metaphor of tourism thus corresponded to certain personal experiences and conditions of everyday life.

Moreover, because tourism was perceived as apolitical, it was a useful image in thinking about the Nazi period: it made it possible to hold on to one's life experience in the prewar years while dissociating oneself from the "politics" of the regime. This is perhaps the reason why the connection between travel, as an image of normal life, and National Socialism became a fundamental mainstay in the way Germans after 1945 have described their lives in the 1930s. This link was used, as we have seen, by tourist associations until the 1950s; it was confirmed in the 1970s and 1980s by the oral history project under the direction of Lutz Niethammer, and was again on display most recently in the television series *Heimat Front*.[29]

More broadly conceived, the link between tourism and normal life appears fundamental in the modern world because tourism functions as a social and cultural activity with enormous symbolic power to legitimize political systems. It is viewed as an entitlement that reflects on the ability of the system to keep the promise of a better life. East and West Germany provide good examples: in 1953, 83 percent of West Germans said in an opinion poll that travel was not a luxury anymore. Still, even in 1960 only one-third of West Germans actually traveled. Thus, although most West Germans did not travel in 1960, most were convinced of the ability of the social market economy to make travel a normal part of modern life. In East Germany, by contrast, the desire to travel subverted the state that prevented its citizens from traveling freely. The end is well known: the East German state collapsed in 1989 as people marched through its cities shouting "Visafrei nach Hawaii" (visa-free to Hawaii). In short, in the modern world people view the ability to travel as a mark of normality.

A word of caution is in order here. Tourism means different things to different people. Traveling has many motivations: people may travel to get away from it all, to forget the past, or just to have fun at the seaside or an Alpine resort. Obviously, I do not argue that all Germans traveled after 1945 to remember the Third Reich, or that my interpretation in any way exhausts the varied meanings of travel in modern society. My aim has been to present one aspect of travel, and how it can illuminate attitudes toward the Third Reich.

The argument posed in this chapter, namely, the links among travel, normality, and perceptions of the past, is certainly speculative. Its essence, in a way, is about the importance of historical investigation into the relative sensibility of happiness between the 1930s and 1950s. It requires further empirical evidence that may, in turn, alter some of its conceptualizations. I am aware of the dilemma I have faced in writing this essay: to provide a solid evidentiary base in order to achieve limited results or to provide a weak evidentiary base in order to achieve original results.[30] My aim was to open new doors and propose new connections. There are several methodological rewards to the argument as well as the approach of this essay, I would argue, when one uses it to think about the period of the 1930s to the 1950s. It is to this topic, then, that I now turn.

Until recently, the common historiographical view has been that West Germans after 1945 repressed the Nazi past. Wolfgang Benz reflects the thinking of a whole interpretive school when he argues that "National Socialism was treated by a whole generation with collective silence and widespread amnesia."[31] The body of work produced by this approach has significantly illuminated how Germans attempted to master their past and how most of them refused to own up to it. In principle, the argument that (some) Germans repressed (some aspects) of the Nazi years is unassailable. But the repression thesis appears to be an exemplary case of the dangers of imposing a laudable moral cause on the vicissitudes and contingencies of historical and human affairs; it has been less successful in explaining Germans' changing attitudes toward National Socialism than in providing a sweeping condemnation of post-1945 German society. As a consequence, the repression approach was often content with an explanation that ignored the complex negotiations between remembering and forgetting. It paid little attention to what Germans did remember of the Nazi past and was quick to use as explanatory devices the terms "denial" and "repression," which are infinitely tricky in elucidating human motivations. Most Germans instead commingled silence and expression in multiple, ambiguous ways. By looking at relative sentiments of happiness and different perceptions of normality, we may learn more about human values and beliefs, and open new possibilities for studying how Germans came to terms with the past.

Moreover, most studies on coming to terms with the past focus on artifacts made specifically to represent the Nazi past (such as novels, films, museums, monuments, and so forth) after 1945. This is certainly an important approach, but it has clear temporal and subject-matter limitations. A true history of coming to terms with the past, it seems to me, implies writing a history of sensibilities: it implies discovering the configuration of what is and what is not considered being normal and happy within a culture at a given moment. This kind of history should, first, encompass the peace and war years, and the postwar era. In other words, studying how Germans came to terms with the Nazi past is a historical topic that should not be bound to the post-1945 era. Patterns of remembrance, perceptions, and sensibilities existed across 1945. In the 1950s, explicit ideological support of National Socialism and anti-Semitism became taboo.[32] But did public silence mean self-conviction in private? Were the 1950s closer in this respect to the Third Reich or to the emerging West German political culture of post-1968?

These are important questions that are not always posed by new studies that have recently shifted the argument concerning postwar German memories from the emphasis on repression to the complex argument about different uses of the Nazi pasts.[33] These studies are mostly interested in how things happened in the postwar era, whereas a history of sensibilities of normality and relative happiness could trace values and beliefs across the signposts of political history (1933, 1945, 1949).[34] A history of coming to terms with the past as a history of sensibilities should go beyond the predictability of certain cultural practices and artifacts. In West Germany, as stated, a candid discussion of National Socialism could not take place in the public sphere. Discretion dictated that certain views about the Nazi regime could not be expressed in public, although they were the norm in private life and everyday behavior. Consequently, we should look for traces of National Socialism not only in artifacts and practices created intentionally to represent it, but also in social practices and representations where they were not directly discernible and fairly unpredictable. These kinds of sources, practices, and representations may ultimately reveal more about attitudes and beliefs.[35]

It is in light of this consideration that I chose to undertake a study of tourism. Tourism is a social practice that takes place in public but has an essential component linked to private life and individual decision making, for the motivations, the impressions, and the experiences of traveling are absolutely private (although the tourist may decide to share them with others). Moreover, tourism, while supported by governments in all political regimes, is a pillar of modern popular culture; it thus enables us to explore intimate values as well as, of course, official posturing. As a social and cultural practice that is determined by experienced memories, not only by the raison d'être of raison d'état, tourism may reveal what people intimately thought about National Socialism (West German government officials, by contrast, *had* to make certain critical statements about the Nazis for foreign consumption). Regimes can forbid people from traveling, but no regime has yet found the trick to force people to travel; there is an element of free will and agency in traveling that is advantageous for the historian who looks for clues about motivations and beliefs.

We have found some of these clues in the pages that describe the multiple attitudes toward National Socialism. The German Central Tourist Association, an official mouthpiece of West Germany's newly instituted democracy, depicted the Nazis as outsiders, invaders of the true Germany symbolized by Goethe. But the members of the Harz Tourist Union, by contrast, remembered fondly the Nazi prewar years, whereas others viewed the years of war and occupation as terrible but were uncritical of the pre-1939 dictatorship. Thus, in a society that silenced public expressions of support for National Socialism, thinking of tourism functioned as a medium to recapture the inalienable personal experience during the Third Reich. In this respect, the fact that tourism was viewed as apolitical was an important factor, for thinking of tourism was a way to connect with one's experience under National Socialism without being politically incorrect.

I would like, finally, to use this discussion of dissonance and normality as an occasion to reflect on the procedures by which we understand the Nazi past and, in particular, on the problem of the place of the Third Reich and the Holocaust within history. Few if any historical periods have been documented and studied so comprehensively as the Nazi era. Our knowledge of the period is so vast that it is difficult to see how the unearthing of new documents can revolutionize our interpretations. (Interpretative revolutions in the study of National Socialism may happen, but they depend on asking new questions, not on finding new documents.) Even the finding of the single most coveted document in modern German history—an order signed by Hitler ordering the Final Solution—will change little. Who, among people who seek truth and who look at the evidence with an open mind, would doubt the centrality of Hitler to the extermination of the Jews? But in spite of this vast knowledge, the Third Reich and the Holocaust present enormous problems of historical understanding and explanation. Our interpretation of the Nazi regime, therefore, is not dependent on finding new evidence but on thinking critically on the methods we use to approach this past.

In this respect, the notion of normality has been central to thinking about the Nazi regime. But using the notion of normality in German historiography has been less fruitful in producing new insights and novel approaches than in illustrating the problems of this historiography.[36] Let me discuss briefly the work of three historians, whose work I hold in high regard. In his debate with Martin Broszat over the historicization of the Nazi regime, Saul Friedländer argued that the Third Reich could not be regarded or analyzed with the same methods as normal history. "Writing about Nazism is not like writing about sixteenth-century France."[37] With this statement, Friedländer is making two points. First, we lack a sense of detachment from the Nazi era, because the enormity of the crime prevents an honest historian from writing about it with a sense of neutrality. This is true but not unique to the Holocaust. Other historical cases present a similar problem of lack of detachment. One can think of the Palestinian catastrophe of 1948–49, of Vichy France, and of Stalin's Russia. Religious history may provide the best examples: Jews and Christians still argue over the historical meaning of a Jewish prophet who founded a church, whereas Catholics and Protestants still argue over the meaning of a heretic who split the Church to refound Christianity. In a sense, Friedländer is correct, for all agree that Nazism is relevant to our lives in a way sixteenth-century France is not, while acknowledging that writing on any historical event is, on a fundamental level, unlike writing about another. But it seems more accurate to argue that on a spectrum of events that test our interpretative abilities, that prevent the detachment necessary for the historian's craft, the Holocaust is an extreme case but not a case *sui generis*. Second, for Friedländer the meaning of his statement is moral: the Nazi regime was unique because it determined who should and who should not inhabit the world. *"This, in fact, is something no other regime, whatever its criminality, has attempted to do."*[38] This is true. But criminality is not a useful yardstick to determine what is or is not part of history; it is part of history, not extraneous to it. Immoral things are also human, although not humane. However big our moral repulsion, this in itself cannot be a historical yardstick to determine what was normal. Normality is thus used by Friedländer as a powerful moral metaphor and yardstick, and less so as a historical tool.[39]

Other historians have seen the Holocaust as abnormal to a degree that puts it beyond the human ability to understand and explain. Dan Diner wrote: "Auschwitz is a no-man's land of understanding, a black box of explanation, a vacuum of extrahistorical significance which sucks in attempts at historiographic interpretation."[40] This statement postulates two kinds of histories: the history of all human events and the outside-of-history story of the Holocaust. Abnormal, outside of time, and in a sphere all its own, the Holocaust thus becomes a matter of belief.

But even historians who pleaded to historicize the Nazi regime found it, in parts, abnormal. Thus, Martin Broszat argued in a seminal essay that alongside the barbarism of the regime were patterns of social "normality"—long-term modernization tendencies, such as patterns of leisure, social policy, and plans for universal insurance—that were influenced by Nazism in various ways but existed before and remained after.[41] This context of a normality of everyday life, stated Broszat, cannot be reduced to being simply an epiphenomenon of Nazi ideology. At the same time, Broszat conceded that "regarding the crimes perpetrated against the Jews . . . everyday life in the Nazi period was probably not as normal after all as it might appear to have been on the surface."[42] But because normality is used but never defined, one wonders what is normal everyday life and where can it be found in the 1930s? In communist Russia, with the terror, trials, and Gulags? In Fascist Italy? Or in America's Jim Crow South? By arguing that everyday life connected to racism and extermination was not normal, Broszat sharply separates normality from barbarity and assumes a schizophrenic existence of everyday life.[43] Perhaps more important, by arguing for the abnormality of some aspects of everyday life and, by extension, of the Nazi period, Broszat undermined his own argument about the integration of the Nazi period into history: either the Third Reich is part of European historical development or it stands outside it as abnormal; it cannot be both.

The notion of normality used by these historians works much better as a moral metaphor than as an analytical tool—as an abstraction whose consequence is to make the Holocaust autonomous of time, space, and agency, than as an illuminating concept. The problem is that normality is taken as a presupposition, not as an object of study; a definition of normal history is assumed to be self-evident and universally accepted. The assertion of abnormality thus becomes a self-fulfilling prophecy. The three cases above impose a morally clear although analytically vague category on a society that had in fact quite different ideas about normality. I wonder whether these historians do not write a history that is quite different from the history that was actually created by people in the past.[44] The Holocaust poses a profound challenge to our ability to understand and explain the human condition; we do often describe it, struggling in vain to find the right words, as abnormal, as an event that is impossible to grasp and to fathom. But, and this is the main point, we should not mistake a term that best describes our own problems in understanding the Nazi regime as a term that actually explains the Nazi regime. Our use of the notion of normality reflects our own thinking about the Holocaust and the perceived enormity of the event.[45]

Instead, the notion of normality can be useful for our historical understanding, first, when we approach it not as a being but as an object of exploration.[46] We need to investigate the relation between historical understanding to the problematizing of normality, to write the history of the formation of normality as an analytical category and heuristic device in our thinking about the Nazi regime. For there is nothing obvious or self-explanatory about the claim, by historians who are trained to look at the past critically, that the Nazi regime was abnormal. The problem is not whether the regime was really abnormal but whether normality (as it is used) has any value as an explanatory device, and how and why has it come to be so prevalent in the historical discourse about the Nazi era. The idea that the Nazi period was not normal (or not entirely normal) has become a ritualistic statement that is at times contradicted by the very analysis of those who argue it. In his balanced book *The Nazi Dictatorship*, Ian Kershaw gives a masterful analysis of our understandings and interpretations of the Nazi regime since the war. His book demonstrates how our thinking about the dictatorship and its crimes, in spite of the profound problems it poses, has developed and been refined. Still, he adds that "Arguably, indeed, an *adequate* explanation of Nazism is an intellectual impossibility."[47] This has the disarming validity of common sense. Arguably, an adequate explanation of the rise of Christianity or the Reformation is also an intellectual impossibility. And was there an adequate explanation of the Reformation sixty years after 1517? Is there now, for that matter?

My point is not that an adequate explanation of the Holocaust is possible but that—if we assume that adequate historical explanations are at all possible, which is open for debate—the Holocaust is not governed by different explanatory categories from other epoch-making historical events. It seems more fruitful to recognize that historical explanations are always complex, incomplete, and still under construction, and that in this respect, again, the Holocaust is an extreme case but not one that stands alone. Kershaw further argues that "it seems plain that . . . the Nazi era . . . cannot be regarded as a 'normal' part of history in the way that even the most barbarous episodes of the more distant past can be viewed. The emotions which rightly still color attitudes to Nazism obviously rule out the detachment with which not only sixteenth-century France (Friedländer's example) but also many more recent events and periods in German history and in the history of other nations can be analyzed."[48] But Kershaw's own book demonstrates that, with all the difficulties, a great amount of historically detached work has been done, also about the Holocaust. And why should we accept detachment from subject matter as a yardstick to determine historical normality? This way of relating Nazism and history seems to invert the relations between cause and effect in historical explanation. It is not that historians argue that National Socialism is abnormal because they have succeeded in explaining it as such, but that they argue that it is abnormal because all our other explanations are unsatisfactory.

I chose to discuss Kershaw's work because he is one of the most distinguished historians of Nazi Germany of his generation. That he also clings to ritualistic statements about the abnormality of the Nazi regime, which add little to historical understanding, is illustrative of a problem of historical argumentation. In the same paragraph where he argues that the Nazi era cannot be regarded as normal, Kershaw writes that the problem of detachment

> does not rule out the application of "normal" historical method [are there abnormal historical methods?] to the social, as well as to the political, history of Germany in the Nazi era. . . . [A] wide-ranging interpretative analysis of the Nazi era based on such methods . . . [can] be written. And, while the historian's relationship to his subject of study is different in the case of Nazism than, say, in that of the French Revolution, it could be argued that, even accepting the uniqueness of the Holocaust, the problems posed by "historicization" are little different in theory to those facing the historian of say, Soviet society under Stalin.[49]

If we can write a wide-ranging interpretative analysis of the Nazi regime, why assume that adequate explanation is an intellectual impossibility? If the problems the Nazi era poses are shared by other historical cases, what is the historical significance of viewing it as abnormal? If a historical topic, however extreme, can be put into a narrative, subjected to interpretative analysis, and compared and contrasted with other historical cases, what, then, is the meaning of arguing that it "cannot be regarded as a 'normal' part of history"?

In fact, the idea of normal history is inadequate. Let us assume, for the sake of argument, that Stalinism and Nazism represent abnormal European histories. One would like to know, then, which countries represent the "norm": Belgium and Portugal? No offense, but Russia and Germany do seem more consequential to modern European history. As for England and France, the view that their history should be seen as normal was demolished two decades ago by David Blackbourn and Geoff Eley. And to write the history of twentieth-century Europe as a self-congratulatory, teleological story of freedom and democracy is a mistake. From the vantage point of 1940, the future of Europe was seen as one of totalitarianism, utopian ideologies, and radical attempts at social engineering based on class and race.[50] The notion of normal history is linked to the Third Reich by a moral concern, which is laudable but has little to advance historical clarification. Kershaw's analysis is always historical, but there exists a point in his discussion after which the logical conclusions of his own argument are not drawn, and instead we fall into a language that has become so familiar in describing the Nazi era, a language that, in one way or another, against the best of intentions, puts the Nazi era beyond history. By questioning our own historical understanding and use of categories, we may cross the impenetrable threshold that sanctifies the Holocaust and puts it and the Nazi era in a historical plain all their own.

The notion of normality can be useful in another, closely related way, namely, by writing the history of the notion from the subjective point of view of perpetrators, survivors, and subsequent generations, as well as in its manifestations in popular culture. For the Nazi regime, and the Holocaust in particular, were viewed by many people as singular right from the beginning. Heinrich Himmler expressed this sentiment when he addressed a group of ss men at Posen in 1943 about the extermination of the Jews: "In our history, this is an unwritten and never-to-be written page of glory." [51] Survivors experienced the concentration camps as, to use the evocative description of the author Ka-Tzetnik in the Adolf Eichmann trial, another planet, "Planet Auschwitz. . . . The inhabitants of this planet had no names, they had no parents or children. They did not dress as people do here, they were not born and did not give birth; they breathed according to different laws of nature, they did not live according to the laws of the world here and they did not die." [52] After the war, but especially from the 1960s and 1970s onward, the uniqueness of the Holocaust became a mainstay of public memory in Israel and among American Jews, among others. This sentiment has been represented in popular culture by annual trips to Poland's concentration camps by young Israelis and American Jews, in films and novels, and in the sanctified place awarded to survivors' testimony. Rather than simply citing these views on the uniqueness of the Holocaust, we need to explore the history of this notion, how it evolved from the perceptions of perpetrators and survivors between 1933 and 1945 and our own days, what have been its ideological and political uses in different contexts and countries, and how it has been linked to popular culture.

I raised doubt about the use of the notion of normality as a historical explanatory device while at the same time, given the centrality of the notion of normality and uniqueness in thinking about the Nazi regime, pleading to write the history of this term. To avoid misunderstanding, let me state my argument again, in different words. The Nazi era and especially the Holocaust are historical cases that test the limits of our interpretations, extreme events that call into question our ability to explain the past in any satisfactory way.[53] This, I believe, is beyond doubt, and to argue differently is either naive or sinister. The question is, Where do we go from here? One way would be to negotiate, based on this premise, between the Nazi era and the historical method while arguing, at one point along the way, that our ability to understand is not simply limited but that in fact the era stands beyond our comprehension. This view operates within a territory that interprets National Socialism within history while at the same time assigning it, implicitly or explicitly, to an ahistorical realm. A second way is to remain, however difficult it is both emotionally and historically, within the territory of the historian and to attempt to elucidate the era only by negotiating between it and history. There will be many frustrations along the way, many false starts and dead ends. The consolation of assigning the era to a land beyond history is unavailable. The task of remaining within the territory of the historian is more difficult, at times unforgiving, and always unsatisfactory, because historical explanations, as has been observed, are always complex, incomplete, and still under construction, and with the case of the Nazi era and the Holocaust an explanation, however convincing, will continue to evoke in us a sense of moral inadequacy, for the victims of the Holocaust died in complete innocence.[54]

The argument that a historical event, enacted by men and women within known boundaries of space and time, should be regarded as an integral part of history, not as abnormal or outside of historical understanding, is so obvious that if one were to make it about any historical event one would be viewed as naive. But the Holocaust is one historical event about which this statement needs to be said. The reason is that, with regard to the Holocaust, we tolerate statements that are in the realm of faith, therapy, and theology but not in the realm, *sensu strictu*, of history. This is precisely because the Holocaust was a foundational past; historians should study the use of these beliefs to understand the Holocaust, without confusing popular use with explanation. Arguing that the Holocaust is unique and incomprehensible has become part of civic liturgy and, in some quarters, indeed a demonstration of profundity and thoughtfulness. But certainly the Holocaust, as a historical event, stands not outside of history. The fact that the regime and especially the Holocaust have been viewed as extraordinary is significant: it tells us about the depravity of the event and its meaning for the human condition. But the fact that people saw it as unique does not make it, from the historian's point of view, unique. The meaning of history, as a discipline based on methods, theories, and evidence that attempts to find meanings over time and across cultures, cannot be reduced to the subjective sentiments of people. I myself pursue in this chapter an approach that explores the subjective beliefs of post-1945 West Germans with regard to notions of dissonance and normality. But this evidence was not taken at face value; rather, it was subjected to historical questions. Writing the history of the relations between the Holocaust and the notions of uniqueness and incomprehensibility may enhance our self-consciousness as to our own relations to the Holocaust.

I should say what my own view about the Holocaust and history is. The Holocaust is a part of German history, an extreme part but an integral part nonetheless, that is bound, similar to all other historical events, by patterns of explanations based on evidence. To arrive at such an explanation is, as we all know, an arduous task, but it is ultimately possible. The Holocaust represents a rupture in modes of representation and speech, in the faculty to describe meaningfully that which happened, and yet this rupture cannot be, in fundamental terms, considered total and absolute, for the language of rupture itself is intimately connected to the set of images, representations, experiences, and languages that existed before. Survivors, perpetrators, subsequent generations, and even scholars have often perceived "Planet Auschwitz" as outside of time. But the sense of rupture is predicated on the ability to articulate past experience, from which one is severed. The sense of being outside time, outside of history, is predicated on the ability to articulate the notion of being inside time, of being part of history. In this sense, continuity and the notion of being within time—that is, the notion of living within history—is constitutive of the sense of rupture itself.

Admittedly, this has been a long journey from post-1945 tourism to the place of the Nazi era in history. What began as an exploration of a dissonance turned into a reflection on normality. The thread of this chapter was how to think about normality as a historical object, namely, the ways it was perceived by Germans from the 1930s to the 1950s, and as a historiographical object, namely, the ways it was used by historians. The topic of travel was my vehicle for this discussion. What links the theme of traveling and May 8, 1945, with the historical explanation of the Nazi past? One link, on the historical level, is the Germans' sense of having been victims while having been perpetrators. The search for normality after violence (done to Germans and done by Germans) may be seen as a way of putting those difficult and uncomfortable experiences behind them; the selective view of tourism seems to fit in well here. Another link, more broadly, is an awareness, via a discussion of normality, of the danger of psychological anachronism, the greatest historical error, to my mind. Normality, however defined and understood, has been posed as a problem by Germans in the 1940s and 1950s as well as by historians since; it has a past and a present. Historians have explored in the past generation a dazzling array of new topics, such as miracles, sexuality, asylums, witchcraft, and fear, but a history of normality, as far as I know, has yet to be written. The philosopher Georges Canguilhem, Michel Foucault's mentor, observed in his classic essay *The Normal and the Pathological* (1943) that "The normal is not a static or peaceful, but a dynamic and polemical concept."[55] This chapter, I hope, elucidated precisely that, although I am well aware that there are no final words on normality, however lucid, or shall we say "normal," they may seem.

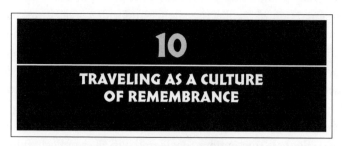

10

TRAVELING AS A CULTURE
OF REMEMBRANCE

Traces of National Socialism in West Germany, 1945–1960

For a long time, too long perhaps, the central question in *Vergangenheits-bewältigung* studies—that is, studies exploring the ways in which Germans have attempted since 1945 to master their Nazi past—has been *whether* Germans came to terms with the past or not. This is an important question, underlined by its moral urgency. But, as a historical question, it has severe limitations. Recently, it has slowly been replaced by more comprehensive questions: what did Germans remember of the Nazi past, how was it remembered, and who remembered what? Building on these new research questions, this chapter is conceived as a critical reflection on *Vergangenheits-bewältigung* studies. My focus is on postwar West German society between 1945 and 1960. It is an attempt to explore how the topic of mastering the past can further an understanding of postwar German society and culture. The first part of the essay discusses critically problems of method in old and new interpretations. In the second part, I use the social and symbolic practice of tourism as a methodological vehicle to illuminate postwar values and beliefs concerning National Socialism. My aim is to be suggestive, not comprehensive. I do not state this to preempt criticism. Rather, I view this chapter, as well as the test case of tourism, as an attempt to think through a useful way in which to conceive of mastering Germany's past. For there is no one "correct" way of conceiving of this topic. Some trips, to use a metaphor from the world of traveling, actually have a final stop. Historical understanding, a trip of unexpected consequences if ever I knew one, is not one of them.

ON REPRESSION

How did West Germans remember the Nazi past in the period after 1945? The common view, shared by scholars, journalists, and laypersons, has been for a long time that, as one historian argued, "National Socialism was treated for a whole generation with collective silence and wide-spread amnesia."[1] This interpretation, full of moral concern, was first formulated in Germany in the 1960s, when the sons and daughters rebelled against the war generation of their parents. The argument, as well as the atmosphere of the period, has been successfully captured by novels from and about the period. Thus, Bernhard Schlink describes in *The Reader* the sentiments of the hero, Michael Berg, who attends a war-crimes trial during his law studies: "Exploring the past! We students in the seminar considered ourselves radical explorers. We tore open the windows and let in the air, the wind that finally whirled away the dust that society had permitted to settle over the horrors of the past. . . . The [war and reconstruction] generation . . . was in the dock."[2]

A foundational text of this interpretation and its vocabulary was the 1967 study by Alexander and Margarete Mitscherlich, *The Inability to Mourn*, which analyzed postwar West German society in Freudian terms. While Germans' moral duty after the war was "working through" their crimes and guilt, they chose instead to repress the traumatic Nazi past and to channel their energy to the material construction of West Germany.[3] In different renditions and various degrees of sophistication, this view dominated the historiography: the argument was that most Germans repressed the Nazi past; the mode of proceeding was to look for traces of memory in the records of cultural artifacts, war-crimes trials, and political acts (such as the restitution for Holocaust survivors); the basic assumption was that a trauma like the Third Reich must and should be overcome for Germany to lead a normal life. The body of work produced by this approach has significantly illuminated how Germans attempted to master their past and how most of them refused to own up to it.

In principle, the argument that (some) Germans repressed (some aspects) of the Nazi years is unassailable. But the question is what are the theoretical consequences of using the repression approach as a dominant explanatory device. As much as the repression thesis described a poignant historical condition, it also possessed several methodological pitfalls. It appeared at times to be an exemplary case of the dangers of imposing a laudable moral cause on the vicissitudes and contingencies of historical and human affairs; it was less successful in explaining Germans' changing attitudes toward National Socialism than in providing a sweeping condemnation of post-1945 German society. The myth of repression was, in moral terms, so seductive that even scholars who cited evidence of engagement with the Third Reich ended up interpreting it as a form of denial.[4] As a consequence, the repression ap-

proach was content with an explanation that ignored the complex negotiations between remembering and forgetting. It was founded, in a sense, on an
explanatory framework that countered repression with atonement: in this dichotomous relationship, Germans after 1945 could either fully atone for their
crimes or else they were repressing them. There was little middle ground between the two extremes. But this appears to be an imposition of our own
moral values and expectations on a historical situation—and on an image of
the past—that was significantly more complex.

Moreover, although studies of the repression approach provided new and
valuable information, they also closed down new, original ways of understanding the past. A foundational argument of this approach was to explain
the postwar repression by the continuation of anti-Semitism and, more generally, by Germans' unwillingness to view the Third Reich as a criminal regime. But scholars did not originate, on the basis of these findings, new
questions and assumptions. For if anti-Semitism was still so strong, and
if most Germans viewed the Nazi period as acceptable, then the focus on
mastering the past seems misplaced for it attributes present-day concerns
to people in the past who had in fact very different values and beliefs. Rather
than asking why Germans did not remember their criminal past, a better
question would be what in fact they did remember of the Nazi period.

As a result, by relentlessly directing attention to sins of omission and repression, we are in danger of not understanding what did take place and
why. The basic historical assumption of the interpretation that emphasizes
repression, whose origins lay more in moral indignation than in historical work, is questionable: why, one wonders, are we to expect at all that
those who committed or supported crimes during National Socialism should
atone for their deeds just several years later? The argument seems to be
based on a logic according to which what seems immoral to us must also be
viewed as such by others; as if the defeat of May 1945 were a moral revolving
door that transformed, literally overnight, Germans' values and beliefs; this
seems something of a magical feat. If one takes seriously Germans' ideology
during the Third Reich, as well as the possibility that many Germans viewed
their lives as good, lawful, and just, then the fundamental premise of the repression thesis becomes doubtful.

Furthermore, let us assume, for the sake of the argument, that Germans
did repress their criminal Nazi past. This only begs the question: what, then,
did they remember of the years 1933–45? For it seems improbable that Germans repressed everything, that no traces of the past remained in public and

private life. Traces of the past must have remained. The question is where and how to find them. When we abandon the myth that Germans repressed the past we can begin appreciating the complexity of attitudes toward National Socialism. My argument is not that Germans never repressed the Nazi past or that they talked openly and incessantly about their Nazi experience; repression and denial obviously existed. Rather, my argument is that the notion of repression as an explanatory device tends to obscure rather than reveal human motivations where silence and expression coexisted in ambiguous, multiple ways. Long ago, in his 1959 essay "What Does Coming to Terms with the Past Mean?" Theodor Adorno wrote: "The effacement of memory is more the achievement of an all-too-wakeful consciousness than it is the result of its weakness in the face of the superiority of unconscious processes."[5] Capturing this agency—of an awake memory that attempts to extinguish itself, of the will to forget that emerges dialectically only as a consequence of an animated memory—has not always been successful.

The problem of motivation is shared even by the most erudite studies of a new approach that intermingles memory, repression, and working through. Take for example the work of Dominick LaCapra who, making specific use of psychoanalysis, investigated the transferential relations between the historian and the Nazi past as a traumatic event. He has often been insightful, but not when he argues that the Holocaust was the "uncanny return of the repressed in the form of phobic ritualism and paradoxical sacrificialism."[6] Perhaps, and perhaps not. I am not sure how revealing this statement is. Be that as it may, LaCapra leaves this statement hanging in the air because he provides us with no theoretical and methodological understanding of what might be involved in repression and in a return of the repressed. Moreover, it seems to presume that the Holocaust came after its repression (something, once, was repressed; the Holocaust was the "uncanny return" of this repressed thing and was, in turn, repressed as well); but LaCapra does not say how exactly this happened, what the implications of this argument are, and whether it is at all possible, logical, and chronologically reasonable. Above all, it seems to me to be the kind of explanation that—as a result of the enormity of the Holocaust; the difficulties in understanding, explaining, and interpreting it; and the sanctified status it possesses in our culture—only Holocaust studies can tolerate. Had LaCapra's statement been used to describe any other historical event, I am quite certain it would have been unceremoniously dismissed as ahistorical.

Recently there has been a shift in the argument concerning postwar German memories—from the emphasis on repression to the complex argument about different uses of the Nazi past. As Robert Moeller has thoughtfully put it, "the apparent failure of West Germans to pay the high psychic costs demanded by the Mitscherlichs did not mean that they fled headlong from the past or suffered from collective amnesia. There were many accounts of Germany's 'most recent' history that circulated in the 1950s; remembering selectively was not the same as forgetting."[7] Studies have insightfully shown that the Nazi past was very much present: in memories of expellees from Eastern Europe and of prisoners of war; in cinema, autobiographies, and pedagogical circles; in the legal system, preoccupied with the denazification and war-crimes trials; in cultural representations such as cemeteries and concentration camps; in issues of public policy concerning, for example, welfare for wounded soldiers and widows; and in debates of political and cultural leaders about the meaning of National Socialism.[8] One important finding that emerges from this literature is that most Germans ultimately believed their nation was a victim of the war, not its perpetrator.[9] Moral concern about Nazism ended quickly after 1945 as the result of a combination of circumstances: domestically, coming to terms with the past was extremely unpopular, while internationally, the Cold War shifted attention away from the Nazis and onto the communists.

These new findings are interesting not only for what they show about post-1945 German society but also because they enable us to locate the repression thesis in a broader context. Significantly, the sources used by the new historians were mostly available for historians of the repression thesis for decades. Many of the sources, far from being clandestine, recorded events, statements, and actions in the public sphere, including documents such as Bundestag debates, intellectuals' writings, and expellees' memory books. That historians and laypersons neglected this evidence for so long is, perhaps, a measure of their repression, a repression that answered several needs. For young Germans coming of age in the 1960s and thereafter, the repression thesis served as a moral buffer between themselves, who remembered, and the Third Reich generation, who failed to own up to its past. For Europeans, the adoption of the repression approach fitted within a convention that answered a general need to remove the war from being at the center of a serious moral and political discussion; the partial silence in Germany about the Third Reich accorded with similar silence, albeit with different contents and domestic reasons, in France about Vichy, in Italy about fascism, and in all continental countries about the Holocaust.[10]

Building on this new scholarship, I would like to take the discussion further. The shift in argument, from the emphasis on repression to the complex argument about different uses of the Nazi past, has been only to some degree accompanied by a systematic shift in methods, sources, and subject matter. Some studies, which discuss illuminatingly the commingling of silence and memory, suffer from the current weakness of cultural history, namely the emphasis on cultural representations at the expense of social relations, mediation, and reception. An exemplary case of this problem is Y. Michal Bodemann's fine essay "Eclipse of Memory." Bodemann's aim is to explore how "Auschwitz and the final solution were represented in the public arenas of postwar Germany . . . [as a] nexus of silence and memory."[11] His method is to analyze several cultural artifacts as representatives of larger discourses in German society. Thus, Eugen Kogon's *The SS State*, published in 1946, represented the Nazis as criminals and the Jews as victims. A second discourse, found in memoirs and novels, reversed or blurred the roles of victims and perpetrators. A third narrative, epitomized in Carl Schmitt's *Glossarium*, provided apologetics for the Third Reich, while a narrative of silence pervaded postwar German sociology. Bodemann presents a complex picture of varying attitudes toward the past, while avoiding the false dichotomy between silence and memory. But this is an analysis of culture that is devoid of social conditions. Images of the Nazi past circulate in an autonomous sphere of representations, while their analysis ignores social differentiation, roles, and structures, as well as class, gender, generational, and other relations that made these representations possible and gave them meaning. We thus learn more about memory than about the effects of memory on the organization, hierarchy, and arrangements of social and cultural relationships; more about cultural representations than about their effects on social processes; more about single artifacts and discourses than about the relations among them. The picture that emerges is of several narratives of the Nazi past in symbolic and cultural isolation, instead of one that elucidates how they built together a German symbolic universe with opposing crosscurrents and conflicting imageries.

Thus, for Bodemann, a book stands for the discourse of society as a whole. This kind of cultural analysis—of an autonomous cultural sphere disconnected from social experience—is widespread in studies of mastering the past, as well as in cultural history. The problem with this mode of proceeding is that an object—or, better, the person who created the object—is instinctively seen as representative of larger trends. The fallacy is evident, and it is worthwhile remembering here the words of Karl Mannheim:

> We cannot jump straight from the general observation of individuals and their psychic mechanisms to the analysis of society. The psychology of society is not a million times that of an individual. . . . What for our purpose is needed is an historically-differentiated psychology by which the changes in attitudes, motivations and symbol-transmutations in different periods among different classes and under different social situations will be made plain.[12]

Some studies using the new approach that commingled silence and memory have made a concerted effort to bring into the picture everyday life, the private sphere, and unofficial sentiments.[13] But the picture that emerges from many other studies on mastering the past is often that of political and cultural leaders rather than of ordinary Germans, of the public rather than of the private sphere, of official rather than of popular culture, of the representation of cultural artifacts rather than of their reception.[14] The limits of this approach are evident when we recognize that scholars universally agree that, as Norbert Frei put it, "the open ideological and political belief in National Socialism and anti-Semitism became a taboo."[15] For if a candid discussion on National Socialism could not take place in the public sphere, then the historiographical focus should shift more decisively to exploring the private sphere and, more importantly, the dialectics between public and private. Discretion dictated that certain views about the Nazi regime could not be said in public, although they were the norm in private life and everyday behavior.

I would like to elucidate this point by discussing Claudia Koonz's thoughtful essay "Between Memory and Oblivion: Concentration Camps in German Memory." Koonz argues that "Germans constructed a new identity based on a fresh start or a clean break with the past . . . silence about genocide, terror and racism settled in." But several pages later she recounts the following story: "One afternoon in the fall of 1960, I visited Dachau with a fellow student, who, having grown up in Bavaria, could talk freely with local men around their *Stammtisch*. He suggested that if I remained silent my accent would not betray me and I would hear a conversation I would never forget. He was right. The men laughed boisterously about the 'good old days' when the 'riffraff' got what was coming to them and the village prospered. With private memories like these . . ."[16] The lesson of this story, it seems, is not heeded, for Koonz goes on to analyze public memories (ceremonies, monuments, and museums) in concentration camp sites. To be sure, Koonz is sensitive to the various forms of memory: "[I]t makes sense to distinguish popular memory (as reflected for example, in the media, newspapers, oral histories, memoirs and opinion polls) from official memory (as expressed in ceremonies and leaders' speeches). Public memory is the battlefield on which these two compete for hegemony."[17] But this distinction is not entirely satisfactory, for these various forms of memory have more in common than meets the eye at first glance. They only include objects whose meaning was linked to being displayed *openly* in the public sphere. Consequently, the *Stammtisch*, as well as a whole range of activities in the private sphere, finds no place among these memory definitions.[18] Moreover, her analysis is restricted to cultural artifacts and social practices whose very purpose was, to begin with, to represent the Third Reich. But if there is something to be learned from Koonz's afternoon at Dachau's *Kneipe* (the local pub) it is that memories of National Socialism were often expressed in roundabout ways, through social practices that were not immediately, or even primarily, linked to representing National Socialism.

Consequently, we should not look for traces of National Socialism only in artifacts and practices created intentionally to represent it, for this leads to a certain predictability. And we should not look for the memory of the Third Reich only in the visible sources, in social and political meeting points where memory is explicit and its meaning palpably manipulable. Rather, because some views about Nazism could not be made public, we should look for their expression in social practices and representations where they were not directly discernible, but fairly unexpected. These kinds of sources, practices, and representations may ultimately reveal more about attitudes and beliefs.[19]

In light of this consideration I chose to undertake a study of tourism. Because tourism, as a social and cultural practice of modern popular culture, can reveal individual motivations and intimate values (the experiences of traveling are private), as well as the ways governments in all political regimes attempt to use traveling to shape national identity, to foster legitimacy, or to bolster ideology. Tourism may thus reveal what people intimately thought about National Socialism. This investigation calls for a mixture of imagination and speculation. There are many sources on tourist activities, but most are not by tourists. Think about yourself: when you travel you experience a multitude of emotions, motivations, fantasies, but you rarely leave behind a trail of written documents. My emphasis is on words, but also on observable actions. My aim is to attempt to catch a sensibility—attitudes and characteristic styles and emotions—that came to be expressed in public action: How did tourists translate intimate thoughts into public action? How did they carve a space for different, opposing, perceptions about National Socialism? And how did memory and silence coexist in private and public spheres?

NATIONAL SOCIALISM AS
VICTIMHOOD AND FOND MEMORIES

After 1945 tourist activities and organizations were revived quickly. The first postwar tourist association was founded in Baden in December 1945. In the same month, the old tourist association in Dortmund resumed its activities. And the preparatory meeting for the foundation of the German League of Tourist Associations and Spas (Bund deutscher Verkehrsverbände und Bäder) took place in June 1946. Overall, by February 1947 thirteen tourist associations were active in the western occupation zone in Württemberg, the Rhineland, Westphalia, Bavaria, and other regions.[20] Moreover, lively discussions on tourist issues took place in the associations' newspapers and journals, as well as in conferences and meetings.[21]

After the war, as we have seen in the previous chapter, tourism became a medium for thinking about Germany's recent past, about what was normal and what exceptional in one's everyday as well as national experience.[22] Even before there had been significant actual traveling, there had already been a significant rhetoric of tourism that represented several overlapping, and at times contrasting, attitudes toward the Third Reich. The rhetoric was produced by activists in tourist associations and the tourist trade, mostly middle-class men, liberal professionals (writers, lawyers, journalists) and businessmen who had been connected to the tourist industry for decades, including in the Nazi period. The social composition of German tourism remained, from the 1920s to the 1950s, unchanged: most of the tourists were from the upper and middle classes; some workers traveled, but overall workers remained underrepresented. By the mid-1950s tourism had reached the peak levels of the interwar years; the end of the 1950s is considered the beginning of mass tourism in Germany.

The rhetoric of tourism represented, first, the prewar Nazi years (1933–39) as overwhelmingly positive. The fiftieth anniversary of the Tourist Union of the Harz (Harzer Verkehrsverband) in 1954 provided a suitable occasion for drawing up a historical balance sheet. A special commemorative booklet was published, in which members of the tourist union remembered the period as one of great improvements: "German tourism in general, and with it the tourism in the Harz, experienced strong growth through the decline of unemployment, the general economic activity, and the rapid increase of motor vehicles."[23] The visible symbol of progress was the "Harz highway" project: "In terms of landscape, the highway is one of the most beautiful in northern and central Germany, and will be a particular attraction for motor vehicle tourism in the Harz."

Indeed, postwar descriptions of tourism in the Third Reich were painted either in the professional language of the trade, which had existed since the beginning of modern tourism in the nineteenth century (who visited where and when) or in a poetic language that is part of tourism discourse everywhere. Either way, the language of tourism disclosed nothing of the real drama of German society in those years: the accommodation with a murderous system, the striving for world domination, and the persecution of Jews. For traveling, similar to every other sphere of life in the Third Reich, was an integral part of the period's systematic terror. The 1935 Nuremberg Laws forbade most hotels to accept Jewish guests.[24] A decree of the Ministry of Interior from July 24, 1937, posed extreme restrictions on the presence of Jews in spas; an additional decree from June 16, 1939, made participation impossible. Given what we know of Nazi ideology, this information is quite predictable. More significant is the evidence of grass-roots activity, before the Nazi legislation, to remove Jews from tourist sites and hotels. Massive discrimination started in the fall of 1934. The case of Neustrelitz stood for many communities in Germany during the period: the town's hotel owners together with the local tourist and transportation bureau agreed "to post everywhere the inscription: the admission of Jews is unwelcome." In contrast to the postwar silence over this past, descriptions of the conditions of tourism under Allied occupation were dramatic, often expressing self-pity. Thus, tells us one writer in 1954, conditions for the revival of tourism in the Harz after 1945 were terrible: first, all beds were confiscated by the occupation forces. Then, "the occupying army disposed 480 percent more than the annual, normal timber production in the Harz forest." The result: "It seems as if fate overtook not only human beings but also nature."[25] West Germans seemed to have been more affected emotionally by the years of postwar reconstruction than by the peace years of the Third Reich.[26]

At the same time, tourist rhetoric also represented the Nazi period in a commingling of distancing and victimhood; the Nazi Party had thus been a foreign entity that had imposed a dictatorship and a war on an innocent people. The German Central Tourist Association (Deutsche Zentrale für Fremdenverkehr), founded in 1948 as West Germany's national tourist organization, articulated this creed clearly in the first postwar tourist campaign aimed at foreigners, the "Goethe Year 1949" campaign. The organization complained that the task of bringing tourists to Germany was very difficult

> because the years of the Nazi dominion made Germany the least beloved country in the world. . . . The German Central Tourist Association must show foreign tourists a way that will enable them to meet again the true Germany. . . . The true Goethe's Germany was, is, and remains immortal and indestructible. In this Germany we believed in the period of rape [*Vergewaltigung*], in this Germany we believe today.[27]

Thus the same period when "rape" became an accusatory metaphor to describe the Allied occupation of Germany—as well as a harsh reality for many German women, especially in the Soviet zone—the German Central Tourist Association chose this same word to describe the Nazi regime. It achieved two aims: it distinguished between the Nazis and the Germans, as if Nazis were not "true" Germans; and it drew a semantic likeness between the Allies and the Nazis.[28] West Germans made tourism a medium in which the nation could be considered an innocent victim of war and occupation. According to this view, National Socialism was an aberration from the German history of cultural and artistic accomplishments.[29]

Perceiving themselves as victims, Germans originated a particular meaning to the common view of tourism as a vehicle for world peace. According to this view, tourism was fundamental to "creat[ing] the conditions for the longed-for world peace and happy future" because the effect of face-to-face meetings was "to dispel prejudices."[30] This belief, expressed here by the leading tourist journal *Der Fremdenverkehr* (Tourism), was very common in Germany after 1945. But whose prejudices were these? The term "to dispel prejudices" became in West German society a code word for the need of others to rid their minds of prejudices about the Germans, and not for the need of Germans to account for their role during the Nazi period, which was the source of most of the Germans' own prejudices. *Der Fremdenverkehr* expressed this sentiment clearly in its opening statement on the first issue in July 1949: it wanted to attract tourists to Germany so that "people abroad will get to know Germany and the German people as they are today, and, as a result, will be freed of their prejudices."[31] The term "to dispel prejudices" thus became a euphemism that meant the persistent persecution of Germany via the unjust association of the country with "this un-German Germany," namely, National Socialism.[32]

Significantly, this argument was itself appropriated from the Nazis. A 1939 booklet, entitled *Tourism and Hospitality in the New Germany*, complained:

"How much nonsense is still written about our Germany everywhere in the world, and how much of this nonsense is still believed. But all the efforts of the tendentious instigators would be futile had it been possible for every member of other nations to form an independent opinion about the German people and the German land."[33] Misunderstood then, misunderstood now. Given the overwhelming continuity of personnel among members and leaders of local, regional, and national tourist associations, it is hard to believe that the post-1945 use of this argument was not inherited from the previous period. Moreover, in the 1930s the alleged anti-German propaganda by "tendentious instigators" referred to the Jews, who presumably were spreading this "nonsense" about Germany. The use of a similar language after the war manifested not simply insensitivity among some Germans but the view of the continuing threat posed to Germany by the "Jewish problem": while before 1945 it was the presence of the Jews that victimized Germany, after the war it was their absence, blamed on Germany, that unjustly victimized it.

It would be an oversimplification to impose uniformity on Germans' attitudes toward National Socialism. Tourism became a metaphor that both claimed the Nazi past and separated the present from it. Hans Christoph Seebohm, secretary of transportation, articulated this duality well. In the first German Tourism Convention (Deutscher Fremdenverkehrstag) in 1950, he stated that tourism "[makes us] feel what it means to be members of a big community that strives for peace and understands the words 'to be German' as a task to raise ourselves to become European."[34] Distancing himself from the Third Reich, he portrayed an image of a new, cooperative Germany in a peaceful Europe. At the same time, however, he argued that Jews and Germans had experienced the same kind of persecution and were thus morally equal: "The methods that were used by the National Socialist leaders against the Jews and that we most vehemently condemn are on a par with the methods that were used against the German expellees."[35] Although he condemned the "methods" against the Jews, Seebohm, by denying relations of cause and effect, displayed a basic reluctance and moral inability to grasp the essence of the Nazi regime — and of the agency of Germans, not of "methods," who had actualized it: the Jews had been innocent victims, while the expulsion of Germans from the East had been a result of Hitler's murderous war.

I have described the discourse of tourism after the war as a way of embracing as well as denying the Third Reich. Was the meaning of post-1945 tourist revival, then, a flight from reality? This is not a helpful argument. Far from being a flight from reality, tourism was a symbolic practice by which Germans gave meaning to their lives. Viewed in this way, the discourse of tourism after 1945 allowed Germans to identify with the Third Reich, and, at the same time, to place this experience within the context of postwar conditions. Tourism became a medium for making sense of the past and the present; it made possible a coexistence of different, even contradictory, perceptions: of the good, old Nazi tourist days of the peace years, as well as of the nation as an innocent victim of war and occupation. We may not agree with these views, but they cannot be defined as a flight from reality or as repression. Germans did not keep the Nazi past hermetically sealed. The problem with viewing tourism as a flight from reality is that the subjective meaning of the tourist experience is largely lost, while concepts like irrationalism and manipulation take center stage as explanatory devices. It is, therefore, to some aspects and implications of the tourist experience that I would now like to turn.

NATIONAL SOCIALISM EMBRACED AND REMOVED

How did West Germans, through traveling, articulate their views of the Third Reich? The methodological problems of getting to the tourist experience are, as we have pointed out, significant because we need to sift meaning from a tenuous combination of observable behavior and written sources. My argument, raised by way of hypothesis, concerns the nexus between tourism and war, as experience and as memory, as it was played out among two generations—the war soldiers and the youth coming of age in the 1950s.

In the 1950s, when improved economic conditions made traveling widespread, many Germans traveled primarily to forget the war, to resume normal life, to avoid what was perceived as the pernicious effect of politics. For the historian, the behavior and motivations behind this traveling are the most difficult to document, for, unlike anger or happiness, apathy and effacement leave few traces. But through sources such as films, novels, and autobiographies, among others, we can reconstruct this sentiment with accuracy. Mass traveling to sunny Italy, Yugoslavia, and Spain provided an outlet to a war-weary generation. This seemingly banal tourist behavior—the passionate quest for sea, beach, and sun—led Hans Magnus Enzensberger to write his classic essay "A Theory of Tourism," in which he called tourism a "mass fraud." [36] The depoliticized tourist appeared to Enzensberger a result of capitalist, consumerist brainwashing. But this judgment may be too harsh and simplistic, for silence over the past, the desire to forget, was not the only reaction.[37]

Indeed, when economic conditions in the 1950s improved, the generation of the war soldiers began traveling also to places it had experienced in the war. Here was a vital purpose of post-1945 traveling: for some West German men traveling after the war became a way of capturing recollections from the good old days of the Third Reich. Mass tourism, strictly speaking, began in Germany in the late 1950s. But the first time German men traveled on a mass scale had been two decades before, in the first half of the 1940s: under different conditions, to be sure, carrying different ideological baggage and exposed to different risks. An unexpected function of the German army was to operate the biggest travel agency in German history. Most Germans saw Prague, Paris, Rome, Athens, Crete, and Tobruk for the first time during their military service.

The connection was clear enough to contemporaries. "Until now this war has been one big Strength through Joy trip," wrote one soldier after the campaign in France in May 1940.[38] He was referring to the Strength through Joy organization (Kraft durch Freude, or KdF), which was established in 1933 with the aim of providing all German workers with paid vacation. Another, who belonged to the forces preparing the campaign against the Soviet Union, described to his parents in March 1941 his feelings about the war: "I can tell you, in order to requite your understandable curiosity, that I have behind me a very big trip until the Russian border. We drove through half of Europe, no exaggeration. Again, many new impressions pour in and again one gets to know many new and interesting things. My military service so far has been almost entirely an educational trip."[39] I am not suggesting that war equaled a pleasure trip. But it did introduce many German men (and some women), willingly or not, to new experiences, cultures, landscapes, foods, and customs. Soldiers, when crisscrossing Europe, looked around at times with a tourist's gaze. Certainly, a word of caution is in order: in Stalingrad and the like, German soldiers were not looking around with a tourist's gaze. This argument does not presume to include all German soldiers at all times during World War II. It applies better to the years of triumphs, 1939–41, than to the years of total war, 1942–45, to the western front than to the eastern front; and after 1945 traveling was possible only in Western Europe, not behind the Iron Curtain. But this argument does capture an important experience of some German soldiers during the war.

Some occupied cities enjoyed special tourist status. Paris immediately became a tourist attraction. Reporting about the fall of Paris, William Shirer observed that "most of the German troops act like naive tourists . . . it seems funny, but every German soldier carries a camera."[40] German soldiers, men and women, went into a shopping frenzy, helped by the favorable exchange rate, for goods unavailable at home. "Ils nous prennent tout," complained the Parisians.[41] Hitler, of course, himself toured Paris. His plane landed at dawn on June 23, 1940, for a blitz visit that ended at nine o'clock that evening.[42] During the visit he confided to Albert Speer: I have always dreamed of visiting Paris. Perhaps as a result, he decided to offer all his troops a holiday in Paris—the plum of his conquests.[43] The German military authorities established by the late summer 1940 a special unit of the Wehrmacht to organize tours in Paris. According to *Der Deutsche Wegleiter*, a biweekly German-language guide to occupied France, by May 1941, 1 million Germans had been served by the unit. An additional organization, "Jeder einmal in Paris" (Everybody in Paris once) arranged soldiers' tours. And a special office of the KdF was also operating. Units of soldiers from as far as North Cape, Greece, and the Ukraine were brought to Paris to tour and relax. As late as April 1944, tours to Chantilly, Rambouillet, and Fontainebleau took place. For many soldiers the encounter with foreign lands during the war was the first in their life and made a lasting impression.

For some West German men, therefore, traveling in the post-1945 period was not a discovery of uncharted territory. On the contrary, it was a reunion with familiar sites, sites of recollections—shall we say fond recollections?— and lost emotions. It brought back memories of youth, adventure, and domination. The *Frankfurter Allgemeine Zeitung* carried a story in 1953 of a German couple who, during a trip to Amsterdam, rang the bell of a beautiful villa, explaining to the owners that the man wanted to show his wife where he had lived during the war.[44] In several oral interviews I conducted, interviewees emphasized the element of discovery in seeing new countries and often told of the desire to visit them again after the war. Alfred, a Wehrmacht soldier, was first sent to the eastern front but was then moved to Thessalonica.[45] He was eighteen, on his first stay abroad. After the war he used to recount to his family about Greece, the food, wine, and women. He always promised his son, whom I interviewed, to take him to Greece when he turned eighteen. The trip never came to pass. The family took its first trip in 1959 to northern Germany and later used to travel to Italy. When Alfred's son was eighteen, in the late 1960s, he was not interested in traveling with his father. Thus, while some did travel to wartime places, like the German couple in Amsterdam, others only fantasized about it. Regardless, the motivation was there, and the hidden aspirations are as important for historians to understand perceptions of National Socialism as the public behavior.

Significantly, this post-1945 traveling to sites of past experiences and lost emotions was articulated in one favorite medium that emerged in the 1950s with the explicit aim of expressing popular sentiments about the Third Reich. This was the illustrated magazine, such as *Quick* and *Stern*, that carried in weekly fiction series stories that romanticized the war, portraying it as an adventure while presenting the German soldier as dignified and honorable. A popular *Stern* series was *Die Katze* (The cat), about espionage, resistance, collaboration, and good German soldiers in occupied France. The hero was Hugo Bleicher, a counterespionage soldier who served in Paris. Ten years after the end of the war, goes one episode of *Die Katze*, Bleicher returns to Paris, accompanied by the coauthor of his memoirs, on a trip to the past. He meets Madame Blavette who, as a resistance fighter, had been jailed by Bleicher. He explains to her his past motives—"Only for the sake of truth"—and apologizes. "But there is nothing to apologize for," smiles Madame Blavette, "there was after all a secret messenger in my home who worked against the Germans. You, Monsieur Bleicher, and the other Germans did then only your duty, nothing else." Here is the best of all possible worlds: Bleicher absolved by his victim.[46] The story is not about actual traveling, but about a traveling fantasy: it reflects some of the period's inner desires and emotions. It brings back to Bleicher and to the reader the sense of sheer power that Germans felt as conquerors of the continent in the early 1940s, as well as the sense of the *anständiger Soldat*, the respectable, decent soldier. It provides a dénouement to the war story, namely the war as an event where all did their duty, Germany was forgiven, and Europe could move ahead. In this narrative, tourism functioned as a symbolic practice in which German men embraced the experience of the Third Reich without being, in the new Western Europe, politically incorrect.

This way of putting the relations between the "traveling" of World War II and post-1945 tourism questions the validity and usefulness of the concept of a Zero Hour (*Stunde Null*); it goes beyond the shibboleth that "memory was sealed off in post-traumatic oblivion behind the 'Zero Hour' of 1945."[47] Across the divide of 1945, some Germans traveled and formed ideas about themselves as well as about others. For some among the generation of soldiers, traveling after 1945 was a way of connecting with past experiences, of traveling, in reality or in the imagination, to capture the lost world of the Third Reich.

And yet, at precisely the same time, a different generation was forming very different ideas about National Socialism. By the 1950s memories of war and occupation commingled with Germany's new commitment to West European peace and prosperity. A new social group began to travel in the 1950s:

the youth. They hitchhiked across Europe, crisscrossed the continent thanks to low-priced train tickets, and discovered the charm of camping.[48] But their traveling was different in style and content from the traveling of their parents or older siblings. If for some among the older generation travel was an occasion to recapture, in private, memories of adventurous youth, for many among the younger generation tourism became a public pilgrimage of atonement, a voyage in time and space to distance oneself from the Third Reich, from the fathers and mothers, in order to build a bridge to a new Europe. Tourism became a social practice impelled by the idea that by traveling one learns about and experiences the Other. At the same time traveling was also a way for others to know Germans and perhaps even to forgive. This new traveling culture, together with its sentiments of radicalism, innovation, undisclosed rage at the older generation, and condemnation of Nazism, was captured by autobiographies, such as Bernward Vesper's *Die Reise* (The journey). Vesper was born in 1938 as "a child of middle-class parents who hung on to an idiotic dream of a thousand-year Reich."[49] His father, Will Vesper, was a Heimat blood-and-soil poet during National Socialism. *Die Reise*, praised by the German author Peter Weiss as the "intellectual high point of the '68 movement," portrays sensitively the emerging culture of youth tourism in the 1950s:

> I met on the streets, in the youth hostels, in the cars Danes, Norwegians, Swedes, English, Americans, and French. And while I set out with the angst of being humiliated, which I felt as a German whose land was occupied, humbled, and hated by the enemy, I found myself instead in an international brotherhood. . . . And what was revealed precisely before the monument for the Danish resistance fighters murdered by the Germans, and later in Coventry and Oradour, was that all of us viewed the war as a matter of the older generation.[50]

While this description may underestimate the persistence of anti-German memories in countries such as France, Holland, and Denmark, it does show how the war created in West Germany in the 1950s two different traveling experiences across generational lines. While some among the older generation traveled in order to (among other things) recapture a lost past, for the younger generation tourism was a way of distancing itself from this same past. While the older generation used traveling to express its views on National Socialism in a private, almost clandestine mode, the younger generation used this same practice to express its views in public.

Why was tourism adopted as a way of relating to the past? It is clear from the approach presented here that I do not share Enzensberger's view of tourism as a "mass fraud." In the modern world, tourism has become a fundamental social and cultural practice by means of which people construct ideas about the self, society, nation, the past, and others. But tourists are not social scientists: we cannot expect them to construct an objective view of the world. In traveling, like in film, literature, and art, we deal primarily not with accurate representations of social reality but essentially with an artistic representation of the world, with an "experiencing of fictional environments."[51] In this respect, tourists' perceptions should be understood together with other human symbolic productions: art, ritual, and play. Viewed from this perspective, the practice and discourse of traveling can enrich our understanding of German and other societies.

The point of departure of this essay has been the attempt to show how some members in West German society transformed inner beliefs about National Socialism into a symbolic and social practice under conditions that restricted open, public articulation of support for that regime. I intentionally chose a common, even banal, everyday social practice such as tourism to show how the multiple ways in which Germans related to National Socialism conflicted and commingled. In terms of subject matter and approach, through the investigation of tourism I wished to move beyond the by now predictable list of research topics, such as museums, monuments, novels, films, plays, and commemorations, which share the characteristic of being purposefully originated to represent the Third Reich. This mode of proceeding brought us closer to people's hidden values and beliefs: because attitudes toward National Socialism were a contested and political issue, the common sources used to explore them often hide as much as they reveal the real motivations and ideas of people, who attempted to conceal, appropriate, and manipulate. Tourism, in contrast, is a social activity that leaves ample space for exercising private, profound values. As tourists, people reveal about themselves more than they might have wished. In this respect, the investigation of the tourist experience takes us beyond the world of official discourse and the public sphere, but also beyond the world of the private sphere—and into an area that shared both private and public. Tourism, as a practice that allows people to hide as much as to reveal, collapses the dichotomy between public and private experiences and offers different possibilities of expressing one's intimate emotions. Exploring these kind of practices, where Germans acted out their emotions about National Socialism, makes the study of mastering the past truly rewarding.

It may be argued that the group of World War II soldiers who traveled after 1945 represented only a small minority when compared with the entire population of West Germany (only half of the population was male, minus all the dead who never returned and the POWs, minus those who had fought on the eastern front and could not travel behind the Iron Curtain, minus those who traveled to forget the past and have fun under the Italian sun). A similar argument of unrepresentativeness can be made with regard to the young travelers of the 1950s. This is certainly correct, but also irrelevant. The articulation of different attitudes about National Socialism among different, even small, social groups is not a problem but, in a sense, the solution to a historiography that was all too often content to generalize about the entire German population. The starting point of this essay has been precisely Mannheim's notion that what we need is a historically differentiated psychology by which different attitudes and motivations are made clear. Three groups were discussed: tourist leaders and activists operating in associations and journals, World War II soldiers who traveled after 1945, and youth coming of age in the 1950s. They represent men more than women and the upper and middle classes more than the lower classes.

Underlying this approach was the attempt to avoid the temptation to interpret contradictions, inconsistencies, and ambivalences in terms of irrationalism, escapism, denial, and repression. Tourism reflected perceptions of National Socialism on various levels, as we have seen. The German Central Tourist Association, an official mouthpiece of West Germany's newly instituted democracy, depicted the Nazis as outsiders, invaders of the true Germany symbolized by Goethe. Members of the Tourist Union of the Harz, in contrast, remembered fondly the prewar Nazi years, while some soldiers used traveling to recapture an inalienable personal experience of the war, expressed in terms of youth, adventure, and discovery. In all these cases, aspects of the Third Reich were both embraced and rejected. A different attitude was evident among the 1950s generation, where tourism became a cultural practice that represented the attempt to build a new Germany within the new Europe and a pilgrimage to atone for the sins of their fathers and mothers.

In reality, after 1945 many Germans perceived the prewar years of the Third Reich as positive. At the same time, many, often the same people, also recognized, with various degrees of hostility and support, the historical conditions existing in occupied, defeated Germany, namely the building of democratic institutions and civil society. They commingled, not without tensions, the irreducible, and basically acceptable, experience of the peace years and for some also the war years of the Third Reich with the transformations underway in post-1945 West Germany. We have seen that there is more than one way of constructing an image of the past and that people construct more than one image of the same past. Differently put, tourism reflected a kind of a dual consciousness with regard to the Third Reich: holding on to some notions of this past, while simultaneously cultivating notions of distancing and even victimhood. These two sets of perceptions reinforced each other. The image of victimhood made no sense without the image of the good life that preceded it; the memories of the good old days shone through only in light of present misery, of defeat and occupation. Tourism thus became a metaphor that both claimed aspects of the Nazi past and insulated the present from it.

Exploring traces of National Socialism in the culture of traveling, this chapter has hoped to capture an unpredictable facet of post-1945 German memories and to constitute a new space of memory possibilities. Above the surface there have been considerably more discussions on the Third Reich in public life and academic circles after the 1970s than before. But the earlier period may be the more interesting and challenging for scholars. Here existed genuine tensions about National Socialism and its crimes, for this was after all a society of, among others, many murderers and many more bystanders. In this society tensions flared between perpetrators and honest Germans (of the Nazi period: because perpetrators of the Third Reich turned into honest, law-abiding citizens in East and West Germany, which created for some another tension—within themselves), between Auschwitz and moral taboos, between guilt and belief in God, between personal memories and public silences, between shooting children and educating your own. The years after the war, which are so often uncomplicatedly labeled as years of denial and repression, may be much more important than previously thought for molding the memories of dictatorship, war, and genocide. Many of these memories were not displayed in public. But they did leave indelible traces in dreams, nightmares, and, also, in a culture of traveling. This history of German dreams and nightmares of the period, and of traveling as a culture of hidden fantasies, still awaits its chronicler.[52]

NOTES

Abbreviations

BAL	Bundesarchiv Lichterfelde
HStAS	Hauptstaatsarchiv Stuttgart
Ncm, IfT	Noncataloged material at the Historisches Archiv zum Tourismus am Willi Scharnow-Institut für Tourismus der Freien Universität Berlin

Prologue

1. Saul Friedländer, *When Memory Comes* (1979; New York, 1991).

2. Bryce Lyon, "Henri Pirenne's *Réflexion d'un solitaire* and His Re-evaluation of History," *Journal of Medieval History* 23, no. 3 (1997): 285–99.

3. That some would argue that the Holocaust is *the* signifying event of our age is a measure of the centrality of the event. At the same time, the importance of the Holocaust is bounded in space to mostly Europe, North America, Israel, and countries such as Australia, which is linked to European civilization and has a Jewish community. It is less pronounced in Asia from China through India to Jordan, Africa, and Central and South America. This essay reflects on the historian's representations within the tradition of Western historical writing.

4. Obviously, a historian of Carolingian kingship can write about it without reflecting on the Holocaust. But if this historian is aware of current trends in, and debates about, historical method, theory, and representation in public and professional circles, he or she would not be able to ignore the centrality of the Holocaust. The opposite case is not necessarily true.

5. Eugen Weber, *My France: Politics, Culture, Myth* (Cambridge, Mass., 1991).

6. "The past is never dead. It's not even past": the sentence appears in William Faulkner, *Requiem for a Nun* (New York, 1951), 92. Strictly speaking, the sentence had nothing to do with southern history, but is part of a scene that depicts an animated discussion over sentencing a woman to death for killing a child. C. Vann Woodward, I believe, first gave this sentence a southern collective memory spin in his 1956 essay "The Historical Dimension" that was later included in his *The Burden of Southern History* (Baton Rouge, 1960). See ibid., 36. I am grateful to Scot French for this information.

7. On July 16 and 17, 1942, 13,152 Jews—including 3,118 men, 5,919 women, and 4,115 children—were rounded up by the French police at the Vélodrome d'Hiver (known as Vél' d'Hiv') in Paris, later to be deported for extermination. It symbolizes the active participation of Vichy in the Final Solution. In the small village of Izieux, between Lyon and Chambery in the Loire region, 44 Jewish children hid in a remote house in the middle of the mountains. On April 6, 1944, the Gestapo led by Klaus Barbie came to take the children and seven of their leaders. All were deported to Auschwitz. Only one adult survived, one child was able to escape, and one released because he was not Jewish. It stands as a symbol for the pre-

meditated nature of the Final Solution; the event had no contingent or contextual motives. Its only "justification" was the plan and desire to exterminate all the Jews in Europe and the world. Louis Malle's film *Au revoir les enfants*, about the tragic fate of a Jewish child who takes refuge in a Catholic school, was released in 1987.

8. Furet directed this sentence toward understanding *histoire des mentalités*, but it is valid for history in general. François Furet, *In the Workshop of History* (Chicago, 1984), 15–16.

9. Fernand Braudel, *The Mediterranean and the Mediterranean World in the Age of Philip II* (London, 1972) and *The Identity of France*, vol. 1, *History and Environment* (New York, 1988), 15.

10. I am grateful to Lenard Berlanstein for his thoughts on this issue.

11. Eric Hobsbawm, *Nations and Nationalism since 1780: Programme, Myth, Reality* (Cambridge, 1991), 12–13.

12. Elie Wiesel, "Trivializing the Holocaust: Semi-Fact and Semi-Fiction," *New York Times*, April 16, 1978, B1, B29. Wiesel wrote this piece in reaction to the television series *Holocaust*.

13. See, for example, Ian Kershaw, *The Nazi Dictatorship: Problems and Perspectives of Interpretation*, 4th ed. (London, 2000), chaps. 1, 9.

14. Saul Friedländer, "The 'Final Solution': On the Unease in Historical Interpretation," in *Lesson and Legacies: The Meaning of the Holocaust in a Changing World*, ed. Peter Hayes (Evanston, Ill., 1991), 31–32. *Nazi Germany and the Jews* balances personal involvement and historical detachment: "For my generation, to partake at one and the same time in the memory and the present perceptions of this past may create an unsettling dissonance; it may, however, also nurture insights that would otherwise be inaccessible." Saul Friedländer, *Nazi Germany and the Jews: The Years of Persecution* (London, 1997), 1.

15. See the insightful book of Constantin Fasolt, *The Limits of History* (Chicago, 2004).

16. See on this issue Dan Stone, *Constructing the Holocaust: A Study in Historiography* (London, 2003).

17. A clear distinction does not exist, for we know the things that happened only once we narrate them. But *res gestae* and *historia rerum gestarum* are not identical, for narrations of the past are not all equally illuminating.

18. Marc Bloch, *The Historian's Craft* (New York, 1953), 187–88.

19. Ibid., 123.

20. Victor Klemperer, *I Will Bear Witness: A Diary of the Nazi Years, 1933–1941*, vol. 1 (New York, 1998), 314.

21. Hayden White, *The Content of the Form: Narrative Discourse and Historical Representation* (Baltimore, 1987), 75.

22. Ian Thomson, *Primo Levi: A Life* (New York, 2002), 227–35.

23. Raul Hilberg, *The Politics of Memory: The Journey of a Holocaust Historian* (Chicago, 1996), 105–19, 156.

24. Nicholas Berg, *Der Holocaust und die westdeutschen Historiker: Erforschung und Erinnerung* (Göttingen, 2003), 343, 447–63.

25. Hans-Ulrich Wehler, "Das Ende des deutschen 'Sonderwegs,'" in *Umbruch und Kontinuität: Essays zum 20. Jahrhundert* (Munich, 2000), 84.

26. François Furet, *L'atelier de l'histoire* (Paris, 1981). In English, Furet, *In the Workshop of History*.

27. Of course, much of this transformation has already been evident in the work of Furet

himself, who left behind the ossified rendition of social history in favor of history of discourse and power. The two historiographical moments described here were thus blended, not clearly separated. Accentuating their differences serves only to identify changes and articulate the transformation.

28. Isaiah Berlin, "Historical Inevitability," in *Four Essays on Liberty* (London, 1969), 43.

29. Bloch, *The Historian's Craft*, 195.

30. Blaise Pascal, *Pensées* (Paris, 1670), 277.

Part I

1. Benedict Anderson, *Imagined Communities: Reflections on the Origins and Spread of Nationalism* (1983; revised and extended ed., London, 1991); Ernest Gellner, *Nations and Nationalism* (Ithaca, N.Y., 1983).

2. This is true even for the best theoretical contributions, such as Partha Chatterjee *The Nation and Its Fragments: Colonial and Postcolonial Histories* (Princeton, N.J., 1993); Eugen Weber, *Peasants into Frenchmen: The Modernization of Rural France, 1870–1914* (Stanford, Calif., 1976). A similar approach is also evident in the multivolume history of the Italian regions published by Einaudi. See Carl Levi, "Introduction: Italian Regionalism in Context," in *Italian Regionalism: History, Identity and Politics*, ed. Carl Levi (Oxford, 1996), 5.

3. Jürgen Kocka, "Probleme der politischen Integration der Deutschen 1867 bis 1945," in *Die Rolle der Nation in der deutschen Geschichte und Gegenwart*, ed. O. Büsch and J. J. Sheehan (Berlin, 1985), 118–36.

4. For an overview of this interpretative transformation, see Celia Applegate, "A Europe of Regions: Reflection on the Historiography of Sub-National Places in Modern Times," *American Historical Review* 104, no. 4 (October 1999): 1157–82.

5. Thus the term "regionalism" entered French political debates only in the last years of the nineteenth century. Anne-Marie Thiesse, "L'invention du régionalisme à la Belle Époque," *Le Mouvement Social* 160 (July–September 1992): 11–32. See also her book *La Création des identités nationales. Europe XVIIIe–XXe siècle* (Paris, 1999).

6. See the eye-opening book of Abigail Green, *Fatherlands: State-Building and Nationhood in Nineteenth-Century Germany* (Cambridge, 2001).

7. Notable examples are Peter Sahlins, *Boundaries: The Making of France and Spain in the Pyrenees* (Berkeley, 1989); Celia Applegate, *A Nation of Provincials: The German Idea of Heimat* (Berkeley, 1990); Caroline Ford, *Creating the Nation in Provincial France: Religion and Political Identity in Brittany* (Princeton, N.J., 1993); Charlotte Tacke, *Denkmal im sozialen Raum: Nationale Symbole in Deutschland und Frankreich im 19. Jahrhundert* (Göttingen, 1995); Heinz-Gerhard Haupt and Charlotte Tacke, "Die Kultur des Nationalen: Sozial- und kulturgeschichtliche Ansätze bei der Erforschung des europäischen Nationalismus im 19. und 20. Jahrhundert," in *Kulturgeschichte Heute*, ed. Wolfgang Hardtwig and Hans-Ulrich Wehler (Göttingen, 1996), 255–83; Anne-Marie Thiesse, *Ils apprenaient la France: L'exaltation des régions dans le discours patriotique* (Paris, 1997); Stefano Cavazza, *Piccole Patrie. Feste popolari tra regione e nazione durante il fascismo* (Bologna, 1997); Heinz-Gerhard Haupt, Michael Müller, and Stuart Wolf, eds., *Regional and National Identities in Europe in the XIXth and XXth Centuries* (The Hague, 1998); John Dickie, *Darkest Italy: The Nation and Stereotypes of the Mezzogiorno, 1860–1900* (London, 1999); the forum in the *American Historical Review* 104,

no. 4 (October 1999): 1183–1220, on "Bringing Regionalism Back to History": Applegate, "A Europe of Regions"; Kären Wigen, "Culture, Power, and Place: The New Landscapes of East Asian Regionalism"; Michael O'Brien, "On Observing the Quicksand"; and Vicente Rafael, "Regionalism, Area Studies, and the Accidents of Agency"; Xosé-Manoel Núñez, "The Region as Essence of the Fatherland: Regionalist Variants of Spanish Nationalism (1840–1936)," *European History Quarterly* 31, no. 4 (2001): 483–518; Michael Müller and Rolf Petri, eds., *Die Nationalisierung von Grenzen. Zur Konstruktion nationler Identität in sprachlich gemischten Grenzregionen* (Marburg, 2002); Oliver Zimmer, *A Contested Nation: History, Memory and Nationalism in Switzerland, 1761–1891* (Cambridge, 2003); Ron Robin and Bo Stråth, eds., *Homelands: Poetic Power and the Politics of Space* (Brussels, 2003); Stéphan Gerson, *The Pride of Place: Local Memories and Political Culture in Nineteenth-Century France* (Ithaca, N.Y., 2003); Eric Storm, "Regionalism in History, 1890–1945: The Cultural Approach," *European History Quarterly* 33, no. 2 (2003): 251–65; Rolf Petri, ed., "Regioni Plurilingue e frontiera Nazionali," special issue, *Memoria e ricerca* 14 (2004).

8. In this respect, the work of Ajay Skaria is exemplary. See, for example, "Homeless in Gujarat and India: On the Curious Love of Indulal Yagnik," *Indian Economic and Social History Review* 38, no. 3 (2001): 271–97. See also Arjun Appadurai, "The Production of the Locality," in *Modernity at Large* (Minneapolis, 1996), 178–99.

9. Alon Confino, *The Nation as a Local Metaphor: Württemberg, Imperial Germany, and National Memory, 1871–1918* (Chapel Hill, N.C., 1997).

10. Applegate, *A Nation of Provincials*, 6.

11. For studies of the Heimat idea as a primary human condition of loyalty, security, and social orientation, see, for example, Ina-Maria Greverus, *Der Territoriale Mensch. Ein literatur-anthropologisches Versuch zum Heimatphänomen* (Frankfurt am Main, 1972), and Klaus Weigelt, "Heimat—Der Ort Personaler Identitätsfindung und sozio-politischer Orientierung," in *Heimat und Nation. Zur Geschichte und Identität der deutschen*, ed. Klaus Weigelt (Mainz, 1984), 15–25.

12. See, for instance, Klaus Bergmann, *Agrarromantik und Großstadtfeindschaft* (Meisenheim am Glan, 1970); Hermann Glaser, *The Cultural Roots of National Socialism [Spießer-Ideologie]* (London, 1978); Anton Kaes, *From Hitler to Heimat: The Return of History as Film* (Cambridge, Mass., 1989), 163–66; Dieter Kramer, "Die politische und ökonomische Funktionalisierung von Heimat im deutschen Imperialismus und Faschismus," *Diskurs* 6–7, nos. 3–4 (1973): 3–22. Werner Hartung, *Konservative Zivilisationskritik und regionale Identität. Am Beispiel der niedersächsischen Heimatbewegung 1895 bis 1919* (Hannover, 1991), 56–57.

13. On Heimat, regionalism, and nationhood, see Jost Hermand and James Steakley, eds., *Heimat, Nation, Fatherland: The German Sense of Belonging* (New York, 1996); James Retallack, ed., "Saxon Signposts," special issue, *German History* 17, no. 4 (1999); George Kunz, *Verortete Geschichte: Regionales Geschichtsbewußtsein in den deutschen Historischen Vereinen des 19. Jahrhunderts* (Göttingen, 2000); James Retallack, ed., *Saxony in German History: Culture, Society, and Politics, 1830–1933* (Ann Arbor, Mich., 2000); Maiken Umbach, ed., *German Federalism: Past, Present, Future* (New York, 2002); Glenn Penny, *Objects of Culture: Ethnology and Ethnographic Museums in Imperial Germany* (Chapel Hill, N.C., 2002); Jennifer Jenkins, *Provincial Modernity: Local Culture and Liberal Politics in Fin-de-Siècle Hamburg* (Ithaca, N.Y., 2003); Siegfried Weichlein, *Nation und Region. Integrationsprozesse im Bismarckreich* (Düsseldorf, 2004); Nancy Reagin, "Recent Work on German National Identity: Regional? Imperial?

Gendered? Imaginary?," *Central European History* 37, no. 2 (2004): 273–89; and also see Abigail Green, "The Federal Alternative? A New View of Modern German History," *Historical Journal* 46, no. 1 (2003): 187–202.

14. On various appropriations of the Heimat idea, see Will Cremer and Ansgar Klein, eds., *Heimat. Analysen, Thesen, Perspektiven* (Bielefeld, 1990); Edeltraud Klueting, ed., *Antimodernismus und Reform. Zur Geschichte der deutschen Heimatbewegung* (Darmstadt, 1991); Dietmar von Reeken, *Heimatbewegung, Kulturpolitik und Nationalsozialismus: Die Geschichte der 'Ostfriesische Landschaft'* (Aurich, 1995); Katharina Weigand, ed., *Heimat: Konstanten und Wandel im 19./20. Jahrhundert. Vorstellungen und Wirklichkeiten* (Munch, 1997); Rudy Koshar, *Germany's Transient Pasts: Preservation and National Memory in the Twentieth Century* (Chapel Hill, N.C., 1998); Jan Palmowski, "Building an East German Nation: The Construction of a Socialist Heimat, 1945–1961," *Central European History* 37, no. 3 (2003): 365–99; Thomas Schaarschmidt, *Regionalkultur und Diktatur. Sächsische Heimatbewegung und Heimat-Propaganda im Dritten Reich und in der SBZ/DDR* (Cologne, 2004); Willi Oberkrome, *"Deutsche Heimat." Nationale Konzeption und regionale Praxis von Naturschutz, Landschaftsgestaltung und Kulturpolitik in Westfalen-Lippe und Thüringen (1900–1960)* (Paderborn, 2004).

On the Heimat idea in film, literature, architecture, and the arts, see Matthew Jefferies, *Politics and Culture in Wilhelmine Germany: The Case of Industrial Architecture* (Oxford, 1995), chap. 2; Heide Fehrenbach, *Cinema in Democratizing Germany: Reconstructing National Identity after Hitler* (Chapel Hill, N.C., 1995), chap. 5; Irmgard Wilharm, "Der Heimatfilm in Niedersachsen," in *Von der Währungsreform zum Wirtschaftswunder. Wiederaufbau in Niedersachsen*, ed. Bernd Weisbrod (Hannover, 1998), 47–56; Christopher Wickham, *Constructing Heimat in Postwar Germany: Longing and Belonging* (Lewiston, N.Y., 1999); Elizabeth Boa and Rachel Palfreyman, eds., *Heimat: A German Dream: Regional Loyalties and National Identity in German Culture, 1890–1990* (Oxford, 2000); Robert Moeller, *War Stories: The Search for a Usable Past in the Federal Republic of Germany* (Berkeley, 2001), chap. 5; Peter Blickle, *Heimat: A Critical Theory of the German Idea of Homeland* (Rochester, N.Y., 2002); Habbo Knoch, ed., *Das Erbe der Provinz. Heimatkultur und Geschichtspolitik nach 1945* (Göttingen, 2002); Robert Moeller, "Sinking Ships, the Lost *Heimat* and Broken Taboos: Günter Grass and the Politics of Memory in Contemporary Germany," *Contemporary European History* 12 (2003): 1–35; Maiken Umbach and Bernd Hüppauf, eds., *Vernacular Modernism: Heimat, Globalization and the Built Environment* (Stanford, Calif., 2005); Johannes von Moltke, *No Place like Home: Locations of Heimat in German Cinema* (Berkeley, 2005).

On the Heimat idea and nature, see John Williams, "'The Chords of the German Soul Are Tuned to Nature': The Movement to Preserve the Natural Heimat from the Kaiserreich to the Third Reich," *Central European History* 29, no. 3 (1996): 339–84; Matthias Frese and Michael Prinz, eds., *Politische Zäsuren und gesellschaftlicher Wandel im 20. Jahrhundert. Regionale und vergleichende Perspektiven* (Paderborn, 1996), 401–543; William Rollins, *A Greener Vision of Home: Cultural Politics and Environmental Reform in the German Heimatschutz Movement, 1904–1918* (Ann Arbor, Mich., 1997); Thomas Lekan, *Imagining the Nation in Nature: Landscape Preservation and German Identity, 1885–1945* (Cambridge, Mass., 2004).

On the Heimat idea and anthropology, see Kaspar Maase, "Nahwelten zwischen 'Heimat' und 'Kulisse.' Anmerkungen zur volkskundlich-kulturwissenschaftlichen Regionalitätsforschung," *Zeitschrift für Volkskunde* 94, no. 1 (1998): 53–70. And see the comprehensive review by Rolf Petri, "Deutsche Heimat 1850–1950," *Comparativ* 11, no. 1 (2001): 77–127.

Chapter One

Chapter 1 originally appeared as "The Nation as a Local Metaphor: Heimat, National Memory and the German Empire, 1871–1918," *History and Memory* 5, no. 1 (1993): 46–86; reprinted with permission of Indiana University Press.

1. The seminal study has been Benedict Anderson, *Imagined Communities: Reflections on the Origin and Spread of Nationalism* (1983; revised and extended ed., London, 1991).

2. Karl Deutsch, *Nationalism and Social Communication* (Cambridge, Mass., 1966).

3. Ernest Gellner, *Nations and Nationalism* (Ithaca, N.Y., 1983); Anthony Smith, *The Ethnic Origins of Nations* (Oxford, 1986); Eric Hobsbawm, "Introduction: Inventing Traditions" and "Mass-Producing Traditions," in *The Invention of Tradition*, ed. Eric Hobsbawm and Terence Ranger (Cambridge, 1983), 1–14, 263–307.

4. Eugen Weber, *Peasants into Frenchmen: The Modernization of Rural France, 1870–1914* (Stanford, Calif., 1976).

5. Eric Hobsbawm, *The Age of Empire, 1875–1914* (New York, 1987), 148.

6. Anderson, *Imagined Communities*, 5. Ernst Kantorovitz argued as much in a brilliant, though forgotten, article back in 1951, "*Pro Patria Mori* in Medieval Political Thought," *American Historical Review* 56 (1951): 472–92.

7. An illustration of this problematic state of the research was the excellent study by Anderson who treated the nation, "in an anthropological spirit, as kinship or religion," but ignored the relations between the imagined national community and other imagined communities that exist in the nation such as regional and religious.

8. Anderson, *Imagined Communities*, 15.

9. For an overview on the state of the concept and the research, see Nathan Wachtel, "Memory and History: An Introduction," *History and Anthropology* 2 (1986): 207–24; Philippe Joutard, "Mémoire collective," in *Dictionnaire des sciences historiques*, ed. André Burguière (Paris, 1986), 447–49; Pierre Nora, "Mémoire collective," in *La nouvelle histoire*, ed. Jacques Le Goff, Roger Chartier, and Jacques Revel (Paris, 1978), 398–401, and "Between Memory and History: *Les Lieux de Mémoire*," *Representations* 26 (1989): 7–25; David Lowenthal, *The Past Is a Foreign Country* (Cambridge, 1985), 185–259; John Gillis, "Memory and Identity: The History of a Relationship," in *Commemorations: The Politics of National Identity*, ed. John Gillis (Princeton, N.J., 1994), 3–24; Patrick Hutton, *History as an Art of Memory* (Hanover, N.H., 1993), chap. 1, "Placing Memory in Contemporary Historiography."

10. Henri Bergson, *Matter and Memory* (New York, 1988); Marcel Proust, *Remembrance of Things Past* (London, 1983); Jack Goody, *The Domestication of the Savage Mind* (London, 1977) and "Mémoire et apprentissage dans les sociétés avec et sans écriture: La transmission du Barge," *L'Homme* 17: 29–52; Roger Bastide, "Mémoire collective et sociologie du bricolage," *L'année sociologique* 21 (1970): 65–108.

11. Maurice Halbwachs, *Les cadres sociaux de la mémoire* (Paris, 1925); *La topographie légendaire des Évangiles en Terre sainte. Étude de mémoire collective* (Paris, 1941). For an English version, see Halbwachs, *On Collective Memory*, ed., trans., and introd. Lewis Coser (Chicago, 1992); *The Collective Memory*, trans. Francis Ditter and Vida Yazdi Ditter (New York, 1980). On Halbwachs's formulation and use of collective memory, see Hutton, *History as an Art of Memory*, chap. 4.

12. Several discussions with the late Amos Funkenstein helped to refine my argument.

See his illuminating article "Collective Memory and Historical Consciousness," *History and Memory* 1, no. 1 (1989): 5–26.

13. Extremely influential has been the magisterial work edited by Pierre Nora, *Les lieux de mémoire*, vol. 1, *La République*; vols. 2–4, *La Nation*; vols. 5–7, *Les Frances* (Paris, 1984–92). For a critique of Nora's approach, see Steven Englund, "The Ghost of Nation Past," *Journal of Modern History* 64 (June 1992): 299–320.

14. James Sheehan, *German History, 1770–1866* (Oxford, 1989), 1.

15. With historical hindsight we know that the memory of the nation-state shaped in 1871 has remained to this day the principal way for Germans to imagine the nation. There were two important attempts to redesign German nationhood in the twentieth century: the *Anschluß* in 1938 (the forced unity between Austria and Germany) and the annexation of territories to the Third Reich between 1939 and 1945, and the existence of two Germanys between 1949 and 1990. The unification of 1990 demonstrated that, in spite of these attempts, Germans' idea of the nation-state has remained connected to the boundaries of 1871.

16. Richard Evans, *Death in Hamburg: Society and Politics in the Cholera Years, 1830–1910* (Oxford, 1987), 1–2.

17. Hans Mommsen, "History and National Identity: The Case of Germany," *German Studies Review* 6 (October 1983): 575.

18. "Peculiarity"—but similar to the peculiarities of other nations. In my view neither this nor other peculiarities that existed between 1871 and 1914 predetermined 1933.

19. See Keith Robbins, *Nineteenth-Century Britain: Integration and Diversity* (Oxford, 1988).

20. The regional variegation of the German Empire was also a reflection of power relationships between Bismarck, William I, and the Prussian army, on the one hand, and the German states, on the other, relationships that in themselves were influenced by particularist identities. Significantly, in 1871 Bismarck did not attempt to incorporate the German states into Prussia—that is, to depose the German princes as he did in Hannover and Hessen-Nassau, which were annexed to Prussia in 1866—because he recognized that such an attempt would lead to armed resistance and popular revolt based on sentiments of local identity and anti-Prussianism. For Bismarck's annexationist policy in 1866, see Hans Schmitt, "From Sovereign States to Prussian Provinces: Hannover and Hesse-Nassau, 1866–1871," *Journal of Modern History* 57 (March 1985): 24–56.

The regional diversity of the European nation-states has been for too long passed over by historians who saw themselves as delegates of the indivisible nation. British historiography has been for a long time dominated by the conception that English history was British history, thus ignoring Scotland and Wales. Contra this assumption, Linda Colley argued in *Britons* that "Great Britain was invented only in 1707" with the Act of Union that united Scotland with England and Wales, and that the new national identity did not replace old loyalties as "Britishness was superimposed over an array of internal differences" without obliterating the Welsh, Scottish, and English distinct identities. See Linda Colley, *Britons: Forging the Nation, 1707–1837* (New Haven, 1992), 6, 373. See also Hugh Kearney, *The British Isles: A History of Four Nations* (Cambridge, 1995), and Krishan Kumar, *The Making of English National Identity* (New York, 2003).

In German historiography the idea of the centralized nation was expressed in the notion that the German Empire was Prussia and Prussia the German Empire. James Sheehan has observed of the historiographical tendency, now in decline, to treat the German Empire as a centralized state that "It is remarkable that France, Europe's most centralized nation, has been dissolved by its historians into regions, while Germany, Europe's most fragmented polity, is treated as if it were a cohesive entity." In "What Is German History? Reflections on the Role of the *Nation* in German History and Historiography," *Journal of Modern History* 53 (March 1981): 21.

21. This sentence has usually been attributed to Massimo d'Azeglio, prime minister of the Kingdom of Sardinia before Cavour, who allegedly said it after the Italian unification. In fact, the famous sentence was uttered by Martini. See Simonetta Soldoni and Gabriele Turi, eds., *Fare gli Italiani. Scuola e cultura nell'Italia contemporanea*, vol. 1, *La nascita dello stato nazionale* (Bologna, 1993), 17.

22. *Schwäbisches Heimatbuch* (1940): 146.

23. See Verschönerungsverein Eningen, HStAS, J 2, no. 624, and *Bericht über die Entwickelung und Thätigkeit des Verschönerungsverein der Stadt Stuttgart in den ersten 25 Jahren seines Bestehens 1861–1886* (Stuttgart, 1886).

24. Wilhelm Seytter, *Unser Stuttgart. Geschichte, Sage und Kultur der Stadt und ihrer Umgebung* (Stuttgart, 1904), 4–5.

25. *Unsere Heimat in alter und neuer Zeit. Heimatkunde für Schule und Haus* (Giengen an der Brenz, 1914), 85.

26. Karl Mayer, *Heimat-Buch für Kirchheim u. Teck und Umgebung*, 3rd ed. (Kirchheim unter Teck, 1920), 5 (the first edition was published before 1914).

27. *Arbeitsplan des Württembergischen Landesausschußes für Natur- und Heimatschutz* (Stuttgart, n.d.), 5. The booklet was published in 1911.

28. *Unsere Heimat in alter und neuer Zeit*, 85.

29. "Geschichte der Gründung des Bundes für Heimatschutz in Württemberg und Hohenzollern," *Schwäbisches Heimatbuch* (1919): 9–10. Emphasis added.

30. See the reprint, Karl Bohnenberger, *Volkstümliche Überlieferungen in Württemberg* (Stuttgart, 1980).

31. Angelika Bischoff-Luithlen, *Von Amtsstuben, Backhäusern, und Jahrmärkten. Ein Lese- und Nachschlagebuch zum Dorfalltag im alten Württemberg und Baden* (Stuttgart, 1979), 255–56.

32. Friedrich Wagner, ed., *Heimatkunde für Stadt und Oberamt Hall* (Schwäbisch Hall, 1912), 33.

33. Bischoff-Luithlen, *Von Amtsstuben*, 256.

34. *Unsere Heimat in alter und neuer Zeit*, 50.

35. Hermann Fischer, *Schwäbisches Wörterbuch*, vol. 1 (Tübingen, 1904), vii.

36. This number of local historical museums is impressive even for a large and populated country like Germany. The figure is from Erika Karasek, *Die volkskundlich-kulturhistorischen Museen in Deutschland. Zur Rolle der Volkskunde in der bürgerlich-imperialistischen Gesellschaft* (Berlin [East], 1984), 225–26. Karasek, who provided a Marxist-Leninist interpretation of Heimat museums between 1890 and 1945, reached this figure by using the information available in *Jahrbuch der deutschen Museen* 8 (1938). In the overall period between 1890 and 1918, 76 new Heimat museums were founded between 1890–99; 178 museums between 1900–1909; 103 museums between 1910–14, and predictably only 14 during the First World

War. Definitive numbers for the pre-1890 period are unavailable, though partial evidence illustrates a clear pattern by which the post-1890 wave of Heimat museums constituted a quantitative as well as a qualitative change with respect to foundations of local historical museums in preceding decades. In the regions that constituted West Germany, 14 local historical museums were founded before 1871, 15 between 1871–80, and 31 between 1881–90. Altogether, 46 new museums were founded between 1871 to 1890 (on West German territory) compared with 371 for the entire Germany between 1890 and 1918. I calculated the data from Hanswilhelm Haefs, *Die deutschen Heimat-museen* (Frankfurt, 1984).

37. *Oettinger Amts- und Wochenblatt*, June 6, 1908.

38. Documents in my possession sent by the Städtisches Heimatmuseum in Reinfeld on August 3, 1990.

39. *Oettinger Amts- und Wochenblatt*, July 1, 1908.

40. D. Hohnholz, "Das Heimatmuseum im Schloß zu Jever," in *Die Tide. Monatsschrift für Nord-, Ost- und Westfriesland, Oldenburg, Friesische Inseln und Helgoland* (Wilhelmshafen, 1921), 115.

41. Peter Barteit, "Heimatverein Vilsbiburg 1928–1978," in *50 Jahre Heimatverein Vilsbiburg 1928–1978*, ed. Fritz Markmiller (Dingolfing, 1978), 4.

42. *80 Jahre Heimatverein "Niedersachsen" e.V. Scheeßel, 1905–1985* (Scheeßel 1985), 6–7.

43. Celia Applegate, *A Nation of Provincials: The German Idea of Heimat* (Berkeley, 1990), 93–96.

44. Eisele and Köhle, *Geschichtliche Heimatkunde für den Oberamtsbezirk Göppingen und seine Umgebung* (Göppingen, 1908).

45. Karl Rommel, *Reutlinger Heimatbuch. Bilder, Sagen und Geschichten aus Stadt und Amt* (Reutlingen, 1929); G. Eppinger, *Beschreibung, Geschichte und Führer von Fellbach* (Fellbach, 1908). In 1910 Reutlingen had 29,763 inhabitants, Fellbach 6,780.

46. *Aufruf zur Gründung eines Bundes Heimatschutz*, HStAS, E 151/07, 584.

47. *Um die Heimat. Bilder aus dem Weltkrieg 1914*, collected by J. Kammerer, 9 vols. (Stuttgart, 1915–17); *Die Heimat. Neue Kriegsgedichte* (Jena, 1915). The booklets cost sixty pfennings.

48. *Die Heimat. Neue Kriegsgedichte*, 48.

49. Ibid., 35, 49.

50. Ibid., 35, 48, 50; *Um die Heimat*, vol. 2, *Der westliche Kriegsschauplatz* (Stuttgart, 1915), 131.

51. See Alain Corbin, *Village Bells: Sound and Meaning in the 19th-Century French Countryside* (New York, 1998).

52. See John Gillis, *A World of Their Own Making: Myth, Ritual, and the Quest for Family Values* (New York, 1996), on the invention of the home and family in the West.

53. *Um die Heimat*, vol. 7 (no title) (Stuttgart, 1917), 119; *Die Heimat. Neue Kriegsgedichte*, 69.

54. The association of women with coziness and home was prevalent in that period in Europe and North America. See Erna Hellerstein, Leslie Hume, and Karen Offen, eds., *Victorian Women: A Documentary Account of Women's Lives in Nineteenth-Century England, France, and the United States* (Stanford, Calif., 1981), esp. pt. 2.

55. Also in England nation, home, and women were related metaphors. See Jane Mackay and Pat Thane, "The Englishwomen," in *Englishness: Politics and Culture, 1880–1920*, ed. Philip Dodd and Robert Colls (London, 1986), 191–93, 223–24.

56. Ernst Jünger, "Der Kampf als inneres Erlebnis," in *Werke*, vol. 5 (1922; Stuttgart, 1960), 87.

57. The person in figure 3 is of particular interest since its gender is not clear and it appears to be androgynous. Interestingly, the artist was a woman, a rarity among artists of war posters.

58. By linking Heimat with women and by countering them to war, the Heimat idea reflected a pervasive notion in Germany and Europe that women were invested with a peaceful and nonaggressive character that made them inherently opposed to war. See Richard Evans, *Comrades and Sisters: Feminism, Socialism and Pacifism in Europe, 1870–1945* (Brighton, Sussex, 1987) and *The Feminist Movement in Germany, 1894–1933* (London, 1976); Darryn Kruse and Charles Sowerwine, "Feminism and Pacifism: 'Women's Sphere' in Peace and War," in *Australian Women: New Feminist Perspective*, ed. Ailsa Burns and Norma Grieve (Melbourne, 1986), 42–58.

59. Grant McCracken observed that "Confronted with the recognition that reality is impervious to cultural ideals, a community may displace these ideals. It will remove them from daily life and transport them to another cultural universe, there to be kept within reach but out of danger." Grant McCracken, *Culture and Consumption: New Approaches to the Symbolic Character of Consumer Goods and Activities* (Bloomington, Ind., 1988), 106. See his chapter 7 on displaced meaning.

60. Carl Schorske, *Fin-de-Siècle Vienna: Politics and Culture* (New York, 1981).

61. See chapter 4 about the East German communists' appropriation of the Heimat idea.

62. Vernon Lidtke, *The Alternative Culture: Socialist Labor in Imperial Germany* (New York, 1985), chap. 2.

63. Hartmann Wunderer, "Der Touristenverein 'Die Naturfreunde'—Eine sozialdemokratische Arbeiterkulturorganisation (1895–1933)," *Internationale wissenschaftliche Korrespondenz zur Geschichte der deutschen Arbeiterbewegung* 13 (December 1977): 513; Dieter Langewiesche and Klaus Schönhoven, "Arbeiterbibliotheken und Arbeiterlektüre im Wilhelminischen Deutschland," *Archiv für Sozialgeschichte* 16 (1976): 182–89.

64. *Die neue Heimat. Ein Gruss aus dem neuen Deutschland an die aus der Gefangenschaft heimkehrenden Deutschen* (Berlin, 1918), 5.

65. Kurt Tucholsky, "Heimat," in *Heimat. Ein deutsches Lesebuch*, ed. Manfred Kluge (Munich, 1989), 27.

66. See Hobsbawm, "Introduction: Inventing Traditions" and "Mass-Producing Traditions: Europe, 1870–1914," in *The Invention of Tradition*, 1–14 and 263–307.

67. Hermann Hesse, "Heimat. Calw," in Kluge, *Heimat*, 21.

Chapter Two

Chapter 2 originally appeared as "Edgar Reitz's *Heimat* and German Nationhood: Film, Memory, and Understandings of the Past," *German History* 16, no. 2 (June 1998): 185–208, © 1998 Edward Arnold (Publishers) Ltd., <www.hodderarnoldjournals.com>; reprinted with permission. It was also presented in the annual Cinema and History workshop of the Trento Group in Trento, Italy, on November 1994. I should like to thank the members of the group for their critical advice: Aldo Bernardini, Ilana Bet El, Valeria Camporesi, Lia Beltrami, Kyoko Hirano, Jerry Kuehl, and Pierre Sorlin. My special thanks go to Francesca Fiorani.

1. Anna Mikula, "Edgar Reitz, ein Deutscher," *Die Zeit Magazin*, October 26, 1984, 42.

2. Edgar Reitz, "Unabhängiger Film nach *Holocaust?*," in *Liebe zum Kino* (Cologne, 1984), 100.

3. Kenneth Barkin, "Modern Germany: A Twisted Vision," *Dissent* 34 (Spring 1987): 254.

4. Timothy Garton Ash, "The Life of Death," *New York Review of Books*, December 19, 1985, 28.

5. Gertrud Koch, "How Much Naiveté Can We Afford? The New Heimat Feeling," *New German Critique* 36 (1985): 13. See also Anton Kaes, *From Hitler to Heimat: The Return of History as Film* (Cambridge, Mass., 1989), 186.

6. See, for example, Eric Santner, "On the Difficulty of Saying 'We': The Historians' Debate and Edgar Reitz' *Heimat*," in *Framing the Past: The Historiography of German Cinema and Television*, ed. Bruce Murray and Christopher Wickham (Carbondale, 1992). Christopher Wickham, "Representation and Mediation in Edgar Reitz's *Heimat*," *German Quarterly* 64, no. 1 (1991): 35–45, esp. 38–41; Thomas Elsaesser, "Subject Positions, Speaking Positions: From *Holocaust*, *Our Hitler*, and *Heimat* to *Shoah* and *Schindler's List*," in *The Persistence of History: Cinema, Television, and the Modern Event*, ed. Vivian Sobchack (New York, 1996), 145–83.

7. Celia Applegate insightfully recognized this when she observed that "Reitz has been criticized (often by Americans) for consigning Nazism in general and Nazi atrocities in particular to the periphery of his characters' lives. But this criticism surely misses the point. . . . *Heimat* has never been a word about real social forces or real political situations. Instead it has been a myth about the possibility of a community in the face of fragmentation and alienation." Celia Applegate, *A Nation of Provincials: The German Idea of Heimat* (Berkeley, 1990), 19.

8. Kaes, *From Hitler to Heimat*, 165.

9. Ibid., 170. The statement of Rob Burns and Wilfried Van Der Will, to give another example—that "Reitz was, of course, fully aware of the ideological baggage attached to the concept of *Heimat* and of the perversion it had undergone"—is, as we shall see, not accurate. In fact, Reitz's awareness of the Heimat idea was very selective. See Rob Burns and Wilfried Van Der Will, "The Federal Republic 1968 to 1990: From the Industrial Society to the Culture Society," in *German Cultural Studies: An Introduction*, ed. Rob Burns (New York, 1995), 318.

10. Mikula, "Edgar Reitz, ein Deutscher," 42.

11. *Satzungen des Bundes "Heimatschutz*," HStAS E151/07, 584 (emphasis added).

12. See, for example, the statement in *Heimatschutz* 10, no. 1 (1915): 2, the journal of the German League for Heimat Protection.

13. On the eve of 1914 all the important German regions prided themselves on having Heimat organizations. See *75 Jahre Deutscher Heimatbund* (Siegburg, 1979).

14. Karl-Heinz Brackmann and Renate Birkenhauer, *NS-Deutsch. "Selbstverständliche" Begriffe und Schlagwörter aus der Zeit des Nationalsozialismus* (Darmstadt, 1988), 39.

15. For an excellent selection of Nazi Heimat literature, see Ernst Loewy, *Literatur unterm Hakenkreuz: Das Dritte Reich und seine Dichtung. Eine Dokumentation* (1966; Frankfurt am Main, 1987), part II.

16. A good example is the interpretation of Heimat in the otherwise superb project on Heimat films led by Wolfgang Kaschuba: Projektgruppe Deutscher Heimatfilm, *Der deutsche Heimatfilm. Bildwelten und Weltbilder: Bilder, Texte, Analysen zu 70 Jahren deutscher Filmgeschichte* (Tübingen, 1989). The project argued that "Heimat = Fatherland" (16) in the na-

tionalist, imperialist sense, and viewed this meaning of the Heimat idea as beginning immediately after the unification in 1871. This is an oversimplified interpretation of the Heimat idea, its origination, development, and appropriation.

17. On West Germany's use of the Heimat idea, see chapter 3; on the different career of the idea in East Germany, see chapter 4.

18. Kaes, *From Hitler to Heimat*, 127–28.

19. Reitz, "Unabhängiger Film nach Holocaust?," 99.

20. Ibid., 102.

21. Ibid.

22. Mikula, "Edgar Reitz, ein Deutscher," 42. I used the translation of Kaes, *From Hitler to Heimat*, 256.

23. Edgar Reitz, "The Camera Is Not a Clock (Regarding My Experiences Telling Stories from German History)," in *West German Filmmakers on Film: Visions and Voices*, ed. Eric Rentschler (New York, 1988), 137–38.

24. Wilhelm Seytter, *Unser Stuttgart. Geschichte, Sage und Kultur der Stadt und ihrer Umgebung* (Stuttgart, 1904), 4–5.

25. Emil Utitz, "Ein neues Museum," *Museumskunde* 6 (1910): 196.

26. Peter Jessen, "Das Museum für Kunst- und Kulturgeschichte in Lübeck," *Museumskunde* 12 (1916): 59.

27. Cited in Klaus Geobel, "Der Heimatkundeunterricht in den deutschen Schulen," in *Antimodernisums und Reform. Zur Geschichte der deutschen Heimatbewegung*, ed. Edeltraud Klueting (Darmstadt, 1991), 100.

28. Modris Eksteins argued in his original book *Rites of Spring: The Great War and the Birth of the Modern Age* (New York, 1989) that Nazism "was an aestheticizing of existence as a whole," whose "point of departure [was] the subjective self, feeling, experience, *Erlebnis* . . ." (304, 311).

29. Loewy, *Literatur unterm Hakenkreuz*, 149. Schlageter was a communist who was killed by the French in 1923 during the German passive resistance to the occupation of the Ruhr. He became a hero for nationalists from both left and right.

30. In Geobel, "Der Heimatkundeunterricht in den deutschen Schulen," 103–4.

31. Applegate, *A Nation of Provincials*, 243–44.

32. Projektgruppe deutscher Heimatfilm, *Der deutsche Heimatfilm*, 11. And see Heide Fehrenbach, *Cinema in Democratizing Germany: Reconstructing National Identity after Hitler* (Chapel Hill, N.C., 1995), chap. 5.

33. Reitz, "The Camera Is Not a Clock," 137, 140.

34. Gideon Bachman, "The Reitz Stuff," *Film Comment* 21, no. 4 (1985): 19. Emphasis added.

35. In his discussion of Reitz's conception of history, Kaes, for example, cites Walter Benjamin's *Thesis on the Philosophy of History*: "To articulate the past historically does not mean to recognize it 'the way it really was' (Ranke). It means to seize hold of a memory as it flashes up at a moment of danger." He then concludes that "Reitz adopted this concept of history based on memory for his series" (Kaes, *From Hitler to Heimat*, 172.) But Benjamin's words leave a lot to be interpreted. Should we conclude that history is identical to memory? Does Reitz "articulate the past historically" like historians, and if not, what are the differ-

ences? Can we articulate the past historically only when memory "flashes up at a moment of danger"? Kaes remains silent on these issues.

36. Christopher Browning, *Ordinary Men: Reserve Police Battalion 101 and the Final Solution in Poland* (New York, 1992).

37. Thomas Elsaesser, *New German Cinema: A History* (New Brunswick, N.J., 1989), 277.

38. Bachman, "The Reitz Stuff," 19.

39. Reitz adds presumptuously that "Art is ambiguous, an eternal mystery for schoolteachers." In Reitz, "The Camera Is Not a Clock," 139.

40. Maurice Halbwachs, *The Collective Memory* (New York, 1980), 78–87, 105–7. On Halbwachs's conceptions of history and memory, see Patrick Hutton, *History as an Art of Memory* (Hanover, N.H., 1993), 73–90.

41. An interview with Joachim von Mengershausen, Tel Aviv, Israel, December 21, 1992. I should like to thank von Mengershausen for his patience in answering my questions and for his illuminating discussion of various aspects of the film.

42. My following discussion of the motives of the Heimat films owes to Projektgruppe deutscher Heimatfilm, *Der deutsche Heimatfilm*. All quotations are from p. 11.

43. Kaes, *From Hitler to Heimat*, 16.

44. Edgar Reitz and Peter Steinbach, *Heimat. Eine deutsche Chronik* (Nördlingen, 1985), scene 566.

45. Pierre Nora, ed., *Les lieux de mémoire*, vol. 1, *La République*; vols. 2–4, *La Nation*; vols. 5–7, *Les Frances* (Paris, 1984–92).

46. Pierre Nora, "Between Memory and History: *Les lieux de mémoire*," *Representations* 26 (Spring 1989): 7, 14.

Chapter Three

Chapter 3 originally appeared as "'This lovely country you will never forget.' Kriegserinnerungen und Heimatkonzepte in der westdeutsche Nachkriegszeit," in *Das Erbe der Provinz. Heimatkultur und Geschichtspolitik in Deutschland nach 1945*, ed. Habbo Knoch (Göttingen, 2001); reprinted with permission.

1. On various appropriations of the Heimat idea, see Celia Applegate, *A Nation of Provincials: The German Idea of Heimat* (Berkeley, 1990); Heide Fehrenbach, *Cinema in Democratizing Germany: Reconstructing National Identity after Hitler* (Chapel Hill, N.C., 1995), chap. 5; Matthew Jefferies, *Politics and Culture in Wilhelmine Germany: The Case of Industrial Architecture* (Oxford and Washington, D.C., 1995), chap. 2; Jost Hermand and James Steakley, eds., *Heimat, Nation, Fatherland: The German Sense of Belonging* (New York, 1996); Katharina Weigand, ed., *Heimat: Konstanten und Wandel im 19./20. Jahrhundert. Vorstellungen und Wirklichkeiten* (Munich, 1997); William Rollins, *A Greener Vision of Home: Cultural Politics and Environmental Reform in the German Heimatschutz Movement, 1904–1918* (Ann Arbor, Mich., 1997); Rudy Koshar, *Germany's Transient Pasts: Preservation and National Memory in the Twentieth Century* (Chapel Hill, N.C., 1998); Siegfried Weichlein, "Das Spannungsfeld von nationaler und regionaler Identität," in *Politische Kultur in Ostmittel- und Südosteuropa*, ed. Werner Bramke (Leipzig, 1999), 241–52, and "Saxons into Germans: The Progress of the National Idea in Saxony after 1866," in *Saxony in German History: Culture, Society, and Politics, 1830–1933*, ed. James Retallack (Ann Arbor, Mich., 2000), 166–79; Christopher Wickham, *Con-*

structing *Heimat in Postwar Germany: Longing and Belonging* (Lewiston, N.Y., 1999); Robert Moeller, *War Stories: The Search for a Usable Past in the Federal Republic of Germany* (Berkeley, 2001), chap. 5; Thomas Schaarschmidt, *Regionalkultur und Diktatur. Sächsische Heimatbewegung und Heimat-Propaganda im Dritten Reich und in der SBZ/DDR* (Cologne, 2004); Willi Oberkrome, *"Deuesche Heimat." Nationale Konzeption und regionale Praxis von Naturschutz, Landschaftsgestaltung und Kulturpolitik in Westfalen-Lippe und Thüringen (1900–1960)* (Paderborn, 2004); Thomas Lekan, *Imagining the Nation in Nature: Landscape Preservation and German Identity, 1885–1945* (Cambridge, Mass., 2004).

2. See Applegate, *Nation of Provincials*, 63–65, 71–72; Rudy Koshar, *From Monuments to Traces: Artifacts of German Memory, 1970–1990* (Berkeley, 2000), chap. 1, *German Travel Cultures* (Oxford, 2000), and *Germany's Transient Pasts*; Alon Confino, *The Nation as a Local Metaphor: Württemberg, Imperial Germany, and National Memory, 1871–1918* (Chapel Hill, N.C., 1997), 113–14, 119–20, 179–82; Kirsten Belgum, *Popularizing the Nation: Audience, Representation, and the Production of Identity in Die Gartenlaube, 1853–1900* (Lincoln, 1998), 45; Pieter Judson, "'Every German visitor has a völkisch obligation he must fulfill': Nationalist Tourism in the Austrian Empire, 1880–1918," in *Histories of Leisure*, ed. Rudy Koshar (Oxford, 2002), 147–68.

3. *Der Fremdenverkehr* 5, nos. 13–14 (1955): 12. The journal represented also the League of German Travel Associations (Bund Deutscher Verkehrsverbände), regional travel associations, and the German Travel Agents Association (Deutsches Reisebüro-Verband).

4. For arguments against this shibboleth, see Moeller, *War Stories*, 1–20, and chapter 10 in this volume. For traces of National Socialism in the postwar period, see Koshar, *Transient Pasts*, chap. 5; Fehrenbach, *Cinema in Democratizing Germany*; Frank Biess, *Homecomings: Returning POWs and the Legacies of Defeat in Postwar Germany* (Princeton, N.J., forthcoming); Maria Mitchell, "Materialism and Secularism: CDU Politicians and National Socialism, 1945–1949," *Journal of Modern History* 67 (June 1995): 278–308; Peter Dudek, *"Der Rückblick auf die Vergangenheit wird sich nicht vermeiden lassen." Zur pädagogischen Verarbeitung des Nationalsozialismus in Deutschland (1945–1990)* (Opladen, 1995); Elizabeth Heineman, "The Hour of the Women: Memories of Germany's 'Crisis Years' and West German National Identity," *American Historical Review* 101 (April 1996): 354–95; Norbert Frei, *Vergangenheitspolitik: Die Anfänge der Bundesrepublik und die NS-Vergangenheit* (Munich, 1996); Helmut Peitsch, *"Deutschlands Gedächtnis an seine dunkelste Zeit." Zur Funktion der Autobiographik in den Westzonen Deutschlands und den Westsektoren von Berlin 1945 bis 1949* (Berlin, 1990).

5. A. R. Lingnau, "Widersehen mit Deutschland: Nach Deutschland zu jeder Jahrzeit," *Der Fremdenverkehr* 6, nos. 7–8 (1954): 2.

6. *German Review: The Journal of the German Central Tourist Association* (*Deutscher Zentrale für Fremdenverkehr*), September 1952, a promotional advertisement on back of front cover; and p. 1, an opening letter from Hans Christoph Seebohm, federal minister of transportation. The German version of the first quotation was somewhat different from the English one. Instead of "this lovely country you will never forget," the German text had the toned-down, generic phrase "Reisen vermitteln unvergessliche Eindrücke" ("travel [in Germany] gives unforgettable impressions"). In Seebohm's letter, the German version had a didactic tone of informing Germans of proper postwar international behavior.

7. Mitteilungen der Z.F.V.: Warum Deutschland-Werbung mit Goethe, n.d. [late 1948], 1–2, Ncm, IfT.

8. *Der gute Kontakt: Bemerkungen zum "Ersten Deutschen Fremdenverkehrstag,"* n.d., p. 1, Ncm, IfT.

9. On distancing the Heimat idea from National Socialism, see Koshar, *Transient Pasts*, 235–37.

10. Die Geltung Deutschland im internationalen Fremdenverkehr, 10, Ncm, IfT.

11. *Abschrift. Referat des verbandsdirektor Stadtrat a.D. Ochs . . . am 6.9.1946 auf der Hohensyburg betreffend Vorbereitung der Gründung des Bundes deutscher Verkehrsverbände und Bäder*, 7, Ncm, IfT.

12. *Die Arbeit für die deutsche Heimat. Die Reden und Vorträge bei der Arbeitsgemeinschaft Deutscher Heimat-, Wander- und Naturschutzbünde am 22. März 1954 im Bundesratsaal in Bonn* (Stuttgart, 1954), 9.

13. Cited in Constantin Goschler, *Wiedergutmachung. Westdeutschland und die Verfolgten des Nationalsozialismus (1945–1954)* (Munich, 1992), 203. Seebohm used the word "Judenschaft" that was part of the language of the Third Reich. It assumed that Jews possessed an essential group characteristics. See also Michael Wolffsohn, "Globalentschädigung für Israel und die Juden? Adenauer und die Opposition in der Bundesregierung," in *Wiedergutmachung in der Bundesrepublik Deutschland*, ed. Ludolf Herbst and Constantin Goschler (Munich 1989), 161–90.

14. Various German postwar identity questions were articulated in gender terms and displaced onto women. On the gendered image of postwar German victimhood, see Heineman, "The Hour of the Women" and *What Difference Does a Husband Make? Women and Marital Status in Nazi and Postwar Germany* (Berkeley, 1999), chaps. 4–5; Moeller, *War Stories*; Uta Poiger, *Jazz, Rock, and Rebels: Cold War Politics and American Culture in a Divided Germany* (Berkeley, 2000), 5, 35; Atina Grossmann, "A Question of Silence: The Rape of German Women by Occupation Soldiers," *October* 72 (April 1995): 43–63.

15. *Die Arbeit für die deutsche Heimat*, 9. Arnold's speech had clear signs of Third Reich language, confirming that while postwar Germans thought and acted in some new ways, they articulated these in familiar terms. He spoke about *Volkstum* to denote nationhood and described Heimat feeling in biological terms (*angekränkelt*).

16. Moeller, *War Stories*, 36.

17. See Pretti Ahonen, *After the Expulsion: West Germany and Eastern Europe, 1945–1990* (Oxford, 2004). Adenauer himself had few illusions about the feasibility of regaining any time soon, if at all, the former German territories in the East.

18. *Jubiläumsschrift des Harzer Verkehrsverband E.V. zu seinem fünfzigjährigen Bestehen* (Braunschweig, 1954), 7.

19. Deutsche Zentrale für Fremdenverkehr, *Deutschland*, edited by Dr. Heinz Graefe (Frankfurt am Main, n.d.). The book has no date of publication or page numbers: was the intention to represent the German Heimat as eternal and without chronological markers?

20. On practical measures to rebuild towns and on reconstruction as a return to normality, see Koshar, *Transient Pasts*, 204, 207–8, 219–21. On postwar normality, see Richard Bessel and Dirk Schumann, eds., *Life after Death: Approaches to a Cultural and Social History of Europe during the 1940s and 1950s* (Cambridge, 2003).

21. A revanchist state of mind of some expellees is still very much alive, as demonstrated by Rolf-Josef Eibicht, ed., *50 Jahre Vertreibung. Der Völkermord an den Deutschen Ostdeutschland-Sudetenland. Rückgabe statt Verzicht* (Tübingen, 1995). Fifty years after the

war, some people have forgotten nothing and have learned nothing. The book discusses the "genocide" against innocent Germans and demands their right of return and of property restitution because all those involved were victims "of the terrible decade from 1938 to 1948" (note the periodization). Indeed, "a victim remains a victim, no matter whether one had acted before as perpetrator!" (9, 28). How morally convenient. Jörg Haider, the right-wing Austrian politician, provided an introduction "A Right for Heimat," and Eibicht the final essay: "Germany as a Victim of History." This is the rhetoric of moral vacuousness and self-pity.

A similar case is the book of Walli Richter, ed., *Letzte Tage im Sudentenland* (Munich, 1989), which is a collection of Germans' accounts of their expulsion from Czechoslovakia. While it mentions the discrimination of the Jews and of "political unwanted people" (13), this discrimination has no agency. The tone is nostalgic and self-pitying, and the sense is that Sudeten Germans were multiple victims: of the Nazis, of the war, and of the Czechs. The prehistory of the expulsion, the period of 1938 and the war, is dealt with in 80 pages, while the story of victimhood is told over 400 pages. The book begins with a recollection about 1938: "The Year in Paradise." This sentiment was true for many Sudeten Germans, but standing alone, with no context and agency, it is apologetic. It should be noted that both books appropriate current discourses of European peace and reconciliation, of victimhood, and of the Holocaust to argue their case.

22. For a recent exhibition on the subject, see *Flucht, Vertreibung, Eingliederung. Baden-Württemberg als neue Heimat* (Stuttgart, 1993). An interesting case of historical comparison is that of the Palestinian refugees of 1947–48. Many refugees refused to settle down and set roots after 1948 because of the implied significance of abandoning the belief in, and intention to, returning to the old home in Palestine. At the same time, unlike West Germany, some host states (such as Lebanon, Syria, and Egypt) denied refugees the possibilities of setting roots.

23. Moeller, *War Stories*, 129–40, on these two films; the film reviewer's opinion is from p. 139.

24. Fehrenbach, *Cinema in Democratizing Germany*, 160–61.

25. Matthias Thömmes, "Lernt Deutschland Kennen!," *Der Fremdenverkehr* 8, nos. 9–10 (1956): 11.

26. Ibid., 12.

27. Hermann Opitz, "Knigge für Touristen," *Frankfurt Allgemeine Zeitung*, July 2, 1953.

Chapter Four

1. Cited in *Bild der Heimat. Die Echt-Foto-Postkarten aus der DDR*, ed. Erasmus Schröter with text by Peter Guth (Berlin, 2002), 9. "Unsre Heimat, das sind nicht nur die Städte und Dörfer, / unsre Heimat sind auch all die Bäume im Wald, / unsre Heimat ist das Gras auf der Wiese, das Korn auf dem Feld / und die Fische im Fluss sind die Heimat. / Und wir lieben die Heimat, die schöne. Und wir schützen sie, weil sie dem Volke gehört, / weil sie unserem Volke gehört."

2. Karlheinz Blaschke, "Die Marxistische Regionalgeschichte. Ideologischer Zwang und Wirklichkeitsferne," in *Die DDR-Geschichtswissenschaften als Forschungsproblem*, ed. Georg Iggers (Munich, 1998), 341–68.

3. Cited in Thomas Schaarschmidt, *Regionalkultur und Diktatur. Sächsische Heimatbewegung und Heimat-Propaganda im Dritten Reich und in der SBZ/DDR* (Cologne, 2004), 331.

4. On Heimat and nature associations in the Cultural League, see Hermann Behrens et al., eds., *Wurzeln der Umweltbewegung. Die "Gesellschaft für Natur und Umwelt" (GNU) im Kulturbund der DDR* (Marburg, 1993). On the Cultural League, Magdalena Heider, *Politik, Kultur, Kulturbund: Zur Gründungs-und Frühgeschichte des Kulturbundes zur Demokratischen Erneuerung Deutschlands 1945–1954 in der SBZ/DDR* (Cologne, 1993); Eberhart Schulz, "Auffassungen und Aktivitäten des Kulturbundes zur Wiederherstellung der Einheit Deutschlands (1949 bis 1952)," *Beiträge zur Geschichte der Arbeiterbewegund* 42, no. 2 (2000): 31–43.

5. The GDR used from the 1960s the notion of "socialist Heimat" to construct feelings of loyalty; new studies have begun to explore this and other aspects of GDR Heimat. This essay is not so much interested in the attributes of the notion of socialist Heimat but in placing these attributes within the Heimat symbolic manual that goes back to imperial Germany. On East Germany's idea of Heimat, see Schaarschmidt, *Regionalkultur und Diktatur*; Willi Oberkrome, *"Deuesche Heimat." Nationale Konzeption und regionale Praxis von Naturschutz, Landschaftsgestaltung und Kulturpolitik in Westfalen-Lippe und Thüringen (1900–1960)* (Paderborn, 2004); Jan Palmowski, "Building an East German Nation: The Construction of a Socialist Heimat, 1945–1961," *Central European History* 37, no. 3 (2003): 365–99. Other works on the Heimat idea in the GDR are Frank Hafner, *'Heimat' in der sozialistischen Gesellschaft* (Frankfurt am Main, 1992); Renate Herrmann-Winter, ed., *Heimatsprache zwischen Ausgrenzung und ideologischer Einbindung. Niederdeutsch in der DDR* (Frankfurt am Main, 1998). And also the essay by Peter Sonnet, "Heimat und Sozialismus. Zur Regionalgeschichsschreibung in der DDR," *Historische Zeitschrift* 235, no. 1 (1981): 121–35.

For the Heimat in GDR films, see Harry Blunk, "The Concept of 'Heimat-GDR' in DEFA Feature Films," in *DEFA: East German Cinema, 1946–1992*, ed. Seán Allan and John Sandford (New York, 1999), 204–21; Elizabeth Boa and Rachel Palfreyman, *Heimat: A German Dream; Regional Loyalties and National Identity in German Culture, 1890–1990* (Oxford, 2000), chap. 4. And see Johannes von Moltke, *No Place like Home: Locations of Heimat in German Cinema* (Berkeley, 2005), chap. 5, on GDR film in the 1950s. I am indebted to Johannes von Moltke for making his work available to me.

6. See Everhard Holtmann, "Heimatbedarf in der Nachkriegszeit," in *Von der Währungsreform zum Wirtschaftswunder. Wiederaufbau in Niedersachsen*, ed. Bernd Weisbrod (Hannover, 1998), 31–45.

7. Schaarschmidt, *Regionalkultur und Diktatur*, 506–7; Adelheid von Saldern, "Herrschaft und Repräsentation in DDR-Städten," in *Inszenierte Einigkeit. Herrschaftsrepräsentationen in DDR-Städten* (Stuttgart, 2003), 27–30, here 28.

8. For Saxony, see Schaarschmidt, *Regionalkultur und Diktatur*, 294–95.

9. The image has generic features, but its location, in this specific case, is identifiable. It represents the "Drei Gleichen," an ensemble of castles between Erfurt and Gotha, which are quite striking because one can see them from afar. They are located in the Thuringian Valley. I am indebted to Jan Palmowski's excellent Heimat geography.

10. This image of Thuringia raises an important question about the relations between Heimat iconography and representations of the region. People do have a very distinct sense of their own region, which cannot be represented interchangeably very easily. One could

argue, How could one represent Thuringia, but with the Thuringian Forest and a folk costume? You cannot represent it after all with a terrain of volcanic origin from the Harz or with a Baltic landscape. This is true. Heimat images of regions work within constraints, for a certain resemblance to the given region is necessary, to give the Thuringian a sense of familiarity. The choice in figure 6 of the Thuringian Forest and folk costume thus makes sense. But the point is that it "made sense" within a tradition of the Heimat symbolic manual, of certain iconographic elements that were shared among Heimat images of different regions. More important, the SED in Thuringia could represent the region with images of workers or of peasants toiling on the land. It did not. Instead, it appropriated this symbolic language.

11. For a comprehensive discussion of Heimat iconography and cityscapes between 1871–1918, see Alon Confino, *The Nation as a Local Metaphor: Württemberg, Imperial Germany, and National Memory, 1871–1918* (Chapel Hill, N.C., 1997), chap. 7.

12. The SED used a familiar, generic image of pre-Nazi Erfurt in order to represent the town when the Nazis took over. For a similar image from the Third Reich, see *Deutsche Werbung* 2, no. 6 (1936): 386.

13. Oberkrome noted that the Heimat idea had also masculine representations related to radical and xenophobic notions of space and nationhood. This is a useful corrective, which does not seem to alter the basic representation of the Heimat idea as something you defend and protect but not something you go to war with. Oberkrome, *"Deuesche Heimat"*, 144.

14. See Victoria Bonnell, *Iconography of Power: Soviet Political Posters under Lenin and Stalin* (Berkeley, 1997), chap. 6.

15. The union, possessing only marginal political power, emphasized those who were persecuted for political reasons. Those who suffered under Nazism for nonpolitical reasons, such as the Jews, were marginalized. For the East German regime this group was of lesser importance, for its persecution did not fit within the class struggle historical vision. These victims did not find a home at the VVN and founded the Berlin Federation of the Victims of the Nuremberg Laws (Berliner Verband der Opfer der Nüremberg Gesetze). Note the use in the title of the word "Opfer" (which means victim and also sacrificial offering) in the title instead of "Verfolgten" (one who is persecuted, a word with more of a political resonance). See Martin Broszat and Hermann Weber, eds., *SBZ-Handbuch* (Munich, 1990), 749–51. The VVN was dissolved in February 1953 and was followed by the Committee of Antifascist Resistance Fighters, which was governed by the SED. The party thus achieved mastery over the interpretation of the Third Reich's past.

16. See an additional poster for this exhibition with the same themes by the same artist, Albert Jahn, in Deutsches Historisches Museum, *Das politische Plakat der DDR 1945–1970*, CD-ROM (Berlin, 1995), digital reproduction 0162054.

17. In Soviet iconography, the image of the male blacksmith was a central figure from the Revolution until 1930, when he was replace by the deheroized, everyman shock worker. Bonnell, *Iconography of Power*, chap. 1. Several aspects of the immediate postwar East German iconography, such as the workers and peasants dressed in work clothes, resembled Soviet iconography of the 1930s more than that of 1945 to 1953.

18. See Wilhelm Schutz, *Den Feinden zum Trutz/der Heimat zum Schutz* (Defying the enemy, protecting the Heimat), in *Das Plakat* 10 (January 1919): table 23. The poster is reproduced in Confino, *The Nation as a Local Metaphor*, color tip-in.

19. Broszat and Weber, eds., *SBZ-Handbuch*, 382.

20. Note that the representation of the little child is gender unidentified, just like the First World War knight in figure 3.

21. See Palmowski, "Building an East German Nation," 377, 381, and "Mecklenburg, Where Is Thy Sting?—Regional Identities and the Limits of Democratic Centralism in the GDR," *Journal of Contemporary History*, forthcoming. I am grateful to Jan Palmowski for sharing with me his work and thoughts.

22. Schaarschmidt, *Regionalkultur und Diktatur*, 346–47.

23. See chapter 1.

24. *Junge Touristen. Material zur Anleitung der Wanderbewegung der Junge Pioniere und Schüler* (Berlin, 1954), 5.

25. Ibid., 4.

26. On historical perceptions in the GDR, see Iggers, *Die DDR-Geschichtswissenschaften als Forschungsproblem*; Martin Sabrow, ed., *Verwaltete Vergangenheit. Geschichtskultur und Herrschaftslegitimation in der DDR* (Leipzig, 1997).

27. Monica Gibas, "'Die Republik, das sind wir!' Das propagandistische 'Gesamtkunstwerk.' Zehnter Jahrestag der DDR als nachholendes Initiationsritual," in *Parteiauftrag: Ein neues Deutschlands. Bilder, Rituale und Symbole der frühen DDR*, ed. Dieter Vorsteher (Berlin, 1996), 228.

28. BAL, DY 34/5968, "Information zum Abschluß der Touristischen Suchfahrt 1964," n.d.

29. On tourism and Heimat, see chapter 3, note 2.

30. BAL, DY 34/5962, "Dem 20. Jahrestag der DDR entgegen," 1969, n.d.

31. On the Discovery Tour, see BAL, DY 34/5962, "Durchführung der 'Entdeckungsfahrt durch die DDR,'" 16.2.1966. On the Vacation Tombola, BAL, DY 34/5968, KTW, Beschluß 1966, n.d.; DY 34/5967, Vorlage des KTW, 27.11.1964.

32. *Junge Welt*, August 29, 1962. For the Heimat book of Kirchheim unter Teck, see chapter 1, note 26.

33. BAL, DY 34/5962, 16/17.3.1967, 2. This was expressed in a meeting of leaders of the Committee for Tourism and Traveling, of state officials on youth policy, and of directors of youth hostels.

34. See Richard Bessel, "Hatred after War: Emotion and the Postwar History of East Germany," *History and Memory* 17, nos. 1–2 (2005): 195–216.

35. BAL, DY 34/5967, 27.11.1964, 1.

36. BAL, DY 34 29/1091/5146, "Jedem Jugendlichen und Touristen 1957 einen interessanten und frohen Urlaub in der DDR," 2.

37. See Paul Betts, "The Twilight of the Idols: East German Memory and Material Culture," *Journal of Modern History* 72, no. 3 (September 2000): 731–65.

38. *Junge Welt*, November 25–26, 1961.

39. Schröter, *Bild der Heimat*, 6–7.

Chapter Five

1. *Die Zeit*, December 29, 1999, 8.

2. *Junge Touristen. Material zur Anleitung der Wanderbewegung der Junge Pioniere und Schüler* (Berlin, 1954), 4.

3. The national meaning behind the motto "Get to Know Germany!" was not unique to

Germany. See Marguerite Shaffer, *See America First: Tourism and National Identity, 1880–1940* (Washington, D.C., 2001).

4. *Schwäbische Kronik*, July 11, 1912.

5. Gustav Ströhmfeld, *Gedenkschrift des Vereins für Fremdenverkehr in Stuttgart E.V zur Feier seines 25 jährigen Bestehens 1885–1910* (Stuttgart, 1910), 19.

6. Gustav Ströhmfeld, *Aufgaben und Pflichten der Fremdenverkehrspflege* (Stuttgart, 1911), 70.

7. On the KDF, see Kristin Semmens, *Seeing Hitler's Germany: Tourism in the Third Reich* (New York, 2005); Shelley Baranowski, *Strength through Joy: Consumerism and Mass Tourism in the Third Reich* (Cambridge, 2004); Rudy Koshar, *German Travel Cultures* (Oxford, 2000), chap. 3. And the pioneering work of Hasso Spode, "Arbeiterurlaub im Dritten Reich," in *Angst, Belohnung, Zucht und Ordnung: Herrschaftsmechanismen im Nationalsozialismus*, ed. Carola Sachse, Tilla Siegel, Hasso Spode, and Wolfgang Spohn (Opladen, 1982), 275–328; "'Der deutsche Arbeiter reist!' Massentourismus im Dritten Reich," in *Sozialgeschichte der Freizeit: Untersuchungen zum Wandel der Alltagskultur in Deutschland*, ed. Gerhard Huck (Wuppertal, 1980), 281–306; and "Ein Seebad für zwanzigtausend Volksgenossen: Zur Grammatik und Geschichte des fordistischen Urlaubs," in *Reisekultur in Deutschland: Von der Weimarer Republik zum "Dritten Reich,"* ed. P. J. Brenner (Tübingen, 1997), 7–47.

8. *Kraft durch Freude. Die Deutsche Arbeitsfront. Gau Saarpfalz* (July 1936): 10; and an article from a KDF journal, "KDF-Wandern heißt: Die Heimat suchen!," BAL, NS/5/VI DAF 6249.

9. *Landesfremdenverkehrsverband Baden: Jahresbericht 1935/36* (n.p), 3, 6–7.

10. Matthias Thömmes, "Lernt Deutschland Kennen!," *Der Fremdenverkehr* 8, nos. 9–10 (1956): 12.

11. *Deutsche Werbung* (June 1935): 1076.

12. See Alon Confino, *The Nation as a Local Metaphor: Württemberg, Imperial Germany, and National Memory, 1871–1918* (Chapel Hill, N.C., 1997), 174–77.

13. *Der Fremdenverkehr* 5, nos. 13–14 (1953): 9–10.

14. See also the identity map printed on a commemorative kerchief and scarf for the tenth anniversary of the GDR. Monica Gibas, "'Die Republik, das sind wir!' Das propagandistische 'Gesamtkunstwerk.' Zehnter Jahrestag der DDR als nachholendes Initiationsritual," in *Parteiauftrag: Ein neues Deutschlands. Bilder, Rituale und Symbole der frühen DDR*, ed. Dieter Vorsteher (Berlin, 1996), 228.

15. Heinrich Hoffmann, ed., *Deutscher Osten — Land der Zukunft. Ein Ruf des Ostens an die Heimat!* (Munich, 1942), 4. The map included economic and industrial signs, which represented German technological progress and innovation over Polish and Jewish backwardness.

16. Deutschen Ausland-Institut, ed., *Das deutsche Weichselland* (Berlin, 1940), 24.

17. *Die Schöne Heimat: Bilder aus Deutschland* (Taunus, 1961).

18. The game is available at the Haus der Geschichte der Bundesrepublik Deutschland, Bonn catalog number 1990/5/044.

19. A poster published by Landkreis Nordvorpommern, *Ferienland an Ostsee und Boddenküste* (1997), in my possession.

20. *Charivari. Die Zeitschrift für Kunst, Kultur und Leben in Bayern* 16, no. 5 (May 1990): 61.

21. Josef Winckler, "Gedanken bei einer Dichterfahrt durch Deutschland," in *Deutsche Heimat. Bilder aus Stadt u. Land*, ed. M. Paul Block and Werner Linder (Berlin, 1926), 1.

22. Friedrich Arnold, *Anschläge: Deutsche Plakate als dokumente der Zeit 1900–1960* (Ebenhausen bei Munich, 1963), poster IV/8 "Wählt meine Partei."

23. See also the 1960 poster to attract foreign tourists "Sunny days await you. The German federal railroad." *Der Fremdenverkeher* 12, no. 5 (1960): 20.

24. On the Heidelberg poster, see *Der Fremdenverkeher*, nos. 3–4 (1955): 11; on the Bingen poster, *Der Fremdenverkeher*, no. 6 (1965): 42.

25. Alain Weill, *The Poster: A Worldwide Survey and History* (Boston, 1985), 107, 110, 134, 172.

26. *Deutsche Werbung* (March 1939): 323.

Part II

1. Two important reference points are Pierre Nora's seven-volume project *Les lieux de mémoire* (Paris, 1984–92) and Benedict Anderson, *Imagined Communities: Reflections on the Origins and Spread of Nationalism* (London 1983; revised and extended ed. 1991). For an English translation of Nora's project, see *Realms of Memory*, vol. 1, *Conflicts and Divisions*; vol. 2, *Traditions*; vol. 3, *Symbols* (New York, 1996–98); and *Rethinking France—Les Lieux de Mémoire* (Chicago, 2001).

2. John Gillis, *A World of Our Own Making: Myth, Ritual, and the Quest for Family Values* (New York, 1996), 4.

3. Brewster Chamberlin, "Doing Memory: Remembrance Reified and Other Shoah Business," *Public Historian* 23, no. 3 (Summer 2001): 74. Jay Winter attempted to analyze "the memory boom" as something "more than a passing fashion." Jay Winter, "The Memory Boom in Contemporary Historical Studies," *Raritan* 21, no. 1 (Summer 2001): 52–66, here 53.

4. Some notable exceptions are Allan Megill, "History, Memory, Identity," *History of the Human Sciences* 11, no. 3 (1998): 37–62; Kerwin Klein, "On the Emergence of *Memory* in Historical Discourse," *Representations* 69 (2000): 127–50; Peter Fritzsche, "The Case of Modern Memory," *Journal of Modern History* 73, no. 1 (March 2001): 87–117; Wulf Kansteiner, "Finding Meaning in Memory: A Methodological Critique of Collective Memory Studies," *History and Theory* 41 (May 2002): 179–97; and the brilliant essay of Gabrielle Spiegel, "Memory and History: Liturgical Time and Historical Time," *History and Theory* 41 (May 2002): 149–62.

5. "Entre Mémoire et Histoire" was originally published in Nora, ed., *La République*, XVII–XLII. For an English translation, see "Between History and Memory: Les Lieux de Mémoire," *Representations* 26 (Spring 1989): here pp. 8–9. For critical evaluation of Nora's work, see Berthold Unfried, "Gedächtnis und Geschichte. Pierre Nora und die *lieux de memoire*," *Österreichische Zeitschrift für Geschichtswissenschaften* 2, no. 4 (1991): 79–98; Steven Englund, "The Ghost of Nation Past," *Journal of Modern History* 64 (June 1992): 299–320; Lucette Valensi, "Histoire nationale, histoire monumentale. *Les lieux de memoire* (note critique)," *Annales HSS* (November–December 1995): 1271–77; Nancy Wood, "Memory's Remains: Les lieux de mémoire," *History and Memory* 6 (1994): 123–49; John Bodnar, "Pierre Nora, National Memory, and Democracy: A Review," *Journal of American History* 87, no. 3 (December 2000): 951–63; Hue-Tam Ho Tai, "Remembered Realms: Pierre Nora and French National Memory," *American Historical Review* 106, no. 3 (June 2001): 906–22.

Somewhat close to Nora is the view expressed by Patrick Hutton in *History as an Art of Memory*: "[T]he problem for the historian . . . is how to proceed in the quest to recover lost traditions and how to reconcile them with long-standing historiographical positions." In the Renaissance, the art of memory was "a resource for recovering lost words. In that sense, I wondered, was not history the art of memory for the modern age?" Patrick Hutton, *History as an Art of Memory* (Hanover, N.H., 1993), xvi–xvii.

6. They write: "Knowledge of the past, however small, begins with memory. Because people have a memory, they know from experience that there was a past. . . . [W]e credit memory with the verification of there having been a past." Joyce Appleby, Lynn Hunt, and Margaret Jacob, *Telling the Truth about History* (New York, 1994), 258.

7. Susan Crane, "(Not) Writing History: Rethinking the Intersections of Personal History and Collective Memory with Hans von Aufsess," *History and Memory* 8, no. 1 (1996): 5–29, here 23.

8. Herodotus, *The Histories*, trans. Aubrey de Sélincourt, new rev. ed. with introd. John Marincola (London, 1996), 3.

Chapter Six

I am indebted to Ilana Pardes, who first suggested with her customary keen perception that I should read *Moses and Monotheism*.

1. The literature is huge. See, for example, Dorothy Zeligs, *Moses: A Psychodynamic Study* (New York, 1986); Marthe Robert, *From Oedipus to Moses: Freud's Jewish Identity* (London, 1977).

2. Yosef Hayim Yerushalmi, *Freud's Moses: Judaism Terminable and Interminable* (New Haven, 1991); Jan Assmann, *Moses the Egyptian: The Memory of Egypt in Western Monotheism* (Cambridge, Mass., 1997); Richard Bernstein, *Freud and the Legacy of Moses* (New York, 1998).

3. Sigmund Freud, *Moses and Monotheism* (New York, 1967), 151.

4. That is how Freud defined himself in his preface to the Hebrew translation of *Totem and Taboo*. See Yerushalmi, *Freud's Moses*, 14.

5. Yerushalmi, *Freud's Moses*, 4; Bernstein, *Freud and the Legacy of Moses*, 5; Michel de Certeau, *The Writing of History* (New York, 1988), 308–9.

6. On this distinction, see Assmann, *Moses the Egyptian*, 161.

7. Freud, *Moses and Monotheism*, 159.

8. Ibid., 128.

9. Peter Gay, *Freud: A Life for Our Time* (New York, 1988), 647.

10. Yerushalmi, *Freud's Moses*, 30–31.

11. Bernstein, *Freud and the Legacy of Moses*, 46–52.

12. Ernest Renan, "What Is a Nation?," in *Nation and Narration*, ed. Homi Bhabha (London, 1990), 19.

13. Krzysztof Pomian, "Franks and Gauls," in *Realms of Memory*, vol. 1, ed. Pierre Nora (New York, 1996), 30.

14. Ibid., 42.

15. Ibid., 29.

16. Freud, *Moses and Monotheism*, 134.

17. A document in my possession by Hanns Baum, "Das Altertums-Museum in Weinheim" from 1912.

18. Fr. Behn, "Das Heimatmuseum auf Föhr," *Museumskunde* 4 (1908): 194–95.

19. Gioacchino Volpe, *Momenti di storia italiana* (Florence, 1925), vi, 54. Volpe (1876–1971)

played a role in modern Italian historiography. Formed in the postunification liberal era, he first focused his studies on the Middle Ages, and later in his career moved to explore political problems of modern Italy. He held important academic and institutional positions during the Fascist regime and continued to work and publish in postwar Italy. *Momenti di storia italiana* collects writings previously published in various periodicals.

20. Behn, "Das Heimatmusuem auf Föhr," 199.

21. Assmann, *Moses the Egyptian*, 148–49.

22. I should add that Freud's Jewishness is closely linked to this move from the plane of history to the plane of morality. Freud's plan to write *Moses and Monotheism* was speeded up by Nazi anti-Semitism. He wrote the book to explore why the Jews were hated throughout history. For Freud the social scientist, the historical evidence for his theory was not quite there; but Freud the Jew supplemented evidence with historical morality.

23. Freud, *Moses and Monotheism*, 101.

24. Yerushalmi, *Freud's Moses*, 4.

25. On the essential element of human history in Freud's thought, see Patrick Hutton, *History as an Art of Memory* (Hanover, N.H., 1993), 69–70.

26. Bernstein, *Freud and the Legacy of Moses*, xi.

27. Freud, *Moses and Monotheism*, 151 (emphasis added).

Chapter Seven

Chapter 7 originally appeared as "Collective Memory and Cultural History: Problems of Method," *American Historical Review* 105, no. 2 (December 1997): 1386–1403; reprinted with permission. I should like to thank Edward Ayers, Francesca Fiorani, and Sophia Rosenfeld for their insightful critical advice.

1. Also in cases where the use of memory has been insignificant in terms of method and theory, the memory perspective itself has proved to be thought provoking. Take, for example, the recent debate on post-Zionism in Israel, where a group of scholars, called "the new historians," has questioned Zionist historiography's most cherished assumptions. The scholars have criticized, among others, the myth of the heroic birth of Israel, Zionism's role in the Palestinian tragedy, and, more generally, the reduction of historical studies in Israel to an ideological and educational tool of Zionism. These and other claims opened a public debate by scholars and laypersons about the historical meaning of Zionism. At the center of the rethinking of Zionist history has been the term "memory." As Anita Shapira, a leading historian of Zionism and a critic of the "new historians" observed, "the debate is less about historiography than it is about collective memory." But the notion of memory has been used either perfunctorily or as a hollow metaphor defining memory as a monolith in expressions like "the collective memory of early statehood" or "Palestinian collective memory." In terms of method, the debate has centered on the actions, ideology, and motivation of institutions and leading figures, while a social and cultural history of memory's construction and reception has not been taken, as well as the interrelations among different memories within and between Israeli and Palestinian societies. These topics still await their historians. For a good introduction to the post-Zionist controversy, see Gulie Ne'eman Arad, ed., "Israeli Historiography Revisited," special issue, *History and Memory* 7 (Spring–Summer 1995): esp. Anita Shapira, "Politics and Collective Memory: The Debate over the 'New Historians' in Israel,"

9–34; and Ilan Pappe, "Critique and Agenda: The Post-Zionist Scholars in Israel," 66–90. For a collection of essays about the recent historical disputes in Israel, see Robert Wistrich and David Ohana, eds., *The Shaping of Israeli Identity: Myth, Memory, and Trauma* (London, 1995).

2. The literature is enormous. See, for example, Lawrence Langer, *Holocaust Testimonies: The Ruins of Memory* (New Haven, Conn., 1991); Ronald Berger, *Constructing a Collective Memory of the Holocaust: A Life History of Two Brothers' Survival* (Niwot, 1995).

3. The term "vehicles of memory" is used by Yosef Hayim Yerushalmi, *Zakhor: Jewish History and Jewish Memory* (New York, 1989). Pierre Nora's magisterial seven-volume collection *Les lieux de mémoire* provides a cornucopia of memory sites: vol. 1, *La République*; vols. 2–4, *La Nation*; vols. 5–7, *Les France* (Paris, 1984–92).

4. See, for example, Frederick Crews, *The Memory Wars: Freud's Legacy in Dispute* (New York, 1995); James Young, *The Texture of Memory: Holocaust Memorials and Meaning* (New Haven, Conn., 1993); Miriam Hansen, "'Schindler's List' Is Not Shoah: The Second Commandment, Popular Modernism, and Public Memory," *Critical Inquiry* 22 (Winter 1996): 292–312; Diane Barthel, *Historic Preservation: Collective Memory and Historical Identity* (New Brunswick, N.J., 1996); Daniel Sherman, "Objects of Memory: History and Narrative in French War Museums," *French Historical Studies* 19 (Spring 1995): 49–74; Michael Wallace, *Mickey Mouse History and Other Essays on American Memory* (Philadelphia, 1996); *Southern Cultures* 2 (Fall 1995), special issue on memory and the South; Keith Wilson, ed., *Forging the Collective Memory: Government and International Historians through Two World Wars* (Providence, R.I., 1996).

For recent, current, and instant history of memory, see Barbie Zelizer, *Covering the Body: The Kennedy Assassination, the Media, and the Shaping of Collective Memory* (Chicago, 1992); Thomas Johnson, *The Rehabilitation of Richard Nixon: The Media's Effect on Collective Memory* (New York, 1996); Michael Schudson, *Watergate in American Memory: How We Remember, Forget, and Reconstruct the Past* (New York, 1992); Edward Linenthal and Tom Engelhardt, eds., *History Wars: The Enola Gay and Other Battles for the American Past* (New York, 1996).

5. Lynn Hunt warned several years ago against the danger of defining the new cultural history topically: "Just as social history sometimes moved from one group to another (workers, women, children, ethnic groups, the old, the young) without developing much sense of cohesion and interaction between topics, so too a cultural history defined topically could degenerate into an endless search for new cultural practices to describe, whether carnivals, cat massacres, or impotence trials." See Hunt, "Introduction," in *The New Cultural History*, ed. Lynn Hunt (Berkeley, Calif., 1989), 9. The history of memory faces a similar danger.

I was reminded of memory studies when I recently read Jacques Revel's critical evaluation of social history: "'Classical' social history was mainly conceived as a history of social entities. . . . As a result, when one looks through the enormous mass of results accumulated over the past thirty or forty years, one has a certain sense of déjà vu and stagnant categories. From one work to the next, the characters are the same though the cast may vary." Memory studies could also end up being predictable, as yet another memory is subjected to an analysis of its construction, appropriation, and contestation. Jacques Revel, "Microanalysis and the Construction of the Social," in *Histories: French Constructions of the Past*, ed. Revel and Lynn Hunt (New York, 1995), 498.

6. Jacques Le Goff, "Mentalities: A History of Ambiguities," in *Constructing the Past:*

Essays in Historical Methodology, ed. Le Goff and Pierre Nora (New York, 1984), 166. It was first published as "Les mentalités: Une histoire ambigue," in *Faire de l'histoire*, ed. Jacques Le Goff and Pierre Nora, vol. 3 (Paris, 1974).

7. François Furet, "Beyond the Annales," *Journal of Modern History* 55 (September 1983): 405.

8. The French history of *mentalité* was justifiably criticized on grounds that it, first, tended to view every historical problem as a psychological problem and, second, to reduce categories of mentality to social analysis (of hierarchy, income, occupation), a method that reduced beliefs and values to a social structure established a priori. See Carlo Ginzburg, "A proposito della raccolta dei saggi storici di Marc Bloch," *Studi medievali* 3 (1965): 335–53; and Roger Chartier, "Intellectual History or Sociocultural History? The French Trajectories," in *Intellectual History: Reappraisals and New Perspectives*, ed. Dominick LaCapra and Steven Kaplan (Ithaca, N.Y., 1982), 13–46, esp. 22–32. For a critical appraisal, see also Patrick Hutton, "The History of Mentalities: The New Map of Cultural History," *History and Theory* 20 (1981): 237–59.

9. This has been Furet's argument about the study of mentalities. I found Furet's critique of the history of mentality insightful for my thinking about memory. See Furet, "Beyond the Annales," 404–7.

10. Robert Mandrou, "Histoire/L'histoire des mentalités," in *Encyclopaedia universalis* (1971; rpt., Paris, 1985), 9:366.

11. For Warburg's idea of social memory, see Kurt Forster, "Aby Warburg's History of Art: Collective Memory and the Social Mediation of Images," *Daedalus* (Winter 1976): 169–76; E. H. Gombrich, *Aby Warburg: An Intellectual Biography*, 2nd ed. (Chicago, 1986), 239–59. Gombrich presents Warburg's fragmented notion of social memory but does not attempt to provide a comprehensive view. For a critical evaluation of Gombrich's book, see Felix Gilbert, "From Art History to the History of Civilization: Aby Warburg," *Journal of Modern History* 44 (1972): 381–91.

Seventy years after Warburg's death, his writings are still unavailable in English. Fortunately, Kurt Forster is now preparing the English edition of Warburg's collected writings (*Gesammelte Schriften* [Leipzig and Berlin, 1932]), to be published in the Getty Research Institute's book series Texts and Documents. For a selection of Warburg's essays and several critical appraisals of his work, see Dieter Wuttke, ed., *Aby Warburg: Ausgewälte Schriften and Würdigungen* (Baden-Baden, 1980). For some evaluations of Warburg's notions of culture and art history, see Silvia Ferretti, *Cassirer, Panofsky, and Warburg: Symbol, Art, and History* (New Haven, Conn., 1989); Yoshihiko Maikuma, *Der Begriff der Kultur bei Warburg, Nietzsche and Burckhardt* (Königstein, 1985); Kurt Forster, "Aby Warburg: His Study of Ritual and Art on Two Continents," *October* 77 (Summer 1996): 6–24. For an attempted feminist, poststructuralist, and psychoanalytic reading of Warburg, see Margaret Iverson, "Retrieving Warburg's Tradition," *Art History* 16 (December 1993): 541–53. On the reception of Warburg's writings, see Michael Diers, "Warburg and the Warburgian Tradition of Cultural History," *New German Critique* 65 (Spring–Summer 1995): 59–74. On his projected picture atlas of memory, which he called *Mnemosyne*, and which included photographs and reproductions of recurring human figures and gestures, see Dorothee Bauerle, *Gespenstergeschichten für ganz Erwachsene: Ein Kommentar zu Aby Warburgs Bilderatlas Mnemosyne* (Münster, 1988).

12. Peter Burke, "Aby Warburg as Historical Anthropologist," in *Aby Warburg, Akten des*

internationalen Symposiums Hamburg 1990, ed. Horst Bredekamp, Michael Diers, and Charlotte Schoell-Glass (Weinheim, 1991), 39–44; Simon Schama, *Landscape and Memory* (New York, 1995), 209–14; Ron Chernow, *The Warburgs* (New York, 1993), 64–66.

13. Forster, "Aby Warburg's History of Art," 172.

14. Carlo Ginzburg, "From Aby Warburg to E. H. Gombrich: A Problem of Method," in *Clues, Myths, and the Historical Method* (Baltimore, 1992), 21.

15. Maurice Halbwachs, *La topographie légendaire des Evangiles en Terre sainte. Etude de mémoire collective* (Paris, 1941); *Les cadres sociaux de la mémoire* (Paris, 1925). For an English version, see Halbwachs, *On Collective Memory*, ed., trans., and introd. Lewis Coser (Chicago, 1992); *The Collective Memory*, trans. Francis Ditter and Vida Yazdi Ditter (New York, 1980). On Halbwachs's formulation and use of collective memory, see Patrick Hutton, *History as an Art of Memory* (Hanover, N.H., 1993), chap. 4.

16. Marc Bloch, *The Royal Touch: Sacred Monarchy and Scrofula in England and France* (London, 1973), 4.

17. Halbwachs received after World War I a chair of Pedagogy and Sociology at the University of Strasbourg, where he began a close professional friendship with Lucien Febvre and Marc Bloch. When Bloch and Febvre founded the *Annales d'histoire économique et sociales* in 1929, Halbwachs became a member of the editorial board. See Coser, "Introduction," in Halbwachs, *On Collective Memory*, 5–11. About the relation between Warburg and Halbwachs, we know very little. See Jan Assmann, "Collective Memory and Cultural Identity," *New German Critique* 65 (Spring–Summer 1995): 125.

18. Peter Burke poses this question in his discussion of social amnesia. See Burke, "History as Social Memory," in *Memory: History, Culture and the Mind*, ed. Thomas Butler (New York, 1989), 108.

19. Robert Gildea, *The Past in French History* (New Haven, Conn., 1994), 9–10, 44.

20. Henry Rousso, *The Vichy Syndrome: History and Memory in France since 1944*, trans. Arthur Goldhammer (Cambridge, Mass., 1991).

21. Robert Moeller, "War Stories: The Search for a Usable Past in the Federal Republic of Germany," *American Historical Review* 101 (October 1996): 1008–48. The narrative trajectory of Holocaust and World War II memory as one of repression (1950s–60s), awakening (sometime during the 1960s), obsession (the 1970s and after) has an air of predictability. A common argument about Holocaust remembrance in Israel, for example, is that the Adolf Eichmann trial was the watershed between survivors' repression and state indifference before 1961 and growing interest and instrumentalization of the Holocaust later on. But this argument is correct only insofar as we explore the official state level. In everyday life, the Holocaust was everywhere between 1945 and 1961. The fundamental division in Israeli society between those who came from "there" and those who were "here" was often represented in small gestures, as when a survivor's number on the arm drew hisses and furtive glances or when a survivor's behavior was excused with the explanation, "Well, he was there." So far, this aspect has been captured better by writers than by historians. See the novel by David Grossman, *See Under: Love*, trans. Betsy Rosenberg (New York, 1989), and especially the masterful first story, "Momik."

22. My argument is not, in case such a clarification is needed, against every exploration of the political. The study of the political is fundamental because it allows cultural history to link with power and thus avoid being a rendition of the old history of ideas. My critique

is of the particular mode of cultural history that reduces power to politics, and the political to top-down, public, and official manifestations.

23. Rousso, *Vichy Syndrome*, 272.

24. Rousso does not provide in his discussion of transmission any new information that was not already discussed in part 1 about the evolution of the syndrome. We only get more of the same—more films, more books, more commemorations—though it is unclear what are the criteria according to which a source (say, de Gaulle's memoirs) is used to interpret the construction of the syndrome (part 1) rather than its reception (part 2).

25. Rousso, *Vichy Syndrome*, 219 (emphasis added).

26. The danger of looking for evidence in the most visible places is clear when Rousso explains his choice of method in exploring the depth of the syndrome in French society: "Before 1971 . . . polling . . . [about World War II's issues] was practically non-existent. Since polling data are essential for what I want to do here, I have focused in what follows on the 1970s and 1980s" (ibid., 272–73). Instead of posing a problem—how French men and women remembered Vichy—and looking for the answer everywhere, Rousso viewed polling data, which as a source should be a vehicle to establish an argument, as the essential factor, and looked for the answer where polling data existed. This is a little bit like looking for a lost coin under the lamppost because there is light there.

27. The status of evidence in the history of memory has been so far ignored, although this is a crucial issue. See the discussion of James Wilkinson, "A Choice of Fictions: Historians, Memory, and Evidence," *Publications of the Modern Language Association* 111 (January 1996): 80–92, who has a favorable view of Rousso's method.

28. Rousso, *Vichy Syndrome*, 221.

29. Ibid. Rousso himself is conscious of this problem when he writes of his method that it "may at times seem rather circular . . . [and] is intended only as a heuristic tool." One can identify with this argument. Still, we must be clear about the consequences of writing a history of memory by separating memory's construction from its reception.

30. Yael Zerubavel, *Recovered Roots: Collective Memory and the Making of Israeli National Tradition* (Chicago, 1995). Among the growing Israeli discussion of memory, Zerubavel's study seems the most comprehensive and illuminating.

31. Zerubavel makes a concerted effort, often very successful, to get to the everyday level of collective memory. Among the sources she uses are jokes, popular songs, public school textbooks, plays, poems, children's stories, and the experience of trips to Masada and Tel Hai.

32. See, for example, Zerubavel, *Recovered Roots*, 18, 30, 31, 96.

33. Ibid., xix.

34. Let me illuminate this argument with an example. In *The Vichy Syndrome*, the context created in part 1 (memory from above) conditions the exploration in part 2 (ignoring popular construction of memories). But why should we assume that people were limited to the memory delineated in part 1? Instead of exploring how people constructed their own collective memories of Vichy, which at times concurred with and at times opposed the official memory of Vichy, Rousso investigates only how the memory constructed by politicians and intellectuals was received by the public. Thus the Vichy memory from above looks very much like a memory imposed on a public that has no agency.

35. Zerubavel, *Recovered Roots*, 3.

36. My thoughts on the relation between text and context owe a debt in some measure to the work of microhistorians who attempted to provide an alternative to the customary use of context as the "background" of the text. See Giovanni Levi, *Inheriting Power: The Story of an Exorcist* (Chicago, 1988) and "I Pericoli del Geertzismo," *Quaderni storici* (1985): 269–77. And see also Revel, "Microanalysis and the Construction of the Social," 492–502, esp. 500–501.

37. Jacques Le Goff discusses Halbwach's "multiplicity of social time" and its influence on Fernand Braudel in *History and Memory*, trans. Steven Rendall and Elizabeth Claman (New York, 1992), 135.

38. Halbwachs, *On Collective Memory*, 53 (emphasis added). I attempt to break the text-context dichotomy in my analysis of local and national identities in Germany. Instead of understanding local identity as part of national identity, and localness against the background of nationhood, I view local identity as a constituent of national identity and localness as the symbolic representation of the nation. My basic argument is that Germans imagined nationhood as a form of localness. See Alon Confino, *The Nation as a Local Metaphor: Württemberg, Imperial Germany, and National Memory, 1871–1918* (Chapel Hill, N.C., 1997). The present article is a product of my thoughts on memory following the completion of my empirical study.

39. Gildea, *Past in French History*, 340.

40. Zerubavel, *Recovered Roots*, 235.

41. Of the three myths, only Tel Hai is presented as having a rich history of contestation reaching to the 1930s–1940s. The analysis of the contestation of the Bar Kokhba revolt focuses on the early 1980s, that of Masada on the 1960s and 1970s. Possibly, the paucity of contestation is linked more to the specific cases of Masada and Bar Kokhba than to a general attribute of Zionist's construction of the past. Other myths may reveal a different picture.

42. John Bodnar, *Remaking America: Public Memory, Commemoration, and Patriotism in the Twentieth Century* (Princeton, N.J., 1992).

43. Ibid., 13–14, 245, 20.

44. Ibid., 14, 247.

45. Ibid., 253.

46. In fact, Bodnar does use the metaphor of the whole and its parts to explain his views on the relationship of memories. Vernacular culture represents a variety of interests that "are grounded in parts of the whole," namely the nation-state. But for Bodnar, "the component parts of the nation-state [are] its families, classes, ethnic groups, and regions [which] attract loyalty and devotion." The nation-state thus remains an aggregation of sanctified vernacular memories, while official memory remains extraneous to it, a metaphor of "'unitary conceptual framework.'" Ibid., 14, 16.

Chapter Eight

Chapter 8 originally appeared as "Telling about Germany: Narratives of Memory and Culture," *Journal of Modern History* 76 (June 2004): 389–416, © 2004 by The University of Chicago, all rights reserved; reprinted with permission. Paul Betts, Jacques Ehrenfreund, Allan Megill, and Gavriel Rosenfeld read earlier drafts of this essay; I am indebted to them for their insightful and critical comments. I am especially grateful to Michael Confino and Francesca Fiorani, whose wisdom was invaluable.

Books discussed in this essay include (in alphabetic order): Omer Bartov, *Mirrors of De-*

struction: War, Genocide, and Modern Identity (Oxford, 2000); Paul Betts and Greg Eghigian, eds., *Pain and Prosperity: Reconsidering Twentieth-Century German History* (Stanford, Calif., 2003); Robert Gellately, *Backing Hitler: Consent and Coercion in Nazi Germany* (Oxford, 2001); Rudy Koshar, *From Monuments to Traces: Artifacts of German Memory, 1870–1990* (Berkeley, 2000); Pieter Lagrou, *The Legacy of Nazi Occupation: Patriotic Memory and National Recovery in Western Europe, 1945–1965* (Cambridge, 2000); Robert Moeller, *War Stories: The Search for a Usable Past in the Federal Republic of Germany* (Berkeley, 2001); Erna Paris, *Long Shadows: Truth, Lies, and History* (New York, 2001).

1. This was exemplified by the *Sonderweg* debate of the 1980s over Germany's alleged special historical path. The *Sonderweg* approach made the pre-1933 period into an inevitable prehistory of the Third Reich, whereas the critique of the *Sonderweg* argued for an open-ended historical causation and narrative. Both concentrated on Germany before 1933. See David Blackbourn and Geoff Eley, *The Peculiarities of German History: Bourgeois Society and Politics in Nineteenth-Century Germany* (Oxford, 1984).

2. Laura Engelstein formulates a similar question with respect to the Russian Revolution and present-day Russian historiography: "Culture, Culture Everywhere: Interpretations of Modern Russia, across the 1991 Divide," *Kritika* 2 (Spring 2001): 364. See also her "New Thinking about the Old Empire: Post-Soviet Reflections," *Russian Review* 60 (October 2001): 487–96.

3. I owe this distinction to Edward Ayers, "Narrative Form in Origins of the New South," in *C. Vann Woodward: A Southern Historian and His Critics*, ed. John Roper (Athens, Ga., 1997), 39. For narratives of modern German history, see the important book of Konrad Jarausch and Michael Geyer, *Shattered Past: Reconstructing German Histories* (Princeton, N.J., 2003), pt. I. See also Michael Geyer's characteristically imaginative essay, "Germany; or, the Twentieth Century as History," *South Atlantic Quarterly* 96 (Fall 1997): 663–703.

4. While the *Sonderweg* approach is rarely used these days as an interpretative framework, Heinrich August Winkler, who belongs to the founding generation of the approach, does begin his new study by asking, "Was there or was there not the controversial 'German special path'?" (1:1). He ends the study by stating: "There was a 'German special path.' It was the long way to modernity of a country deeply impacted by the Middle Ages" (2:648). Although Winkler qualifies this interpretation in many ways, he cannot go beyond what is originally a limited interpretative framework. Heinrich August Winkler, *Der lange Weg nach Westen*, vol. 1, *Deutsche Geschichte vom Ende des Alten Reiches bis zum Untergang der Weimarer Republic*; vol. 2, *Deutsche Geschichte vom "Dritten Reich" bis zur Wiedervereinigung* (Munich, 2000).

5. The East German writer Christoph Hain describes in his novel *The Tango Player* the ridiculous futility of it all. The protagonist is a disenchanted history lecturer fed up with Marxism-Leninism: "I was supposed to work in modern history, to burn the midnight oil discovering how illegal social-democratic parties managed secretly to print newspapers and row them across lake Constance a hundred years ago. And how the brave workers and artisans of Prague defended themselves against Windischgrätz's cannons with broomsticks and buckets of sand. But it's tiresome when science has nothing more to do than unearth anecdotes": Christoph Hein, *The Tango Player*, trans. Philip Boehm (Evanston, Ill., 1994), 104. After being banished from the university, the lecturer is content to return to his job not because of his conviction about Marxism-Leninism but as a way to regain his social and per-

sonal equilibrium. The limitation of a Marxist-influenced history of twentieth-century Germany has been most clear in the work of one of the century's most distinguished historians, Eric Hobsbawm. The narrative of *The Age of Extremes* is anything but fixed, but it does reduce German history to the struggle between communism and capitalism: Nazism's main achievement "was to liquidate the Great Slump more effectively than any other government, for the anti-liberalism of the Nazis had the positive side that it did not commit them to an a priori belief in the free market. Nevertheless, Nazism was a revamped and revitalized old regime rather than a basically new and different one." Lost in this interpretative framework is the revolutionary nature of the Nazi regime posing a historical alternative to both communism and liberalism, which is well presented in Mark Mazower, *Dark Continent: Europe's Twentieth Century* (New York, 1998). For Hobsbawm's citation, see *The Age of Extremes: A History of the World, 1914–1991* (New York, 1996), 128.

6. The editors of the *Annales* described it well in their 1989 statement, "Let's Try the Experiment" as the movement "toward analysis in terms of strategies, which allow memory, learning, uncertainty, and negotiation to be reintroduced into the heart of social interaction. . . . They remind us that social objects are not things endowed with properties, but, rather, sets of changing relationships within constantly adapting configurations." In Jacques Revel and Lynn Hunt, eds., *Histories: French Constructions of the Past* (New York, 1995), 487, originally published as "Tentons l'expérience," *Annales ESC* 44 (November–December 1989): 1317–23.

7. Rudy Koshar, *From Monuments to Traces: Artifacts of German Memory, 1870–1990* (Berkeley, 2000).

8. Saul Friedländer, ed., *Probing the Limits of Representation: Nazism and the "Final Solution"* (Cambridge, Mass., 1992).

9. Elie Wiesel, "Trivializing the Holocaust: Semi-Fact and Semi-Fiction," *New York Times*, April 16, 1978, B1, B29. Wiesel wrote this piece in reaction to the television series *Holocaust*.

10. See Inga Clendinnen, *Reading the Holocaust* (New York, 1999), 20–21, which is an exceptionally thoughtful meditation on the Holocaust by a historian of the Aztecs.

11. Saul Friedländer, "The 'Final Solution': On the Unease in Historical Interpretation," in *Lesson and Legacies: The Meaning of the Holocaust in a Changing World*, ed. Peter Hayes (Evanston, Ill., 1991), 23, 31.

12. Saul Friedländer, *Nazi Germany and the Jews: The Years of Persecution, 1933–39* (New York, 1997).

13. Friedländer, "The 'Final Solution,'" 32.

14. Robert Conquest recounts a revealing anecdote in his book on the twentieth century: "And then, the mind is a venue of thought, but also of feeling, not always rationally describable. Late in 1997 the Paris *Le Monde* interviewed me by phone. I was asked did I find the Holocaust 'worse' than the Stalinist crimes. I answered yes, I did, but when the interviewer asked why, I could only answer honestly with 'I feel so.' Not a final judgment, let alone to suggest that the Holocaust was much 'worse' than the Stalinist terror. . . . Still, this primary 'feeling,' based indeed on knowledge, has a validity of its own. I would argue, too, that whatever view one takes, without feeling the Holocaust one cannot feel, or understand, Stalinism. The crux is nevertheless that such feelings are only acceptable when based on, or conjoined with, sound knowledge and careful thought." Robert Conquest, *Reflections on a Ravaged Century* (New York, 2000), xii.

15. Clendinnen, *Reading the Holocaust*, 21.

16. Lawrence Langer describes survivors' clinging to a dual sentiment, in which "'you won't understand' and 'you must understand' are regular contenders in the multiple voices" of Holocaust testimonies. Lawrence Langer, *Holocaust Testimonies: The Ruins of Memory* (New Haven, Conn., 1991), xiv.

17. The literature is huge and continues to grow. See, for example, James Young, *The Texture of Memory: Holocaust Memorials and Meaning* (New Haven, Conn., 1993); Saul Friedländer, *Memory, History, and the Extermination of the Jews of Europe* (Bloomington, Ind., 1993); Geoffrey Hartman, ed., *Holocaust Remembrance: The Shapes of Memory* (Oxford, 1994); Alvin Rosenfeld, ed., *Thinking about the Holocaust after Half a Century* (Bloomington, Ind., 1997); Omer Bartov, *Murder in Our Midst: The Holocaust, Industrial Killing, and Representation* (New York, 1996); Hayes, ed., *Lesson and Legacies*. And see note 18.

18. The general trend in the historiography of German memory has understandably been to explore the post-1945 memory of National Socialism; the great majority of these studies focus on West rather than East Germany. Other topics and periods have been marginal in comparison. For German memory of National Socialism, see Gavriel Rosenfeld, *Munich and Memory: Architecture, Monuments, and the Legacy of the Third Reich* (Berkeley, 2000); Jeffrey Herf, *Divided Memory: The Nazi Past in the Two Germanys* (Cambridge, Mass., 1997); Maoz Azaryahu, "Renaming the Past: Changes in 'City Text' in Germany and Austria, 1945–1947," *History and Memory* 2 (Winter 1990): 32–53; Wolfgang Benz, "Postwar Society and National Socialism: Remembrance, Amnesia, Rejection," *Tel Aviver Jahrbuch für deutsche Geschichte* 19 (1990): 1–12; Norbert Frei, *Vergangenheitspolitik: Die Anfänge der Bundesrepublik und die NS-Vergangenheit* (Munich, 1996); Geoff Eley, "Nazism, Politics, and the Image of the Past: Thoughts on the West German Historikerstreit, 1986–1987," *Past and Present* 121 (November 1988): 171–208; Michael Geyer, "The Politics of Memory in Contemporary Germany," in *Radical Evil*, ed. Joan Copjec (London, 1996), 169–200, and "The Place of the Second World War in German Memory and History," *New German Critique* 71 (1997): 5–40; Elizabeth Heineman, "The Hour of the Women: Memories of Germany's 'Crisis Years' and West German National Identity," *American Historical Review* 101 (April 1996): 354–95; Elizabeth Domansky, "A Lost War: World War II in Postwar German Memory," in Rosenfeld, *Thinking about the Holocaust*, 233–72; Y. Michal Bodemann, "Eclipse of Memory: German Representations of Auschwitz in the Early Postwar Period," *New German Critique* 75 (Fall 1998): 57–89; Dominick LaCapra, *History and Memory after Auschwitz* (Ithaca, N.Y., 1998); Harold Marcuse, *Legacies of Dachau: The Uses and Abuses of a Concentration Camp, 1933–2001* (Cambridge, 2001); Claudia Koonz, "Between Memory and Oblivion: Concentration Camps in German Memory," in *Commemorations: The Politics of National Identity*, ed. John Gillis (Princeton, N.J., 1994), 258–80; Klaus Naumann, *Der Krieg als Text: Das Jahr 1945 im kulturellen Gedächtnis der Presse* (Hamburg, 1998); Peter Dudek, *"Der Rückblick auf die Vergangenheit wird sich nicht vermeiden lassen": Zur pädagogischen Verarbeitung des Nationalsozialismus in Deutschland (1945–1990)* (Opladen, 1995); Helmut Peitsch, *"Deutschlands Gedächtnis an seine dunkelste Zeit": Zur Funktion der Autobiographik in den Westzonen Deutschlands und den Westsektoren von Berlin 1945 bis 1949* (Berlin, 1990); Hermann Graml, "Die verdrängte Auseinandersetzung mit dem Nationalsozialismus," in *Zäsuren nach 1945: Essays zur Periodisierung der deutschen Nachkriegsgeschichte*, ed. Martin Broszat (Munich, 1990), 169–83; Manfred Kittel, *Die Legende von der "Zweiten Schuld": Vergangenheitsbewältigung in der Ära Adenauer* (Berlin, 1993); Christa

Hoffmann, *Stunden Null: Vergangenheitsbewältigung in Deutschland 1945 und 1989* (Bonn, 1992); Alf Lüdtke, "'Coming to Terms with the Past': Illusions of Remembering, Ways of Forgetting Nazism in West Germany," *Journal of Modern History* 65 (1993): 542–72; David Case, "The Politics of Memorial Representation: The Controversy over the German Resistance Museum in 1994," *German Politics and Society* 16 (Spring 1998): 58–81. For a journalistic treatment, see Jane Kramer, *The Politics of Memory: Looking for Germany in the New Germany* (New York, 1996), and the intelligent book of Ian Buruma, *The Wages of Guilt: Memories of War in Germany and Japan* (New York, 1994). Studies on East Germany have begun to emerge: see, for example, Thomas Fox, *Stated Memory: East Germany and the Holocaust* (Rochester, N.Y., 1999). A case apart is the *Erinnerungsorte* project that, similar to Pierre Nora's project on French *lieux de mémoire*, covered German memory through the centuries. See Etienne François and Hagen Schulze, eds., *Deutsche Erinnerungsorte*, 3 vols. (Munich, 2001); Pierre Nora, ed., *Les lieux de mémoire*, 7 vols. (Paris, 1984–1992).

19. For studies on German memory prior to 1933, see, for example, Susan Crane, *Collecting and Historical Consciousness: New Forms for Collective Memory in Early Nineteenth-Century Germany* (Ithaca, N.Y., 2000); Christopher Clark, "The Wars of Liberation in Prussian Memory: Reflections on the Memorialization of War in Early Nineteenth-Century Germany," *Journal of Modern History* 68 (September 1996): 550–76; Alon Confino, *The Nation as a Local Metaphor: Württemberg, Imperial Germany, and National Memory, 1871–1918* (Chapel Hill, N.C., 1997); Rudy Koshar's *Germany's Transient Pasts: Preservation and National Memory in the Twentieth Century* (Chapel Hill, N.C., 1998), as well as *From Monuments to Traces*, are rare examples of studies that explore memory in modern German history as a whole.

20. Friedländer, "The 'Final Solution,'" 32–33.

21. Liah Greenfield, *Nationalism: Five Roads to Modernity* (Cambridge, Mass., 1992), 358, 360, 384.

22. Daniel Goldhagen, *Hitler's Willing Executioners: Ordinary Germans and the Holocaust* (New York, 1996), 69, 71.

23. Omer Bartov, *The Eastern Front, 1941–45: German Troops and the Barbarisation of Warfare* (London, 1985) and *Hitler's Army: Soldiers, Nazis, and War in the Third Reich* (New York, 1992).

24. On the debate, see the recent thoughtful contribution of Richard Bessel, "Functionalists vs. Intentionalists: The Debate Twenty Years On; or, Whatever Happened to Functionalism and Intentionalism?," *German Studies Review* 26 (2003): 15–20.

25. Omer Bartov, *Mirrors of Destruction: War, Genocide, and Modern Identity* (Oxford, 2000).

26. It is interesting to note the importance given by Bartov, Goldhagen, and Greenfield to the late eighteenth century for understanding twentieth-century German history. The birth of modernity in the Enlightenment and the French Revolution are seen as unleashing ideas—romantic nationalism, eliminationist anti-Semitism, or the project of perfecting humanity—that led to the Third Reich and the Holocaust two centuries later. Similarly, "the Soviet tragedy" has recently been interpreted by Martin Malia and François Furet as an outcome of the Enlightenment project of perfecting humanity. On a general descriptive level, this ideational link between late eighteenth-century and modern state violence may be illuminating. But on another, it merely confirms that the defining moments of the modern period—that is, the Enlightenment and the French Revolution—influenced major events

after 1789. The danger is to create a narrative—from the Enlightenment via the project of perfecting humanity to the Gulag and the Holocaust—in search of historical "examples." But the late eighteenth century gave rise also to the ideas of feminism, human rights, and democracy. The point, therefore, is to explain why ideas of the Enlightenment were applied so differently in different countries. See François Furet, *The Passing of an Illusion: The Idea of Communism in the Twentieth Century*, trans. Deborah Furet (Chicago, 1999); Martin Malia, *The Soviet Tragedy: A History of Socialism in Russia, 1917–1991* (New York, 1994); Catherine Evtuhov, "Introduction," in *The Culture Gradient: The Transmission of Ideas in Europe, 1789–1991*, ed. Catherine Evtuhov and Stephen Kotkin (London, 2003), 1–10. I am grateful to John Boyer for his insight on this point.

27. See Wulf Kansteiner, "Cultures of Catastrophe: Understanding the History and Memory of Mass Death in Twentieth-Century Europe," *German Politics and Society* 19 (Winter 2001): 87–95.

28. Robert Gellately, *Backing Hitler: Consent and Coercion in Nazi Germany* (Oxford, 2001).

29. Ibid., vii, 259.

30. Ibid., 263.

31. Robert Moeller, *War Stories: The Search for a Usable Past in the Federal Republic of Germany* (Berkeley, 2001).

32. Ibid., 173.

33. Two books that attempt to elucidate the relations between personal memory and public memory are Helmut Peitsch, Charles Burdett, and Claire Gorrara, eds., *European Memories of the Second World War* (New York, 1999), and Graham Bartram, Maurice Slawinski, and David Steel, eds., *Reconstructing the Past: Representations of the Fascist Era in Post-War European Culture* (Keele, 1996). See also David Glassberg, "Public History and the Study of Memory," *Public Historian* 18 (Spring 1996): 7–23.

34. Hans Dollinger, ed., *Kain, wo ist dein Bruder? Was der Mensch im Zweiten Weltkrieg erleiden mußte—dokumentiert in Tagebüchern und Briefen* (Frankfurt, 1989), 221.

35. Pieter Lagrou, *The Legacy of Nazi Occupation: Patriotic Memory and National Recovery in Western Europe, 1945–1965* (Cambridge, 2000).

36. Ibid., 3.

37. Ibid., 6. The book compares, first, the three countries. But Lagrou goes a step further by making the comparison among the three groups the linchpin of the book. Instead of dividing the book into three national case studies, Lagrou organizes it around social groups.

38. Ibid., 16.

39. Ibid., 17.

40. Maurice Halbwachs is an important member of this tradition, as is Karl Mannheim, who observed that "we cannot jump straight from the general observation of individuals and their psychic mechanisms to the analysis of society. The psychology of society is not a million times that of an individual. . . . What for our purpose is needed is an historically-differentiated psychology by which the changes in attitudes, motivations and symbol-transmutations in different periods among different classes and under different social situations will be made plain": Karl Mannheim, "The Psychological Aspect," in *Peaceful Change: An International Problem*, ed. C. A. W. Manning (New York, 1937), 129.

41. I am, of course, using Marc Bloch's celebrated phrase in *The Historian's Craft* (New York, 1953), 26.

42. See Marc Bloch's review of Maurice Halbwachs's *Les cadres sociaux de la mémoire* (Paris, 1925) in *Revue de synthèse* 40 (December 1925): 73–83. I used the Italian translation, "Memoria colletiva, tradizione e costume: A proposito d'un libro recente," in Marc Bloch, *Storici e storia* (Turin, 1997), 215.

43. Erna Paris, *Long Shadows: Truth, Lies, and History* (New York, 2001). See also Allan Megill, "Two Para-Historical Approaches to Atrocity," *History and Theory* 41 (December 2002): 104–23.

44. Paris, *Long Shadows*, 4–5.

45. Ibid., 11. When she is offered the chance to spend a night in a guest room in Berlin's historical Neue Synagoge on Oranienburger Strasse, she accepts with "alacrity: I thought—rightly, as it turns out—that I would not get much closer to the past than in a place that housed so many ghosts." But in this place, Paris is to meet not the ghosts of the past (whatever that means), but her own. Her stories about the different ways people try to link with the past are at times hilarious. Jewish culture has acquired in Berlin in the past decade a certain modishness as Germans try to connect with the city's Jewish past. On Oranienburger Strasse, the center of renewed Jewish life, dozens of Klezmer bands made up entirely of German Christians play to audiences of German Christians. So much for Jewish authenticity. The head of the German branch of the Lauder Foundation, responsible for the renewal of Jewish life in Europe, explained to Paris that "many Germans try to attend every Jewish event. They can't seem to get close enough . . . they seem to be looking for comfort" (ibid., 19–20).

46. Of course, the quest to understand the past is always connected with a quest to understand the self; we are interested in the past in order to illuminate our life in the present, to gain self-consciousness and wisdom. But the past needs to be explored on its own terms, not on ours.

47. Paris's book is mostly about contemporary popular perceptions of the past, which may be different from popular perceptions in the 1950s. But the general point is still valid, whatever popular perceptions of the past in the 1950s may have been.

48. Lagrou, *The Legacy of Nazi Occupation*, 17.

49. Moeller, *War Stories*, 86.

50. This is a classic problem from the atelier of Michel Foucault. Stephen Kotkin, *Magnetic Mountain: Stalinism as a Civilization* (Berkeley, 1995), is an original attempt to tackle this problem with respect to the 1930s Soviet Union.

51. Jan Assmann, "Collective Memory and Cultural Identity," *New German Critique* 65 (Summer–Spring 1995): 125–33, esp. 126–27.

52. Bartov, *Mirrors of Destruction*, chap. 4.

53. This argument, in a sense, takes us back to the classic writings on memory of Maurice Halbwachs. The fundamental idea of *The Social Formation of Memory* is the "multiplicity of social times," as Halbwachs analyzes the collective memory of, among others, the family, the religious community, and the social class. He writes: "But these various modes by which memories become associated result from the various ways in which people can become associated. We can understand each memory as it occurs in individual thought only if we locate each within the thought of the corresponding group. We cannot properly understand their relative strength and the ways in which they combine within individual thought unless we connect the individual to the various groups of which he is simultaneously a member."

Maurice Halbwachs, *On Collective Memory*, ed., trans., and introd. Lewis Coser (Chicago, 1992), 53. Jacques Le Goff discusses Maurice Halbwach's "multiplicity of social time" in *History and Memory*, trans. Steven Rendall and Elizabeth Claman (New York, 1992), 135.

54. Lutz Niethammer, *"Die Jahre weiß man nicht, wo man die heute hinsetzen soll": Faschismuserfahrungen im Ruhrgebiet* (Berlin, 1983); *"Hinterher merkt man, daß es richtig war daß es schief gegangen ist": Nachkriegserfahrungen im Ruhrgebiet* (Berlin, 1983); and *Lebenserfahrung and kollektives Gedächtnis: Die Praxis der "Oral History"* (Frankfurt, 1980). See also Lutz Niethammer, "Erfahrungen and Strukturen: Prolegomena zu einer Geschichte der Gesellschaft der DDR," in *Sozialgeschichte der DDR*, ed. Hartmut Kaelble, Jürgen Kocka, and Hartmut Zwahr (Stuttgart, 1994), 95–115; Lutz Niethammer, Alexander von Plato, and Dorothee Wierling, *Die volkseigene Erfahrung: Eine Archäologie des Lebens in der Industrieprovinz der DDR* (Berlin, 1991).

55. See Mark Roseman, "Introduction: Generation Conflict and German History, 1770–1968"; Alexander von Plato, "The Hitler Youth Generation and Its Role in the Two Postwar German States"; and Dagmar Reese, "The BDM Generation: A Female Generation in Transition from Dictatorship to Democracy," in *Generations in Conflict: Youth Revolt and Generation Formation in Germany, 1770–1968*, ed. Mark Roseman (Cambridge, 1995), 30–36, 210–26, 227–45, respectively. See also Dorothee Wierling, "Von der HJ zur FDJ," *Bios* 6 (1993): 107–18; "The Hitler Youth Generation in the GDR: Insecurities, Ambitions and Dilemmas," in *Dictatorship as Experience: Toward a Socio-Cultural History of the GDR*, ed. Konrad Jarausch (New York, 1999), 307–24; and *Geboren im Jahr Eins. Der Jahrgang 1949 in der DDR: Versuch eine Kollektivbiographie* (Berlin, 2002).

56. On the importance of linking everyday, private memory to public memory, see the thoughtful discussions of Jürgen Danyel, "Unwirtliche Gegenden and abgelegene Orte? Der Nationalsozialismus and die deutsche Teilung als Herausforderungen einer Geschichte der deutschen 'Erinnerungsorte,'" *Geschichte and Gesellschaft* 24 (1998): 463–75, esp. 465–66, and Dan Stone, "Making Memory Work, or Gedächtnis macht frei," *Patterns of Prejudice* 37 (2003): 87–98, esp. 96.

57. Jean Amery, *At the Mind's Limits: Contemplations by a Survivor on Auschwitz and Its Realities*, trans. Sidney Rosenfeld and Stella Rosenfeld (Bloomington, Ind., 1980), 84.

58. Applying Joan Scott's analysis on the notion of experience to memory studies is useful. The notion of "experience" is often used in memory studies to describe a situation, rather than something out of which the individual's sense of self emerges. The experience of the individual is seen as "the authoritative (because seen or felt) evidence that grounds what is known," but not as a social construction of knowledge of people who make themselves as they go along. Joan Scott, "The Evidence of Experience," *Critical Inquiry* 17 (Summer 1991): 773–98, here 789–90.

59. Lagrou, *The Legacy of Nazi Occupation*, 11.

60. Alain Corbin, "A History and Anthropology of the Senses," in *Time, Desire and Horror: Towards a History of the Senses* (Cambridge, Mass., 1995), 181–95, esp. 181–82. The work of Corbin, who studied sensibilities such as smells, sounds, and leisure, stands out in its originality. See *Village Bells: Sound and Meaning in the 19th-Century French Countryside*, trans. Martin Thom (New York, 1998); *The Lure of the Sea: The Discovery of the Seaside in the Western World, 1750–1840*, trans. Jocelyn Phelps (Cambridge, 1994); and *The Foul and the Fragrant: Odor and the French Social Imagination* (Cambridge, Mass., 1986).

61. Paul Betts and Greg Eghigian, eds., *Pain and Prosperity: Reconsidering Twentieth-Century Europe* (Stanford, Calif., 2003), 3.

62. Uta Poiger, *Jazz, Rock, and Rebels: Cold War Politics and American Culture in a Divided Germany* (Berkeley, 2000); Rudy Koshar, *German Travel Cultures* (Oxford, 2000).

63. Changes in identity ultimately depend also on the age of a given social group. Teenagers will acquire new identities much more rapidly than people in their forties and fifties, with their lingering mental habits, nostalgia, and retro mind-set.

64. Christopher Browning's *Ordinary Men: Reserve Police Battalion 101 and the Final Solution in Poland* (New York, 1992) exemplifies the interpretation that highlights circumstances, while Goldhagen's *Hitler's Willing Executioners* illustrates the interpretation that highlights ideology and inner conviction. Many scholars fruitfully commingle these approaches in various ways. Mark Mazower recently argued for a "subtly modulated psychology" in interpreting the perpetrators' motivations, noting "the conceptual rigidities found in some well known discussions of Nazi perpetrators." See his essay on the need to decenter the Holocaust as a model for state violence in the twentieth century, "Violence and the State in the Twentieth Century," *American Historical Review* 107 (October 2002): 1166–67.

65. Corbin, "A History and Anthropology of the Senses," 182.

66. Friedländer mentions two such psychological elements: the *Führerbindung* (the bond to the Führer) and the notion of *Rausch* (the result of the growing excitement of the repetitive act of killing). Friedländer, "'The Final Solution,'" 25, 27. And see Clendinnen, *Reading the Holocaust*, 83–88.

67. Johan Huizinga, *Homo Ludens: A Study of the Play-Element in Culture* (Boston, 1955), 4.

68. Helmut Heiber, ed., *Goebbels-Reden*, vol. 1, *1932–1939* (Düsseldorf, 1971), 111.

69. Wisława Szymborska, *Poems New and Collected, 1957–1997*, trans. Stanislaw Baranczak and Clare Cavanagh (New York, 1998), 198–99.

Chapter Nine

Chapter 9 originally appeared as "Dissonance, Normality and the Historical Method: Why Did Some Germans Think of Tourism after May 8, 1945?," in *Life after Death: Approaches to a Cultural and Social History of Europe during the 1940s and 1950s*, ed. Richard Bessel and Dirk Schumann (Cambridge, 2003), 323–47; reprinted with permission of Cambridge University Press. Earlier versions of this essay were delivered in 1999–2000 at the École des Hautes Études en Sciences Sociales in Paris, the Humboldt University in Berlin, Cambridge University, and the 1999 German Studies Association meeting in Atlanta. I should thank Michael Werner, Wolfgang Hardtwig, and Richard Evans. I am grateful to Kristiane Klemm and Hasso Spode for making the research for this essay possible at the Institut für Tourismus in Berlin. I should also like to thank Omer Bartov and Francesca Fiorani for their critical comments. On the place of National Socialism in history, my discussions with my father, Michael Confino, about this essay and over the years were the most insightful for me.

1. "Ein Dezenium Verbandsarbeit: Berichte der deutschen Fremdenverkehrsverbände," *Der Fremdenverkehr* 11, no. 5 (1959): 26. The permission was received on September 1, then revoked; the association had its first meeting in February 1946.

2. *Jubilaumsschrift des Harzer Verkehrsverband e. V. zu seinem funfzigjährigen Bestehen* (Braunschweig, 1954), 31–32.

3. The remarkable revival of tourist activities and organizations after the defeat con-

firms that this dissonance was not that exceptional. The first postwar tourist association was founded in Baden in December 1945. In the same month, the old tourist association in Dortmund resumed its activities. And the preparatory meeting for the foundation of the German League of Tourist Associations and Spas (Bund deutscher Verkehrsverbände und Bäder) took place in June 1946. Overall, by February 1947, thirteen tourist associations were active in the western occupation zone in Württemberg, the Rhineland, Westphalia, Bavaria, and other regions. For Baden, see "Ein Dezenium Verbandsarbeit," 60. For Dortmund, "50 Jahre Landesverkehrsverband Westfalen," *Der Fremdenverkehr* 10, no. 2 (1958): 15; "Ein Dezenium Verbandsarbeit," 41. On the German League of Tourist Associations and Spas, see *Abschrift: Referat des Verbandsdirektor Stadtrat a. D. Ochs . . . am 6.9.1946 auf der Hohensyburg betreffend Vorbereitung der Grundung des Bundes deutscher Verkehrsverbände and Bäder*, Ncm, IfT. On the newly founded associations, see *Neugegrundete Fremdenverkehrsverbande in Deutschland: Stand vom 10.2. 1947*, Ncm, IfT.

Moreover, lively discussions on tourist issues took place in the associations' newspapers and journals, as well as in conferences and meetings. The German Central Tourist Association (Deutsche Zentrale für Fremdenverkehr) was founded in 1948 as West Germany's national tourist organization. The *Deutsche Zeitschrift fir Fremdenverkehr* was first published in July 1949.

4. Anton Luft, "Erfahrungen mit Pressefahrten," *Der Fremdenverkehr* 8, nos. 3–4 (1956): 10.

5. Edoardo Grendi, "Microanalisi e storia sociale," *Quaderni Storici* 7 (1972): 506–20. The citation is from Giovanni Levi, "On Microhistory," in *New Perspectives on Historical Writing*, ed. Peter Burke (University Park, Pa., 1992), 109. I am indebted to microhistory for thinking about the problematics of the essay and the period.

6. *Jubilaumsschrift des Harzer Verkehrsverband e. V. zu seinem funfzigjährigen Bestehen*, 29.

7. Ibid., 28.

8. Ibid., 29.

9. My discussion is based on Christine Keitz, *Reisen als Leitbild. Die Entstehung des modernen Massen tourismus in Deutschland* (Munich, 1997), 248–49.

10. R. Irmer, "50 Jahre Harzer Verkehrsverband," *Der Fremdenverkehr* 6, nos. 7–8 (1954): 3–4.

11. Elizabeth D. Heineman, "The Hour of the Women: Memories of Germany's 'Crisis Years' and West German National Identity," *American Historical Review* 101, no. 2 (April 1996): 387.

12. *Mitteilungen der Z.F.V: Warum Deutschland-Werbung mit Goethe*, n.d., 1–2, Ncm, IfT.

13. On rape in postwar Germany, see Heineman, "Hour of the Women," and Atina Grossmann, "A Question of Silence: The Rape of German Women by Occupation Soldiers," *October* 72 (April 1995): 43–63.

14. See Michael Hughes, "'Through No Fault of Our Own': West Germans Remember Their War Losses," *German History* 18, no. 2 (2000): 193–213.

15. The Goethe Year campaign should also be seen against the background of the Cold War and the transformation of the Soviet occupation zone into East Germany. For the German Central Tourist Association, Goethe symbolized the true German spirit not only in contrast to the Nazi regime but also in contrast to East Germany's communist regime, which celebrated the Goethe anniversary in Weimar. The German Central Tourist Association at-

tempted to delegitimize the appropriation of Goethe by the East German communists. In this respect, the celebrations in West Germany, which claimed the mantle of the true Germany, took place against a perceived background of two "abnormal" Germanys, the Nazi as well as the Communist regime.

16. Christoph Hennig, *Reiselust: Touristen, Tourismus and Urlaubskultur* (Frankfurt am Main, 1997), 11.

17. For Oberammergau and tourism, see Ian Kershaw, *Popular Opinion and Political Dissent in the Third Reich: Bavaria, 1933–1945* (Oxford, 1983), 136, 197.

18. Shelley Baranowski, *Strength through Joy: Consumerism and Mass Tourism in the Third Reich* (Cambridge, 2004).

19. Cited in Hasso Spode, "Arbeiterurlaub im Dritten Reich," in *Angst, Belohnunt, Zucht and Ordnung: Herrschaftstmechanismen im Nationalsozialismus*, ed. Carola Sachse, Tilla Siegel, Hasso Spode, and Wolfgang Spohn (Opladen, 1982), 314. On tourism in the Third Reich, see also Rudy Koshar, *German Travel Cultures* (Oxford, 2000), chap. 3; Kristin Semmens, *Seeing Hitler's Germany: Tourism in the Third Reich* (New York, 2005).

20. Cited in Spode, "Arbeiterurlaub im Dritten Reich," 314.

21. " 'Wir waren wie eine einzige gluckliche Familie!,' " *Der Enztäler: Wildbader Tagblatt*, August 24, 1996.

22. Mary Nolan, "Work, Gender, and Everyday Life: Reflections on Continuity, Normality and Agency in Twentieth-Century Germany," in *Stalinism and Nazism: Dictatorships in Comparison*, ed. Ian Kershaw and Moshe Lewin (Cambridge, 1997), 324. Nolan's essay is excellent.

23. Kaspar Maase, *Grenzenloses Vergnugen: Der Aufstieg der Massenkultur 1850–1970* (Frankfurt am Main, 1997), 209–10.

24. I cannot discuss here the topic of German tourism in uniform between 1939 and 1945, namely of Wehrmacht soldiers being tourists in conquered countries. This subject is fundamental in providing background and meaning to postwar German tourism and memory. See chapter 10.

25. This discussion is based on Ulrich Herbert, "Good Times, Bad Times: Memories of the Third Reich," in *Life in the Third Reich*, ed. Richard Bessel (Oxford, 1987), 97.

26. Ibid.

27. On the brochures, see Axel Schildt, " 'Mach mal Pause!' Freie Zeit, Freizeitverhalten and Freizeit-Diskurse in der westdeutschen Wiederaufbau-Gesellschaft der 1950er Jahre," *Archiv für Sozialgeschichte* 33 (1993): 397. On Oberammergau, *Niederschrift über die Sitzung des Verwaltungsrats der Deutschen Zentrale für Fremdenverkehr am 5. Februar 1949 im Hotel Lang, Oberammergau*, February 5, 1949, 2–3, Ncm, IfT; *Deutsche Verkehrsblätter*, no. 1 (April 8, 1949): 4; and Kershaw, *Popular Opinion*, 136, 197. The 1934 Oberammergau Passion Play was, as mentioned earlier, a big success. Significantly, in the second half of the 1930s, when relations between the Nazi party and Bavarian Catholics were tense, attending the Oberammergau Passion Play became at times an act of defiance and support of the church. But in 1934 relations between the church and the party were good. Thus, the fashioning of the 1950s Passion Play after the 1934 play was not an act of remembering resistance to the Third Reich, but instead of a great tourist season made possible by the Nazis.

28. "Less people traveled"—again, not considering the soldiers.

29. On Niethammer's project, see Herbert, "Good Times, Bad Times," 97–110. See *Heimat Front*, pt. 1: *Die Mobilmachung* (1998).

30. See Alain Corbin, "A History and Anthropology of the Senses," in *Time, Desire, and Horror: Towards a History of the Senses* (Cambridge, Mass., 1995), 186.

31. Wolfgang Benz, "Postwar Society and National Socialism: Remembrance, Amnesia, Rejection," *Tel Aviver Jahrbücher für deutsche Geschichte* 19 (1990): 12. The essayist Jane Kramer, who argued that Germans "buried the past . . . without a reckoning, without committing the past to history," popularized this view on the pages of the *New Yorker*. See Jane Kramer, *The Politics of Memory: Looking for Germany in the New Germany* (New York, 1996), xv.

32. Norbert Frei, *Vergangenheitspolitik: Die Anfänge der Bundesrepublik und die NS-Vergangenheit* (Munich, 1996), 23.

33. See, for example, Robert G. Moeller, "War Stories: The Search for a Usable Past in the Federal Republic of Germany," *American Historical Review* 101 (October 1996): 1008–48; Heineman, "Hour of the Women"; Heide Fehrenbach, *Cinema in Democratizing Germany: Reconstructing National Identity after Hitler* (Chapel Hill, N.C., 1995); Frank Biess, " 'Pioneers of a New Germany': Returning POWs from the Soviet Union and the Making of East German Citizens, 1945–1950," *Central European History* 2, no. 2 (1999): 143–80; Catherine Epstein, "The Production of 'Official Memory' in East Germany: Old Communists and the Dilemmas of Memoir-Writing," *Central European History* 2, no. 2 (1999): 181–202; and Maria Mitchell, "Materialism and Secularism: CDU Politicians and National Socialism, 1945–1949," *Journal of Modern History* 67 (June 1995): 278–308.

34. I do not mean to imply that these studies subscribe to the argument of zero hour, namely of 1945 as a wholly new beginning in German history. They are sensitive to the social relationships and culture negotiations across 1945. But they do mostly focus on post-1945. For a useful critique of the concept of zero hour, see Robert G. Moeller, "Introduction: Writing the History of West Germany," in *West Germany under Construction: Politics, Society, and Culture in the Adenauer Era*, ed. Robert G. Moeller (Ann Arbor, Mich., 1997), 12.

35. Excellent in this regard is Paul Betts's analysis of industrial design in the 1950s as a way to link Nazi and post-Nazi commodity culture. Paul Betts, "The Nierentisch Nemesis: Organic Design as West German Pop Culture," *German History* 19 (2001): 185–217.

36. Exceptions are the perceptive discussions of Nolan, "Work, Gender, and Everyday Life," 311–42; and Ian Kershaw, *The Nazi Dictatorship: Problems and Perspectives of Interpretation*, 3rd ed. (London, 1993), chap. 9, although Kershaw's discussion, as we shall see, is not without problems. The notion of normality had different implications on Third Reich scholarship. Nolan identified three such implications connected to the debate over whether National Socialism can be historicized. The first question concerns the place of Auschwitz in the historical evaluation of the Nazi regime; the second problem involves whether the Nazi era can be at all understood historically; and the third issue is the place of National Socialism in twentieth-century German history (Nolan, "Work, Gender, and Everyday Life," 317). My discussion here touches on all these issues, though especially on the problem of historical explanation and the place of the Nazi regime within the historical method.

37. Saul Friedländer, "Some Reflections on the Historicization of National Socialism," in *Reworking the Past: Hitler, the Holocaust, and the Historians' Debate*, ed. Peter Baldwin (Boston, 1990), 98. My critique notwithstanding, I have found Friedländer's body of work on the

Holocaust to be highly insightful. It stands out as a combination of original thinking and historical writing, and moral voice.

38. Friedländer, "Some Reflections," 100 (emphasis in the original).

39. Our difficulty in understanding Auschwitz is enormous, but sixteenth-century France presents its own violent cases. The Wars of Religion saw unparalleled Catholic zeal for religious massacres. Disfigurement of the dead and mutilation of bodies, expressing a theatricalization of godly damnation, were common, but also common was cannibalism. Catholic killers ate the livers of the Huguenots they murdered, while the fricassees of human ears and grilled hearts were served up during the Saint Bartholomew massacres; human flesh was auctioned in the city of Romans in 1580. Although these facts are monstrous, we don't doubt our ability to explain them. Perhaps the reason lies in our detachment from these events in historical time and space, in spite of our moral revulsion. And so, perhaps, will be one day the case with an explanation for the Holocaust: the distance in time and space will provide the necessary detachment to explain it, while the moral revulsion will remain. But lack of detachment does not make the Holocaust abnormal and cannibalism normal. Indeed, it should be added that genocide and ethnic cleansing were much more common in the twentieth century than cannibalism in the sixteenth. Which case, in truth, better reflects its age?

I have taken the details on sixteenth-century cannibalism from Alain Corbin, *The Village of Cannibals: Rage and Murder in France, 1870* (Cambridge, Mass., 1992), esp. 88–89, an insightful book helpful for thinking about extreme violence and the Holocaust. For the cannibalism cases, see Frank Lestringant, "Catholiques et cannibales: Le thème du cannibalisme dans le discours Protestant au temps des guerres de religion," in *Pratiques et discourses alimentaires à la Renaissance: Actes du Colloque de Tours de mar 1979*, ed. Université François Rabelais, Centre d'études supérieures de la Renaissance (Paris, 1982), 233–47.

40. Dan Diner, "Between Aporia and Apology: On the Limits of Historicizing National Socialism," in Baldwin, *Reworking the Past*, 144. Diner's important work on the Holocaust serves as a testimony to its historicity. The insight of his work, in my reading, lies precisely in his persistent negotiations of the tension between the Holocaust as history and as a "black box." He is one of the few scholars who attempt to understand in historical terms the psychological, also irrational, elements of the Nazis, to bridge between the apocalyptic elements of the Holocaust and a certain rational slant in its historiographical description as an outcome of racial ideology and the context of war. See Diner, *Beyond the Conceivable: Studies on Germany, Nazism, and the Holocaust* (Berkeley, 2000).

41. Martin Broszat, "A Plea for the Historicization of National Socialism," in Baldwin, *Reworking the Past*, 77–87. See the judicious discussion of Kershaw, *The Nazi Dictatorship*, 180–96.

42. Broszat, "A Plea," 125.

43. The work of Detlev Peukert has been fundamental in integrating normality with barbarism, everyday life with racism. See *Inside Nazi Germany: Conformity and Opposition in Everyday Life* (London, 1987), and "Alltag and Barbarei: Zur Normalität des Dritten Reiches," in *Ist der Nationalsozialismus Geschichte? Zu Historisierung and Historikerstreit*, ed. Dan Diner (Frankfurt am Main, 1987), 51–61. But, then, Peukert helps to normalize the Nazi regime in one theoretical move, while making it abnormal again in another, for he sees the period as

a whole as a prototype of the pathologies of modernity. Normalities and pathologies thus dominate the historical discourse on the Third Reich.

44. Paradoxically, Saul Friedländer's masterful narrative of the years of persecution belied his own moral, theoretical view of the incomprehensibility of the Third Reich and of its uniqueness. He could conceive and write his study, and we can understand it, only on the basis of a shared historical discourse (of history as a discipline, I mean) and of a shared notion of what modern history has been like, excesses, crimes, and mass murders included. Had the Nazi era been abnormal and unique it would have left us no methods, narratives, and approaches to write about and comprehend it. While it is difficult to write about the Nazi regime, and problems of representation and language are significant, it is not wholly impossible, as Friedlander's book successfully demonstrates. See *Nazi Germany and the Jews: The Years of Persecution, 1933–1939* (New York, 1997).

45. Using the notion of abnormality also serves, perhaps, as a mechanism to distance us from the Holocaust by labeling it as the absolute other, utterly different from our own values, ways of life, and conditions of modernity.

46. See the original attempt of Andrew Bergerson, *Ordinary Germans in Extraordinary Times: The Nazi Revolution in Hildesheim* (Bloomington, Ind., 2004).

47. Kershaw, *Nazi Dictatorship*, 3 (emphasis in original).

48. Ibid. 193.

49. Ibid., 194.

50. David Blackbourn and Geoff Eley, *The Peculiarities of German History: Bourgeois and Politics in Nineteenth-Century Germany* (Oxford, 1984). On a history of Europe without the teleology of freedom and liberty, see Mark Mazower, *Dark Continent: Europe's Twentieth Century* (New York, 1999).

51. Cited in Klaus Fischer, *Nazi Germany: A New History* (New York, 1995), 513.

52. Cited in Hanna Yablonka, *The State of Israel vs. Adolf Eichmann* (New York, 2004), 110.

53. On this, see the excellent collection by Saul Friedländer, ed., *Probing the Limits of Interpretation: Nazism and the "Final Solution"* (Cambridge, Mass., 1992).

54. Eva Hoffman put it eloquently: "However one understands the motivations of the Nazis in carrying out the Holocaust, their perverted ideology, technological prowess, or their sheer sadism, the victims of the Final Solution did not have a chance to die for a cause or for a belief. They died in innocence." Eva Hoffman, "The Uses of Hell," *New York Review of Books*, March 9, 2000, 23.

Of course, historical descriptions of sensitive historical events, and perhaps of all historical cases, often commingle elements of faith and elements of the historian's craft. The Holocaust is not singular in presenting this mixture. But descriptions, by historians and other scholars, that put the Holocaust, in various degrees, beyond history are more prevalent in Holocaust historiography than in others.

55. Georges Canguilhem, *The Normal and the Pathological* (New York, 1989), 239.

Chapter Ten

Chapter 10 originally appeared as "Traveling as a Culture of Remembrance: Traces of National Socialism in West Germany, 1945–1960," *History and Memory* 12, no. 2 (Fall–Winter

2000): 92–121; reprinted with permission of Indiana University Press. I am indebted to Omer Bartov for his illuminating critical comments. I am also grateful to the Humboldt Foundation, whose fellowship enabled me to conduct research in Germany in 1999–2000.

1. Wolfgang Benz, "Postwar Society and National Socialism: Remembrance, Amnesia, Rejection," *Tel Aviver Jahrbuch für deutsche Geschichte* 19 (1990): 12.

2. Bernhard Schlink, *The Reader*, trans. Carol Brown Janeway (New York, 1997), 91–92.

3. Alexander Mitscherlich and Margarete Mitscherlich, *The Inability to Mourn: Principles of Collective Behavior*, trans. Beverley R. Placzek (New York, 1975), xvi.

4. See, for example, Benz, "Postwar Society." The danger of using the concept of repression as an explanatory device is that it is an interpretation that is closed within itself. One sets out to find evidence for what has been already predetermined, namely that Germans repressed the past; in an interpretive vicious circle, one reads into the evidence what has been already decided. It is hard to find independent variables that can help establish whether an engagement with the past — say, a war-crimes trial or restitution to the survivors — means denial or something else. For, with a little bit of self-convincing, everything can be seen as a case of denial.

5. Theodor W. Adorno, "What Does Coming to Terms with the Past Mean?," in *Bitburg in Moral and Political Perspective*, ed. Geoffrey H. Hartman (Bloomington, 1986), 117.

6. Dominick LaCapra, *History and Memory after Auschwitz* (Ithaca, N.Y., 1998), 3.

7. Robert Moeller, "War Stories: The Search for a Usable Past in the Federal Republic of Germany," *American Historical Review* 101, no. 4 (October 1996): 1012–13.

8. See, for example, ibid.; Heide Fehrenbach, *Cinema in Democratizing Germany: Reconstructing National Identity after Hitler* (Chapel Hill, N.C., 1995); Frank Biess, " 'Pioneers of a New Germany': Returning POWs from the Soviet Union and the Making of East German Citizens, 1945–1950," *Central European History* 2, no. 2 (1999): 143–80; Catherine Epstein, "The Production of 'Official Memory' in East Germany: Old Communists and the Dilemmas of Memoir-Writing," ibid., 181–202; Maria Mitchell, "Materialism and Secularism: CDU Politicians and National Socialism, 1945–1949," *Journal of Modern History* 67 (June 1995): 278–308; Peter Dudek, *"Der Rückblick auf die Vergangenheit wird sich nicht vermeiden lassen": Zur pädagogischen Verarbeitung des Nationalsozialismus in Deutschland (1945–1990)* (Opladen, 1995); Elizabeth Heineman, "The Hour of the Women: Memories of Germany's 'Crisis Years' and West German National Identity," *American Historical Review* 101 (April 1996): 354–95; Norbert Frei, *Vergangenheitspolitik: Die Anfänge der Bundesrepublik und die NS-Vergangenheit* (Munich, 1996); Helmut Peitsch, *"Deutschlands Gedächtnis an seine dunkelste Zeit": Zur Funktion der Autobiographik in den Westzonen Deutschlands und den Westsektoren von Berlin 1945 bis 1949* (Berlin, 1990); Hermann Graml, "Die verdrängte Auseinandersetzung mit dem Nationalsozialismus," in *Zäsuren nach 1945: Essays zur Periodisierung der deutschen Nachkriegsgeschichte*, ed. Martin Broszat (Munich, 1990), 169–83; Manfred Kittel, *Die Legende von der "Zweiten Schuld": Vergangenheitsbewältigung in der Ära Adenauer* (Berlin, 1993); and Christa Hoffmann, *Stunden Null: Vergangenheitsbewältigung in Deutschland 1945 und 1989* (Bonn, 1992).

9. See, for example, Josef Foschepoth, "German Reaction to Defeat and Occupation," in *West Germany under Construction: Politics, Society, and Culture in the Adenauer Era*, ed. Robert Moeller (Ann Arbor, Mich., 1997), 77; Mitchell, "Materialism and Secularism"; Moeller, "War Stories."

10. Henry Rousso, *The Vichy Syndrome: History and Memory in France since 1944* (Cambridge, Mass., 1991); Nicola Tranfaglia, *Un passato scomodo: Fascismo e postfascismo* (Bari, 1996).

11. Y. Michal Bodemann, "Eclipse of Memory: German Representations of Auschwitz in the Early Postwar Period," *New German Critique*, no. 75 (Fall 1998): 59, 63.

12. Karl Mannheim, "The Psychological Aspect," in *Peaceful Change: An International Problem*, ed. C. A. W. Manning (New York, 1937), 129. I owe this citation to an essay of my father, Michael Confino, on history and psychology in the case of the Russian nobility. See "Histoire et Psychologie: A propos de la noblesse russe au XVIII siècle," *Annales* (November–December 1967): 1183.

13. See, for example, Moeller, "War Stories"; Fehrenbach, *Cinema in Democratizing Germany*; Biess, "'Pioneers of a New Germany'"; Heineman, "The Hour of the Women."

14. Some important examples: Jeffrey Herf, *Divided Memory: The Nazi Past in the Two Germanys* (Cambridge, Mass., 1997), explores "how anti-Nazi German political leaders interpreted the Nazi past" (1); Maria Mitchell explores leaders of the CDU in "Materialism and Secularism"; in *Vergangenheitspolitik: Die Anfänge der Bundesrepublik und die NS-Vergangenheit* (Munich, 1996), Norbert Frei focuses on government policy and the public sphere; Peter Dudek, in his book *Der Rückblick auf die Vergangenheit* about mastering the past in the educational system, is interested in educators and teachers, not their students; Christa Hoffmann concentrates on Nazi war-crimes trials in *Stunden Null*; in "Coming to Terms with the Past: Interpreting the German Church Struggles, 1933–1990," *German History* 16 (1998): 377–96, John Conway explores church historians, intellectuals, and leaders, not rank-and-file believers; and Joyce Marie Mushaben's "Collective Memory Divided and Reunited: Mothers, Daughters and the Fascist Experience in Germany," *History and Memory* 11, no. 1 (Spring–Summer 1999): 7–40, focuses on the link between gender identity and coming to terms with the past among East and West German women activists and intellectuals, not among "ordinary" women.

15. Frei, *Vergangenheitspolitik*, 23.

16. Claudia Koonz, "Between Memory and Oblivion: Concentration Camps in German Memory," in *Commemorations: The Politics of National Identity*, ed. John Gillis (Princeton, N.J., 1994), 262–63.

17. Ibid., 261.

18. The *Stammtisch* is a social practice that takes place in public but its meaning is restricted to a close group of friends. *Stammtisch* friends do not expect their conversations —certainly those on National Socialism—to become public knowledge. This is fundamentally different from all the artifacts mentioned by Koonz: the media, newspapers, oral histories, memoirs, opinion polls, ceremonies, and leaders' speeches—all receive meaning by becoming public.

19. See Omer Bartov, "'Seit die Juden weg sind': Germany, History, and Representations of Absence," in *A User's Guide to German Cultural Studies*, ed. Scott Denham, Irene Karandes, and Jonathan Petropoulos (Ann Arbor, Mich., 1997), 209–26.

20. For Baden, see "Ein Dezenium Verbandsarbeit: Berichte der deutschen Fremdenverkehrsverbände," *Der Fremdenverkehr* 11, no. 5 (1959): 60; for Dortmund, see ibid., 41, and "50 Jahre Landesverkehrsverband Westfalen," *Der Fremdenverkehr* 10, no. 2 (1958): 15. On the German League of Tourist Associations and Spas, see *Abschrift: Referat des verbandsdirektor*

Stadtrat a.D. Ochs . . . am 6.9.1946 auf der Hohensyburg betreffend Vorbereitung der Gründung des Bundes deutscher Verkehrsverbände und Bäder, Ncm, IfT. On the newly founded associations, see Neugegründete Fremdenverkehrsverbände in Deutschland: Stand vom 10.2.1947, Ncm, IfT.

21. The German Central Tourist Association (Deutsche Zentrale für Fremdenverkehr), was founded in 1948 as West Germany's national tourist organization. The Deutsche Zeitschrift für Fremdenverkehr was first published in July 1949.

22. The following discussion is partly based on a section from chapter 9.

23. Jubiläumsschrift des Harzer Verkehrsverband E.V. zu seinem fünfzigjährigen Bestehen (Braunschweig, 1954), 29.

24. My discussion is based on Christine Keitz, Reisen als Leitbild: Die Entstehung des modernen Massentourismus in Deutschland (Munich, 1997), 248–49.

25. R. Irmer, "50 Jahre Harzer Verkehrsverband," Der Fremdenverkehr 6, nos. 7–8 (1954): 3–4.

26. Heineman, "The Hour of the Women," 387. This sentiment emerged clearly years later in Edgar Reitz's TV series Heimat. See chapter 2 of this book.

27. Mitteilungen der Z.F.V.: Warum Deutschland-Werbung mit Goethe, n.d. [late 1948], 1–2, Ncm, IfT.

28. On rape in postwar Germany, see Heineman, "The Hour of the Women"; Atina Grossmann, "A Question of Silence: The Rape of German Women by Occupation Soldiers," October 72 (April 1995): 43–63.

29. The Goethe Year campaign should be also seen against the background of the Cold War and the transformation of the Soviet occupation zone into East Germany. Goethe symbolized the true German spirit not only in contrast to the Nazi regime but also in contrast to East Germany.

30. Der Fremdenverkehr 11, no. 5 (1959): 2; "Vorurteile auszuräumen," ibid. 5, nos. 9–10 (1953): 2.

31. Statement of Dr. Hermann Punder, director of the managing board, Der Fremdenverkehr 1, no. 1 (1949): 1.

32. Der gute Kontakt: Bemerkungen zum "Ersten Deutschen Fremden-verkehrstag," n.d., p. 1, Ncm, IfT.

33. M. Hoffmann and W.-O. Reichelt, Reiseverkehr und Gastlichkeit im neuen Deutschland (Hamburg, 1939), 25–26.

34. Deutscher Fremdenverkehrstag, 1950 (Bonn, 1950), 26–27. The first German Tourism Convention met in Bonn, April 28–30, 1950.

35. Cited in Moeller, "War Stories," 1019.

36. Hans Magnus Enzensberger, "Eine Theorie des Tourismus," in Einzelheiten, vol. 1 (Frankfurt am Main, 1962), 196.

37. The coexistence of silence and memory following the cataclysmic events of the 1930s and 1940s was strong not only in Germany. Edward Said tells in his autobiography Out of Place of the reaction of his parents, Christian Palestinians who lived in Moslem Cairo, to the fall of Palestine in 1948–49. The subject was hardly discussed: "[T]he repression of Palestine in our lives occurred as part of a larger depoliticization on the part of my parents, who hated and distrusted politics." But Said simultaneously tells of his Aunt Nabiha, who worked tire-

lessly in Cairo for suffering Palestinian refugees: "[I]t was through Aunt Nabiha that I first experienced Palestine as history and cause." Edward Said, *Out of Place: A Memoir* (New York, 1999), 117, 119. See Alon Confino, "Remembering Talbiyah: On Edward Said's *Out of Place*," *Israel Studies* 5, no. 2 (Winter 2000): 182–98.

38. Certainly, this sentiment coexisted with other, terrifying, sentiments. Close to 60,000 soldiers died in the Western campaign and the horrors of war were real. But the horror commingled with a certain fascination with the campaign as an adventurous military victory and as a trip to a foreign land. Horror and fascination were not mutually exclusive.

39. Klaus Latzl, "Tourismus und Gewalt: Kriegswahrnehmungen in Feldpostbriefen," in *Vernichtungskrieg: Verbrechen der Wehrmacht, 1941–1945*, ed. Hannes Heer and Klaus Naumann (Hamburg, 1995), 448–49. The approach of this essay is stimulating.

40. William Shirer, *"This is Berlin": Radio Broadcasts from Nazi Germany, 1938–40* (New York, 1999), 328 (dispatch from June 17, 1940). See also Gilles Perrault and Pierre Azéma, *Paris under the Occupation* (New York, 1989), 11, and Bertram Gordon, "Ist Gott Französisch? Germans, Tourism, and Occupied France, 1940–1944," *Modern and Contemporary France* 4, no. 3 (1996): 287–98.

41. David Price-Jones, *Paris in the Third Reich: A History of the German Occupation* (New York, 1981), 10–11, 95.

42. Perrault and Azéma, *Paris under the Occupation*, 66.

43. The following discussion is indebted to ibid., 17; Bertram Gordon, "Warfare and Tourism: Paris in World War II," *Annals of Tourism Research* 25, no. 3 (1998): 621, 627; and Price-Jones, *Paris in the Third Reich*, 88.

44. Hermann Opitz, "Knigge für Touristen," *Frankfurter Allgemeine Zeitung*, July 2, 1953.

45. Interview with Heinz Schulz, son of Alfred Schulz, by author, April 8, 2000. Names were changed for confidentiality.

46. Cited in Michael Schornstheimer, *Die leuchtenden Augen der Frontsoldaten: Nationalsozialismus und Krieg in den Illustriertenromanen der fünfziger Jahre* (Berlin, 1995), 129–30.

47. Koonz, "Between Memory and Oblivion," 265.

48. Again, novels capture this phenomenon and state of mind very well. Thus, Schlink's hero Michael Berg uses a two-week break in the war trial "to go away. If I had been able to leave for Auschwitz the next day, I would have gone. But it would have taken weeks to get a visa. So I went to Struthof in Alsace. It was the nearest concentration camp. . . . I hitchhiked, and remember a ride in a truck with a driver who downed one bottle of beer after another" (*The Reader*, 149).

49. Bernward Vesper, *Die Reise: Romanessay*, ed. Jörg Schröder and Klaus Behnken (Jossa, 1979), 238. *Die Reise* was first published posthumously in 1977, six years after Vesper committed suicide.

50. Ibid., 525. On the youth travel culture of the 1950s, see Rainer Schönhammer, "Unabhängiger Jugendtourismus in der Nachkriegszeit," in *Goldstrand und Teutonengrill: Kultur- und Sozialgeschichte des Tourismus in Deutschland 1945 bis 1989*, ed. Hasso Spode (Berlin, 1996), 117–28. Peter Weiss's evaluation is cited in Andrew Plowman, "Bernward Vesper's *Die Reise*: Politics and Autobiography between the Student Movement and the Act of Self-Invention German Autumn: The Critical Reception of *Die Reise*," *German Studies Review* 21, no. 3 (October 1998): 507.

51. See Christoph Hennig's brilliant book, *Reiselust: Touristen, Tourismus, und Urlaubs-kultur* (Frankfurt am Main, 1997), 13.

52. See the fascinating book, *Das Dritte Reich des Traums* (Munich, 1966), by Charlotte Beradt, a German journalist who, between 1933 and 1939, interviewed about 300 people about their dreams. She emigrated to the United States in 1939, taking her valuable material with her.

INDEX

—associations of: League for Heimat Protection in Württemberg and Hohenzollern (Bund für Heimatschutz in Württemberg und Hohenzollern), 36, 40, 44, 63; German League for Heimat Protection (Deutscher Bund Heimatschutz), 36, 44–45, 63, 76; Committee for Nature Conservation and Heimat Protection (Landesausschuss für Natur- and Heimatschutz), 39; Württemberger Folklore Association (Württemberg Vereinigung für Volkskunde), 40; Saxon Regional Association for Heimat Protection (Landesverein Sächsischer Heimatschutz), 92

—in East Germany: embraced and rejected after 1945, 92–95; and symbolic manual, 93–95; continuation of old symbols, 95–99; and expellees, 99; redefined according to communism, 100–102; tension between socialism and nationhood, 102–8; impregnates spirit of GDR, 108–11

—in imperial Germany: vehicles of, 35–36; social composition of, 36–38; and history, nature, and folklore, 38–42; in museums, 42–45; as representation of nation, 45–51; and tourism, 47; as apolitical image, 51–55; and religion, 53; and modernity, 55; as local metaphor, 55–56; and associations, 63; based on idea of experience, 67

—symbolic manual: characteristics of, 28; of localness and nationhood, 61–65; used by Nazis, 64; in West Germany, 64; of history, 65–69; in East Germany, 93–95; powerful regardless of ideology, 115

—in Third Reich: and race, 64; based on idea of experience, 68, 116–24 passim

—and tourism: in imperial Germany, 47, 79, 116; in West Germany, 82–84, 87–88, 90–91, 118–24 passim; in East Germany, 105, 108–11, 118–24 passim; as national lexicon, 115–24; in Third Reich, 116–24 passim

—in Weimar: based on experience, 67–68

—in West Germany: representing the local versus the national, 64; avoiding historical causality, 68–69; represented as victim after 1945, 82–86; and expellees, 84–90; representing the divided nation, 87–90; and Heimat films, 89–90; representing relations with Western Europe, 90–91

Heimat films: relation to *Heimat*, 76–78; and postwar identity, 89–90. See also *Heimat*; Heimat idea

Heraclitus, 6

Herman the Cheruskian, 121

Herodotus, 156

Hesse, Hermann, 55

Heuß, Theodor, 84

Hilberg, Raul, 13

Himmler, Heinrich, 231

Historians: animal metaphors of, xiii; as traveling jugglers, xiii–xiv; speaking truthfully about past, 1, 12–15; perceptions of past, 2–7; strange and familiar to past, 6–7; and cultural Archimedean point, 1, 9, 75, 157–58, 164; as artists and scientists, 12, 74–75; as artisans or jugglers, 17; finding disciplinary redemption in memory, 156–58. *See also* Experience; Historical explanation; Memory

Historical explanation: and evidence, 1, 12–15, 45, 47–48, 71–72, 75, 94–95; excessive expectations of, 8; principles of understanding and contingency, 10–11; transcending and conditioned by culture, 12–17; of relations between text and context, 18, 26–27, 208–9; and limits of identity, 195–99; and overlapping memories, 206; and context of experience, 208; and exceptional normal, 214–17; of Holocaust as normal history, 226–34. *See also* Experience; Historians; Memory

Hitler Youth (Hitler Yugend), 103, 205, 211

Hitler, Adolf, 14, 106, 226

Hobsbawm, Eric, 6, 29

Hoffmann, Heinrich, 119
Hohlwein, Ludwig, 123
Hollywood, 57, 65–66, 69–70, 72, 78
Holocaust (television series), 57, 65–66, 70
Holocaust: and problem of familiarization and explanation, 8–12; and historical relativism, 13–15; and *Heimat*, 58, 60–61, 73, 80; compared to Germans' expulsion, 85; as problem of narration, 192–94; and explanation and memory, 192–95, 211–13; and explanation and identity, 195–99; and historical dissonance and normality, 226–34. *See also* Experience; Heimat idea; Historical explanation; Memory; Third Reich
Holtzhauer, Helmut, 92–93
Huizinga, Johan, 213
Hunt, Lynn, 156

India, 17
Israel, 168
Italy, 4
Izieux, 5

Jacob, Margaret, 156
Jena, 109
Jerusalem, 19
Jever, 43
Jünger, Ernst, 54

Kaes, Anton, 61, 73
Kershaw, Ian, 229–30
Kirchheim unter Teck, 39, 110
Klemperer, Victor, 11
Kneschke, Karl, 104
Koch, Gertrud, 60, 73
Kocka, Jürgen, 24
Kogon, Eugen, 240
Koonz, Claudia, 241–42
Koshar, Rudy, 191–92, 194
Kovno, 157
Kurdistan, 20

LaCapra, Dominick, 238
Lagrou, Pieter, 201–4 passim

Lanzmann, Claude, 177
Le Goff, Jacques, 3, 172
League of German Girls (Bund Deutscher Mädel), 103, 205, 211
Localness: local turn in nationalism historiography, 23–27; in German historiography, 27–28; as nationhood in imperial Germany, 45–51; as nationhood in East Germany, 92–113; representing German nationhood in twentieth century, 118–52; representing the global, 123–24. *See also* Heimat idea; Nationalism
Lodz, 119, 123
London, 34

Malle, Louis, 5
Malraux, Andre, 177
Mannheim, Karl, 241
Martini, Ferdinando, 34
Marx, Karl, 93
Memory: collective, 31–32; and German unification, 33–34, 188–89; as genuine and invented, 69–71; paradigm shift from "society" to "memory," 153–56; innovation of *Moses and Monotheism*, 166–68; as history of mentalities, 171–73; and Aby Warburg, 173–76; sacrificed to the political, 176–78; and issue of reception, 178–82; relations of memories in society, 182–86; relations of public and private, 199–208; as description and explanation, 208–10. *See also* Experience; Historians; Historical explanation; Holocaust; Third Reich
—in Germany: and historiography, 188–89; as closed and open narratives, 189–92; and explanations of Holocaust, 192–99; limits of identity as explanation, 195–99; relations of individual and collective memories, 199–208; repression thesis of Third Reich, 224–26
Mickey Mouse, 170
Mitscherlich, Alexander and Margarete, 236
Moeller, Robert, 199–204 passim, 239

Moses and Monotheism: interpretations of, 159; concept of nationhood, 160–64; and Heimat idea, 161–62; representing national idea and scholarship, 161–64; setting new relations between past and present, 164–66. *See also* Nationalism

Moulin, Jean, 177

Munich, 120

Museums: of Heimat in imperial Germany, 42–45, 67; German National Museum (Germanisches Nationalmuseum), 43; Rhine-Westphalia Archaeological Museum (Museum rheinisch-westfälischer Altertümer), 43; Roman German Central Museum (Römisch germanisches Zentralmuseum), 43; of Heimat and *Moses and Monotheism*, 161–62. *See also* Heimat idea

Mussolini, Benito, 4

Napoleon III, 161

Nationalism: and local turn, 23–27; interpretations of, 29–31; as religion, 30; as visual image, 45–51, 92–113, 118–52; and *Moses and Monotheism*, 161–64. *See also* Heimat idea; Localness

Niethammer, Lutz, 205

Nora, Pierre, 79, 156

North Rhine–Westphalia, 84, 87

Oettingen, 42

Palestinians, 20, 168

Paris, Erna, 203–4

Pirenne, Henri, 2–3

Poland, 87, 120

Pomerania, 40, 118, 120

Posen, 231

Potsdam, 118

Prague, 109

Princeton University Press, 13

Proust, Marcel, 31

Reagan, Ronald, 60

Reitz, Edgar, 57, 59–60, 62–80 passim

Renan, Ernest, 29, 160–61, 164

Renningen, 48, 123

Reutlingen, 44, 47–48, 122–23

Rhine, 122

Ribbentrop-Molotov Agreement, 9

Riga, 157

Rome, 13, 19

Rousso, Henry, 176–81 passim

Russia, 87

Russian Revolution, 9

Rwanda, 154

Saxony, 92, 96, 99–100

Schabbach, 57, 62, 73, 76

Scheeßel, 43

Schiller, Friedrich von, 119

Schlink, Bernhard, 236

Schmitt, Carl, 240

Schorske, Carl, 52

Second World War, 199-204 passim

Seebohm, Hans Christoph, 85

Seven Year Plan, 119

Sheehan, James, 33

Silesia, 87–89

Smith, Anthony, 29

South Africa, 155, 166

South Tyrol, 84

Soviet Union, 99

Stalin, 98

Steinbach, Peter, 59

Strength through Joy (Kraft durch Freude), 116–17, 220–22, 248

Stresemann, Gustav, 106, 122

Ströhmfeld, Gustav, 116–17

Stuttgart, 36, 38, 44, 66, 116

Szymborska, Wisława, 213

Teutoburg Forest, 121

Third Reich: and problem of strangeness and familiarity, 7–12; as civilization, 10; and principle of historical understanding, 10; and *Heimat*, 64, 68; and Heimat symbolic manual, 116–24 passim; and tourism, 218–24; and repression thesis, 224–26, 235–38; as commingling of silence and memory, 239–43; as victimhood and fond memories, 243–47. *See also* Heimat idea; Holocaust; Memory

Thömmes, Matthias, 90, 117

Thuringia, 40, 96, 99, 109

Tocqueville, Alexis de, 11

Todt, Fritz, 218

Tourism: image of historians, xiii–xiv; in imperial Germany, 47, 79, 116; in East Germany, 105, 108–11, 115–24 passim; in Third Reich, 116–24 passim, 218–24; as symbolic practice, 220, 242–43. *See also* Experience; Heimat idea; Third Reich

—associations of: Friends of Nature (Die Naturfreunde), 53; German Central Tourist Association (Deutsche Zentrale für Fremdenverkehr), 82, 88, 90, 219, 253; Association for German Heimat, Travel, and Nature Protection (Deutsche Heimat-, Wander-, und Naturschutzbünde), 84; German League of Tourist and Spa Associations (Bund deutscher Verkehrsverbände und Bäder), 84, 243; Tourist Association of the Harz (Harzer Verkehrsverband), 87, 217, 253; German League of Tourist Associations (Bund deutscher Verkehrsverbände), 90, 117; Association for Tourism in Württemberg and Hohenzollern (Württembergisch-Hohenzollerische Vereinigung für Fremdenverkehr), 116; Baden's Federation of Regional Tourism (Landesfremdenverkehrsverband Baden), 116; Central Reich Railway for German Tourism (Reichsbahn Zentrale für den deutschen Reiseverkehr), 118; Regional Tourist Union of East Friesland (Landesverkehrsverband Ostfriesland), 214; Regional Tourist Union of the Harz (Landesfremdenverkehrsverband Harz), 214; Working Group of Spas and Health Resorts in the Harz (Arbeitsgemeinschaft Harzer Heilbäder and Kurorte), 214–15; Nordmark Regional Tourist Union (Landesfremden-Verkehrsverband Nordmark), 215

—and West Germany: after May 1945, 214–17; embracing and denying Nazism, 217–20, 247–51; Nazism as victimhood and fond memories, 243–47

Tucholsky, Kurt, 55

Turin, 13

Tuttlingen, 39

Two Year Plan, 94, 100

Ulbricht, Walter, 103, 106

Vatican, 155, 166

Vesper, Bernward, 251

Veyne, Paul, 74

Vienna, 52

Vilna, 157

Vilsbiburg, 43

Vistula, 119

Wagner, Richard, 118

Warburg, Aby, 171, 173–76, 187

Warsaw, 109

Weber, Eugen, 4–5, 24–25, 30

Wehler, Hans-Ulrich, 15

Weimar, 119

Weiss, Peter, 251

White, Hayden, 74

Wiesel, Elie, 7

William II (German emperor), 54, 106

Wölfflin, Heinrich, 174

Woodward, C. Vann, 5

Wulf, Joseph, 13

Württemberg, 24, 99, 124

Yerushalmi, Yosef Hayim, 160, 167

Yugoslavia, 154

Zerubavel, Yael, 180–84

Zionism, 19–20, 163, 180–82, 184